KYOTO AREA STUDIES ON ASIA
CENTER FOR SOUTHEAST ASIAN STUDIES, KYOTO UNIVERSITY
VOLUME 25

Grassroots Globalization

KYOTO AREA STUDIES ON ASIA

Center for Southeast Asian Studies, Kyoto University

The Nation and Economic Growth:
Korea and Thailand
Yoshihara Kunio

One Malay Village:
A Thirty-Year Community Study
Tsubouchi Yoshihiro

Commodifying Marxism:
The Formation of Modern Thai Radical Culture, 1927–1958
Kasian Tejapira

Gender and Modernity:
Perspectives from Asia and the Pacific
Hayami Yoko, Tanabe Akio, Tokita-Tanabe Yumiko

Practical Buddhism among the Thai-Lao:
Religion in the Making of a Region
Hayashi Yukio

The Political Ecology of Tropical Forests in Southeast Asia:
Historical Perspectives
Lye Tuck-Po, Wil de Jong, Abe Ken-ichi

Between Hills and Plains:
Power and Practice in Socio-Religious Dynamics among Karen
Hayami Yoko

Ecological Destruction, Health and Development:
Advancing Asian Paradigms
Furukawa Hisao, Nishibuchi Mitsuaki, Kono Yasuyuki, Kaida Yoshihiro

Searching for Vietnam:
Selected Writings on Vietnamese Culture and Society
A. Terry Rambo

Laying the Tracks:
The Thai Economy and its Railways 1885–1935
Kakizaki Ichiro

After the Crisis:
Hegemony, Technocracy and Governance in Southeast Asia
Shiraishi Takashi, Patricio N. Abinales

Dislocating Nation-States:
Globalization in Asia and Africa
Patricio N. Abinales, Ishikawa Noboru and Tanabe Akio

People on the Move:
Rural–Urban Interactions in Sarawak
Soda Ryoji

Living on the Periphery:
Development and Islamization among the Orang Asli
Nobuta Toshihiro

KYOTO AREA STUDIES ON ASIA

CENTER FOR SOUTHEAST ASIAN STUDIES, KYOTO UNIVERSITY

Myths and Realities:
The Democratization of Thai Politics
TAMADA Yoshifumi

East Asian Economies and New Regionalism
ABE Shigeyuki and Bhanupong NIDHIPRABA

The Rise of Middle Classes in Southeast Asia
SHIRAISHI Takashi and Pasuk PHONGPAICHIT

Farming with Fire and Water:
The Human Ecology of a Composite Swiddening
Community in Vietnam's Northern Mountains
Trần Đức Viên, A. Terry RAMBO and Nguyễn Thanh Lâm

Re-thinking Economic Development:
The Green Revolution, Agrarian Structure and Transformation in Bangladesh
FUJITA Koichi

The Limits of Tradition:
Peasants and Land Conflicts in Indonesia
URANO Mariko

Bangusa and Umma:
Development of People-grouping Concepts in Islamized Southeast Asia
YAMAMOTO Hiroyuki

Development Monks in Northeast Thailand
Pinit LAPTHANON

Politics of Ethnic Classification in Vietnam
ITO Masako

The End of Personal Rule in Indonesia:
Golkar and the Transformation of the Suharto Regime
MASUHARA Ayako

Grassroots Globalization:
Reforestation and Cultural Revitalization in the Philippine Cordilleras
SHIMIZU Hiromu

The World Heritage Listed Rice Terraces of Ifugao

Top: View of rice terraces and mountain range taken from Kidlat's humble hovel at Patpat, Hapao, Hungduan, in northern Luzon. The long narrow road that is visible in the distance halfway up the side of the mountain on the right links the remote mountain village of Hapao with Banaue. At the end of the Asia-Pacific War, some 50,000 Japanese troops under the command of General Yamashita Tomoyuki invaded the farthest reaches of Ifugao and dug in there to make their last stand. (March 21, 2002)

Middle: Rice planting in the terraces. The terraces are constructed at an altitude of 1,000–1,500 meters. (March 2, 2000)

Bottom: Everyday life in an Ifugao village. After the rice has been dehusked in a mortar, it is shaken in a winnowing basket to separate the white rice from the remaining debris. (March 6, 2000)

Lopez Nauyac, The Man Who Plants Trees

Lopez Nauyac, founder and president of the Ifugao Global Forest City Movement, an NGO promoting reforestation in Hapao (referred to hereafter as 'Global'). Here he is planting saplings of species indigenous to the mountains of Hapao while wearing full Ifugao dress. (March 12, 2002)

Nauyac distributing the illustrated booklet *Ang Bantay ng Mahiwagang Gubat* (Guardian of the Enchanted Forest) to students at an elementary school in Nungulunan, next to Hapao, in which he calls on them to plant trees. After he explains the importance of reforestation, they all take a pledge to plant trees. The booklet was produced by IKGS, a Japanese NGO that supports 'Global' work. (March 15, 2006)

Grassroots International Cooperation and Networking With Japan

Top: View of one of the sites reforested with support from the JICA Partnership Program. (March 6, 2004)

Bottom left: Nauyac explaining the progress of the project to members of a JICA survey team at the same reforestation site. Key 'Global' member Santos Bayucca makes a video recording of the scene. Santos's father was a former policeman in Banaue who became involved with the illegal NPA guerillas in the early 1970s and was shot dead by the Philippine Constabulary at his home in Uhaj, Banaue. Santos, too, became active in the NPA for about one year. Ifugao has also provided an arena, though small, for the communist movement's global-wide activities. (August 13, 2005)

Bottom right: A group of woodcarvers and carpenters from Hapao organized by Kidlat and Nauyac participate in the Fourth Echigo-Tsumaari Art Field Triennale in Niigata, Japan. They built a traditional Ifugao house and erected a totem pole amid the rice terraces in a Japanese mountain village. (July 24, 2009)

Villagers Deploying Across the Globe as Migrant Workers

Of the 1,751 individuals from 338 households in Hapao (based on 2006 data), more than 150 have migrated to work in a total of twenty-seven countries in Asia, the Middle East, Europe, North America and Australia; 80 percent of them are women and many work as live-in domestic helpers, caregivers or factory workers (assembling consumer electronics etc.). (All of these photographs were taken around 2010. I borrowed them from Santos Bayucca and made scanned copies with his permission.)

Adela Dao-ay in Canada

Boni Buyagao in South Korea

Christine Tayaban in Hong Kong

Gideon Vicente in Dubai

Jonalyn Taguyungon in Taiwan

Rosa Ipan in Australia

KYOTO AREA STUDIES ON ASIA
CENTER FOR SOUTHEAST ASIAN STUDIES, KYOTO UNIVERSITY
VOLUME 25

Grassroots Globalization

Reforestation and Cultural Revitalization in the Philippine Cordilleras

By

SHIMIZU Hiromu

Translated by
Alexander Brown

Kyoto University Press

First published in Japanese by Kyoto University Press, Japan.

This English edition published in 2019 jointly by:

Kyoto University Press
69 Yoshida Konoe-cho
Sakyo-ku, Kyoto 606-8315, Japan
Telephone: +81-75-761-6182
Fax: +81-75-761-6190
Email: sales@kyoto-up.or.jp
Web: http://www.kyoto-up.or.jp

Trans Pacific Press
PO Box 164, Balwyn North
Victoria 3104, Australia
Telephone: +61-(0)3-9859-1112
Fax: +61-(0)3-8611-7989
Email: tpp.mail@gmail.com
Web: http://www.transpacificpress.com

© SHIMIZU Hiromu 2019.

Edited by Cathy Edmonds.

Designed and set by Sarah Tuke, Melbourne, Australia.

Printed by Asia Printing Office Corporation, Nagano, Japan.

Distributors

Australia and New Zealand
James Bennett Pty Ltd
Locked Bag 537
Frenchs Forest NSW 2086
Australia
Telephone: +61-(0)2-8988-5000
Fax: +61-(0)2-8988-5031
Email: info@bennett.com.au
Web: www.bennett.com.au

USA and Canada
Independent Publishers Group (IPG)
814 N. Franklin Street
Chicago, IL 60610
USA
Telephone inquiries: +1-312-337-0747
Order placement: 800-888-4741
  (domestic only)
Fax: +1-312-337-5985
Email: frontdesk@ipgbook.com
Web: http://www.ipgbook.com

Asia and the Pacific (except Japan)
Kinokuniya Company Ltd.
Head office:
3-7-10 Shimomeguro
Meguro-ku
Tokyo 153-8504
Japan
Telephone: +81-(0)3-6910-0531
Fax: +81-(0)3-6420-1362
Email: bkimp@kinokuniya.co.jp
Web: www.kinokuniya.co.jp
Asia-Pacific office:
Kinokuniya Book Stores of Singapore
Pte., Ltd.
391B Orchard Road #13-06/07/08
Ngee Ann City Tower B
Singapore 238874
Telephone: +65-6276-5558
Fax: +65-6276-5570
Email: SSO@kinokuniya.co.jp

The translation and publication of this book was supported by a Grant-in-Aid for Publication of Scientific Research Results (Grant Number 17HP6004), provided by the Japan Society for the Promotion of Science, to which we express our sincere appreciation.

All rights reserved. No reproduction of any part of this book may take place without the written permission of Kyoto University Press or Trans Pacific Press.

ISSN   1445–9663 (Kyoto Area Studies on Asia)
ISBN   978–1–925608–84–7

Author's Biography

SHIMIZU Hiromu
Professor Emeritus of Kyoto University
Visiting Professor of Faculty of Policy Studies, Kansai University
President of the Japanese Society of Cultural Anthropology (2018–)

SHIMIZU Hiromu specializes in cultural anthropology and emphasizes the importance of the 'anthropology of response-ability'. He has published academic works in Japanese and English, including *Funka no kodama* (Echoes of the eruption) (Kyushu University Press, 2003) and *Kusanone globalization* (Grassroots globalization) (Kyoto University Press, 2013, the original work of this book). *Kusanone globalization* won the Japan Academy Prize in 2017, the most prestigious academic publication prize in Japan, which was bestowed upon a cultural anthropologist for the first time. The book also received the eleventh Japanese Society of Cultural Anthropology Award in 2016.

Contents

Preface	xiv
Acknowledgements	xviii
1 Thinking about Globalization at the Periphery: An Attempt at an Anthropology of Response-ability	1

Part I: Five Hundred Years of Negotiating with Global Powers

2 The Ifugao Lifeworld: A Fascination for Anthropologists and Communist Guerillas	31
3 Life amid the Blessings of Forests: Rice Terrace Cultivation and Woodcarving	65
4 Confronting Global Power from the Margins: Invasions and Resistance	91

Part II: Re-establishing the Connection between the Local and the Global

5 The Praxis of Meaning in Lopez Nauyac's 'Global' Gaze	131
6 Memories of Overdevelopment: Kidlat Tahimik's 'Circumnavigation of the World'	179
7 The Politics of Representation: Culture as a Resource	235

Part III: Negotiating with Globalization

8	Working Overseas and Reviving Tradition: Spreading Wings and Putting Down Roots	293
9	International Cooperation: From Entanglement to a Participatory Anthropology	337
10	Grassroots: Regional Networks and the Anthropology of Response-ability	407

Bibliography	441
Index	458

Preface

Rapidly advancing globalization is having a significant effect and impact on indigenous people all over the world. In the case of my own long-term research since 1998, I have never felt this advance more keenly than when I lived in a remote village in steep mountains far from the capital city of a developing country. My own field site, Hapao village, Hungduan Municipality, Ifugao Province, the Philippines, is about 250 kilometers north of Manila, nestled deep in the valley of the upper Magat River in the Cordillera Mountains. Since 1998 I have conducted ongoing research ranging from one to five weeks almost every year. I have been very much fascinated by the village because the people have confronted, experienced, and actively and aggressively taken their chances in globalization.

The effects and impacts of globalization are explicit in Hapao village. As of 2007, among 1,750 residents, more than 150 villagers, mainly women (almost three-quarters of them), work as domestic helpers and caregivers, and have been abroad to twenty-seven countries, mainly in Asia but also in the Middle East, Europe, Canada, the United States of America and Australia. The number has been steadily increasing since then. A villagers' organization has implemented a grassroots reforestation project, under the banner Ifugao Global Forest City Movement (IGFCM), in close cooperation with International Kudzu Green Sannan (IKGS), a small Japanese non-governmental organization (NGO) in Hyōgo Prefecture. It received 86 million Japanese yen (about US$800,000) between 2001 and 2008 from five Japanese funding agencies for reforestation and social development projects. Therefore, 'Global' is a popular word in this village and echoes in the experiences of villagers and members who stay overseas. The world-renowned film director Kidlat Tahimik has been so deeply inspired by the words and deeds of Lopez Nauyac, the founder and the leader of this movement, that he has produced several documentary films, which have been shown at numerous international film festivals.

Hapao itself is located at the center of a steep mountain range and it was to Hapao, during the Second World War, that the main force of the

Preface xv

Japanese army (which occupied the Philippines under General Yamashita Tomoyuki, with tens of thousands of soldiers) retreated and entrenched itself for three months before surrendering. The villagers still clearly remember the suffering caused by bombing, food shortage and epidemics such as dysentery. Lopez insists that world peace was born in Hapao and the surrounding areas when General Yamashita finally gave up fighting to surrender. Hapao is one of five clusters of rice terraces in Ifugao that were inscribed on the United Nations Educational, Scientific and Cultural Organization (UNESCO) World Heritage List in 1995 as living cultural heritage. A scene of the rice terraces in Banaue is printed on the back of 1,000-peso notes, the largest denomination bills, which were first issued in 1991 to praise this national cultural heritage.

Twenty years have passed since I first met the central character in this book, Lopez Nauyac, in 1997 in Baguio. My acquaintance with Kidlat Tahimik extends back even further, to our first meeting thirty-five years ago at a party held by the Japan Foundation for guests of the first South Asian Film Festival in 1982 in Tokyo. It has taken far longer than I expected

Kidlat Tahimik making an acceptance speech after receiving the Fukuoka Prize. Prince and Princess Akishino are seated on stage to the right. (September 13, 2012)

to finish writing this book. While there were reasons and unforeseen circumstances behind these delays, when I look back I can say that this is just how long the process has taken. I have come to understand that the practice of anthropology is slow work. Thanks to these delays, I finished writing the manuscript for the Japanese edition at around the time it was announced that Kidlat had won the 23rd Fukuoka Asian Culture Prize in 2012. His work has been the subject of great interest and praise in recent years. At the Twelfth Jeonju International Film Festival (South Korea) in 2011, eleven of Kidlat's works were shown as part of a special screening and in 2009 a Kidlat Tahimik Retrospective at the University of the Philippines Film Institute featured twelve films. He also won the Caligari Film Prize in 2015 for his lifework film *Balikbayan #1: Memories of Overdevelopment Redux III* at the 2015 Berlinale, or Berlin International Film Festival.

The main research for the Japanese book extended over a period of twelve years from 1997 to 2009. I visited Hapao at least once a year (except in 2007). After that, I resumed my visits to Ifugao almost every year from 2014 to 2018 to add information for this English version. However, from the beginning, each visit lasted no more than five weeks and sometimes were as short as one week. At no point was I able to spend an extended period in the field. For this reason, I was unable to master the Ifugao language beyond a few basic greetings. With my four friends-cum-collaborators who provided me with most of the knowledge and information in this book, I spoke English with Kidlat, English and Tagalog (Filipino) with Nauyac, and Tagalog with Orlando Mahiwo and Santos Bayucca. Most of my conversations with the young villagers were in Tagalog and sometimes also in English, and also in English with the elders.

During initial field trips in 1998, I asked Rowena Nakake, who later became the Hungduan municipal employee in charge of tourism development, to act as my interpreter and research assistant but, since then, I have had neither. In Hapao I lodged with Nauyac at his 'Global' office-cum-home in the Boyyod area. After he moved to Danghai on the outskirts of Lagawe town in 2002, I stayed in the home of Orlando Mahiwo, who continued the movement as Nauyac's right-hand man and built a house next to the office. People involved in 'Global', as well as other villagers, would gather there almost every day and so, just by being there, I was able to obtain all sorts of information. In the evenings we often purchased a bottle of gin from Santiago's *sari-sari* store (general store) next door and continued our conversation over a couple of quiet drinks. Of course, I also made sure to go out into the village and walk around to talk with the villagers every day.

I became interested in Hapao because of the intriguing name Nauyac gave to his 'Global' reforestation movement and the meanings it contained. I was also fascinated by Nauyac on my first meeting with him at his home in Baguio and inspired by Kidlat's role in the movement and the way he positioned himself as Nauyac's disciple. The initial research theme was the reforestation movement and the conservation of the rice terraces and the natural environment. Later, however, my interests expanded to development and when I joined a number of Grant-in-Aid for Scientific Research projects funded by the Japan Society for the Promotion of Science (JSPS), my interests and the object of my research grew wider to include history, out-migration, cultural revitalization, international aid and so on. However, while my interests expanded (or perhaps diffused) with the passage of time, the fact that they converged on the theme of globalization, as indicated by the title of this book, means that I seem to have returned in the end to my original intention.

By 'original intention' I mean that vivid first impression I had on meeting Nauyac and my own personal interest in globalization impacts as an urgent research theme on *dekigoto* (event or impact). I began thinking about events in my first ethnography on Mount Pinatubo Aetas (Asian-type Negritos with shifting cultivation and hunting-gathering for their subsistence), *Dekigoto no minzokushi* (Ethnography of the event) (Shimizu 1990), and continued in *Bunka no naka no seiji* (Politics in culture) (Shimizu 1991), where I looked at the People Power Revolution in the Philippines in 1986 as a religious, cultural and political event, and *Funka no kodama* (Echoes of the eruption) (Shimizu 2003), where I looked at the events surrounding the eruption of Mount Pinatubo in 1991, the biggest eruption in the twentieth century. Globalization, the theme of this book, can also be considered as a major event in recent years in the line of my lifework on event and its impact on socio-cultural transformation.

Acknowledgements

My research trips to the Philippines for this book were as follows. I made my first trip to Baguio during the May holidays in 1997, when I met with Kidlat and Nauyac and spent a week conducting preliminary research there. I made a total of fourteen visits to Hapao in March 1998, September–October 1998, March 1999, March 2000, March 2001, March 2002, February–March 2003, March 2004, August 2005, March 2006, March 2007, April and June 2008, and July 2009, before completing the ethnography in Japanese to be published (Shimizu, 2013). These visits lasted between one to five weeks for a total of 230 days in the field over twelve years. When I was making my way to and from Hapao I stopped off in Baguio and spent a number of nights staying in Nauyac's home in the Asin Road Barangay, where I conducted research with the migrant Ifugao community. I also visited Sannan town in Hyōgo Prefecture three times, where, as well as interviewing IKGS members, I visited the offices of the NGO to consult relevant documents. Since completing the Japanese edition of this ethnography, I have continued to visit the field almost every year for the past several years.

Other than the first visit, which I made at my own expense, funding for this project came from my membership in the following JSPS research projects: JSPS Research for the Integrated Research Project for Future 'Impact Analysis of Metropolitan Policies for Development and Environmental Conservation in the Philippines' (Chief Investigator: Ohmachi Tatsuo, Tokyo Institute of Technology), 1997–2001; Ministry of Education, Culture, Sports, Science and Technology Grant-in-Aid for Scientific Research (A) 'Development in Southeast Asia's Island Regions and the Peripheral World: Minorities, Boundaries, Gender' (Chief Investigator: Katō Tsuyoshi, Kyoto University), 2002–04; MECSST Grant-in-Aid for Scientific Research on Innovative Areas 'The Generation and Utilization of Cultural Resources' (Chief Investigator: Yamashita Shinji, University of Tokyo), 2004–06, and an Kyoto University individual travel grant in 2007; and the Global Center of Excellence Program, 'In Search of Sustainable Humanosphere in Asia and Africa' (Chief Investigator: Sugihara Kaoru, Kyoto University), 2008. In August 2005 and June 2008, I made my research visits as head of the evaluation team for the Japan International Cooperation Agency (JICA).

After publishing the monograph in Japanese, I visited Hapao and the Hungduan area with JSPS Grant-in-Aid for Scientific Research (A) 'Issues on Constructing Civil Societies in Asia and International Politics' (Chief Investigator: Takenaka Chiharu, Rikkyo University/Saint Paul's University), 2011–2014; and I also received a JSPS Grant-in-Aid for Scientific Research (A) 'Anthropology of Response-ability: In Search for a New Style of Engaged Anthropology' (Chief investigator: Shimizu Hiromu, Kansai University), 2015–2018.

During my research trips I received the full cooperation of Lopez Nauyac and Orlando Mahiwo, who allowed me to stay in their homes and to go around with them to anywhere to observe their activities, and from their family and kin, Kidlat Tahimik and Katrin de Guia who were kind enough to offer any help and information necessary for my research, Santos Bayucca, the son-in-law of Nauyac, the members of 'Global' and all the people of Hapao, especially elders such as Teofilo Gano, a *monbaki*, Victor Melon, Angelina Gano and Joseph Nakake, who was a younger brother of my good old friend, the late Sylvano Mahiwo (1951–2015), a professor at the Asian Center, University of the Philippines, Diliman, as well as municipal mayors of Hungduan, Hilario Bumangabang and Pablo Cuyahon Sr. On the Japanese side, I owe much to Tomita Kazuya, Tomita Eriko, Segawa Chiyoko, Ōtake Asuka and Fujimura Masami of the NGO NEKKO, which continuously supported not only Nauyac's reforestation movement but also my research in Hapao and Japan. I owe them my most sincere thanks.

In preparing the Japanese manuscript for publication, Suzuki Tetsuya of Kyoto University Press offered many helpful comments and suggestions. Thanks to him, I was able to make many changes and improvements, including a major reorganization of the chapter structure. Thanks to Takase Momoko of the editing office of Tōyōsha for correcting mistaken and missing characters, as well as pointing out numerous repetitions and overlaps in the text. In April 2010, I began serving as Director of the Center for Southeast Asian Studies at Kyoto University while I was still correcting, revising and proofing the manuscript. This led to lengthy delays and created many headaches for the publisher. It is only thanks to the cooperation of Mr Suzuki and Ms Takase that I was able to compete the manuscript. I thank them from the bottom of my heart.

And last but not least, I would like to express my sincere gratitude to Dr. Alexander Brown, a JSPS International Research Fellow at Japan Women's University and an Honorary Fellow at University of Sydney, and a freelance editor Ms Cathy Edmonds for their careful and meticulous works of translation and copyediting. And also again to Kidlat Tahimik, who read through my draft of Chapters 6 and 7, corrected factual errors and provided constructive suggestions.

1 Thinking about Globalization at the Periphery
An Attempt at an Anthropology of Response-ability

This book is an ethnography of a small grassroots reforestation, cultural revival and social development movement that has been underway since the late 1990s in Hapao, a village in the Municipality of Hungduan in Ifugao Province, high up in the Cordillera Mountains in the north of the Philippine island of Luzon. By looking at the way globalization has penetrated the village and how the villagers have become entangled in it, I

Watching the sunset in the front garden of a house in Hapao, where I conducted my research. One boy plays guitar while another sends a text message on his mobile phone. They turned to face me when I greeted them from behind. (6 June, 2008)

1

consider the extent to which globalization has penetrated even the remote mountains of the Philippines at the grassroots level, its influence over the village and its people, and the significance of this process. I refer to globalization having 'penetrated' in the past tense because, in the broadest sense, the phenomenon we refer to as globalization first emerged in Ifugao as far back as the end of the sixteenth century when Spain colonized the Philippines. However, since around 1990, and coinciding almost exactly with the end of the Cold War, the villagers of Hapao have been swept up in a new wave of rapid globalization as they depart the Philippines to become overseas migrant workers.

As well as examining the micro-level reality of globalization in the households of a village located on the global periphery and its impact on the way of life of its inhabitants, this book contributes to anthropology by challenging it to take more seriously the 'participation' component of the discipline's foundational methodology of participant observation. In recent years, calls for a public anthropology have taken place both in the United States and in Japan. Anthropologists have been asked to make a real commitment to addressing social problems and to contribute to finding solutions. However, addressing these issues in the anthropologist's home country oftentimes seems more pressing. Of course, we cannot ignore the fact that anthropologists ought to face up to the culture and society from which they come. However, it is also true that for the people who offer their cooperation to the anthropologist when he or she spends an extended period of time in the field, either by helping with the research or simply living there day to day, it is just as important that the anthropologist responds to their hopes, expectations, requests and demands. I call this the anthropology of response-ability and I have done my best to put it into practice.

This book is an account of my attempt at the anthropology of response-ability over the twenty-year period from 1997 to 2017 and constitutes a reflexive synthesis of my long-term commitment to the field. I spent a total of 290 days – during annual trips that lasted for as long as one month or as little as a week – at my primary field site of Hapao, which, during that time, has undergone major social and economic change. This book is the result of trial and error and an attempt at a new cultural anthropology. It is an attempt at a comprehensive ethnography containing an overview of various aspects of the field site, including its history, ecology, livelihood, culture and social movements.

Thinking about Globalization at the Periphery

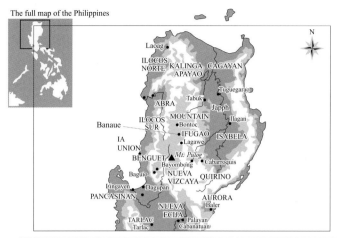

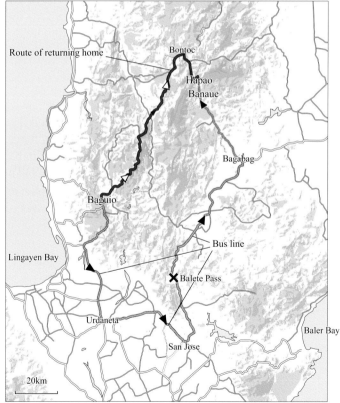

Map of northern Luzon

Confronting globalization in the deep mountains

For the majority Filipinos known as the lowland Christians, who make up nearly 90 percent of the archipelago's population of 100 million, particularly for those who live in Metro Manila, the Ifugaos, with their different cultural traditions, seem very remote, both psychologically and culturally. Like the Muslims who make up 5 percent of the total population of the nation and live in the southwest part of Mindanao and farther south on islands in the Sulu Archipelago, the Ifugaos represent an exotic other. However, even the indigenous Ifugao villages of the high mountains have been inundated by the wave of globalization that has washed over them since the early 1990s in the form of development projects funded by foreign governments, migrant work, inbound tourism from overseas, satellite broadcasts, films and music on video and DVD, and mobile telephony. The villagers have confronted this wave and have gone along for the ride, making use of the things that globalization has brought while struggling to defend and improve their way of life. Globalization has been accompanied by major changes in the villagers' way of life and in the configuration of their social networks.

The argument in this book centers on the work of two men who were in their late and mid-50s when I began my research in 1997, and it draws extensively on narratives of their activities as they recounted them to me. The first is Lopez Nauyac, the leader of the reforestation movement in Hapao. The second is Kidlat Tahimik, a world-renowned filmmaker who received an American-style education delivered in English and absorbed the influence of the United States in his way of thinking and his sensibilities. In his quest to remake himself as an authentic Filipino, he reveres Nauyac as a soul brother and spiritual guru. He purchased a traditional Ifugao-style house and relocated it to Patpat, the *sitio* (territorial enclave) in Hapao where Nauyac was born. He visits the village frequently and has produced documentary films in full collaboration with Nauyac as part of the reforestation movement. Kidlat has shown a number of these films first at the Yamagata International Documentary Film Festival and later at other international film festivals.

My field site of Hapao is a remote mountain village deep in the Cordillera Mountains, 250 kilometers to the north in a straight line from Manila. It is famous for its splendid rice terrace landscapes that were included on the UNESCO World Heritage List in 1995 as an example of living cultural heritage. Furthermore, at the end of the Asia-Pacific War,

General Yamashita Tomoyuki, commander-in-chief of the Philippines Area Army, led the main body of the Japanese forces (typically referred to as the Shobu Group) to the village, where his force of approximately 60,000 soldiers made their last stand. Drawing on this history, when Nauyac founded a non-governmental organization (NGO) in 1996 to initiate the reforestation movement, he called it the Ifugao Global Forest City Movement. The NGO's articles of incorporation loudly proclaim that life in Hapao was already deeply imbricated with global events and global political and economic flows.

Nauyac's skillful and convincing explanation of the significance of the reforestation movement enabled him to secure significant assistance funding from the Philippine government, a number of private foundations in Japan and the Japan International Cooperation Agency (JICA). The NGO began its work the year after it was established and implemented successive reforestation and social development projects over more than ten years. The word 'Global', a shortened form of the NGO's name, became an everyday expression in the village and was on everyone's lips. While money and projects from global NGOs flowed in, out of a village containing 338 households and 1,750 individuals (according to the

Commemorative photograph of Nauyac (left) and Kidlat in full Ifugao dress at Hapao (Photo provided by Kidlat Tahimik, Hapao, 1999).

2006 figures from the Hungduan municipal government), over the past nearly quarter of a century more than 150 migrant workers from Hapao, mostly women working as live-in domestic helpers, have left the village and traveled overseas to twenty-seven countries. Life in the village now depends on income and information obtained overseas via an extensive global network that extends beyond the village, beyond Ifugao Province and across the oceans, leading to changes in their way of life.

I chose the village of Hapao as a field site because of my interest in two prominent individuals whose activities I discuss in this book and because of the different forms of globalization taking place there. Three points, in particular, are worth noting. First, Kidlat has great respect and interest in Nauyac's ideas and work, and has been making documentaries to record his efforts towards reforestation and cultural revival for more than twenty years. Kidlat's own character developed for the first half of his life as an honors student receiving his education in English amid a successfully established elite in the Philippines. He sees Nauyac as someone who would surely guide him in decolonizing his Americanized soul and considers him to be a font of inspiration and a model for attempts to temporarily dissolve and then reconstruct his own identity. Over the past twenty years, Kidlat has produced nearly ten documentary films about Nauyac. I am particularly interested in Kidlat's life, his quest to live as an authentic or an indigenous Filipino, and his earnest but always good-humored attempt to reconstruct himself as such. I am likewise fascinated by the creative process whereby he makes his documentaries in collaboration with Nauyac.[1]

---

1 I first became interested in Kidlat Tahimik when his first film *Perfumed Nightmare* was screened at the Japan Foundation Film Festival in September 1982. When I met him at the reception party at the New Otani Hotel, I thought that with his Beatles mop top haircut and somewhat disheveled appearance he looked less like a famous director and more like an aging hippie. When I started talking with him, he said that he was feeling uncomfortable staying in the hotel. He felt suffocated and quite unwell in the cold and artificial hotel atmosphere where one could not smell the rain or feel the wind against one's skin or hear the sound of children playing. I invited him to stay with me in the rental house I was living in in Hayama, Kanagawa Prefecture, and he spent a couple of days with my family. He carried my then nine-month-old daughter when we visited the temples of Kamakura and when we walked along the beach. When he grew tired of walking and rested under the great ginko trees that line the stairs up to the Tsurugaoka Hachiman shrine, he sat for a while doing nothing and just stared blankly at the setting sun. Suddenly

Three main characters of this ethnography, Shimizu, Kidlat and Nauyac (from left), celebrating a happy new year at Uhaj guest lodge. (January 1, 2017)

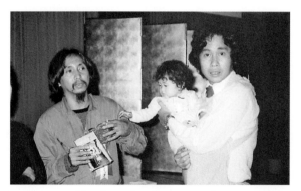

Kidlat, myself and my daughter at a welcome party in New Otani Hotel as part of a South Asian film festival organized by the Japan Foundation. (15 October, 1982)

he said, 'I can feel the cosmic vibrations. My soul feels at peace.' This scene and his words left a deep impression on me and I still remember them vividly. Later, I realized that being inspired by the 'cosmic vibrations' was a keyword in his way of life and in his filmmaking. I later lost contact with him after I moved house a number of times. When we met again in Baguio in the Philippines in May 1997, where I went at my own expense in order to carry out some preliminary research, he took me to visit Lopez Nauyac's house. During my time in Baguio, I rekindled the old friendship with Kidlat and once more became interested in his life and work. This, and my growing interest in Nauyac's plans for the reforestation project in Hapao, led to my research on their activities and to my fieldwork there.

When considering the problems of representation – of who speaks about indigenous culture, society and way of life and the manner in which it is portrayed – for nearly twenty years Nauyac has been expressing himself and his views eloquently and assertively as an indigenous person through Kidlat's lens. In this sense, Nauyac is no longer a mere subject in Kidlat's films and has become a co-producer and co-conspirator with him as they attempt to give voice to the contemporary indigenous experience and philosophy. He speaks confidently as he talks about the meaning of the reforestation movement, his own identity as an indigenous person and in praise of Ifugao culture. Through this storytelling and his approach to explaining his culture, as well as his praxis of self-determination in matters of representation, he clearly demonstrates a strategy for indigenous people living in the modern world as our contemporaries. When I interviewed him, he also demonstrated the eloquent self-expression and self-advocacy that has been strengthened through his relationship with Kidlat – in particular, through their everyday conversations and casual question-and-answer sessions. He spoke frankly with me about his memories of the time when the Japanese army came to the village at the end of the last world war and asked me about Japan today. He made it clear that he expected to receive some assistance from Japan and made specific demands and requests of me directly.

In terms of the problem of representation, I conceived this book as an attempt to respond sincerely to Nauyac's expectations and questions.[2] This ethnography is based on the understanding that Nauyac and the people of Ifugao are my contemporaries, for although we live in different places, in a broader sense we live in the shared space and time of the contemporary world in which our lives are connected both directly and indirectly by the spread of globalization.

The second important point of interest in this study is Nauyac's search for a way for the villagers of Hapao to take pride in themselves as indigenous people maintaining their native culture in the era of globalization and to enrich their lives. Nauyac grasps that the great wave of globalization is

---

2 However, having met Nauyac's expectations and his requests, I had no intention of becoming a kind of billboard to spruik his activities. While Nauyac and Kidlat focus on the wonders of Ifugao traditional culture, adopting a stance that might be called strategic essentialism, my own position is different. I respect Nauayc's work and the strategy that underpins it but I emphasize the contemporaneity of the Ifugaos and the hybridity of their way of life.

looming over Hapao and rather than trying to run away from it, he confronts it and seizes the opportunity to actively make use of it and derive some benefit from it. Since the Spanish colonization of the Philippines, Ifugao has continually been subject to interventions by forces acting on behalf of global political and military powers, and Ifugaos have determined a defensive strategy to protect the lands of their ancestral domain. However, what makes the recent great wave of globalization so different is that it has enabled the villagers to pursue an offensive strategy, whereby individuals leave their native villages to work all over the world, as can be seen in the migrant work undertaken by the villagers of Hapao. To continue with the military metaphor, it is as if the field of battle on which the flesh-and-blood human beings fight their daily battles with globalization has spread out

An elderly couple model their ethnic dress in front of the rice terraces in Banaue while a tourist takes a souvenir photograph. They ask for 5–10 pesos (11–22 cents) as a model fee. The photographer is an older Japanese man (late sixties) who has come sightseeing with his thirty-something-year-old Filipina wife. (March 1, 2000)

from Hapao and its neighboring villages in the remote mountains on the periphery of the Philippines to incorporate places all over the wide world.[3]

Using Mary Pratt's (1992) term, this new field of battle can be referred to as a contact zone.[4] Contact zones are 'social spaces where cultures meet, clash and grapple with each other, often in contexts of highly asymmetrical relations of power, such as colonialism, slavery' (Pratt 1992: 2). Drawing on Pratt's definition, Tanaka (2007: 32) suggests that today, with the rapid advance of globalization, contact zones can be thought of as appearing not only on the 'colonial periphery' but everywhere, even in the cities of the former colonial powers. As Tanaka points out, the traditional anthropologist, like a scientific traveler, refused to see the field as a contact zone where different powers interact with one another, but instead wrote about and dissected the world of the other as entirely self-contained while placing him or herself in a position of transcendence.

In reality, however, the field is a contact zone. By placing his or her body in the field and participating in and observing the daily life and activities of the people there, the anthropologist necessarily practices a form of contact within in the contact zone. Furuya (2001: 16–22), who was the first person to introduce Pratt's notion of the contact zone to Japan and who developed his argument in the context of Latin America (specifically Brazil), points out that 'an individual's history, place and positionality cannot be erased from theory' – and goes on to assert that anthropological fieldwork is 'a site of negotiation… where people negotiate the terms of their own culture with others' and that, therefore, 'an ethnography is simply a record of that negotiation'.

To elaborate on what Tanaka and Furuya are saying, it is neither intellectually nor ethically possible to practice ethnography while eliding the anthropologist in the name of guaranteeing objectivity or to ignore the ways in which the field site interfaces with the world outside. Nor should

---

3 Focusing on the mass migration of human beings on a global scale, from the end of the sixteenth century ten to twenty million people were taken from west Africa to the Americas over three centuries as part of the slave trade. Furthermore, in the period between the middle of the nineteenth century and the First World War, thirty to forty million Europeans crossed the Atlantic Ocean (Masamura 2009: 40, 51).

4 Pratt explains that her use of the term 'contact zone' is often synonymous with the 'colonial frontier' but because the term 'frontier' implies a set of power relations that situate the frontier in relation to the unilateral gaze of the ruler at the center, she avoids the term in favor of the notion of contact, with its implication of a mutually negotiated encounter (Pratt 1992: 6–7).

the anthropologist seek to portray the field as a self-contained microcosmic other. Instead, the onus is on contemporary anthropology to chronicle the way people who are fighting for a better life and for their place in the world negotiate within the constraints that are imposed on them by the existing relations of power that have developed through history.

Applying this perspective to my field site of Hapao, I can say that I became deeply entangled in the field as a site of negotiation between various actors right from the beginning of my fieldwork. From the perspective of the people of Hapao, I was a person from Japan, a country that once sent a great army under the command of General Yamashita to their lands but that now has a rich economy and provides generous foreign assistance through JICA. I appeared to be a person with great potential utility. I confronted this reality directly and accepted it, becoming entangled in the field site and deeply involved in their struggle as an active supporter and collaborator. As well as introducing a Japanese NGO to them, I became a member of their reforestation and cultural revitalization movement and served as a point of contact with the Japanese side, as well as an embedded reporter.

In this book I report reflexively on Nauyac's villager-led, bottom-up reforestation movement based on my observations and on information and documents that came to hand during my involvement in the project. If, as Furuya (2001) observes, 'people negotiate the terms of their own culture with others', then this book is a record of my entanglement in these negotiations and of my deep engagement in securing assistance from Japan in a contact zone that incorporates Hapao, the municipality of Hungduan and parts of Ifugao Province. It is an attempt to write an ethnography of the anthropology of commitment or the anthropology of response-ability (a neologism I created combining the words response and responsibility) that I describe above.

The third and related point of interest is that the movement for local empowerment that originated with a residents' movement founded and led by Nauyac – and which pursues reforestation, social development and cultural revival – provides a concrete example of the possibilities and pitfalls of participatory development. Nauyac positions the remote village of Hapao in northern Luzon within a network of global relationships and emphasizes, in particular, the deep historical links it has with both Japan and the United States. By means of this positioning, he cleverly drew me into the movement as a companion and collaborator in order to obtain grant funding from Japanese NGOs and JICA. He successfully expanded a grassroots reforestation movement that began with money from his own pocket in the mid-1990s into a project that drew in municipal and provincial governments. Beginning in 2000, the movement obtained 86 million Japanese yen (equivalent to US$800,000; $1 floated between ¥105 and ¥130 between 2001 and 2008) in grant funding from Japan over an eight-year period.

I have been deeply involved in Nauyac's reforestation movement from the beginning. At first, I helped him to find a counterpart NGO in Japan and acted as an intermediary between the two. When it came time to put forward a project proposal and apply for funding, I lent my full support by providing documents and ideas to help with the application process. When the JICA Partnership Program commenced in 2002, the 'Global' reforestation movement was the first proposal accepted under the Support Type program and the only proposal to be accepted in that first year. JICA publicized the project widely in various publicity materials. The work of a small NGO based in the mountains of Hikami in Hyōgo Prefecture, Japan, supporting a locally led reforestation movement to protect the UNESCO World Heritage-listed rice terraces and improve local livelihoods in the Philippines was presented as the first model case of the type of grassroots international collaboration that JICA was looking to promote. After the completion of the project, JICA asked me to head the post-implementation stage evaluation team and to carry out a pre-implementation stage evaluation when it was selected for continued funding under the Partner Type scheme. As part of these evaluations I compiled lengthy reports with the assistance of JICA staff.

Looking back over the process of my involvement, I began an engaged anthropology just by chance in June 1991, when Mount Pinatubo in western Luzon erupted. I happened to be at the beginning of a one-year research sabbatical in the Philippines. My involvement on the ground in providing emergency aid and later reconstruction assistance to the indigenous Aeta people, who were the worst affected by the disaster, led me quite unexpectedly to make an exploratory trial run of 'entangled anthropology'. I made a further step towards embracing the challenge of an anthropology of commitment or response-ability in Ifugao, where I was directly involved in seeking development assistance. In other words, I took the pursuit of participant observation to its extreme (or perhaps back to its roots) as I unhesitatingly threw myself into the project as it unfolded. When a group of people from Hapao sought to expand their

Thinking about Globalization at the Periphery 13

Upper left: Nauyac reinforcing the key points for planting saplings to a group of students from the elementary school in Hapao at the reforestation site.

Upper right: Students carrying two saplings each head to the reforestation site near the Hungduan municipal offices. The adults who are helping them bring greater quantities of saplings separately.

Middle right, left: The children planting the saplings.

Bottom: This reforestation activity is part of JICA's Partnership Program. Three female Japanese university students who spent a year in Hapao also take part in the planting.

(These five photographs provided by Ōtake Asuka, one of the Japanese volunteers). (August 25, 2004)

initial efforts to protect the rice terraces and forests that are the basis of their livelihood – and of their society and culture – and to improve their standard of living, I undertook fieldwork while also actively cooperating in planning for the project and obtaining funding from Japan, and during the implementation I attempted to intervene in dialogue and to understand what was happening in Ifugao.

The above-mentioned keywords of representation, globalization, social development and commitment are directly connected to a broader problem. Each aspect is important and each is the subject of a chapter or chapters in this book. However, as I have tried to show through this book's title, when it comes to the phenomena of globalization that spread rapidly at the end of the twentieth century and its problems, the most interesting point that can be derived from the example of Hapao is the alternative perspective that this small village provides – the perspective of the indigenous peoples who live in the deep mountains of the Philippines, on the periphery of a developing country. It enables us to see and understand another global flow that is led not from New York, London, Beijing or Tokyo in the center of the globe, nor from above by the power elites of multinational corporations and empire, but from the periphery, from below, by the poor and overlooked.

The global and the local through history

Globalization, in the classical definition proposed by cultural anthropologists Jonathan Inda and Renato Rosaldo (2008: 4), refers to the mass circulation of people, capital, goods, information and images across national borders that results in a condition of intimate connectivity between disparate places and regions of the globe. The term 'globalization' and the phenomena to which it refers began to attract significant interest in the 1990s, when the Cold War division of the world into East and West came to an end, symbolized by the collapse of the Berlin Wall in 1989 and the dissolution of the Soviet Union in 1991. However, scholarly opinion is divided as to what constitutes globalization and when it first began. Broadly speaking, the arguments can be divided into those that look for the origins of globalization in pre-modern times, those that focus on the beginning of modernity in the sixteenth century (the Age of Exploration), and those that emphasize the changes that have taken place since the 1970s (Steger 2003).

If we were to focus on human migration and take a long view of history, we could see globalization as having begun 70–80,000 years ago when contemporary humanity's ancestors, the first modern humans (who emerged more than 100,000 years ago following the Australopithecines, primitive man and Neanderthal stages), moved out of Africa and across the surface of the globe (Chanda 2007).[5] Alternatively, the Age of Discovery that began at the end of the fifteenth century can also be seen as the forerunner to what we now call globalization, as symbolized in Magellan's circumnavigation of the globe in 1519–22. Following the Age of Discovery, as the Western powers divided up and colonized the globe, they initiated a complete political and economic change at a global scale. From the Age of Discovery through the sudden rise and flourishing of industrial capitalism that built on colonialism up until the recent information technology revolution, people, things and information have moved on a global scale beyond the local communities to which they were once bound. The instantaneous flow of information that resulted from the information revolution and the mass movement of people and goods at high speed that has been enabled by developments in logistics have been particularly important in bringing rapid and fundamental change to the objective nature of time and space. This has led to the rapid development of what David Harvey (1989: 260–307) aptly describes as 'time-space compression'.[6] In 1958 Hannah Arendt had pointed out that while the

---

5 Robertson (1997: 12–13) criticizes Giddens' idea that globalization is a product of modernity, arguing instead that it is a very long-term process that has continued over many centuries. In this sense, the mass migration of the Mongoloid peoples out of the African continent at the end of the last ice age 20,000 years ago, when the Bering Sea was frozen over, could be seen as a single episode in the spread of humanity across the world and as part of the process of globalization, as could the migration of people 1000 years ago from the Malay world in the islands of Southeast Asia across the sea to the islands of the South Pacific and as far as Madagascar. Today, human beings are the only biological organisms to make their home in every possible environment on the surface of the globe, from the frozen north to the tropical equator and from the coral atolls of the South Pacific, just a few meters above sea level, to the Andes and Himalaya mountains 4000 meters above sea level.
6 Harvey (1989: 338–42) refers to this as the condition of postmodernity. He believes that because it was brought about by flexible accumulation during the era of post-Fordism, postmodernity can be adequately understood using a historical materialist approach and he has conducted a bold analysis of it based on Marx's critique of modernity.

original intention of the explorers and navigators of the Age of Discovery was to enlarge the globe, their voyages resulted in the final conquest of space by speed, leading distance to become meaningless. She pointed out that we 'now live in an earth-wide continuous whole', resulting in what she described as the 'shrinkage of the globe' (Arendt 1958: 250).

However, if we differentiate the stages of globalization more rigorously, in the sixteenth and seventeenth centuries it mainly involved the trade in specialty goods between separate cultural spheres, each with its own distinct economy. In the eighteenth and nineteenth centuries, globalization was driven by a system of free trade that was based on the theory of comparative advantage, and from the nineteenth to the twentieth centuries it was connected with imperialist attempts to capture resources and markets. By comparison, globalization today is characterized by the way the market economy, with its free movement of technology, information, goods and finance across national borders, drives the standardization and harmonization that creates intimate connections between different places on the earth and the people who live there and leads them to become mutually dependent on and to influence one another. Robertson (1992: 8) describes how globalization also brings about 'the compression of the world as a whole and the intensification of consciousness of the world as a whole'.

An alternative view of the same contemporary world that Harvey and Robertson describe is that people living in different places (localities) and the events that take place there, as well as the ways in which their societies and ways of life are organized, have become tightly bound up with one another and mutually influential. Giddens (1990: 64) emphasizes this aspect in his definition of globalization, which describes it as 'the intensification of worldwide social relations'. In other words, globalization strengthens mutual interaction. Rather than leading to a homogeneous world created through the free play of the unidirectional influences of powerful actors (multinational corporations, empires), it is a many-sided phenomenon that is accompanied by complex processes. Giddens points out the antagonism between the way globalization is pulled upwards by the centers of power and downwards by the diverse forces of resistance to them, and that it possesses not only a vertical but also a horizontal dynamic at both the domestic and transnational levels (Giddens 1999). Furthermore, whether power is exercised from above or from below, vertically or horizontally, it is bidirectional and reciprocal.

Castells (2001) takes a similar approach. He understands the interactions and cooperative relationships that connect across national borders between not only individuals but also businesses, social movements, experts and various other groups as the appearance of a 'network society'. Other theorists understand the problematic of globalization using terms such as 'deterritorialization' (Tomlinson 1999; Deleuze and Guatarri 1972) and 'the retreat of the state' (Strange 1996). The notion of 'cultural imperialism' tends to be used synonymously for the penetration into local cultures of an American culture that is seen as hegemonic and its absorption into the local – a problematic that is similarly conceptualized as 'McDonaldization', as production systems predicated on the relentless pursuit of rationalization spread and come to interact with and absorb traditional cultures (Tomlinson 1999; Ritzer 2000; Watson 1997). What each of these theorists is trying to capture through the word 'globalization' is the phenomenon whereby multilayered political, economic and cultural 'scapes' spread across the globe, transforming and reconfiguring the world as a whole as they penetrate and subsume it (Appadurai 1996).[7]

In contrast to this macroscopic view, research in anthropology has tended to mainly focus on the interface between the global and the local. Anthropologists carry out micro-level studies that look at the way subjective agents have reconfigured particular societies that experience globalization against the background of their own unique historical conditions. How have their cultural characteristics and way of life changed? Have they

---

7 The characteristics of the new organization of the world and of the great global process of transformation of recent years, which journalists and others have tried to capture through the use of the term 'globalization', include the widespread permeation of influences originating from the center on a global scale and the discord and change that they bring about. It is true that today, if you take the big picture perspective, the West continues to maintain absolute supremacy in terms of political, economic and military power, just as it did in the Age of Discovery. The interventions of multinational companies and international organizations – as well as governmental agencies headquartered in the major political, economic and cultural centers of the world, such as New York, Paris, and London – and their influence reach to the far corners of the earth. Furthermore, the global market economy is led by the West and organized in such a way that profits flow back to the Western world. The preponderance of theoretical work that take a macroscopic perspective on the process of globalization as a whole is also related to the subsumption of the world at large within neoliberal economics and the intricate web of relationships this has created.

adapted to global influences by accepting some while rejecting others? How has the reality of their daily lives changed as a consequence of all this? Anthropologists try to see globalization not simply as an overwhelming power that creates a unidirectional flattening of the world but by paying attention to the conflict that emerges as people actively respond, both by resisting globalization and by taking advantage of it within the unique conditions of their own local circumstances (Inda and Rosaldo 2008: 6–7).

The macroscopic viewpoint described above resembles the gaze of an astronaut looking down from a satellite floating in space. It takes a wide view of the makeup of the whole world on a global-scale, treating the activities of multinational companies and states as the primary unit of analysis. However, even an astronaut cannot see clearly everything that is taking place on earth and so it might be better to compare this approach to that of the view of the earth from the surface of the moon. By contrast, the micro-level viewpoint is that of a person riding in an airplane or a helicopter, or standing on the summit of a mountain, who has a bird's-eye view of a particular locality. My own perspective belongs naturally to the latter group. Furthermore, I have spent a lot of time up close with Nauyac in the 'Global' office that also serves as his home and followed him around Hapao neighboring villages to observe the daily lifeworld of the villagers. Having seen this world clearly through my observations, my perspective is even coarser than that of a bird's-eye view – it is the perspective of an ant running about on the surface of the earth. In this book I try to give the bug's-eye view, just like an ant reporting on what he sees in the immediate world around him.

As Beck (2002: 23) observes, to consider globalization as contained within the movement or flow of people, things, money and information in a space floating above the surface of the earth where flesh and blood humanity lives, inevitably results in a one-sided view. It is not the reality. Globalization is inseparable from the simultaneous process of localization and it is impossible to think about globalization without referring to particular sites and localities. One outcome of the debate on globalization is that we have once again recognized and reclaimed the importance of the concept of place. Robertson (1992) uses the concept of glocalization to talk about the dialectical process that operates between the global and the local. Similarly, Appadurai (1996) urges us to remember that the historical process that gives rise to locality is ultimately subject to the dynamics of the global. The logical conclusion to this is that 'there is nothing mere about the local' (Appadurai 1996: 18).

It is impossible to overstate the importance of the local for people who are living today in a time where the spread of globalization depends upon the different cultural traditions, social structures and historical processes of development that prevail in different places around the globe. However, the bug's-eye view that is produced by focusing on one particular place, no matter how detailed it may be, provides a narrow and limited picture of the world. No matter how many hundreds of such maps we might draw, we would be unable to capture the reality of the globalization that is currently taking place. Because globalization at the global scale is always accompanied by localization, the multilayered and complex connections between the separate local lifeworlds at the micro level and the global societal reconfiguration at the macro level must be taken into account

The 'Global' headquarters, also Nauyac's home. This traditional Ifugao-style house was moved and reassembled here from his birthplace in Patpat. Kidlat records the scene with the Bolex movie camera while Nauyac and his nephew Orlando Mahiwo, who is an unpaid volunteer, sort the native plant seeds they have collected. (March 23, 1998)

when arguing about globalization. No matter how closely the picture of an Ifugao village is drawn and presented in miniature in this book, neither the villagers nor their way of life are contained within the village, so it will necessarily be a particularly narrow and fragmentary map. Therefore, while I carried out the bulk of my fieldwork in Hapao, I also did some research in the Asin Road Barangay in Baguio, where many Ifugao migrants now make their homes, and at the offices of the NGO in Sannan town, Hikami-gun, Hyōgo Prefecture, Japan (which later merged into the municipality of Sasayama), that supports the reforestation movement in Hapao (this was both fieldwork and a kind of homework). In tracing the life journey and the work of Kidlat, who documents Nauyac's activities with his video camera, I conducted a number of long-form interviews with him both at his homes in Hapao and Baguio and in Japan. In addition to giving depth and breadth to my bug's-eye view of Hapao, this supplementary research attempts to show that the specific characteristics of the way globalization has unfolded in a single society located on the periphery has both an individual specificity and a broad generality.

The landscape of globalization from the remote mountains

I did not choose to focus on the Ifugao village of Hapao, an indigenous village located in the remote mountains far from the Metro Manila center of the Philippines, because it constitutes a unique exception to the Filipino majority. The reality is quite the opposite. The impact that the era of globalization has had in the high mountains can also be seen in the remote countryside all over the Philippines. Indeed, it is even more dramatic and striking there and the changes that have been brought about by globalization appear in concentrated form. In 2016, of the total Philippine population of around 100 million, approximately 10 million or about 10 percent of Filipinos were working abroad. Of these, about 50 percent had permanent residency overseas, 40 percent were regular employees and 10 percent worked in casual and temporary jobs. According to the *Bangko Sentral ng Pilipinas*, the Philippine Central Bank, overseas Filipinos (migrant workers) remitted a total of US$25.767 billion (approximately 2.9307 trillion yen) in 2015, constituting 9.8 percent of gross domestic product. In that year, 1.8 million people left the country to work overseas and approximately the same number returned following the conclusion of their contracts. Overall, the number of overseas Filipinos is increasing gradually. Since the 1970s, from the Marcos presidency through to the current Duterte administration, the Philippine government has consistently promoted migrant work as a matter of national policy. Successive presidents have heaped praise on these migrant workers and referred to them as national heroes because they play such an important role in supplementing the national coffers.

A significant amount of research on Filipino migrant workers looks at them from the perspective of globalization. However, most of this research has looked at the majority lowland Christians and considered their working conditions overseas; issues related to their adjustment or maladjustment to the host society; the reorganization of social relations that occurs when they are working overseas or upon their return; the problems faced by the families and children they leave behind; the maintenance, strengthening and reconstruction of identity; and the way migrant work transforms their understanding of the world (Aguilar Jr. 2009; Bonus 2000; Choy 2003; Constable 1997; Espiritu 2003; Parreñas 2001, 2005; Hall 2001; Tyner 2009; Nagasaka 2009). By contrast, this book looks at the reforestation and social development projects led by a native intellectual (he might also be called an idealist or a dreamer) who has a very clear understanding that we are living in an era of globalization. I consider these projects as a means of actively confronting and responding to globalization as it advances into the depths of the mountains. My reason for documenting and trying to understand Nauyac's attempt to maintain and strengthen the forests, rice terraces and traditions that form the basis of the Ifugao way of life and the context of the village in which it takes place, is not simply an attempt to fill a gap in the existing research on globalization, which usually looks at the majority Filipino society (and mostly at migrant work overseas, the impact of migration and international marriage). Beyond this, as Hall and Fenelon (2009) argue, by rethinking globalization from the perspective of the indigenous peoples who are positioned on the periphery of the world system, or even outside it, we can gain new understandings and expand our vision.[8]

---

8 Hall and Fenelon have used world systems theory to consider the movements of resistance and cultural revival by indigenous peoples in response to the spread of globalization. They find that world systems theory is an effective way to think about these movements, but they are critical of its blind spots regarding women and indigenous peoples. They find that in its attempt to capture the whole, it leaves out perspectives and analysis from below – particularly the way the aftereffects of colonialism persist within social science – and ghettoizes the study of indigenous

I also think of Hapao as an example of the 'grassroots globalization' or 'globalization from below' on which Appadurai places his hopes for a better future. As well as describing in detail what has been taking place in Hapao, this book is a report on my own active involvement in these events.[9] The example examined in this book is an initiative of globalization from the periphery and from a peripheral ethnicity. It is an introduction to and analysis of the villagers' confrontation with the wave of globalization that has come from above and from the center.[10] I hope to show that despite the fact that we live in different places that have traced their own unique historical pathways, we are all deeply connected in the contemporary era of globalization and that it therefore gives us the potential to reconstruct and reconfigure social relations on a new basis. I also believe that we can explore the potential for a new anthropology that allows itself to become involved in the movements and circumstances taking place in the field. The significance of the practices in which we engage to achieve this, no matter how small, and in the problems we encounter along the way, as well as through the human relations that are created through fieldwork, open up the potential for an anthropology of commitment.

Looking back at the way globalization has unfolded through history from the perspective of the Ifugaos, their entanglement in the global political and economic system, as well as their opposition and resistance and attempts to negotiate with it, began with the imposition of colonial rule by Spain. It seems likely that many Ifugao ancestors were people who escaped up into the mountains along the Magat River from the Cagayan

---

peoples within the category of ethnography, leaving them out of theoretical discussions in sociology, political science and international relations (Hall and Fenelon 2009: 12).

9 Kataoka (2006) adopts a similar perspective in *Shita kara no gurōbarizēshon* (Globalization from below).

10 Shimizu Akitoshi's (1998) edited collection on peripheral ethnicities points out the importance of the view from the periphery. The term 'peripheral ethnicities' refers to those groups that have been looked down upon, discriminated against and excluded as social minorities and who represent an often invisible face of the world's social structure. As a result, the historical processes by which they have been forced to the periphery and their current circumstances highlight the hidden structure of the contemporary world. Shimizu emphasizes that without recognizing this, it is impossible to understand the world today (Shimizu Akitoshi 1998: 5).

Valley region to avoid the poll tax and *corvée* (unpaid) labor imposed on those regions under Spanish rule (Keesing 1962: 322–3, 338–9). They may have followed a similar historical trajectory to the ethnic minorities of the mountainous region of the Southeast Asian mainland that Scott (2009) describes as Zomia. They are the descendants of people who fled in disgust at the imposition of *corvée* labor and tribute by the ruling powers in the lowlands and who wanted to preserve the freedom and independence of their world. However, they did not live entirely separately from the territories under Spanish control. They obtained luxury goods such as Chinese urns (used for making rice wine or salt-cured meats), Italian glass beads (for necklaces) and mother of pearl from the South Sea Islands (for decorating belts) by bartering with traders and continued to maintain trade relations for this purpose. Furthermore, in the nineteenth century the cultivation of tobacco became an important source of revenue for the Spanish colonial government and tobacco cultivation spread to the Ifugao region, which thereby became connected to the edge of a global network of tobacco distribution.

The ethnic minority highlanders who live in the remote mountains, away from the outside world and who might appear at first glance to lead an isolated life while maintaining their traditional customs, have also been undergoing a dynamic social reorganization that is intimately bound up with changes in the global political economy. Renato Rosaldo's (1980) book *Ilongot Headhunting, 1883–1974: A Study in Society and History* contains a detailed exploration of this point. The Ilongot people who live in Nueva Vizcaya Province adjacent to Ifugao organized their society in the mountains around swidden agriculture and headhunting, which they continued to practice until the 1960s. However, the periods when they carried out frequent headhunting raids into neighboring villages and down into the lowlands, and the consequent blood feuds, were found to alternate with periods when peace was maintained through treaties and marital exchange between the villages. Furthermore, the frequency of headhunting was closely tied to changes in the situation in the world outside. In other words, headhunting became more frequent in times of public discord in the lowland society, such as during the Philippine Revolution that sought independence from Spain (1898), the Great Depression (1929) and the guerilla struggle against Japanese military incursions into the Philippines (1944–45). It was the proclamation of martial law by President Marcos (1972), combined with the imposition of Philippine

Constabulary patrols, that finally caused the Ilongot people to abandon the custom of headhunting.[11]

When we consider the contemporary phenomenon of globalization that emerged in Ifugao about a quarter century ago, a number of changes distinguish this period from the forms of globalization that went before. Together with the Philippine government, foreign NGOs began actively providing development assistance. They also put energy into providing aid to people at the grassroots level, directly implementing small infrastructure projects, together with their Philippine counterparts, to improve the welfare of local people. In Boyyod along the main road where Nauyac's office-cum-house is in Hapao, a German NGO installed a tank to store water from a spring near the village and constructed a water supply system in 2002. Up until that time, people used nearby springs and wells to obtain water. As part of a large-scale agricultural development project (Central Cordillera Agricultural Programme) in northern Luzon, the European Union also installed irrigation equipment and encouraged a small-scale finance system (micro-credit) in the early 2000s, with some solid results.

Moreover, as already explained, nearly 10 percent of the population of the village have been abroad and the number is increasing. These migrations are noteworthy because, unlike in the past, the flows associated with the most recent wave of globalization have led from inside out, at least as far as the movement of people is concerned. Up until approximately 110 years ago – that is, until the beginning of American colonial rule – the Ifugaos also practiced headhunting and, within Ifugao, movement across large distances was almost entirely confined to men. For some time after the end of the Asia-Pacific War, it was still almost solely men who went out into the outside world. However, today most migrant overseas workers are women and they outnumber men four to one. Apart from those few who have married foreigners or obtained permanent residency visas or citizenship overseas as nurses or through other professional qualifications, the migrants who make up this outgoing flow leave for two or three years before returning home. But in the past such journeys were almost unheard of.

---

11 However, according to recent research, Ilongot headhunting continued to recur sporadically and intermittently even in the 2000s. Their antagonism towards the New People's Army's led to a number of heads being taken (Yang 2011).

The fact that these villagers return with the money and the experiences they have gained is of great significance.[12] This has led to an expansion of the consciousness of being Ifugaos and their sphere of action on a global scale. Simultaneously, they have begun to pay greater attention to traditional rituals, games and skills within the village, and to celebrate with great fanfare the culture that makes visible and concrete their identity as Ifugaos. The expansion of their consciousness to incorporate the outside world and its extension to their inner world – their growing concern with the history and culture that supports their way of life and their existence within the everyday world of the village, and the revival and performance of those cultural traditions – have taken place almost exactly at the same time. The Ifugao way of life and culture that constitutes their identity and roots as individuals and as members of an indigenous ethnic group is deeply rooted in their subsistence lifestyle and the landscape in which they live, which is based on the rice terraces. They see themselves as inextricably linked to their natural environment and globalization has only strengthened this awareness. They are affirming and discovering once again that just as plants sink their roots deep into the earth, the way of life of their people, which is symbolized by rice terrace agriculture, rests on the sweat of the ancestors who built the terraces out of stone and maintained them over many generations, on the water from the forests and the soil in the terraced paddies, and on the blessings of the gods.

The structure of this book is as follows. In Chapter 2, I give a general overview of the Municipality of Hungduan and the village of Hapao. In Chapter 3, I explain the unique rice terrace landscape of Hapao, which stretches up the mountain slopes from the river below, and the privately owned forests known as *pinugo* located above them that together make up a single ecosystem that provides the basis for the villagers' way of life. I also cover the woodcarving industry that was formerly the villagers' main

---

12 In the countries where they work, Ifugao migrant workers are regarded simply as cheap labor-power within a globally integrated economy. For the villagers, however, migrant labor is a chance to earn cash income and presents them with an opportunity to improve their standard of living by taking advantage of the wave of globalization. In places such as Hong Kong or Singapore, they form organizations based on regional and ethnic commonalities and share news and occasionally hold parties. They also raise money for charitable projects back home. Migrant workers from Hapao, for example, raised funds to pay for the construction of a new church in the village.

source of cash income and remains important for the poorer villagers who do not receive a higher education and spend their entire lives living in the village.

In Chapter 4, I argue that the Ifugao region as a whole and Hungduan in particular are not isolated from the outside world but have been subject to the direct intervention and influence of the great empires. During the period of Spanish colonial rule, the Ifugaos were subject to repeated incursions by punitive expeditionary forces that sought to subdue them and bring them under the dominion of the colonial government but were repulsed each time as the Ifugaos withdrew into the forest and fought back using guerilla warfare. During the American colonial period, the American governors skillfully won the Ifugaos over, creating a degree of trust and friendship that continues to be remembered fondly on both sides. In place of the Americans, at the end of the Asia-Pacific War, the main body of the Japanese forces under the command of General Yamashita retreated to Hungduan. The people of Hapao were forced to flee their homes and spend more than two months hiding in the forest. Because the Japanese troops ate all their seed rice and sweet potatoes, many people died of starvation and disease during that period and for some time afterwards. For Japan, the number of people lost in the Philippines campaign (498,000 people) made up nearly a quarter of their entire losses during the Asia-Pacific War. The progress of the war in the Philippines came to replicate in miniature the fate of Japan's war as a whole.

In Chapter 5, I draw on Nauyac's own words to explain his historical consciousness, his consciousness of himself as an Ifugao, the circumstances that led him to establish the reforestation movement and the reason he called it the 'Ifugao Global Forest City Movement'. I consider his use of words as a conscious practice of meaning making. Like Kidlat's technique in his documentary films, where Nauyac speaks directly to the camera, I avoid speaking for Nauyac by instead including the text of my interviews with him largely unaltered, making only minor edits such as removing repetition.

In Chapters 6 and 7, I explain the course of Kidlat Tahimik's life, some of the films he has made, and his attempt to reconstruct anew the body and soul that he regards as having been too thoroughly Westernized. As a world-famous filmmaker and a devotee of Nauyac and collaborator in his movement, I also place Kidlat here in a major supporting role in order to provide another way for Nauyac – who is the main character in this book – to demonstrate his historical consciousness, his awareness of himself as an Ifugao and his worldview.[13] For nearly thirty years, Kidlat has been recording Nauyac's activities and introducing him at film festivals around the world through his documentary films, communicating Nauyac's profound philosophy of nature, his historical consciousness, and his understanding of and love for the forests and trees. In this sense, through Kidlat's role as an intermediary – we might even call him a kind of spirit medium – Nauyac and his work have been launched from the territory of Ifugao and from people located on the periphery to be circulated, even in a small way, through international film festivals and the global networks of film culture, where he has caused quite a stir.

In Chapter 8, I introduce the profiles of migrant workers from Hapao who have experienced grassroots globalization firsthand and explain the circumstances that led them to journey from their remote mountain village out into the world. The majority are from relatively wealthy households and their university and other tertiary qualifications and the ability to speak English have enabled them to obtain work overseas. The flipside of

---

13 The appeal of non-Western indigenous culture to Western artists and intellectuals as a means of defamiliarizing their contemporary advanced global culture is by no means confined to Kidlat. For example, Nagafuchi (1998) conducted an insightful analysis of the resonances and sympathies that developed between the Western gaze and the people of Bali within a network that encompassed Bali, Paris and New York from the 1920s to 1930s. According to Nagafuchi, within the relationship of power between the metropole and the colony, while the civilized West looked down on the undeveloped Balinese, there were groups of Balinese artists who used this gaze for their own interests, demonstrating their dances for their Western opposites and creating arts and crafts for sale. He argues that tacit cooperation between the two groups 'created a global landscape for knowing and embodying culture', in which Bali was positioned as an 'island of art' and a 'secret island' (Nagafuchi 1998: 13). What makes Kidlat's case different is that he has rejected the job and social position he held as an elite who received his education in English and deliberately transgressed against Western civilization. Reverting to a colorless and neutral existence, he treats Nauyac as his spiritual guide on the path to resurrecting himself and his own Filipino identity. By placing Nauyac above himself spiritually and acknowledging his superiority, he also gains his active cooperation. As a comrade who works together with him to advance the reforestation and cultural revival movements, Kidlat creates documentary films with Nauyac's tacit collusion. He thereby deftly evades the predicament of positionality that has been problematized in post-colonial anthropology by maintaining an equal power relationship. This is the reason their friendship has continued for more than thirty years and it has given his films their characteristic frankness, familiarity, warmth, kindness and softness.

the rapid growth in migrant work since the 1990s has been the revival of the *Tungoh*, a traditional festival in Hungduan that confirms and displays their identity as Ifugaos. I explain how the municipal government came to lead this revival and celebrate the festival.

In Chapter 9, I explain how, in response to Nauyac's urging, I personally introduced him to a small Japanese NGO that went on to support his reforestation movement. Through this NGO, the movement received more than 80 million yen in grant funding from five organizations, including JICA. I consider the successes and failures of this project and the problems that it generated. The relationship with the Japanese-based NGO created direct connections between two remote mountain communities – one in Japan and one in the Philippines – and bypassed the great cities of Osaka and Manila. The fact that people from these two small villagers began to interact with one another is one small example of grassroots globalization.

In Chapter 10, I provide a summary of the book as a whole and reflect on the nature of grassroots globalization based on my study of Hapao. In the past the people of Hapao resisted the intervention of the great global political powers and were forced to wage a defensive struggle to protect their native land. By contrast, the recent wave of globalization has provided individual villagers with the opportunity to fight an offensive campaign as they sally forth as migrant workers. In addition, their cooperation with international NGOs has created a network that links them with Japan and other parts of Asia, the Middle East, Europe and the United States. I consider the wide-ranging and thorough-going reorganization of people's daily lives and their consciousness, both spatially and historically, that this has created. Finally, I reflect on my own attempt to respond sincerely to the people of Hapao, to whom I became connected through the relationships developed during my fieldwork. For the discipline of cultural anthropology that bases itself on fieldwork as a methodology, this approach is becoming an essential and, indeed, an inescapable part of the practice of fieldwork. While it does impose some restraints, it nevertheless opens up a wide range of possibilities.

Part I
Five Hundred Years of Negotiating with Global Powers

Rowena Nakake is watching afar from steps on a stone wall of a rice terrace in Ba-ang, a neighboring *barangay* of Hapao across the river. (March 11, 1999)

2 The Ifugao Lifeworld
A Fascination for Anthropologists and Communist Guerillas

As a people who have maintained their indigenous cultural traditions since before the coming of the Spanish, the Philippine state regards the Ifugaos as a source of national pride. The 1,000 peso note, which was the highest value paper currency when it was first issued in 1991, featured a scene of the Ifugao rice terraces of the Municipality of Banaue covering half of the reverse side. In 2010 the Philippine currency was completely redesigned and the Banaue rice terraces now appear on the back of the new twenty peso note, which has the lowest value of the paper currency but is the most frequently used by ordinary people for everyday economic transactions.

In 1995 UNESCO inscribed five clusters of rice terraces in Ifugao Province on its World Heritage List as living cultural landscapes.[1] This prompted the Philippine government to establish a committee on the Ifugao rice terraces. Both the Philippine government and a number of foreign aid organizations have implemented policies intended to conserve the terraces. In 2001 UNESCO also recognized the *hudhud* chants of Ifugao,

---

1 The five clusters on the World Heritage List are
(i) the Nagacadan terrace cluster in the municipality of Kiangan, a rice terrace cluster manifested in two distinct ascending rows of terraces bisected by a river; (ii) the Hungduan terrace cluster that uniquely emerges into a spider web; (iii) the central Mayoyao terrace cluster which is characterized by terraces interspersed with traditional farmers' bale (houses) and alang (granaries); (iv) the Bangaan terrace cluster in the municipality of Banaue that backdrops a typical Ifugao traditional village; and (v) the Batad terrace cluster of the municipality of Banaue that is nestled in amphitheatre-like semi-circular terraces with a village at its base. (UNESCO World Heritage Centre 1995)
Although Hapao is not mentioned in this brief synthesis, a sign reading 'UNESCO World Heritage Site' is situated beside a viewing deck in Hapao that provides panoramic views of the rice terraces.

which are recited at funerals and at harvest time, as Masterpieces of the Oral and Intangible Heritage of Humanity, and incorporated them in the Representative List of the Intangible Cultural Heritage of Humanity in 2008.

The term 'Ifugao' originally referred to an ethnic group living in an area of the Cordillera Mountains of northern Luzon and to their language. While consolidating its system of colonial administration in the nineteenth century, the Spanish began to refer to the administrative district where the group lived as Ifugao. When the United States took over the Philippine colony from the Spanish at the beginning of the twentieth century, it took a special interest in the Cordillera Mountains. In 1905 Ifugao was separated from Nueva Vizcaya Province and made into a separate territory with Captain Jefferson Davis Gallman as governor. In 1908 it was incorporated as a sub-province of Mountain Province. In 1966 Ifugao was elevated to the status of an independent province and it remains so today.

Since the beginning of American colonial rule, the Ifugao have attracted the particular interest of American administrators and anthropologists. Of all the indigenous peoples of the Cordillera, the relative ease of access to the Ifugaos from the lowlands of the Cagayan Valley, the splendor of their rice terraces and the way they have preserved their traditional culture have all contributed to this fascination. Of the 14–17 million indigenous people belonging to 110 ethno-linguistic groups that live in the Philippines (according to the Indigenous Peoples' Rights Act of 1997), the Ifugaos have been the subject of a disproportionately large number of research papers and have featured frequently in newspaper and magazine articles.

Apart from a small low-lying area in the southeast of the province, Ifugao is mostly mountainous. Most of the valleys occupied by the Ifugaos are located in the highlands 700–1,400 meters above sea level. The highest rice terraces are located at around 1,600 meters above sea level. The languages spoken by the Ifugaos can be broadly classified into three groups: the Ibulao group in the west, the Alimit group in the east and the central group (Conklin 1980: 3, 37–8). Hungduan Municipality, which includes the village of Hapao, is in the western part of the province and belongs to the Ibulao group.

According to data provided by the Philippine Statistics Authority (2015), Ifugao Province is made up of eleven municipalities, which are further divided into 175 *barangays* (the smallest administrative division in the Philippines), and has a population of 202,802. In 1990 the population stood at 147,281, in 2000 it had grown to 161,623 and in 2010 it was 191,078. This

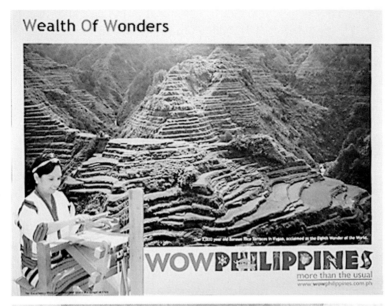

Top: Tourism promotion poster featuring President Gloria Macapagal Arroyo (2001–10) dressed in Ifugao ethnic dress and sitting at a loom with the Banaue rice terraces in the background.

Bottom: The reverse of the 1,000 peso note. On the left are the Banaue rice terraces, on the right is a 2,800-year-old Chinese jar adorned with figures of two men in a small boat that was discovered in the Manunggul cave on Palawan Island (a national treasure) and a langall, an Islamic place of worship in the Sulu Archipelago of Mindanao.

indicates population growth of nearly 40 percent over a period of twenty-five years. The population of Hungduan Municipality in the same three years was 7,254, 9,380 and 9,933 respectively. In 2015 the population was 9,400, which suggests population growth has basically leveled off.

In this chapter, after surveying the existing literature on the Ifugao, I give an overview of the geography and history of the *barangay* of Hapao in Hungduan, where I conducted the fieldwork for this study.

A brief survey of the existing literature

The Ifugaos possess a highly sophisticated customary law and a dazzling mythology, which, with more than a thousand deities, rivals that of the Greeks. These factors, along with their elaborate ritual knowledge and sacrificial practices and the beautiful views of their splendid rice terraces, mean that of all the indigenous peoples of the Philippines, they are the most studied by anthropologists. Conklin's *Ifugao Bibliography* (1968), compiled fifty years ago, includes more than 650 studies, from academic dissertations and books to government reports and articles in periodicals. Since then, an enormous quantity of research has continued to be performed on the Ifugao.

An exhibit titled 'The Filipinos and their Rich Cultural Heritage (*Kinahinatnan*)' at the National Museum of the Philippines contains the following introduction: 'this ethnographic exhibit focuses on the Philippines as a land of diversity, crossroads, and a tapestry of cultures'. The exhibit includes displays of the lifestyle and culture of the Muslim Maranao people of the island of Mindanao, as well as that of the Ifugaos (including everyday items, woodcarvings and ornaments). It also contains a diorama of the rice terraces. Although it may not have been the museum's intention, the Maranao and the Ifugaos are positioned in such a way that they appear as representatives of the Muslim and indigenous peoples of the Philippines respectively. There is also a note in the museum's official guidebook that 'Ifugao woodcarving is concentrated in Hapao village. It is required for lidded ritual boxes, food containers, bowls, spoons and ladles' (Castro 2005: 40).

One of the major studies of the Ifugaos is Barton's *Ifugao Law* (1969[1919]). This was a study of how the Ifugaos maintained social order and harmony on the basis of customary law and taboos, despite their lack of a systematic government or authority structure. Fred Eggan, who wrote the foreword to Barton's work, lists Barton's major contribution as the description and analysis of kinship as the main foundation of Ifugao society (Barton 1969[1919]: xiii–xiv). Barton (1946) also wrote on Ifugao religion and ceremony and edited a compilation of autobiographies of individual Ifugaos (1938).

Lambrecht's series of studies, 'The Mayawyaw Ritual 1–7' (1932–57), was written over a period of more than twenty years. It includes 1,500 pages of detailed description and reflection on ritual practices in Mayawyaw (Mayoyao) village in eastern Ifugao. Lambrecht divides his

Ifugao exhibit at the National Museum of the Philippines. (March 15, 2007)

study into seven themes, such as customs and rituals surrounding rice cultivation, marriage, death and healing rituals. He then breaks each theme into a further seven sections, giving an outline and analysis of the central ideas in the prayer texts, ritual knowledge and ritual procedures.

Of direct relevance to the current study is Conklin's *Ethnographic Atlas of Ifugao* (1980). This is an important foundational text for understanding the Ifugao world, with its basis in rice cultivation. The book draws on research conducted during thirty-eight months of fieldwork in Ifugao between 1961 and 1973. In addition to preparing detailed maps, Conklin worked with the full cooperation and participation of local people. This enabled him to complete an ethnography covering rice cultivation, ecology, society and culture. Featuring 180 documentary photographs, including numerous aerial shots alongside diagrams, and more than 100 maps accompanied by succinct and accurate commentaries, it would not be an exaggeration to describe the book as flawless.

In recent years, a number of Ifugao intellectuals have carried out research on their own people's history and culture. Dumia, who was born in barrio (*barangay*) Mompolia on the outskirts of Lagawe, has published numerous articles on Ifugao history and culture in magazines and newspapers, as well as his 1979 book *The Ifugao World*. This book explains the characteristic features of Ifugao social life and belief, and gives an overview of Ifugao history from the period of Spanish rule until 1970.

Lourdes Dulawan's *Ifugao: Culture and History* (2001), published by the National Commission for Culture and the Arts, is a testimony of eighty-four years lived as a Kiangan Ifugao and provides an overview of Ifugao history and contemporary society. Manuel Dulawan fears that 'the Ifugao are losing their distinct cultural heritage as an ethnic group'. His compilation of literature from the Ifugao oral tradition, also published by the National Commission for Culture and the Arts, is divided into six categories: folklore, legends, myths, chants, songs and rhymes. He writes angrily that, 'Indeed, the acculturation of the Ifugao has been thorough and deep. They have been brainwashed in the schools and in the churches and made to believe that their culture is backward and not worth keeping or learning. As a result, their sense of cultural values is disoriented' (Dulawan 2005: 17).

Carlos Medina, who completed his masters and doctoral studies at the University of Leuven in Belgium, now teaches and conducts research at the Saint Louis University in Baguio. He has published three books on the cycle of Ifugao prayers, myths and legends that is known as *abu'wab*, including an annotated version of the 160-part Ifugao language text collected by Lambrecht (with English translations and commentaries) (Medina 2001, 2002a, 2002b). *Abu'wab* is a collection of tales about the Ifugao creation gods Uvigan and Bugan and their creations. They are recited by a *monbaki* (ritual specialist/priest) as a prayer for divine favor at various stages during the cycle of rice cultivation and on other occasions such as weddings, the healing of the sick, funerals and when hunting. Medina's *Understanding the Ifugao Rice Terraces* (2003) includes an empirical and theoretical analysis of journalistic and academic modes of reporting on the Ifugao world, changes in the Ifugao worldview under the influence of American colonial rule since the early twentieth century, and social construction of Ifugao ways based on the theory by Berger and Luckmann (1967).

Sylvano Mahiwo was born in Hapao and studied international relations at the University of Tokyo under Hirano Kenichirō. In 1991 he received his doctorate for a dissertation, *Postwar Japan's human and cultural foreign policy: a focus on the ASEAN*, and became a professor in the Asian Center, University of the Philippines. In 1991 he began a large research project on the Ifugao rice terraces with funding from the Toyota Foundation. The project aimed to consider the terraces as an example of a sociocultural approach to ecological and environmental problems (although the final report from this project has yet to be published). Born in 1951, Mahiwo is the same age as me. He departed for the University of Tokyo as a Japanese Ministry of Education scholarship student not long after I first arrived at Ateneo de Manila University on a similar Ministry of Education scholarship program designed to send students to other parts of Asia. Our friendship dates from that time, long before I began my fieldwork in Hapao. When I did start my fieldwork, Mahiwo took the time to teach me the history of the village and describe the current situation there. Furthermore, his younger siblings still live in the village. Thanks to an introduction by their older brother, they were kind enough to help me with my research. Though we have lived in different places in societies and cultures that have followed different paths of historical development, I feel that my Ifugao contemporary and I have nevertheless shared similar experiences and sensibilities during almost thirty-five years of friendship.

This realization has been the basis of my understanding of the Ifugaos as contemporaries with 'other' culture.[2]

Mahiwo's niece, Rowena Nakake, who married in Ifugao and lives there to this day, worked as his research assistant and played a key role in

---

2 Mahiwo's own personal history reflects the changes that have taken place in Hapao in a concentrated form. Born and raised in Hapao, he attended the village primary school before going on to the Immaculate Conception High School in Banaue. During the week, he stayed with relatives in Banaue and on the weekends he would walk the five or six hours back to Hapao. In 1969 he graduated from high school and entered Saint Louis University in Baguio. While he was a student there, he passed the examination for the Japanese Ministry of Education scholarship. When he went to Manila for the first time in his life, in order to sit the exam, he got lost there and had no idea where he was. He was overwhelmed by the size of the great city.

From April 1971 he went to Tokyo University of Foreign Studies (TUFS) as an exchange student and studied for one year in a specialist Japanese language course. The next year he was accepted into the Japanese Studies department. In 1973 he transferred to the international studies department at Sophia University, where he graduated the following year (having received recognition of prior learning for subjects undertaken in the Philippines and at TUFS). Upon returning to the Philippines, he worked in the Japan Chamber of Commerce and Industry in Manila. In 1976 he entered the politics program in the graduate school of the University of the Philippines. He continued his studies while working and received his master's degree in 1979. In 1981 he received an international exchange scholarship and returned to Japan. After being accepted into the graduate school at the University of Tokyo as a research student, in 1983 he received permission to transfer to the doctoral program. He obtained a scholarship from the Tokyu Foundation and, in 1991, received his doctorate in international relations.

As part of the Toyota Foundation research project, Mahiwo collected vast quantities of data on the technical, cultural, environmental and ecological knowledge related to Ifugao rice cultivation and the construction and maintenance of the rice terraces. He also collected detailed information about *monbaki* ritual knowledge and other subjects. Unfortunately, Mahiwo has yet to publish his interim findings or produce the final report for this project. According to Mahiwo, the purpose of the project was not only scholarly research – he also hoped to show the sophistication and subtlety of Ifugao culture, technology and knowledge and to reaffirm the basis of his own identity and roots. However, his background in international relations and international politics meant that he lacked the knowledge of cultural anthropology and folklore needed for the project. He therefore encountered difficulties in organizing and analyzing the information for research purposes, which is why the report remains incomplete. However, he always said that he intended to undertake the necessary study and would complete the report when time allowed. He passed away on July 20, 2015, at the age of sixty-four.

Top: Sylvano Mahiwo's mother's house amid the rice terraces of Hapao. On the left the new church is under construction on the same place where an old one used to be. (March 13, 2002)

Bottom: Hungduan Mayor Pablo M Cuyahon Sr. (left) and Sylvano Mahiwo relaxing while they drink some *tapuy* (rice wine) at Sylvano's mother's home. (April 18, 2008)

collecting materials for his research project. She also conducted her own research on the transformation of Ifugao rice cultivation and agricultural ritual through surveys and interviews with villagers. Her results were included in her graduation thesis from the University of the Philippines Baguio, *Change in traditional farming practices and its effects on socio-economic conditions in Hapao, Hungduan, Ifugao* (Nakake 1997). She concluded that population instability due to out migration and other factors, the penetration of the cash economy, school education and Christianity have all influenced agriculture in Ifugao. The result has been a dramatic reduction in or complete change to the performance of agricultural customs and rituals such as *baddang* (free labor), *ubbu* (labor exchange) and many different types of *baki* (ritual). This has led to a weakening of the solidarity between villagers and a decline in agricultural productivity. This point is also emphasized by Rhodora Gonzalez, who I mention in Chapter 9.

Nevertheless, although there has been a reduction in collective agricultural labor and in the number and complexity of agricultural rituals, this does not necessarily reflect a comparable decline in other types of individual rituals, such as those related to sickness or household funereal customs (for example, bone washing). In households where one family member has gone to work abroad, the family's wealth generally increases. In these households, ritual sacrifices involving large pigs are carried out with great ceremony. For example, on my second visit to Hapao, for a little more than three weeks in March 1999, I was able to join in three rituals that involved sacrifices of large pigs. The first was conducted for a couple to ask to be blessed with a child after seven years of marriage. The second was conducted by a group of siblings on their homecoming from Manila and Baguio to give thanks for their father's good health and to pray for his longevity. The third was a bone-washing ritual conducted to heal a skin condition in a man in the prime of life. This ritual was conducted on the understanding that the cause of the condition was the death of his mother following the man's own difficult birth forty years prior. In each case, a *monbaki* was called to recite the names of the creator god Kabunian and his host, as well as those of the ancestral spirits, to give thanks and to ask for divine protection.

On each occasion, the *monbaki* carefully answered my questions about the purpose of the ritual and its component parts. The family members and other villagers who participated in the rituals explained, without my asking, that the rituals were not only important in terms of Ifugao tradition but were also legitimate for them to perform as Christians. They seemed apprehensive that the sacrifice of a pig might be perceived by an outsider as a barbaric heathen custom. According to their explanations, Kabunian and the Christian God are but two names for the same deity. This is simply the result of the fact that the Israelites and the Ifugaos speak different languages and so call their god by different names. They also emphasized that the sacrifices were legitimate because they were not intended to curse anyone with misfortune or illness but to pray for health, fertility and good fortune.

They hate the way the Ifugaos have been saddled with the image of an exotic ethnic group completely different from the majority Christian Filipino lowlanders and the derision and discrimination towards them that is the result of this image. The vast majority of anthropological research on the Ifugaos until now has primarily concerned Ifugao traditional culture. While these researchers were certainly sincere in their quest to deeply understand the inner world of the Ifugaos, by focusing on the uniqueness of Ifugao culture in their presentation of it, they have unintentionally

The carcasses of a pig and chickens from a ritual sacrifice. In front of an earthenware pot containing *tapuy*, a *monbaki* (sitting on the right) prays for a child for the young couple of the house. (March 6, 1999)

contributed to the positioning of Ifugao culture as an exotic 'other' within the majority Filipino society. This discomfort with the biased gaze of anthropologists and journalists has sometimes been expressed to me directly, but mostly indirectly.

The Ifugaos are our contemporaries. They live in these times of rapid globalization just as we do. I based my research on this understanding and adopted it as my basic stance when interacting with the Ifugaos in their villages. My student exchange from the University of Tokyo to Ateneo de Manila University and Mahiwo's exchange from the Philippines to the University of Tokyo on the same Ministry of Education scholarship program (indeed, he even enrolled in the same department as I had done in Tokyo) placed us in a reciprocal relationship, like two opposing mirrors. My stance as a researcher of the Philippines is the natural result of this reciprocity. Mahiwo is a friend with whom I feel completely at home. When we drink and talk together, I feel no sense of unease or separation.

When I spend time in Hapao, the fact that General Yamashita had retreated to the mountains that are part of the *barangay*, the numerous trips that have been conducted by veterans and families of the Japanese war dead since the end of the war in search of their remains, the stories of Yamashita's gold and the provision of Japanese development assistance to Hapao in more recent years serve as continual reminders to me that the people of Hapao and Japan are tightly bound together as contemporaries. However, at the same time I feel that we have followed a different path of historical development. We therefore face different constraints and enjoy different possibilities. My basic approach as a researcher in the field has been informed by the idea that we must examine both our resemblances and our differences in a multifaceted way and try to understand one another, just like those two opposing mirrors. This book is written from this perspective.

My fieldwork and this book are intended to re-examine Ifugao history and society in terms of their relationship to the outside world. I pay particular attention to direct interventions by the outside world on the Ifugaos and their indirect influences, and the way Ifugaos have resisted, negotiated, accepted and taken advantage of the outside world proactively and assertively. In response to the strategic essentialism of Kidlat and Nauyac, which I consider in Chapters 6 and 7, I try to understand the composition of the contemporary Ifugao way of life and their way of thinking based on an understanding of today's practices. As a result, I see a reality of intermingling of different elements where the traditional and the globalizing modern coexist. This is what I try to depict in this book.

Now I briefly summarize the existing studies on the Ifugaos that have been carried out by Japanese researchers. The *barangay* of Ba-ang is located on the steep hills on the other side of Hapao along the Luboong–Bokiawan river, a tributary of the Ibulao River. Focusing on this *barangay*, Kumano Takeshi is conducting ongoing fieldwork on the worldview of its people and their ritual knowledge and practices. His findings have been published in articles on *dopap* wrestling (a special form of wrestling that involves hopping on one leg to invoke the judgment of the gods to assist in conflict resolution), Ifugao textile culture, shamanism and, in more recent years, female migrant workers (Kumano 1999a, 1999b, 2006a, 2006b). Kumano's work mainly explores anthropology's traditional themes and I have sought to avoid overlapping it in my own research. The fact that my friend Mahiwo is from the same academic cohort as me, and the feeling that he could almost be my double, led me to notice not so much the otherness of the Ifugaos but to develop a sense of commonality with them. I therefore decided to adopt contemporary themes such as the reforestation movement, cultural revitalization, migrant work and development assistance as the focus for my own research.[3]

Goda Toh's (1997) ethnography *Ifuga: Ruzon-tō sanchimin no juso to henyō* (Sorcery and change among the highlanders of northern Luzon) is based on his fieldwork on kinship, illness and sorcery in Ifugao. The material for the book was collected during six field trips undertaken by Goda to Ducligan in eastern Banaue and Gohan in the west, as well as to the central Banaue *barangay* of Poblacion and its surrounds between 1984

---

3 When my fascination with Kidlat and Nauyac brought me to Hapao for the first time, I carelessly failed to notice Kumano conducting fieldwork in Ba-ang on the other side of the valley. I learned about his work on my second visit, a discovery that left me embarrassed due to my own ignorance and lack of adequate preparation. Nevertheless, my main concern was to find out how Kidlat, Nauyac and the villagers in Hapao, a place far removed from my own and with different strategies and tactics, were charting a course through the rapid globalization that was sweeping the world and bringing us face to face with similar types of problems. Therefore, Kumano's fieldwork, with its focus on religious ritual knowledge and practice, addresses different research questions from my own. Furthermore, to avoid any overlap with Kumano's research, I decided to avoid digging deeply into religious or ritual knowledge and practices that might relate to his work.

and 1996. This book aims to understand the 'contemporary' social structure, religion and political culture of the highlands people of northern Luzon and how they have survived and adapted to the changes resulting from the 'transformation' of regional society in response to nation-building efforts after the end of the Marcos regime (Goda 1997: 9).

Goda states that another objective of this study was 'to consider the validity and limitations of the methodology of structural-functionalism, which originates in English social anthropology, and attempt its deconstruction' (Goda 1997: 9). However, his conclusion after comparing Ducligan and Banaue can be seen plainly in the book's subtitle, *juso to henyō* (sorcery and transformation). He argues that Ifugao religious practices transformed from witchcraft to sorcery in response to the entanglement of Ifugao society in modernization and the nation-state, a structural-functionalist interpretation that lacks any hint of deconstruction. He argues that in traditional Ifugao society, it is essential to cooperate with neighbors and to take great care not to arouse the jealousy or ill will of others in order to avoid becoming a target of *funi* (sorcery). In this way, 'the *funi*-belief functions to suppress momentums for social stratification within an agricultural society' (Goda 1997: 165). However, Goda concludes that in the Poblacion *barangay* and its surrounds, tourism development, greater investment in education, urbanization and the new resources that have become available through local politics have brought about 'changes in the types of conflict over resources, prestige and authority' – as a result, 'there has been a shift in etiological beliefs within Ifugao society from the *funi* sorcery-beliefs that are centered on kin and neighbors to the reburial ritual with the dead's bone cleaning, which seems to be a primitive form of ancestor worship and witchcraft beliefs (*halopey*)' (Goda 1997: 162). Like Kumano, Goda explores decidedly 'traditional' themes and theoretical frames.[4]

In recent years, four important doctoral theses and books focusing on development-related issues have appeared. These are discussed in further detail in Chapter 9.

---

4 In terms of his attempt to portray the 'present' of our Ifugao contemporaries, my research question is similar to Goda's. However, his work contains a few not-so-small factual errors and presents different perspectives from my own.

Hapao today

Hungduan is one of the eleven municipalities that make up Ifugao Province. It is divided into nine *barangays*, of which Hapao is the largest, with 381 households and a population of 2,138 (Hungduan Municipal Office 2007). Hapao was formerly part of the Municipality of Banaue. It was transferred to the jurisdiction of Hungduan in 1983, along with four neighboring *barangays* nestled in a valley on the same side of a ridge that constitutes the border with Banaue. This was part of a broader reorganization that took place when the Municipality of Tinoc was created in 1982 and eleven of Hungduan's fifteen *barangays* were transferred to it. The administrative realignment of the whole of Ifugao Province at that time brought its administrative units geographically closer together to strengthen the functions of government and counter the control of the Communist Party of the Philippines-New People's Army (CPP-NPA) over the region (Hungduan Municipal Office 2007: 7). Control by the New People's Army (NPA) meant that its members could generally operate freely within the *barangays* of Hungduan. When companies of the Philippine Constabulary were stationed in the municipality to carry out operations against the NPA, the communist guerillas (armed wing of Communist Party of the Philippines) would take temporary refuge in the mountains. When the opportunity presented itself, the guerillas would carry out surprise attacks on the government soldiers, forcing them to retreat so they could once again come down from the mountains and re-establish control over the area.

Ifugaos recognize both the maternal and paternal family line. This network of relatives (kindred) plays an important social and economic role. Like other Ifugao mountain villages, the main occupation in Hapao is agriculture. Rice-paddy cultivation is practiced in rice terraces that are built on the mountain slopes. However, most families cannot secure enough rice for their yearly household consumption from single-season cropping in their terraces. In the past, they supplemented their diet of rice by cultivating sweet potatoes and corn in swidden fields on the mountain slopes further away from their villages. In recent years, however, the relative importance of swidden agriculture has been in decline. Instead, the villagers leave the village for work or produce woodcarvings to sell for cash during the agricultural off-season. There are more and more cases of people purchasing their rice from the village shops. Hapao is also a major center for the production of carved wooden statues and ornaments for the tourism industry and for export. Many people engaged in this craft and it is still an important source of cash income. If we include those who work as carvers as a secondary income source during the off-season, there are more than 100 households where the men do woodcarving work.

In the Philippines the mere mention of Ifugao evokes images of rice terraces. This landscape, alongside white sand beaches and blue seas, is one of the standard images used by the Department of Tourism on posters produced to promote tourism. On government tourist brochures and guidebooks, the rice terraces are described as one of the 'Eight Wonders of the World', alongside the pyramids of Egypt and the Great Wall of China. Furthermore, while the pyramids and the Great Wall were built by slaves and forced labor, the rice terraces were built by the Ifugao ancestors working together to improve their own lives using simple tools and the power of their imaginations. As I mentioned at the beginning of this book, the Ifugao rice terraces were recognized by UNESCO as a World Heritage site in 1995, the third site in the Philippines to be included on the World Heritage List.

The UNESCO website explains the definition and purpose of World Heritage as follows: 'heritage is our legacy from the past, what we live with today, and what we pass on to future generations. Our cultural and natural heritage are both irreplaceable sources of life and inspiration' (UNESCO World Heritage Centre n.d.). According to the Convention Concerning the Protection of the World Cultural and Natural Heritage, adopted unanimously by UNESCO in 1972, sites that are recognized as having 'outstanding universal value' can be included on the World Heritage List (UNESCO World Heritage Centre 1972). In 1973 the United States was the first state to ratify the convention, which came into force in 1975 after it had been ratified by twenty states. The Philippines ratified the convention in 1985, while Japan signed the convention in 1992, twenty years after it was first adopted, making it the 125th state party to the convention. There are three main types of World Heritage: 'cultural sites' (monuments, groups of buildings, sites), 'natural sites' (listed for their natural features) and 'complex sites'. In 2016 the World Heritage List contained 1,073 sites, including 832 cultural sites, 206 natural sites and 35 complex sites.[5]

---

5 The process for obtaining World Heritage listing begins when national governments submit tentative lists to UNESCO. UNESCO then asks its advisory bodies, the International Council on Monuments and Sites (for cultural heritage) and the

Top: Looking down over the road to Hapao from the ridge above. The river running through the middle forms the border between the municipalities of Banaue on the right and Hungduan on the left. (June 5, 2008)

Middle: The entrance to Hapao as seen from Bokiawan. The road traverses the mountainside to the left. (March 14, 2003)

Below: The jeepney enters Hapao. Patpat is on the right. (July 29, 2009)

When the convention was adopted in 1972, the Club of Rome issued *Limits to Growth* (Meadows 1972), a book that sounded an alert about the depletion of natural resources, worsening environmental pollution and explosive population growth. The United Nations Conference on the Human Environment was also held that year in Stockholm with the theme 'Only One Earth'. Amid fierce competition between the Eastern and Western bloc countries over economic growth under the geopolitical framework of the Cold War, in this period the world first began to show a shared concern for the natural environment and the severe burden that human activity (including both production and consumption) was placing on it. The text of the convention states that World Heritage-listed sites remain part of the territory of their respective state but that 'it is the duty of the international community as a whole to co-operate' in their protection, without violating national sovereignty or property rights (Article 6.1) (Audrerie, Souchier and Vilar 2005: 17). The text of this article shows an awareness of World Heritage as part of the shared treasury of human society, with a common destiny symbolized in the phrase 'Spaceship Earth' (see Chapter 10 of this book). In a sense, the convention appears to suggest that it might be possible to trigger an awareness of humanity's commonality via the common ownership of this heritage.

Five World Heritage sites are in the Philippines. Two are beautiful national parks with stunning natural landscapes – the Tubbataha Reefs located in the middle of the Sulu Sea (listed in 1993) and the Puerto Princesa Subterranean River National Park on Palawan Island (listed in 1999). Two other listings comprise historical buildings, relics of Spanish colonial rule. The first is the four Baroque Churches of the Philippines (listed in 1993), which are scattered across the archipelago.[6]

International Union for Conservation of Nature (for natural heritage), to conduct technical evaluations as to whether proposed sites meet the criteria for World Heritage listing. The advisory bodies submit the results of their investigations in the form of recommendations to UNESCO. The advisory bodies can recommend listing, ask for further information, recommend that listing be postponed or recommend not to list a site. The UNESCO World Heritage Committee then meets and makes decisions based on the original submissions by state parties and the recommendations of the advisory bodies (Matsuura 2008: 96–99).

6 The churches are the San Agustín Church in Intramuros in Manila, Miagao Church in Miagao on Iloilo Island, the Church of Nuestra Señora de la Asuncion in Santa Maria, Ilocos Sur Province, and the Church of San Agustín in Paoay, Ilocos Norte Province.

The other is the Historic City of Vigan (listed in 1999), located in Ilocos Sur Province in northwestern Luzon. Of the five sites, the Ifugao rice terraces is the only site to have been listed for its indigenous cultural heritage, as structures that were built and maintained by 'the indigenous people of the Philippines' with their own creativity and imagination and unflagging effort.

The reasons for the listing that are included on the UNESCO World Heritage Centre (1995) website state that 'the Ifugao Rice Terraces epitomize the absolute blending of the physical, socio-cultural, economic, religious, and political environment. Indeed, it is a living cultural landscape of unparalleled beauty.' The website also notes:

> the Ifugao Rice Terraces are the priceless contribution of Philippine ancestors to humanity. Built 2000 years ago and passed on from generation to generation, the Ifugao Rice Terraces represent an enduring illustration of an ancient civilization that surpassed various challenges and setbacks posed by modernization.

The text goes on to explain;

> the maintenance of the living rice terraces reflects a primarily cooperative approach of the whole community which is based on detailed knowledge of the rich diversity of biological resources existing in the Ifugao agro-ecosystem, a finely tuned annual system respecting lunar cycles, zoning and planning, extensive soil conservation, mastery of a most complex pest control regime based on the processing of a variety of herbs, accompanied by religious rituals.

Before they were recognized and applauded by UNESCO, Ifugao leaders and intellectuals already had a strong sense of the cultural importance of the terraces, which they emphasize are the pride of their people. Ordinary Ifugaos, too, see the rice terraces as the basis for a chain of connection that links the current generation with the ancestors. The terraces are a physical manifestation of the intimate community of the living and the dead and provide visible proof of the security of that continuity (Dumia 1979: 2–3). The particular beauty of the stone rice terraces of Hapao is acknowledged even within the wider Ifugao community and is a source of great pride for the people of Hapao. Unlike the earthen-walled Banaue rice terraces, which have become famous as a tourist destination, the Hapao terraces are made of stone. Furthermore, they are remarkable for their size, extent and magnificence. Conklin (1980: 19) hypothesizes that about 30 percent of all Ifugao rice terraces are made of stone, but in Hapao stone terraces account for more than 95 percent of the total.[7]

The road connecting the national highway in the lowlands of the Cagayan Valley with the main destination for rice terrace tourism in Banaue (1,200–1,500 meters above sea level) was concreted at the beginning of the 1980s. When I began my fieldwork in Ifugao at the end of the 1990s, express buses to Banaue operated direct from Manila and Baguio, with one service running from each city every morning and evening. The alternative to the express is to take a bus along the national highway that traverses northern Luzon from Manila to Tuguegarao or Aparri in Cagayan Province in the far north as far as Bagabag in Nueva Vizcaya Province and then change to a jeepney to Banaue. At the fork in the road at Bagabag stands a large road sign that reads, 'Welcome to the Gateway of the 8th Wonder of the World Banaue'.

To get to Hapao from Banaue one takes a jeepney to Hungduan that leaves from beside the marketplace. After climbing a winding mountain road for about thirty minutes, one reaches the pass. For the next twenty minutes the road winds down and then travels along the river on a mostly level road for about ten minutes. The journey takes about an hour in total. Continuing for about another ten minutes past Hapao, one arrives at Hobbong in the center of the municipality, where there is a cluster of general stores. Another fifteen minutes takes one to the base of a plateau on top of which the municipal offices are located. Surfacing of the road between Banaue and Hungduan has been progressing slowly since 2000. By 2010 the portion from Banaue to the pass was mostly complete. On the Hungduan side, only those parts of the road that pass through hamlets were paved initially, but since 2010 the surfacing of the road has proceeded rapidly and as of 2017 almost all parts of the road were cemented. However, with heavy rainfall during the rainy season, landslides along the road frequently cut access. It is not uncommon for repairs, conducted using

---

7 According to Nauyac, the rice terraces of Banaue have earthen walls because the river that runs through the valley is only small and contains no stones suitable for building terrace walls. Fortunately, the earth there is a special clay known as *dulmog*, which is very sticky and resistant to crumbling.

bulldozers, to take two or three days. When I visited the field in July 2009 for a short stay, torrential rain in the area ten days prior created landslides in more than forty places between Banaue and Hungduan. This stopped traffic along the road for several days.[8]

In the Hobbong district, the commercial center of Hungduan, the road was wide and already surfaced for some 200 meters when I first visited there in 1998. About ten *sari-sari* stores (general stores) and billiard halls are lined up on each side. Behind the main street is a small knoll, where facilities such as the municipal office building, the hospital, and the primary and secondary schools are located. Every morning, the first jeepney departs Hobbong for Banaue at about five o'clock and several more continue to depart until about seven. They return from Banaue as soon as they fill with people who have finished their errands, such as shopping or visiting the government offices. The first jeepney arrives back in Hapao at ten or eleven o'clock at the earliest, but often just after noon. The last jeepney returns at about six in the evening.

In Hapao a large river flows along the bottom of a long, narrow V-shaped valley. The rice terraces begin just above the riverbank and continue about halfway up the mountain slopes on both sides. On one side of the valley, a number of relatively comfortably appointed houses are dotted along a road that traverses the mountainside a little above the riverbank. In places, several houses are joined, with their eaves butting up against one another. These houses along the road receive electricity from the Ifugao Electric Cooperative, Inc. (IFELCO) and many use propane gas for cooking. Most of these wealthier houses belong to families that originally owned large areas of terraced land and were able to sustain themselves for the whole year on their rice harvest. Many also have family members who work in local government or as teachers. With the salary they earn from these jobs, they send their children to study at universities in Baguio or further afield. Once they have graduated from university, these children go on to work as teachers, municipal workers or public servants. Others use their English-language skills to go overseas for work. These families thereby gain an even more stable source of cash income. Over the past decade or so, some of those who have built houses using money saved while working

---

8 Until the mid-1960s, the road connecting Banaue with Hungduan was only passable on foot. It was too steep and narrow to allow entry by car. That is why General Yamashita built his final holdout there.

overseas have not followed the traditional Ifugao style but have built their houses in the style typical of lowland Filipinos, and some with a fashionable, Western-style taste and appearance.

The rice terraces lining the slopes on either side of the valley surrounding Hapao define its outlook. Here and there, small hamlets made up of a few houses clustered together are dotted among them. These houses are not connected to the electricity grid and most use firewood for cooking.[9] Apart from these few houses, twenty to thirty terraces fill the lower mountain slopes up to around the halfway point. Gazing on the scene, one has the feeling that the entire horizon is filled with rice terraces. For the villagers, the terraces are not only the basis of their livelihood as rice farmers but possess multiple layers of important meanings: socio-political meanings concerning issues of property ownership and prestige; religious meanings connected with agricultural ritual; cultural meanings based on ethnic identity and pride; and meanings related to their historical consciousness of inheritance and ancestor worship.

Twenty years under CPP-NPA control

As I explain further in the next chapter, the Ifugaos suffered great loss of lives and property under the Japanese army's occupation of Hungduan at the end of the Asia-Pacific War. Twenty years later, the NPA, the armed wing of the Maoist CPP, came to establish a base of operations in Hungduan for much the same reasons that had led the Japanese there. Jovel Francis Ananayo, a native of Hungduan, conducted a series of interviews on the activities of the NPA and the response of the villagers and the Philippine Constabulary as part of his graduation thesis at the University of the Philippines Baguio. According to his research, seventeen NPA guerillas appeared in Hapao for the first time at the beginning of the 1970s. When

---

9 In the Patpat district of Nungulunan on the other side of the valley from Hapao, electricity has been available since February 2002, thanks to a small-scale hydroelectric project funded by the Ifugao provincial government (200,000 pesos) and Benguet State University (800,000 pesos). Eighty households receive electricity from the scheme (which is only available at night and is limited to forty watts per household). Each month they pay twenty-five pesos to maintain the equipment, which they manage collectively. Small-scale hydroelectric projects also brought electricity to Ba-ang, on the other side of the valley from Hapao, in 1996, and Lubo-ong in 2001.

they arrived, they approached the local people with a helpful and friendly attitude and were soon welcomed into the community.

Although there was a primary school in Hungduan at that time, the villagers had no access to other government services such as health and medical services or development assistance: 'The period 1960s was the time at which there was no presence of insurgency and counter-insurgency operations...The municipality's conditions during this period [are] characterized as neglected and poor although the residents enjoyed...peace and order condition' – in other words, 'the existence of a government was almost not felt by the Hungduan residents in the 1960s because of the absence of social services' (Ananayo 1999: iii).

In Tinoc, marijuana was cultivated as a cash crop, making use of the municipality's remoteness, which meant it was not subject to police surveillance. Until the mid-1960s, the narrowness of the road to Hungduan meant that it was impossible to reach by car. It took five or six hours at a fast pace to get to Banaue in the east or Kiangan in the south by walking along the narrow and precipitous mountain roads. In such a remote place, the NPA guerillas began by helping the locals with their farm work in the rice terraces and swidden fields and providing other kinds of labor. They also offered health and medical services and taught literacy and other skills. These activities eased the suspicions of the local villagers and the NPA guerillas were accepted into the community (Ananayo 1999: 16, 37–9).

In the first three months, the NPA guerillas conducted a 'social survey' into the socioeconomic conditions of the villages and the degree of military and police control in the area. Having established a basic understanding of conditions in the municipality and the local way of life, the NPA guerillas turned to propaganda work, publishing a regular periodical called *Dangadang* (meaning 'struggle' in the local Ilocano language). They also created a number of '*barrio* organizing committees' to address health, educational, infrastructure and justice services, mirroring the government's own village-level administration. They replaced the central government as the real provider of local administration. Furthermore, they not only went into the fields with the villagers and worked alongside them, but also marshalled them to help clear and maintain roads and assisted the locals to write petitions and appeals to regional and central government bodies to obtain funding for various development projects. These organizational structures developed into '*barrio* revolutionary committees'.

These committees enabled the CPP to wrest administrative authority from the central government and develop a grassroots administrative structure for the CPP's own shadow government.[10]

Many of the NPA guerillas were former student activists from Manila and quite a few were former students of the University of the Philippines. They organized regular village assemblies in the Catholic Church in Poblacion, where they held rallies and study groups. They also frequently organized activities in neighboring Tinoc. In order to try and deal with the activities of the guerillas, in 1972 Municipal Mayor Lopez Pugong recruited thirty volunteers who were sent to the provincial capital Lagawe to receive military training. After completing their training, they formed a Civil Home Defense Force (CHDF). The CHDF, with the support of the Philippine Constabulary (with primary responsibility for domestic law and order), took over responsibility for keeping the peace and carrying out surveillance. The NPA responded by avoiding Hungduan for a time (Ananayo 1999: 40–1).

However, in 1974 the NPA set fire to the Hungduan municipal office building and burned it to the ground. Part of this building had served as barracks for the police and Philippine Constabulary. The municipal government and the police were forced to withdraw to Lagawe, the entrance to the Ifugao mountains on the edge of the lowlands. The CHDF assumed responsibility for maintaining order in Hungduan, but only had a few older-style rifles (M1 Garands). These were almost useless against the NPA, which had the latest weaponry, including PSL and M16 rifles. NPA control in Hungduan therefore continued from the late 1970s. In 1980, twelve Constabulary soldiers on patrol were killed in an assault by NPA guerillas

---

10 For a detailed account of the way of life, organizing activities and fighting tactics (mainly ambush attacks) of the NPA guerillas in the indigenous regions of the northern mountains, see Nomura (1981). Nomura spent nearly four months between August and December 1979 embedded with an NPA company in Kalinga-Apayao Province, neighboring Ifugao. At that time, protests by local Kalingas against the construction of four large dams on the Chico River were spreading. When the Philippine Constabulary was sent to quell the protests, the NPA guerillas offered support to the locals and commenced a guerila war. While undertaking preliminary fieldwork, I spent just over two weeks in Lubo, a village in the Tanudan River valley in Kalinga-Apayao in March 1977. When there was an ambush by NPA guerillas nearby, Constabulary soldiers began an operation to clear the area of guerillas.

in Poblacion (Ananayo 1999: 42; Hungduan Municipal Profile 1997). For the Constabulary, the logistical burden of maintaining sufficient personnel and weapons in Hungduan at all times was simply too great.

According to Ananayo's interviews, there was a major change in NPA strategy in 1982. Until then, the guerillas had concentrated on capturing the hearts and minds of the local people and organizing them by helping with work and providing health and educational services. After 1982, with a sudden shift in priorities, the NPA began to focus on tightening organizational discipline, recruiting fighters and carrying out aggressive military operations. The NPA established military training camps in the villages of Kamandag in Kiangan and Sadanga in Mountain Province. They also formed ad hoc platoons and companies on top of the existing guerilla companies that serve as their basic operational units. However, to reorganize itself into an army and increase its military strength, the NPA needed both capital and provisions. To secure them, the guerillas raised a revolutionary tax on the villagers and commandeered government vehicles. Much of this activity centered on Hungduan but also occurred in neighboring Banaue, Kiangan, Hingyon and in Lamut in the lowlands (Ananayo 1999: 42–4).

The 1980s were a time of upheaval in Hapao and Hungduan. As the Philippine central government grew weaker, the CPP-NPA grew proportionally stronger. There were numerous armed clashes between the two sides as they struggled for control of the region. The turning point was the Iranian Revolution of February 1979 (in which the Pahlavi monarchy fell and Ayatollah Khomeini became president). The revolution triggered the second oil shock, which dealt a severe blow to the Philippine economy. Until then, the Marcos regime had maintained economic growth at 6–8 percent through a combination of martial law and developmentalism. The oil shock ushered in a period of economic recession. In addition, in August 1983, in the midst of economic and social instability, former Senator Benigno Aquino Jr. (known affectionately as Ninoy) returned to the Philippines from exile in Boston in the United States. He was assassinated in broad daylight at Manila International Airport as he entered the country, which became the 'beginning of the end' for the Marcos regime by igniting anger and compassion of citizens in Manila to hold demonstration and rally on the street.

Ninoy had promised to give up his safe and comfortable life in exile to be with his fellow Filipinos suffering under Marcos's tyrannical rule and to devote himself to their liberation. He knew he risked his life by returning home. First Lady Imelda Marcos had attempted to dissuade Ninoy from returning by warning him that he might be assassinated should he do so. He declared that he had accepted that he would be assassinated but had decided nevertheless to return. His China Airlines flight landed in the middle of the day and as he walked down the jet bridge, he was shot in the back of the head by one of the soldiers who was escorting him. In mass media reports, the story of Ninoy's death was compared with Jesus Christ or José Rizal, who had also accepted their own deaths out of dedication to their homelands. These stories were disseminated widely and, following the assassination, the middle class, which had remained silent under martial law, began to take an active part in street demonstrations and rallies against the Marcos regime. (The events leading from the stories about Ninoy's knowledge that he would be assassinated and of his sacrifice to the People Power Revolution three years later are analyzed in depth in my book *Bunka no naka no seiji: Firipin 'nigatsu kakumei' no monogatari'* (Politics in culture: The story of the 'February Revolution' in the Philippines) (Shimizu 1991).)

The ensuing political chaos and uncertainty had a devastating effect on the economy. Economic growth slowed significantly to –7 percent in 1984 and remained at –5 percent in 1985. The economic stagnation of the early 1980s and the Marcos regime's loss of legitimacy led to the rapid expansion of the CPP-NPA forces throughout the country. According to estimates by the Philippine Constabulary, the NPA had 3,000 fighters in 1981. This increased to 6,000 in 1983 and 15,000 in 1984 (the U.S. Department of State estimate is 20,000). The Constabulary did not release an estimate in 1985 but the U.S. Department of State estimates that the NPA swelled to 25,000 combatants. Fears that the CPP-NPA's rise to power might lead to a real communist revolution in the Philippines motivated the urban middle class in Metro Manila and other cities to become more involved in politics and participate in rallies and demonstrations against the Marcos regime. This eventually led to the February 1986 People Power Revolution.

Marcos increased the size of the Philippine Constabulary, which formed the powerbase for the martial law system, from 54,000 in 1972 to 156,000 in 1985. At the same time, in an attempt to shore up support for his regime among high-ranking officials and guarantee their loyalty, he appointed current and former officers to the communications, transport, electricity, energy and defense-related firms that he had seized under martial law. However, in order for the national troops to gain control against the guerillas, military leaders insisted that they would need a force ten times that of the guerillas, as well as equipment such as vehicles and helicopters. Despite Marcos's strengthening of the Constabulary, by 1982 its supremacy over the NPA was starting to falter. The change in strategy adopted by the NPA units in Hungduan was a response to this changing situation in the Philippines as a whole and to the new strategic direction set by the CPP's central leadership. The CPP's basic strategic objective had been to achieve a 'strategic stalemate' by the mid-1980s and then by the latter half of the 1980s to commence its 'strategic offensive' (Chapman 1987: 108).

In Hungduan, the balance of power that had been established between the NPA and the Constabulary by the mid-1980s resulted in what well might be called a 'strategic stalemate'. In February and July 1990, this stalemate collapsed, leading to open conflict. On February 24, about 300 people, including members of the CPP's political bureau and NPA guerillas from northern Luzon, gathered in Hungduan for a joint congress. When the Constabulary received information about the gathering and dispatched a company of soldiers, they were ambushed by the NPA. Sixteen hours of fierce fighting ensued. When the fighting was over, thirteen Constabulary soldiers were dead (the number of NPA dead and injured is unknown) and most of the NPA guerillas returned to their base camps, but a small company of about forty guerillas under the leadership of Ka Jinjin remained in the area. This led to a second conflict in July, in which the deputy mayor of Hungduan and a police officer were killed.

Felipe Lacubawan was the mayor of Hungduan from January 1988 until June 1992. He told me about how the NPA had penetrated Hungduan and established control over the municipality and how the Hungduan municipal authorities had tried their best to avoid armed conflict between the NPA and the Philippine Constabulary on their land. He also told me about the fighting in 1990.[11] When Lacubawan assumed office, he was asked by the

---

11 Lacubawan attended primary and high school in Kiangan and went to university in Lagawe. He has been a strong Christian since his student days. Through membership of organizations such as the Christian Social Movement, he worked in solidarity with the Philippine Rural Reconstruction Movement and was actively involved in organizing for development and to raise the standard of living for local people. From 1981 until 1985 he was a manager at a savings union in Banaue. He received requests from the intelligence wing of the Philippine Constabulary and from the NPA to provide information and other forms of cooperation. However, he managed to maintain friendly relations with both groups while keeping them at a distance.

Constabulary to help them form a Civilian Armed Forces Geographical Unit (CAFGU). He politely refused the request on the grounds that it would create tensions and inevitably lead to fierce fighting in the village. Instead, he asked the military authorities try to keep the peace through dialogue. In 1998 an amnesty program was instituted to allow guerillas who came down from the mountains to resume their former lives without prosecution. Under the scheme, a number of guerilla fighters who were originally from Hungduan gave up their arms. From that point on, all the CPP-NPA guerillas who remained in the area were from outside. Lacubawan only became openly hostile towards the NPA after the 1990 ambush in which the deputy mayor was killed. He was also a key informant in Ananayo's research.

> Prior to my election here as the municipal mayor, Hungduan became an R&R area for the New People's Army. R&R area means rest and recreation [correctly, rest and recuperation, or rest and relaxation] area. It really meant they had a stronghold here in Hungduan. Actually, the first one who brought [the NPA to] this part of the country, Ifugao, is one from Ifugao…Mr Abrino Aydinan. He was then a commander and he brought it here sometime in 1966, and then became very strong in 1971 up to 1984 when they practically had control of the entire municipality of Hungduan, and then they were able to get local recruits from this place and surrounding municipalities. Strangely, most commanders at that time came from Abra, Kalinga, Mountain Province, and, of the intelligence units, most were from Nueva Ecija, especially from the town of Talavella. They stayed here, and after some time they drove out the municipal government and they burned down the municipal building in

---

In 1988 the European Union ambassador Dr. Fernandes was kidnapped by the NPA, along with staff from the Central Cordillera Agricultural Programme (CECAP), and Lacubawan acted as a negotiator (on behalf of Governor Juan Dait) with the NPA commander Ka Roger and obtained their release. In 1989 CECAP received a grant from the European Union of 23 million euros (759 million pesos) and a contribution from the Philippine government of 4.5 million euros (148.5 million pesos). The first stage of the project went for seven years from 1988, followed by a second round of seven years from 1996 until 2003.

While serving as mayor of Hungduan, Lacubawan remained living in his home in Banaue due to the lack of a municipal office building in Hungduan and the danger posed by the guerillas. In 1991, while he was in office, the NPA's control over Hungduan came to an end. Once the new municipal office building was constructed, he returned to live nearby at his in-law's home (Ananayo 1999: 49–50).

1974. And they started the collection of revolutionary taxes. Local government units transferred in Tinoc, but the municipal treasury office was located in Lagawe. So most people here started migrating to the lowlands, particularly Nueva Vizcaya, Quirino and Isabela provinces...Hapao villagers went to Baguio and other places.

...between 1974 and 1984 [Hapao] practically...became a ghost town, in fact, the road was not maintained any more, and most elementary schools were owned and used as headquarters of the NPA – Hungduan Central school, Hapao elementary school and primary schools in other *barangays*. I became an appointed board member of Hungduan on August 16, 1986. In July of 1986 we came here to make a dialogue with the NPA and the community to look for a space for a new government building. The [NPA member] who attended the meeting was Cario, who was one of the NPA spokesmen vehemently against resetting up the municipal government.

I was elected as mayor on January 25, 1988. That was when we made...a temporary ceasefire agreement...It was not written, nor was it approved by the Philippine government nor by the Philippine Constabulary. But, actually,

Felipe Lacubawan shares his memories in a meeting room at the Hungduan municipal offices. (April 18, 2008)

it was secretly approved by different commands of the Philippine Army and Philippine Constabulary. For one month [the NPA was] free roaming around, but after one month the Philippine Army and Philippine Constabulary came into the area in turn.

[In 1990] Major Ramil and his company, seventeen of them, were ambushed along the national road between Hapao and Bokiawan, together with my chief of police and two other policemen from Kiangan, who were all killed. Major Ramil was loved by the people of Hungduan because he was very friendly.

That was the end of the ceasefire. We tried to interview them at the house of then *barangay* captain, Perlita Gaddang. They said that 'we had to show them that we were strong enough. That is why we conducted the ambush in spite of the internal agreement.' That ended the temporary ceasefire agreement. Then in October of 1990, when I was with my children in the jeepney, traveling back to Banaue, after getting a pig from Poblacion for…a wedding, they got us down at Hapao and I was disarmed. So that was the time I came to believe no matter how you tried to be good with [the NPA], they would act treacherously when it served their purpose. So, finally, I told my vice mayor, 'let's organize CAFGU…' We organized it and joined the Philippine Army team, particularly the 48th Infantry Battalion and then the Philippine Constabulary, which is now the Integrated National Police.

There was that firefight in July 1990, when one of the victims was a leader of a composite team, Delta Company, headed by Lieutenant Pakuliba. Lieutenant Dulunuan and my vice mayor was killed in that action at around two o'clock of that fateful day. After his body was retrieved, the fight continued until two o'clock the following day. After that there were still firefighting and encounters. We fought up to Banaue and up to Kiangan. Until such time the [NPA] reinforcement…hardly came into this area because we stopped them at the entry points.

The people in Hungduan suffered so much. Municipal officials, *barangay* officials, as well as civilian leaders had been affected. Many lives were lost, but finally peace was recovered here. I sat in the office of the new municipal building only for half a year. This building is a symbol of peace. This was a staging point for them to harass nearby detachments in Banaue, Kiangan, Asipulo, but not so much in Tinoc. They went to Mountain Province and Benguet…but when they got exhausted they came back here to rest, regroup and recruit members. They conducted teach-ins and trainings. This was a very good area for their training. They recruited outside and brought them in here for training, and then fielded them to different provinces. This was used as the central camp for the NPA for their operation. (Former mayor Felipe Lacubawan (interview conducted by the author), Hungduan Municipal Building, April 18, 2008)

Ananayo suggests that Hungduan became an important base for NPA operations throughout the 1970s and 1980s for the following reasons. First, its location deep in the mountains made access difficult. Second, the NPA was able to obtain the support of local residents by offering assistance and friendly behavior. Third, Hungduan is located at a strategic point on the roads connecting Kiangan, Banaue, Tinoc and Mountain Province. Fourth, Hungduan (and Hapao village in particular) is relatively wealthy (Ananayo 1998: 78).

A microcosm of the world concentrated at the frontier

As I have discussed in this chapter, for nearly twenty years from the early 1970s to the end of the 1980s, Hapao was not a quiet, self-contained world separated from the outside. It was a battleground where Marcos's martial law regime and the revolutionary forces that sought to overthrow it engaged in a quiet battle for supremacy in an attempt to establish control over the region. The Vietnam War on the Southeast Asian mainland had come to an end in 1975 with the victory of North Vietnam. In Cambodia, the Khmer Rouge had taken power under the leadership of Pol Pot. However, only three years later, a number of Khmer Rouge leaders who were suspected of planning a revolt against Pol Pot escaped to Vietnam. They then led a counter-offensive with Vietnamese support and installed a new government under Prime Minister Heng Samrin. In 1979, China, which supported Pol Pot, attacked Vietnam, which supported Heng Samrin, over the Sino-Vietnamese border. This was the beginning of the Sino-Vietnamese War.

While the Cold War transformed into a kind of sibling rivalry between the socialist powers in mainland Southeast Asia, in the Philippines a Maoist-communist force underwent unprecedented expansion and repeatedly engaged in military engagements with the Philippine Constabulary all over the country. Even when the proxy war that burned in the battlefields of Vietnam as part of the larger Cold War had ended, in the Philippines it continued to smolder in the rural and mountain villages. Indeed, in the Philippines in the 1980s, after the assassination of Ninoy (August 1983) and the People Power Revolution (February 1986), the CPP grew in power. Tensions between the central government and the CPP-NPA intensified and there were repeated outbreaks of small-scale military conflict.

As both Ananayo's research and Lacubawan's testimony show, when the CPP-NPA was new and still weak, it began the steady work of building a base in remote rural and mountainous villages such as Hapao, where the eyes and the services of the central government did not reach and where the military and the police did not maintain an adequate presence. This reflects the Maoist revolutionary strategy of the CPP-NPA, adopted by the organization at its foundation, of surrounding the cities from the countryside by organizing in the rural and mountain villages. In just over ten years, the CPP-NPA expanded its power to the point that it could contemplate all-out confrontation with the Philippine Constabulary. Its definite friendliness and devotion during the early days earned it the trust and support of the villagers. Once it had built a degree of support, the approach changed to one of despotic rule based on superior military strength. Many villagers left Hungduan in disgust and out of fear of getting mixed up in the violence.

The reason so many anthropologists have been fascinated by Ifugao society and culture and have gone there to conduct research is much the same as that of the CPP-NPA when it made the strategic decision to base itself in Hapao. To put it simply, it is the geographical importance of the region derived from its location far from the capital Manila in the depths of the inaccessible mountains. For the CPP-NPA, this was an area not completely under state control. Therefore, even in the beginning, when its military power was far inferior to that of the Constabulary, it could build and maintain a base there and steadily accumulate enough power to launch a counter-offensive. Anthropologists see Ifugao as a place where the influence of American culture and the operation of its economic system does not directly reach or, at least, where its influence is weak. It is therefore seen as a place where non-Western things are preserved.

The film director Kidlat Tahimik and the anthropologists I discuss in the first section of this chapter came to Ifugao to carry out fieldwork and to learn from the Ifugaos in the hope that within Ifugao traditional and indigenous culture they might find an example of an alternative, non-Western culture and society. They hoped perhaps to find a hint of how to create a more desirable modernity or an example of it hidden within. One might suggest that the CPP-NPA's fascination with Ifugao is the chance it offered them to build power and overthrow the capitalist-developmentalist Marcos regime, while for Kidlat and the anthropologists (myself included), the fascination comes from a sense that we can learn from the Ifugaos a worldview or a set of ideas that will allow us to gain some perspective on the mainstream thought patterns and social structures of Western modernity. We seek some guidance for understanding our own culture in relation to that of the Ifugaos and for reconstructing our own sense of self.

However, the people who live in Hapao do not in any way see themselves as living in a separate world removed from the Christian lowlanders in Manila and elsewhere. In terms of the preservation of their Ifugao traditions, they certainly see themselves as different from the lowlanders. But since the beginning of the twentieth century, they have been subject to American colonial rule, invasion by the Japanese and rule by the CPP-NPA just like the lowlanders. Even before the Second World War, churches and primary schools were built in Ifugao and the majority of Ifugaos had been baptized and adopted Christianity. At the beginning of the Asia-Pacific War (1942), Japanese teachers were sent to the region, where they taught Japanese for about six months. Even now there are quite a few old people who can sing the *Patriotic March* (Lo! Above the eastern sea clearly dawns the sky…). As the war drew to a close at the beginning of June 1945, Japanese troops under the command of General Yamashita built their last stand on Mount Napulawan, towering behind Hapao. The shells fired by the Americans against the Japanese did great damage to the Ifugao rice paddies and cost many lives. After the war, some Ifugao children went to university and after graduation they found work in Baguio and Manila. Twenty years ago, in a period where globalization was accelerating rapidly, more and more Ifugaos began traveling overseas for work.

In conclusion, precisely because Hungduan is located in the deep mountains and is difficult to access, the minor powers that sought to challenge the ruling power hid themselves away there and built bases from which they hoped to launch their counter-attack. This is why, conversely, the ruling power must extend its military power to the frontier in order to solidify its control over its territory. As a result, tensions between government and anti-government forces, small-scale fighting and micro-conflicts over the daily exercise of authority and influence have slowly smoldered away. In this period of conflict and tension, the year 1990, when the NPA conducted two ambushes, marked a major turning point. As globalization penetrated Ifugao, it changed from a place where domestic political and military confrontations were concentrated to one where the Ifugaos began to ride the wave of globalization out into the wider world.

3 Life amid the Blessings of Forests
Rice Terrace Cultivation and Woodcarving

In Hapao a traditional way of life, where the villagers' means of subsistence and the core of their identity is made up of techniques, knowledge and rituals of rice cultivation that date 'far back beyond living memory', continues to this day. In this chapter I discuss this traditional way of life in which the people derive their basic needs from mountain forests and rice terraces and from the woodcarving industry, which produces carved items for sale as souvenirs in places such as Manila, Baguio and Banaue and for export overseas.

The forests and rice terraces as an ecosystem

The Ifugaos make their living predominantly by growing rice. Annual rainfall in Ifugao is approximately 3,530 millimeters (1974–84 average). During the rainy season from June to November, the average monthly rainfall is 503 millimeters, while during the dry season from December to May the monthly average is 137 millimeters (Roxas 1994). In the past, Ifugao society was divided into a wealthy (*kadangyan*), a poor (*nawowot*) and a middle (*wadwachaan*) class. Today, however, the Ifugaos do not consciously observe such strict social demarcations. In terms of the economic power they derive from cash income, however, contemporary Ifugao society is actually becoming more divided than it was in the past. Wealthy Ifugaos own numerous large terraces located close to the valley floor, while poorer families might own small terraces located higher up in the mountains or none at all. Ifugaos who do not own their own terraces grow sweet potatoes in swiddens on the village commons or work as tenant farmers for their relatives, sharing half their harvest with the landowner.

In addition to practicing swidden agriculture and working as tenants for their wealthier relatives, poor Ifugaos obtain irregular employment as laborers on civil engineering and construction projects initiated by the government or foreign aid organizations. They also earn cash income by producing woodcarvings. Ifugaos who own only one or two terraces still perform wage labor or make woodcarvings during the agricultural off-season. As large trees suitable for carving are unobtainable near the Ifugao villages, some Ifugaos spend two or three months working outside the province in neighboring Nueva Vizcaya or Quirino, where they live in forest camps and devote themselves to carving. For the Ifugaos, rice terraces are extremely important symbolic resources that represent wealth and prestige. For Ifugaos who have the means, either through working overseas or in a successful woodcarving business, their first priority is to send their children to university in Baguio or Metro Manila. Usually, the next thing they will do is to rebuild their houses in reinforced concrete or purchase rice terraces. For the villagers, the symbolic value of the terraces is of greater importance than their economic value but the only buyers who understand this value are other Ifugaos. Therefore, when ownership changes hands, it is almost always through a trade between two Ifugaos from the same or neighboring villages. Similarly, if an Ifugao moves to Baguio or some other far-off place for work and is unable to tend his or her fields, he or she will lease them to relatives or sell them.

Milgram (1997) conducted fieldwork in five villages in the municipality of Banaue in the early 1990s. She found that each household owned an average of 0.5 hectares of cultivated terrace land. Each household dedicated two-thirds of its total labor power to terrace cultivation, but this only provided about half of the household income. The average annual yield per hectare of terraced land between 1985 and 1995 was 2.66–2.88 tons.[1] Apart from the wealthiest families, most households are only able to produce an amount equal to three to six months of their domestic consumption. These households must therefore either earn cash income to purchase additional rice or switch to sweet potatoes for their staple food when their supply runs out. In terms of cash income, the average annual income was 22,558 pesos per household and 78 percent of households fell below the government's established poverty line. This made them the poorest households in

---

1 The government recommends the use of high-yield varieties, but few Ifugaos have adopted them. The reasons they are reluctant to adopt them include their lack of tolerance to the cold temperatures in the highlands, their unsuitability for making rice wine used for ritual purposes, poor flavor, the need for additional fertilizers and their shattering habit that leads to heavy losses.

the mountain provinces of northern Luzon, where the average annual household income was 33,838 pesos (Milgram 1997: 58–69).

According to the Hungduan municipal government handbook for 2006, the average monthly income per household in Hapao was 12,200 pesos. This is about five times that of Hungduan's poorest *barangay*, Bangbang (2,330 pesos), 1.6 times that of the second-wealthiest *barangay*, Poblacion (6,710 pesos), and more than twice the average household income of all nine *barangays* put together (5,650 pesos) (Profile of Municipality of Hungduan 2007: 22). The five villages Milgram surveyed seem much wealthier than Hapao probably because of direct and indirect benefits from the tourism industry, which is mainly concentrated in and around Banaue town proper.

The household incomes in Hapao are so much higher than in other parts of Hungduan for a number of reasons. A significant number of salaried workers in Hapao work for the elementary and secondary school (this high school provides an additional four years of education on top of an elementary education), the municipal hospital and the agricultural college that are located on the hill above the village. Hapao is also home to wealthy shopkeepers who keep the ten grocery and general stores located on either side of the fifty meters of surfaced road in Hobbong. Additionally, as I explain further in Chapter 8, a number of villagers have left to work overseas and their families benefit from the remittances they send back.

Hapao includes 115.2 hectares of irrigated rice terraces and 44.8 hectares of rainfed terraces. This constitutes 16 percent of the irrigated terraces in the whole municipality of Hungduan (700.41 hectares) and 16 percent of the rainfed terraces (270 hectares). In Hungduan as a whole, in 2000 the average yield of rice per hectare was 58 *cavan* (approximately 2.9 tons; one *cavan* is roughly equivalent to one 60-kilogram bag of rice). This compares quite poorly with the Department of Agriculture's target yield of 99 *cavan* per hectare. However, with its additional 270 hectares of rainfed terraces, the Municipality of Hungduan as a whole produces additional rice to meet demand for its staple food. Because most terraced land is located in the highlands at an altitude of approximately 1,000 meters about sea level, it is unsuitable for growing high-yield varieties of rice and the people practice single-season cropping using local varieties. They also practice swidden agriculture, where they grow sweet potatoes, taro and several varieties of legumes. In the past, before Ifugaos began to travel overseas for work, the cultivation of tubers in swidden fields was essential for guaranteeing their staple food supply. However, now that they have more opportunities to earn cash incomes by working overseas or on local development projects, many people have begun purchasing rice rather than practicing swidden agriculture.

Conklin, whose fieldwork in Ifugao from 1961 until the mid-1970s I introduced in Chapter 2, produced a detailed report on traditional terrace agriculture and the surrounding ecosystem. His research concentrated on the region of Banaue in the central-northern part of Ifugao Province. In Hapao, in the west of the province, the people make their living in an almost identical agro-ecosystem. According to Conklin, the annual agricultural calendar is divided into four seasons (off-season, rice-planting, draining and harvest) and fifteen phases, with twenty-two stages of agricultural work and twenty-three associated agricultural rituals to perform. During these rituals, the people recite the names of more than thirty gods and hundreds of ancestors, and make sacrifices and give offerings. Ancestors are recognized along both the maternal and paternal lines and people can recall their parents and their siblings, their maternal and paternal grandparents and their siblings, and their great-grandparents. In the old days, however, the genealogies recited during rituals incorporated at least eight to ten, and in some cases up to twenty, generations in the chain of ancestors who passed the rice terraces down to their present owners (Conklin 1980: 12–13, 38; for a detailed account of the agricultural calendar, see pp. 14–35).

In terms of the solar calendar, the period from January to February coincides with the period of rice planting. Harvest takes place from July to August. If we include every stage in the work, from maintenance of the terraced paddies after harvest to the creation of nursery beds to raise seedlings, transplanting, weeding, harvesting and storage, then at least 650 working days are required per hectare. This includes approximately 200 days of paddy maintenance and terrace repairs, which is the responsibility of the men, and 450 days of agricultural labor, for which the women are usually responsible. When landslides occur, whether due to typhoons or other causes, the men's labor increases dramatically to more than 500 days as they carry out repairs to the irrigation canals and to the embankments and walls of the terraces. In some cases, the amount of labor required can reach 1,000 days (Conklin 1980: 37). Tractors and *carabao* (water buffalo) are almost never used in the steeply sloped terraces. Instead, the Ifugaos work by hand, using shovels and other tools, meaning the burden of labor is both lengthy and arduous. At the bottom of the steeply sloping mountainside, the terraces are large, but they become progressively smaller as they ascend the mountain. The very highest terraces are only one to two meters wide, resembling thin bands wrapped up in the steep slopes. Climbing up and down the terraces, which can have twenty to thirty vertical steps, cultivating the paddies and raising seedlings by hand is grueling physical work.

The yield of unhulled rice from each hectare of terraced paddy varies greatly depending on the conditions. In Conklin's sample, he found a difference in yield of 1.86–6.13 tons per hectare. In an average terraced

Top: General stores in the center of Hobbong, Hapao. (March 5, 1998)

Bottom: Inside a general store in the same area. (March 15, 1998)

paddy, the yield was 2.5–3 tons. Swidden agriculture requires 250 working days per hectare, while maintaining *pinugo* (private forests) requires twenty working days per hectare. The soil in central Ifugao is highly fertile and in productive valleys, where the conditions for terrace agriculture are good, rice and tubers are planted at a ratio of 5:1. On the other hand, on the periphery of the province, where the mountain slopes are steep, the ratio can be as much as 1:5 and averages 2:3. In the region surveyed by Conklin, a typical five-person household owned an average of 0.5 hectares of terraced paddy land, 0.25 hectares of swidden fields and 1.3 hectares of *pinugo* forest. Households invested a total of 400 working days to maintain these resources (Conklin 1980: 35–7). Conklin's work provides a detailed overview of the 'old' system whereby the Ifugaos maintained their livelihoods before the CPP-NPA took over the area and before working overseas and other rapid social and economic changes accompanying globalization had taken root.

Eder (1982), whose fieldwork concentrated mainly on the Banaue area, found that by the 1970s the productivity of terrace agriculture was already falling, mostly due to a lack of irrigation water, and issues such as people abandoning farming were already beginning to emerge. The reason for the depletion of water resources needed for irrigation was a decrease in forest cover due to the felling of trees for swidden agriculture, the need for raw materials for woodcarving and the collection of firewood for cooking fuel. Unfortunately, in Hapao too, terrace agriculture is starting to face many of the same problems that have appeared in Banaue, although they have appeared much later. After the rice terraces of Ifugao were designated as a World Heritage site, they were added to the List of World Heritage in Danger in 2001 due to issues such as the destruction of terraces that had been abandoned by farmers or their use for crops other than rice.

It is possible to list many different reasons for the destruction of the terraces and together they have a cumulative effect. The biggest issue is that rice terrace agriculture involves heavy physical work but produces low yields, so young people do not want to assume responsibility for the terraces from their parents, which leads to a shortage of labor.[2] Even before

---

2 Furthermore, frequent dry spells caused by El Niño in the 1990s (1990–94, 1997–98) meant that there was little rain in the Ifugao territory and large cracks appeared in the dried-out terraces. The onset of the wet season was delayed and when the rains finally came there were torrential downpours. Rain soaked into

Top: Swidden field of taro on the high ground. (March 14, 2000)
Bottom left: Swidden field of sweet potato on a steep slope. (March 12, 2005)
Bottom right: Swiddens amid the forest. (August 14, 2005)

Top left, right: Planting rice in the terraces in Patpat and Poblacion, Hapao. (March 2, 2000; March 1, 2001)

Middle left: Using a mattock to break up the soil for tilling. (March 11, 1998)

Middle right: Repairing a rice terrace that has collapsed in Hapao (March 2, 2007). Both tasks are undertaken by hand without the use of machines.

Bottom: Repairing a terrace embankment in Abatan, Hungduan. (March 1, 2003)

this, as Eder found, increased logging in the forests above the terraces had caused landslides that clogged up the terraces and irrigation canals. Furthermore, mountain forests act as watershed conservation forests. The clearing of these forests for swidden agriculture and to obtain raw materials for woodcarving and lumber for housing reduces their water-holding capacity, leading to a decrease in the amount of water flowing into the irrigation canals. Most young people, including almost all of those who have completed high school, want to leave the village to find employment in larger towns and cities. Just as Japan's mountain villages are being depopulated, farming as a vocation is ageing and the pool of young people to carry it on is decreasing steadily.

As a result of the attention that came with World Heritage listing, and the later listing as World Heritage in Danger, the Philippine government and the Ifugao provincial government, as well as NGOs and other actors, began to propose and then to implement various projects aimed at rice terrace conservation. However, most outside assistance was in the form of infrastructure maintenance, such as paving roads up to the irrigation canals and terraces, and little capital was available in the first place to enhance cultivators' motivation, so many of these schemes were not particularly effective.

Pinugo forests and the system of land tenure

To this day, terrace agriculture is an important vocation for the people of Hapao and is tied to their social position and their identity. Wide fluvial terraces spread out along the river that runs along the valley floor. As they climb the sides of the mountain, the terraces narrow. Above the narrowest terraces, the inclination becomes too extreme and it is impossible to construct further rice terraces. Instead, the slopes above are covered in privately owned forests known as *pinugo* and *muyong*. The terraces have been maintained, together with their surrounding natural environment – in

---

the cracks, resulting in major damage to the terraces, such as crumbling of the surrounding stone walls. Furthermore, masses of large worms that burrowed into the terraces appeared, leading to water leaks (Osawa 2006; Kimura 2006). To repair the terraces involved a huge amount of work. As a result, some people gave up rice cultivation and abandoned their terraces altogether, while others converted them to vegetable crops.

particular, the *pinugo* forests – in a close-knit web. The surrounding forests, particularly the privately owned *pinugo* forests, combine to form a single ecosystem with the rice terraces. This system is exceptional in the overall context of the Philippines and is characteristic of Ifugao forest ownership and management practices.

However, while the *pinugo* forests have been maintained along with the rice terraces for at least the last several hundred years, technically, the property rights of the Ifugaos over their *pinugo* forests are not legally recognized and their customary practices only receive tacit recognition. The Regalian Doctrine, under the terms of which the state is the original owner of all land, has been the core principle of the Philippine system of land tenure since the Spanish conquest and subsequent colonial administration, and remains so today. On this basis, individual or corporate ownership of land is only recognized where it has been granted by the Crown.[3] The mountains, where most of the indigenous peoples of the Philippines live, automatically reverted to state ownership following the promulgation of Presidential Decree No. 705, 'The Forestry Reform Code of the Philippines' (May 19, 1975), during the martial law regime of President Ferdinand Marcos:

> Section 15. *Topography.* No land of the public domain eighteen per cent (18%) in slope or over shall be classified as alienable and disposable, nor any forest land fifty per cent (50%) in slope or over, as grazing land.
>
> Lands eighteen per cent (18%) in slope or over which have already been declared as alienable and disposable shall be reverted to the classification of forest lands by the Department Head…unless they are already covered by existing titles or approved public land application, or actually occupied openly, continuously, adversely and publicly for a period of not less than thirty (30) years…

---

3   In the mid-sixteenth century, at the beginning of colonial rule, the Spanish – just as they had done in the New World – declared that all land in the Philippines was the property of the Spanish crown. The legal basis for this wholesale expropriation was provided by the principle of *derecho de conquista* (right of conquest), which was exercised in all of Spain's colonies around the world at that time and was recognized by the papacy in 1493. The Regalian Doctrine remains the basic principle of the Philippine system of land tenure and was confirmed in the 1987 constitution.

Section 69. *Unlawful occupation or destruction of forest lands.* Any person who enters and occupies or possesses, or makes *kaingin*[4] for his own private use or for others any forest land without authority under a license agreement... be fined in an amount of not less than five hundred pesos (P500.00) nor more than twenty thousand pesos (P20,000.00) and imprisoned for not less than six (6) months nor more than two (2) years for each such offense...[5]

Ifugaos regard *pinugo* forests as private property and part of their ancestral domain that has been handed down through numerous generations, along with the rice terraces. However, while Ifugaos exercise ownership and management of the *pinugo* forests in practice, their property rights are not legally recognized. One workaround to assert ownership over the forests is to declare them as meadows rather than forests on one's income tax return. Furthermore, under the Indigenous Peoples' Rights Act (IPRA) (1997), it is possible for Indigenous Cultural Communities and Indigenous Peoples to claim collective ownership of 'ancestral domains' that have been in their exclusive possession since time immemorial. However, the concept of ownership contained in this law differs from the concept of absolute property rights that typically pertains to private property – rather, the IPRA defines 'ancestral domain' as a form of 'private but communal' ownership by an indigenous group as a whole.

Furthermore, under the Act, ancestral domains 'belong to each and every generation'. Ancestral domains cannot be sold or transferred because they must pass from the ancestors down through the generations to the children and grandchildren. Unlike land ownership in many other indigenous societies, in Ifugao culture, *pinugo* forests are regarded as the private property of an individual (or sometimes of a parent and child or siblings) and therefore do not fit within the notion of collective ownership that is assumed in the IPRA. Furthermore, voluminous paperwork is required to complete

---

4 A Philippine word for swidden.
5 Under this decree, approximately 40 percent of all land in the Philippines was brought into state ownership and rights to logging and mining development were granted to both domestic and foreign corporations by local powerbrokers and politicians. The decree also effectively made the indigenous peoples of the Cordillera Mountains of northern Luzon and the highlands of Mindoro Island, who live in lands rich in forests and mineral resources, into illegal occupants of their ancestral domains and legally stripped them of the rights that form the basis of their livelihoods (Gatmaytan 1992: 19–22; Koshida 1993: 231).

an application under the IPRA. As a result, Ifugaos have made few attempts to file collective applications for ownership of their 'ancestral domains'.

The *pinugo* forests serve to protect the rice terraces on the lower slopes from landslides and topsoil erosion. They also help to guarantee the water supply for the irrigation canals. If the *pinugo* forests disappear, then the water needed to irrigate the rice terraces will dry up. Furthermore, heavy rains will wash the topsoil downhill and clog the upper terraces and the irrigation canals, causing major damage. The most important *pinugo* forests are those located directly above the rice terraces, but those located in the mountain ranges above the terraced valleys and even further away often feed the springs that are channeled into the irrigation canals and so may be just as important. Furthermore, the villagers, who until 2000 relied on spring water for drinking and for all other daily water needs, are well aware that the *pinugo* forests and the mountain forests in general help to store water and are the source of their perennial springs. The *pinugo* forests are also an important source of fuel for cooking, lumber for building and raw materials for the woodcarvings that are sold locally as souvenirs or exported overseas. Without the *pinugo* forests, neither terrace agriculture nor life in the villages would be sustainable.

Further off in the mountains, lands that have poor water storage capacity (the grasslands and secondary forests known as *bilid*) are designated for communal use by the village and anybody has the right to make use of them freely. There the Ifugaos fell timber to build houses or for woodcarving. They also create swidden fields there or use them for hunting. The use of chainsaws for felling timber in Hapao began around the end of the 1970s and apparently some large trees located in communal forests near the village were cut down. However, in most cases only the desired trees were selected for felling and there were only a few cases where the entire forest cover was stripped, leaving nothing but bare earth. As I discuss in Chapter 2, during the 1970s and 1980s the CPP-NPA controlled the Hapao area. While some individuals may have used chainsaws to collect timber, no organized large-scale logging was carried out by timber companies.

Although the *pinugo* forests are regarded as private property, their ownership may extend beyond a single individual and be shared between siblings, or between parents and children. In Poitan, a village near Banaue where Conklin carried out research in the 1960s, there were 209 *pinugo* forests held by 167 owners. Of these, 139 were owned by single persons, while the remaining twenty-eight had shared ownership between family

Life amid the Blessings of Forests

Top: *Pinugo* forests and terraces in Hapao. (March 16, 2000)

Bottom: In some places, the *pinugo* have lost their forest cover. (March 12, 1999)

members (Conklin 1980: 74). More recently, Hayama (2002) surveyed almost every household in Poitan between 1998 and 1999. She found that of 236 households, only fourteen lacked even a single *pinugo* forest. In the remaining 222 households, at least the husband or the wife had one or more forests. However, there was a major difference between Hayama's and Conklin's findings. Hayama found that most people shared ownership of their forests with their kin. Typically, ownership was shared between a parent and child across two and sometimes three generations (Hayama 2002: 20).[6]

According to Hayama, where ownership is shared between siblings, the right to fell timber is sometimes shared equally between them, while in other cases the sibling who actively manages the forest thereby possesses strong rights to utilize them. She also found cases where *pinugo* forests located far from the household's place of residence were neglected, with nobody looking after them or making use of them. Where ownership is shared between a parent and child or between a grandparent, parent and child, the parent usually has the greatest responsibility to maintain the forest and the strongest rights to make use of its resources.

Pinugo forests are usually inherited together with the rice terraces below. Rice terraces and *pinugo* forests were traditionally passed down to the eldest child and this principle generally still applies today. Barton (1969) suggests two reasons for this; first, to maintain the family's status as a powerful family at the center of a wider kinship network that is dependent on them and, second, to prevent succession disputes between siblings. In the case of wealthy families who own numerous rice terraces, inheritance is sometimes decided on occasions such as marriage. The father's property might be passed to the eldest child, while the mother's property may go to the second child. Alternatively, an unequal inheritance pattern might involve the eldest child receiving half of the parents' total property, while the next child receives half of the remainder and the third child the other half.

---

6 Nine *pinugo* forests were owned by a single individual (3.8 percent), eleven were co-owned by siblings (4.7 percent), and 139 were co-owned across two or three generations (58.9 percent). For the remainder, ownership was shared across two generations, including siblings (Hayama 2002: Table 5: Distribution of Private Forest by Type of Holding, 1998–1999).

However, according to Hayama's research and contrary to Barton's assertion, ownership of *pinugo* forests is not necessarily tied to that of the rice terraces below, nor are they always passed down together. Just like the complex patterns of ownership described above, in practice the inheritance of *pinugo* forests and the methods for transferring ownership rights are also complex, as I now explain.

When a *pinugo* forest is the property of an individual, it may be passed to one of his or her children or divided into several portions and shared between children. However, there are cases where several children hold a *pinugo* forest in common or even together with their parents. In the same way, where the ownership of a *pinugo* forest is shared between a number of siblings, once a period of time has passed following the parent's death, ownership may revert to the individual who actively maintains the forest. Alternatively, if the forest is located near the place of residence, even a small *pinugo* forest may be divided into smaller pieces that become the individual property of each sibling. Sometimes ownership rights are also passed to the siblings' own children, resulting in a pattern of collective ownership across multiple generations. The inheritance or transfer of ownership of *pinugo* forests that were originally held by members of two generations becomes even more complex, but in general it follows the same pattern as for co-ownership among siblings. In other words, a single individual may assume ownership or, conversely, the forest might be divided between multiple individual owners. It may also be shared between siblings or across three generations, including grandchildren (Hayama 2002: 22–3).

However, while ownership rights to the *pinugo* forests can be passed on, like the rice terraces, they have been inherited from the ancestors and are considered to be held in trust. Therefore, the owners of *pinugo* forests are not free to dispose of them as they choose. If the owner moves to Baguio or Metro Manila, or to a neighboring province after having been there several times for seasonal work, he or she can no longer carry out the day-to-day maintenance of the forest. In this case, the sibling or relative of the owner who takes the time to look after the forest will come to be seen as its real owner. In such cases, it is usual for the former owner and whoever is maintaining and utilizing the forest to discuss the ownership and use of the forest, possibly with other relatives as well. Furthermore, if the owner of a rice terrace or *pinugo* forest has to sell it because he or she needs money to pay hospital fees or treatment costs for a family member or for a child's education, they much prefer to sell to a close relative. If that is not possible, then they will explore the possibility of selling to ever more distant relatives.

Even when a single individual inherits a *pinugo* forest, if one of the owner's siblings needs to, they can obtain the owner's permission to harvest timber from it. Conversely, while it is the owner's responsibility to maintain the forest, if he or she needs help to do so, he or she can call on siblings. Maintenance of the *pinugo* forests involves regularly cutting the grass, pruning and thinning the trees, and planting saplings after harvesting or wherever there is open space. Demonstrably taking great care to maintain the forest helps the owner to prevent anyone else from harvesting timber from it without permission. However, while the owner's permission is required to harvest a standing tree from a *pinugo* forest, anyone from the village is free to collect fallen branches for firewood or gather other products from the forests.

'*Pinugo*' is usually translated as 'private forest' and this is how the villagers describe it. As I explain further later, however, Nauyac, who initiated the reforestation movement, stresses that *pinugo* are 'man-made forests'. In fact, while new rice terraces are rarely built (though there have been attempts to repair abandoned irrigation canals and thereby revive neglected terraces with the assistance of government or foreign aid agencies), it is relatively easy to gain possession of a *pinugo* forest through methods other than inheritance. The first method is to plant trees and grow a forest after having grown tubers in a swidden field. The second method is to take care of part of a grassland or thicket or even a piece of common forest land (*bilid*) and plant trees there, as one would in a *pinugo* forest, and then assert ownership rights over the newly created forest. In both cases, the resulting *pinugo* forests tend to be located at some distance from the village and are not directly connected to the rice terraces. Nevertheless, even these more distant *pinugo* forests created through the enclosure of common lands are recognized by the village as benefiting both the individual owner and the village as a whole when they are located on higher ground above the rice terraces and create streams that divert water for irrigating the terraces or serve as headwater forests to feed springs.[7]

---

7 However, according to Nauyac, depending on the species, some trees help to store water in the soil while others take water from the soil and then lose it via

From time to time, disputes arise over the ownership or the boundaries of a *pinugo* forest. If the owner neglects to maintain his or her forest for an extended period of time and somebody else starts to think of the forest as part of the common land of the village or as natural forest, and takes over the maintenance and replanting of the forest, then, unless the original owner asserts his or her rights and prevents these intrusions from taking place, the ownership rights will eventually be transferred to the new owner. However, problems can arise if the original owner starts asserting his or her rights to the forest after the new claimant has already put work into it. Another source of disputes is when two family circles related to the original owner begin to proclaim their rights to the same piece of land. In cases such as these, a resolution will be sought with the mediation of villager elders who possess deep knowledge of genealogy and ritual or with *monbaki*, who have religious authority. Recently, an incident occurred where the hereditary owner of a *pinugo* forest had long neglected its proper maintenance and abandoned the forest. A second individual declared the forest on his income tax return with the local government and, using this document as evidence, proclaimed himself as the 'legal' owner of the forest. Mediation by a *monbaki* would have been desirable, but if either side refuses a case to be brought to a *monbaki* because it is a modern legal case, the problem would be beyond the customary law.

There have also been struggles in Hapao over the borders of the *pinugo* forests. In the mid-1990s the Ifugao State College of Agriculture and Forestry, located on a hill in the center of Hapao, wanted to build a branch school. The then governor of Ifugao Prefecture, Lumawig, and the provincial political leadership asked the owners of the *pinugo* forests and grasslands to donate land for the building of the school. The landowners initially agreed, bowing to political pressure. Later, however, they asked the Hungduan municipal government for compensation and for clarity because they had been unable to reach an agreement as to

---

transpiration, rather than helping to store it in the soil. He says that species recommended for use in reforestation by the government, such as *Eucalyptus* and *Gmelina*, belong to the latter type. There are some government-sponsored reforestation projects taking place in Ifugao and they usually plant *Gmelina* species. However, according to Nauyac, it is important to choose a location where water is plentiful when planting these species.

the exact location of the relevant boundaries and there was a lack of official paperwork regarding the transfer of the land. In the end, the issue was resolved when two hectares of land were formally donated to the municipality to build the branch school and the property rights of the owners of other lands were confirmed.

In a separate case, an individual I refer to as HG received permission to create swidden fields in a *pinugo* forest belonging to another individual, BM (a resident of Hapao to whom HG was related by marriage), on the condition that no tree planting take place. However, HG replanted the *pinugo* forest after having harvested the yams from the swiddens in violation of the original agreement. After HG died in the early 2000s, HG's children continued to plant trees in the *pinugo* forest and to carry out regular maintenance. On this basis, they claimed to be the real owners of the forest. The issue has still not been resolved.

Due to the amount of timber that has been harvested in some parts of the *pinugo* and *bilid* forests in the vicinity of Hapao, they are not necessarily in a good state. Nevertheless, the situation is not yet dire and the forests can be adequately restored with appropriate maintenance and replanting. The situation is still relatively good in Hapao for numerous reasons. First, a large number of people have left the village, keeping population growth down. Second, the CPP-NPA, which exercised powerful influence over the area from the end of the 1970s until the early 1990s, valued the forests for their importance in guerilla warfare and prevented excessive harvesting of timber. Third, tourism development has been limited to the Banaue area and has not yet really reached Hapao. Fourth, the shift in lifestyle from supplementing the rice harvest with yams grown in swidden fields to buying rice using money from other work means that new vegetation has overtaken the abandoned swiddens. Fifth, the villagers' forestry technique involves selecting only the necessary trees for harvest. Finally, the owners of rice terraces exercise great care to conserve the *pinugo* forests as a water source.

At the same time, forest cover did begin to decline rapidly in the early 1990s for a number of reasons: first, the introduction of chainsaws to the village at the end of the 1980s allowed for the efficient felling of trees; second, the end of CPP-NPA control at that time made it possible once again to move freely through the forests; and third, harvesting of timber increased to rebuild houses (as households earned additional cash income) or to build new homes for grown-up children. Finally, the penetration of

Christianity and school education means that the villagers have lost their fear of the spirits of the forests.[8]

In this context, as I explain further in Chapter 5, Nauyac launched a resident-led reforestation movement out of concern for the loss of forest cover and the degradation of the rice terraces. The harvesting and conservation of the forest, two forces on completely different vectors, began at more or less the same time. In general terms, the harvesting of forests near the village has led to a loss of cover there, while those located further away have been conserved. When it began, the Ifugao Global Forest City Movement driven by Nauyac received no outside support or subsidy. The reforestation movement proceeded smoothly thanks entirely to the work of the villagers cooperating with one another without pay. They did so because the *pinugo* forests are the private property of the men and women of the villages. They raised the saplings collectively and then took them back to their own homes and planted them in order to restore the damaged *pinugo* forests. Because the forests are privately owned, the owners were very active in undertaking tasks such as weeding after revegetation and other tasks involved in growing the trees.

Woodcarving as a means of earning cash income

The Save the Ifugao Terraces Movement, an NGO that cooperates with the provincial government and foreign aid organizations to carry out

---

8 In the traditional Ifugao worldview, the forests were a gift from the god Maknongan to support human life. Many spirits are believed to live in the forest and human visitors must take care not to anger them. Prohibitions that exist when Ifugaos visit the forest include not speaking in a loud voice or making too much noise, not throwing away rubbish in the forest, not thoughtlessly throwing stones (because you might hit a spirit and cause it harm), not combining spices such as chili, garlic or ginger with offerings to the spirits, and not cutting down large trees because they are where the spirits live.

In the mid-1960s, in the vicinity of Nungulunan, a *barangay* that neighbors Hapao, an American engineer discovered a gold seam and began exploratory excavations. However, fearful that full-scale mining development would cause the watershed for the irrigation canals to dry up, village elders snuck into the tunnels at night and left pieces of ginger there. It is said that this caused the gold to hide itself and the American engineer gave up his plans to develop a mine because the gold seam was much further down than he originally thought.

reforestation and other conservation activities for the rice terraces, conducted a survey in 2005. It identified forty-one individuals who live in Hapao for whom woodcarving is their main source of income. However, their monthly income from woodcarving is generally between 3,000 and 4,000 pesos and they still engage in rice cultivation in the terraces. Where possible, they also earn additional income as day laborers on civil engineering projects. However, about eight of them, while still based in Hapao, spent time working in temporary camps outside the village or even outside the municipality or the province, where raw materials for carving are available. These carvers have a monthly income of between 5,000 and 6,000 pesos. Many other people in the village also practice woodcarving in their spare time. More than fifty people fit into this category. When Nauyac formed the Ifugao Global Forest City Movement in 1997, more than half of the one hundred-plus people who joined the group were engaged in woodcarving in some way.

The villagers use timber with a diameter of twenty to thirty centimeters for carving. They mostly produce statues of animals, gods and human figures, as well as small items such as ashtrays. Most of the large hardwood trees near the village that were suitable for carving have already been felled and very few are left. Furthermore, even where suitable trees are available near the village, they must be brought down from the steep mountain slopes with great difficulty. To obtain the large trees needed for carving life-sized American Indian or Budai (Laughing Buddha) statues, carvers have to leave the village and travel to places where they are available. As a result, residents who work primarily as carvers and who specialize in the production of large statues, or who excel at such work, generally leave Hapao and move to places on major roads near the lowlands that are convenient for the transportation of raw materials and finished products. The survey confirmed that at least twenty-six carvers had left Hapao in search of raw materials. The majority relocated to the Danghai area on a hill on the outskirts of Lagawe or to Bolog near the entrance to Kiangan in Ifugao. Some left the province entirely for places such as Baguio, Quirino Province or Tagaytay in Cavite Province, a well-known location for tourism to Taal Lake. As I explain in Chapter 8, one carver who received recognition for his skill in carving was employed to carve ice sculptures for use in a hotel function room. He later relocated to London, where he obtained a permanent position as an ice sculptor in a hotel.

Woodcarving workshop facing onto the national highway in Danghai, Lagawe. (March 14, 2006)

In Hapao, children become familiar with woodcarving from childhood. (March 18, 2006)

In 1978 about ten woodcarving families from Hapao who did not own their own terraces moved to a place known as Bolog Camp, located near Kiangan. The carvers moved there because, as well as being close to a major national highway, which makes it easy to bring in raw materials and send out finished products, there is a *pinugo* forest of nearly thirty hectares that contains many large acacias and whose owner was well disposed towards them. In the early 2000s they mainly produced life-sized statues of American Indians and Ifugao hunters and couples and were able to earn between 6,000 and 7,000 pesos a month.[9]

According to the villagers, the woodcarvers from Hapao have the greatest skills and were the first to sell their carvings as souvenirs. Even today, they say, more than half of the full-time carvers who live in the Asin Road area are originally from Hapao. Of the ten sections of the ethnic peoples exhibit at the National Museum of the Philippines, the Ifugao section is the most substantial. Next to a large model of a traditional Ifugao house, several carved wooden items are displayed alongside Chinese ceramics. An explanatory panel explains that 'the most popular of the Highland groups is the Ifugao, meaning "people who live on the known earth." They are known for their intricate rituals interwoven with complex beliefs and legal system based on customary law.' The museum's official guidebook also states that the Ifugao woodcarving industry is concentrated in Hapao (Castro 2005: 33).

In the following extract from a type-written mimeographed interview with Nauyac's friend Victor Melon, he explains how Ifugao woodcarvings first came to be sold as souvenirs.

---

9 At the end of the 1990s, the price of a single acacia tree was 500–2,000 pesos. One tree was enough to make five or six life-sized American Indian sculptures. It usually takes three days to carve one sculpture, meaning a carver could make about ten per month. One sculpture sold for approximately 1,500 pesos. After materials, transport and other costs were deducted, the carver could make 600–700 pesos profit on each sculpture. Back in 1985, the price of a single acacia was 300 pesos and the price of an American Indian sculpture was 2,500–3,500 pesos, meaning that the net income a carver can make has decreased significantly.

One villager tells of how his relatives and their colleagues moved to Baler in Quezon Province over the Sierra Madre Mountains on the Pacific coast, where they mainly make Laughing Buddha statues (probably of Budai) for a Taiwanese broker. Other carvers moved in small groups to many different places, both within Ifugao and further afield.

a. The First Trade

The first commercial exchange of woodcarving was in 1917. Baguio City, known as the gateway to the Cordillera region, was then being developed as a center by the Americans as the Summer Capital of the Philippines. The mountains were being tamed for roads and buildings, and Ifugaos, then famous for their skill in sculpting mountainsides into terraces, were constantly hired for stone walling jobs.

The following is from accounts of village people on the first commercial transaction of woodcarving.

Three Ihapos (men from the village of Hapao) during their five-day walk to Baguio City, stopped along the trail to eat their lunch. Their quaint spoons and bowls etched with sacred signets of *hugus* and lizards caught the fancy of two Americans on a logging trip who exchanged silver coins for them. The story of the trade told on their return home excited the other villagers, who soon carved items for traveling Ihapos to sell in Baguio. Those who worked in Baguio carried their chisels to carve items in their spare time.

Victor Melon and Teofilo Gano waiting for mass to begin. (March 14, 2004)

The incident was the first opening of woodcarving to the world of cash economy. Inevitably, their talent was tapped for bigger opportunities, which slowly changed the worldview of the native woodcarver.

Ubowo was the first Ihapo to give woodcarving another dimension other than the depiction of the Ifugao traditional lifestyle. Belgian missionaries, building Baguio City's landmark cathedral, commissioned him to render in woodcarving the fourteen Stations of the Cross. He also carved a Madonna and Child statue for the friars.

Ubowo is remembered as one of the early migrants who came to settle at the outskirts of Baguio in search of choice species. Over the years, woodcarvers' camps have proliferated and become fixtures in a trade structure that has completely reduced the cultural and spiritual aspects of woodcarving to sheer survival in global economics.

b. From Tradition to Commerce

As a full commercial activity, woodcarving is regarded to have flourished in the 1950s with a proliferation of souvenir spoon and fork sets of various sizes used as wall accents for homes. Wooden house implements such as plates and bowls, ashtrays etcetera were also mass produced. Accounts have it that these woodwares had about forty mythical figures carved on them. This period was also about the same time that the rice terraces were gaining distinction as the eighth wonder of the world.

The Asin Woodcarving Village

Baguio City's colorful market, which sold an array of goods from the lowlands and the Cordillera region, was the first major woodcarving market. Ifugao woodcarvers were then beginning to settle around the outskirts of Baguio, supplying the market with wares, and Ifugao students took carving as a part-time job to support themselves through school. Baguio, the summer capital of the Philippines, enjoyed a steady stream of tourists. Curio shops became popular shopping dens for tourists, as Baguio City, being the gateway to the Cordillera region, had access to a collection of heirlooms and ethnic paraphernalia. Foreign tourists, who brought with them their penchant for antiques, contributed to the firming up of a market for collectors' items of antiques and reproductions, with a strong clamor for such hand-carved items.

The Asin Woodcarvers' Village is located three kilometers from the center of Baguio. Around the 1950s, some Ifugaos came to settle down here producing woodcraft of traditional designs. The settlement is traversed by a road that leads to Asin Hot Springs, a major tourist destination area. Finished jobs or carvings in progress that stood in front yards along the road were a catching sight to tourists who were treated to the added thrill of watching the craftsmen at work. Eventually, work areas turned into showrooms and the village became a convenient stopover for tourists on their way to the hot springs or a destination shopping spot for most visitors. Direct exposure of the woodcarvers to tourists continued to evolve design concepts from traditional to universal, as carvers increasingly produced designs specified by the buyers.

The growth of the village can also be considered a major leap of the industry from traditional woodcarving for the local market to a full-scale industry with market-oriented designs and connections with the foreign market. Local businessmen who saw the potential of woodcarving also ventured into deals with the Ifugao woodcarvers and acted as their middlemen.

A woodcarver, Reynaldo Lopez Nauyac, pursued a dream of establishing a business village for the woodcarvers and [received a] land donation of 20,000 square meters, which 55 of the residing Ifugaos divided among themselves. He founded the Ifugao Woodcarvers' General Services and Development Cooperative, which gave more direction to the business interests of the Ifugaos. ('Historical Beginnings of Woodcarving' by Victor Melon, October 7, 1998, at Melon's house, with Nauyac's complementary comments)

Melon's ability to recall the exact year when the first exchange took place shows the long history of the woodcarving industry as a means of obtaining cash income for the Ifugaos and that it began at a very early stage of American colonization. When the United States colonized the Philippines, it immediately began a civil engineering project to develop what is now Baguio, located in the rolling hills at an altitude of 1,000 meters, into a hill station. Many Ifugaos and other highland peoples of the Cordillera were employed as craftsmen to build stone walls against the cliffs to prevent landslides during the building of the Benguet road and in the urban development of Baguio and the construction of its buildings and residences. The highland peoples were widely respected for their superior skills developed through building stone walls for their terraces. Ifugao people first worked for the Americans as stonemasons but, as Melon explains, the Americans quickly came to appreciate the Ifugaos' everyday items, such as wooden bowls, trays and spoons, and began to purchase them for use in their own homes and as souvenirs. Carved wooden bowls, trays and wooden salad servers remain popular as souvenirs to this day.

To summarize the discussion in this chapter, the traditional way of life in Hapao was based on the cultivation of rice in the terraces as a staple food, supplemented by sweet potatoes, legumes and vegetables grown in swidden fields. Although this pattern continues to this day, the importance of swidden agriculture has decreased and people tend to make up any shortfall in the rice harvest from their own terraces by purchasing rice from shops in the village or in Banaue.

To sustain terrace agriculture, the *pinugo* forests located on the mountain slopes above the terraces must be kept in good condition. If the forest cover deteriorates, landslides become more frequent. Not only is it important to maintain the *pinugo* forests that are located directly above the terraces but also the forest cover higher up in the mountains because landslides can block the irrigation canals that bring water from hundreds of meters away, or even one to two kilometers from the terraces. In practice, the villagers conduct annual maintenance of the canals to clear them of earth and fallen leaves. If the forest cover deteriorates, then this burden becomes extreme.

Nauyac's reforestation movement, which I discuss in Chapter 5, aims to protect the *pinugo* and communal forests and, by doing so, to protect the rice terraces and irrigation canals from being clogged with fallen earth. At the same time, the movement aims to guarantee the availability of raw materials for the woodcarving industry, an important source of cash income. When Nauyac explains the significance of his reforestation movement to the Japanese government and Japanese NGOs, he links it with the invasion of Ifugao by Japanese troops under the command of General Yamashita and to their theft of the Ifugaos' food and the diseases that then spread and cost the lives of so many villagers. When he explains it to the villagers, he talks about the need to protect the forests by replanting so as to enable terrace agriculture and woodcarving to continue, so that young people who remain in the village, rather than going on to high school or to work overseas, can still make a living. To Philippine politicians and officials, he emphasizes that the forests of Ifugao are a watershed for dams located downstream. While stressing the value of the Ifugao way of living in harmony with the forest, he argues that the forests are not just for the Ifugaos but also provide useful services and are meaningful for outsiders. In Chapter 9, I explain how the power of this argument led JICA and other NGOs in Japan to support his movement.

4 Confronting Global Power from the Margins
Invasions and Resistance

As I explained in detail in the previous chapter with regards to the historical experience of NPA control over Ifugao, Hapao and the broader Hungduan region are difficult to access from the outside world (i.e. the lowlands), even compared with the mountainous district of northern Luzon more broadly. For this reason, throughout the period of Spanish colonial rule, the colonial government was unable to establish effective control over the region. It was not until the end of the nineteenth century that a military garrison was finally built in Kiangan, a village located in a part of the mountains not so far removed from the lowlands. Following the establishment of the garrison, punitive expeditionary forces were dispatched to the mountains to pacify the Ifugao, who carried out repeated headhunting raids against Christian villages located in the lowlands near the foot of the mountains. However, the expeditionary forces only razed the villages of Hapao and the Hungduan region and their unharvested rice terraces. When soldiers came to their villages, the inhabitants would avoid direct confrontations with them by taking refuge in the mountains. These expeditionary forces did not remain long in the villages. Once they withdrew after the provisions ran out, Ifugaos would rebuild their homes and villages and continue life as before.

Following the Spanish-American War, Spain ceded the Philippines to the United States under the terms of the Treaty of Paris (December 10, 1898). On December 21, 1898, President William McKinley announced America's intention to occupy the Philippines by issuing the proclamation of Benevolent Assimilation. On February 4, 1899, American provocations against the Philippine Revolutionary Army triggered the start of the Philippine-American War. Within a few months, American forces had gained control of the major urban centers that were connected by road and their surrounds. The revolutionaries continued to fiercely resist the Americans, waging a guerilla campaign. However, after the capture of

General Aguinaldo in the Sierra Madre of northeast Luzon on March 23, 1901, the resistance quickly petered out, except for sporadic guerilla attacks for several years.

While shoring up their administrative systems in the majority lowland Christian communities, the Americans also worked to pacify the non-Christian areas and to promote education and socioeconomic development. They also actively tried to pacify and win the populace over to American rule in the mountains of northern Luzon. In the Ifugao region, in particular, American governors and Ifugao elites developed a very good relationship. Unlike in other parts of the mountains of northern Luzon, a succession of four American governors each remained in their posts in Ifugao for more than five years. They were successful in their implementation of what was a well-thought-out policy of persuasion and conciliation. Even today, Ifugaos retain a favorable impression of America.

When the so-called Asia-Pacific War broke out on December 8, 1941, in the midst of the Second World War, Japan dispatched a force of 600,000 men to the Philippines, a strategic position in the region. In October 1944, when Japan's defeat was clearly imminent, General Yamashita Tomoyuki was appointed General Commander of the Philippines Area Army (Fourteenth Army Division) in an attempt to turn the situation around. However, soon after Yamashita took up his post, the Imperial Japanese Navy, upon whose support he depended, was defeated in the Battle of Leyte Gulf (October 23–25, 1944). Having lost control of both the air and sea, the Japanese were forced to retreat from Manila. Yamashita and the main force of his troops retreated to Baguio and then to the depths of the mountains of Ifugao. There they remained for just over two months until the Japanese surrender. They occupied a valley that stretches from Hapao to Abatan and on to nearby Wangwang in Tinoc Municipality.

As 50–60,000 Japanese soldiers forced their way into the area, most residents of Hapao and the other villages escaped up into the mountains in fear. With their supply lines cut off and carrying little or no provisions of their own, the Japanese soldiers fed themselves by taking rice from the Ifugao terraces that were due to be harvested and potatoes from their swidden fields. The villagers, who were hiding in the mountains, were therefore left without food. Many, particularly children and older people, lost their lives due either to starvation or dysentery. The Japanese had taken everything, even their seed rice and potatoes, and so severe food shortages continued to affect the whole Hungduan region for a number of years after the war ended. While few Ifugaos were killed directly during the Japanese offensive, many died of starvation or illness.

As discussed in the previous chapter, the NPA, the armed wing of the CPP, took control of the Hungduan region in the early 1970s. In 1986, after Corazon Aquino took power in the People Power Revolution, the CPP-NPA became much more active and a tense standoff with the Philippine military continued up until around the end of the 1980s.

Hapao is located in the deep mountains, far from the center of Philippine political and economic life in Manila. In other words, it is located on the frontier. Ifugao has therefore become a place where the government (the central authority), which attempts to dominate the region militarily and politically, and anti-government forces that have based their rebellion in the region repeatedly came into conflict. In this chapter, by tracing the history of Ifugao further back than in the previous chapter, I would like to bring its character as a frontier territory to the fore. I show how Ifugao has been both directly and indirectly bound up with the world beyond the seas since the coming of the Spanish. Although it has been influenced by global trends, it has not been swept up by them but has held its own it its dealings with the outside world. As its people struggle to preserve their villages, their rice terraces and their way of life deep in the forests, the Ifugao region has had to confront globalization head on as it saturates and penetrates their world. They have responded to this challenge flexibly, taking in some elements while attempting to modify and to tame others.

Pacification and resistance under Spanish rule

From the beginning of Spanish colonial rule, the central government in Manila tried again and again to penetrate Ifugao. In the oldest recorded attempt, forty-five soldiers under the command of Juan Salcedo conducted a pacification operation in 1572 in the Pangasinan and Ilocos regions (in the western foothills of the Cordillera Mountains on the coast). They retreated following a fierce encounter with highlanders who were working a gold mine south of Benguet (Dumia 1979: 26).

Since the Spanish colonial period, the indigenous peoples of the Cordillera Mountains of northern Luzon, including the Ifugaos, have been referred to as the Igorots. They can be further divided into six ethnic groups based on linguistic and cultural differences: the Kalinga, Apayao

(Itneg), Bontoc, Ifugao, Kankanay and Ibaloi.[1] Even within the same ethnic group, the Igorot peoples possess strong local loyalties. Throughout the three-and-a-half centuries of Spanish rule, they repeatedly carried out headhunting raids and revenge attacks against people of the same ethnicity in different regions and against members of other ethnic groups, as well as against lowlanders. Furthermore, ferocious resistance to Spanish attempts at pacification was carried out in each locality and village. Outside of a confined area near to the lowlands, they refused to surrender to the Spanish. As a result, during the nineteenth century alone, the Spanish carried out at least seventy-five short-term expeditions and pacification operations across the mountainous region (Scott 1974: 7).

For the first fifty years of colonial rule, Spain regularly dispatched expeditionary forces to occupy the Cordillera Mountains in order to capture the gold that is produced there. All these attempts ended in failure. Following the pattern established by Cortés's conquest of Mexico, Spain used small, highly mobile detachments of troops, their bodies encased in steel armor. These troops were able to exercise absolute superiority over the Filipino lowlanders. However, in the rugged mountainous regions, they were unable to make use of their strategic advantage. Furthermore, only small numbers of troops were dispatched across the Pacific Ocean from Mexico and so the expeditionary forces that were sent up into the mountains were necessarily small. Their main weapon, the rifle, had a limited range and poor accuracy. It therefore proved an ineffective weapon against Ifugao warriors, who hid in the forest and planned close-range surprise attacks. When the Ifugaos learned that a Spanish expeditionary force was on its way, they would harvest everything they could from their rice terraces and swiddens and hide in the forest, taking their crops with them, destroying what remained and leaving their villages behind. This meant that expeditionary forces who entered the mountains had to carry all their provisions with them from the lowlands and could not remain in the highlands for long (Scott 1974: 1–2).

---

1 In 1966 the region that had been Mountain Province was broken up into separate administrative districts based on the dominant language and ethnic groups in each region. The new provinces were Kalinga and Apayao provinces (named after the respective ethnic groups), Mountain Province (Bontoc), Ifugao Province and Benguet Province (mainly Kankanay and Ibaloi).

Unable to locate the Ifugao warriors they were sent to punish, the Spanish troops would set fire to their villages, destroy the canals that carried water to the rice terraces, and lay waste to the terraces and swiddens. When the Spanish realized the great difficulties involved in occupying and controlling the gold mines of the Cordillera, they quickly lost interest in the region. For the next 200 years, only sporadic, short-term expeditions were carried out. Otherwise, the Spanish left the region largely to its own devices. Spanish interest in the highlands revived only when the cultivation of tobacco as a cash crop in the lowlands (a crop that spread out to the east and to the west of the Cordillera in the provinces of Cagayan and Ilocos) became a thriving industry and large profits began to flow to the colonial government of the Philippines via its monopoly over the tobacco industry.

In 1782 the Spanish colonial government introduced the Tobacco Monopoly and in 1785 the Real Compañía de Filipinas (Royal Company of the Philippines) was created to oversee it. The monopoly continued for nearly 100 years until 1881 and underpinned the colonial government's finances. Before the hugely profitable Tobacco Monopoly brought the colonial government's finances back into the black, the Philippines had been a drain on the Spanish coffers. To make up for the enormous cost incurred by the colonial government in the Philippines, Spain had used its Mexican colony to prop it up with large subsidies each year. In 1784, for the first time in 219 years of colonial rule, the Philippines was able to remit 23,000 pesos back to the metropole thanks to the profits from the Tobacco Monopoly. The necessity to attain mastery over the Cordillera region arose not to secure the gold mines, as had been attempted during the early years of the colony, nor to proselytize Christianity, but to guarantee the profits from this industry. Once again, the Spanish colonial authorities began making plans to penetrate the region (Scott 1974: 211).

Britain had shown a keen interest in Spain's monopoly of the Manila–Acapulco galleon trade (ships that traded between Manila and Acapulco, Mexico, mainly carrying Chinese silks and ceramic goods and Mexican silver). In 1762, in the midst of the Seven Years' War that rocked Europe from 1756 until 1763, Britain (with the financial and military aid of the British East India Company) attacked and occupied Manila. It was this attack that spurred the establishment of the Tobacco Monopoly. Britain held the Philippines for less than three years, but the attack forced the Spanish colonial government to confront the urgent need to shore up its administration of the Philippines, which rested on an insecure economic base and was weak militarily. The Manila galleon trade, which had been the colonial government's major source of income, had already passed its peak and was no longer as profitable as it once had been. The colonial government also faced fierce resistance from the southern Mindanao Muslims and was compelled to raise large sums to finance this internal conflict. Taking the colonial administrations of the Dutch East India Company and the British East India Company as a model, the colonial government finally adopted a policy of developing local resources for profit via agricultural development and expropriation. This approach of securing the profitability of the colony by means of tobacco cultivation was the start of a shift of focus from the transit trade between China and the New World to the plantation system. This shift began with tobacco and later expanded to include other cash crops, such as sugar cane and rice (Ikehata 1977: 43–4; de Jesus 1980: 23–5).

Members of the Augustinian religious order had brought 200 ounces of tobacco seed to the Philippines from its origin in the New World in the sixteenth century and began its cultivation. Cultivation of the crop soon spread and became a major source of revenue for the colonial government as one of the main items traded by the Manila galleons. The habit of tobacco smoking also spread quickly in the colony, not only among the lowlanders but also into the mountains (Nozawa 2004: 66–7). The Ifugaos cultivated tobacco with great gusto and consumed it as a luxury item but they also regarded it as a valuable commodity to be sold to brokers in order to generate a cash income. For the Spanish colonial government, Ifugao was a menace both because the flow of Ifugao tobacco onto the black market threatened an important revenue source in the form of the Tobacco Monopoly and because Ifugao raids on lowland Christian communities in search of heads and plunder posed a threat to public safety. Combined, these issues demanded a rapid response from the colonial government.

In response to repeated attacks on the villages in the plains of the Cagayan Valley to the east of the Ifugao region, the colonial government began to send punitive expeditions against Kiangan in 1750. Pacification efforts by Spanish forces continued every few years, not only against Kiangan but also other parts of Ifugao. One such expedition was mounted about every ten years. Kiangan is located at a strategic point on the southeast route when entering the Ifugao world from the flatlands of the Cagayan Valley. It occupies an equivalent position to that of Mayoyao on the northeast route. Asserting control over Kiangan and establishing a base station there was to be the first step in the campaign against Ifugao. However, despite numerous expeditions, the Spanish were unable to maintain their hold over Kiangan for long. Within one to two years, the Ifugaos of Kiangan would rebuild the houses that had been razed by the Spanish expeditionary forces and resume both tobacco cultivation and attacks on the lowlanders (Scott 1974: 199–200).

A decline in revenue from the tobacco tax between 1788 and 1793 led the director of the Ilocos bureau of the Tobacco Monopoly to begin sending regular patrols into the Cordillera. However, the Ifugaos and other highland peoples continued to grow tobacco, shifting their activities to fields deep in the mountains that were more difficult to discover and thereby rendering the patrols largely ineffective. In 1796 the Spanish organized a larger expeditionary force and planned incursions and pacification operation in the Cordillera on a grander scale. This policy did produce some temporary success. For example, in 1801 the Dominican Fray Juan Molano first visited Kiangan in order to open peace negotiations. He remained there for two days. During the visit, he poured his energy into visiting neighboring villages and prepared a report in which he expressed wonder at the beauty of the rice terraces and their irrigation systems. According to this report, there were 186 households in Kiangan at the time and twenty and forty households each in neighboring villages such as Paet and Dugung (Scott 1974: 199–200, 211–12).

However, in 1805 Spain suffered a devastating naval defeat by the British at the Battle of Trafalgar. A further invasion by the French in 1808 left Spain with little time to manage its distant Philippine colony and the pacification campaign in the Cordillera had to be abandoned. As a result, the tentative control it had managed to establish quickly collapsed and Ifugao raids on the Christian lowlanders and blood feuds between Ifugao villages recommenced. The Spanish colonial government responded by sending a punitive expedition in 1810. In addition to destroying villages, they captured four Ifugao chiefs who were regional leaders. The chiefs were taken to Manila, where they all died. After that, the occasional expeditions that took place mainly targeted the villages of Kiangan and Mayoyao, the entry points to the Ifugao world (Scott 1974: 201).

Expeditions into the depth of the Cordillera recommenced in 1830, when Guillermo Galvey, who was named Commandante General de Igorrotes, led an offensive to intimidate and punish the highlanders. His mission was to re-establish the Tobacco Monopoly but he appears to have been motivated as much, or perhaps even more, by his own sense of adventure and quest for glory. His forces traversed the Cordillera Mountains from the South China Sea in the west to the Magat Valley in Cagayan Province in the east. Two years later, in 1832, Galvey once more led an expedition to Ifugao. Over two days his forces razed Kiangan and eighteen surrounding hamlets to the ground. Whenever such Spanish attacks took place, the Ifugaos would flee into the forests, as described earlier, and carry out surprise attacks and engage the invaders in close-range combat. Twenty lowland Christian foot soldiers assembled in Bagabag took fright at the Ifugao tactics and refused to follow Galvey's orders, running away under fire. Immediately after Galvey's campaigns in 1833 and 1844, the Ifugaos of Kiangan rallied their forces and attacked the lowland Christian villages at the base of the mountains, carrying away a number of heads. Again in 1835, at least sixteen Christians lost their heads in the outskirts of Bagabag (Jenista 1987: 4–5; Scott 1974: 216–19).

Following these events, in 1841 the Spanish colonial government designated Kiangan and the surrounding area as a 'politico-military zone' of Nueva Vizcaya Province and placed it under military jurisdiction. The colonial government now began its campaign to pacify Ifugao in earnest (Dumia 1979: 28). In 1847 an expeditionary force marched to Mayoyao, destroying homes, rice terraces and irrigation infrastructure along the way, and demanded pledges of obedience and a rice tribute from the Ifugaos. During this campaign, forty prisoners were taken to the lowlands as hostages and forced to pledge their obedience. In 1849 leaders from Mayoyao were called to the Malacañang Palace, where they were ordered to pledge their loyalty. Following this campaign, the villagers of Mayoyao demonstrated their obedience to Spain. In 1850, for example, during an expedition against the hamlet of Cambulo, they worked with Spanish troops, taking the initiative by carrying out raids prior to the Spanish attack and carrying away 120 heads.[2] The Spanish sent further expeditions

---

2 While the Spanish did manipulate divisions between Ifugao villages, some Ifugao groups, too, used cooperation with Spain to gain an advantage over their opponents in the recurrent blood feuds that occurred between people from different villages and regions of Ifugao. In 1851, at the request of the people of Mayoyao, a church (Nuestra Senora de los Dolores del Mayoyao) was built. The residents hoped that the friar in the church would help to protect them from atrocities carried out by colonial troops. However, with the intensification of conflict with Muslims in Mindanao, fewer Spanish troops were posted in Ifugao. In 1854 the church was razed to the ground. Once again, Mayoyao was free from Spanish rule.

against Kiangan in 1849, against Cambulo in 1853, and against Hapao and Bunhian in 1854. Again, they destroyed rice terraces and homes. In the ten years between 1861 and 1871, the Spanish carried out eight punitive expeditions against the villages of Ahin and Hapao (Jenista 1987: 6, 10–11; Scott 1974: 236–9).

In order to carry out their campaigns efficiently and effectively, the Spanish first established a fort in Kiangan in the 1850s and, in 1851, dispatched missionaries to remain in the area. However, the fort came under attack from Ifugao warriors two years later and the missionary Victorino Garcia and a number of soldiers were killed. The Spanish were forced to temporarily close the outpost but continued to send troops, although only in small numbers, to control Ifugao and keep the peace. In 1864 a missionary station was once again opened in Kiangan. However, in 1868 the priest who was posted there was beaten and then killed with a spear after a dispute with an Ifugao to whom he had loaned money. In 1871 three soldiers were killed in the vicinity of Kiangan. In another incident, a priest was speared while in the middle of saying mass and the missionary station had to be closed (Scott 1974: 257–60).

In 1889 the Kiangan Politico-Military Command was re-established and in 1892 permanent guard posts were built in villages including Hapao, Banaue, Ayangan and Alimit. However, the total strength of these detachments did not exceed 160 men. When the Philippine Revolution broke out in 1896, these detachments were almost all recalled to assist in the fight against the revolutionaries. The few soldiers who remained in Kiangan were all killed during an attack by Ifugao warriors that occurred during mass (Jenista 1987: 7, 11).

Then, at the height of the Philippine Revolution, the Spanish-American War broke out in 1898 over the question of Cuban independence in the Atlantic. By defeating the Spanish, the Americans gained the Philippines. The United States then had to focus on defeating the revolutionary government in the Philippine-American War (1899–1902), winning over native elites in Manila and establishing a system of colonial rule over the Philippines. As a result, American rule did not reach the Cordillera Mountains region during the first decade of the twentieth century. In the meantime, hostilities intensified between those groups and hamlets that had supported Spanish pacification efforts and those who had opposed them. Due to the temporary power vacuum that had been created by the withdrawal of the Spanish, there were exchanges of fierce fighting, headhunting raids and blood feuds. For example, following the withdrawal of Spanish troops from Banaue, it was attacked by its enemy, Cababuyan. Although the town managed to repel the attack, the two sides lost more than 200 heads between them (Jenista 1987: 13).

Spain's containment policy had included the building and maintenance of mountain roads to connect major villages at the base of the mountains with the hamlets scattered higher up. Despite considerable delays in their construction, these roads facilitated the transportation of soldiers, ammunition and provisions. By the end of Spanish rule, roads passable on horseback had been built from the Cagayan Valley to Mayoyao and from Bontoc to Banaue and Kiangan via Hapao, accelerating the movement of people and goods. The road that extends from Hapao via Wangwang to Bontoc is known to this day as the Spanish trail. Along with pacification campaigns and Spanish rule came the creation of maps of Ifugao and a growing number of reports compiled by missionaries on the lifestyles and customs of its people.

Nevertheless, despite 150 years of Spanish attempts to penetrate and pacify the Ifugao world, they were never completely successful. At the end of the nineteenth century, the influence of Spanish colonial rule reached only to some villages located close to the lowlands on the margins of the Ifugao world. However, even by basing themselves in these villages under Spanish rule, Spanish troops could not remain for long in the hamlets deep in the deep mountains. When looked at as a whole, Spain's attempt to subdue the Cordillera was a failure. It also left bitter legacies in the strong hatred and antagonism felt by the Ifugaos towards the lowlanders who were forced to join in Spanish expeditionary forces against them. This animosity remained in the Ifugao world to be passed down through the generations (Jenista 1987: 12).

America's successful policy of conciliation

The people of Ifugao felt a tenacious hatred, hostility and suspicion towards the Spanish colonial government and lowland Filipinos. By comparison, after the tensions of the first few years, when the Ifugaos met America's forays into the region with hostility, the Ifugaos regarded America's government of the Cordilleras in the early twentieth century quite favorably overall. The difference between the way the Ifugaos perceived lowland Filipinos and the Americans is expressed eloquently in the tales of General

Emilio Aguinaldo's (president of the revolutionary government) troops, who infiltrated Ifugao at the end of the Philippine-American War, and the American forces who pursued them, acquiring food from them.

General Aguinaldo, one of the leaders of the Philippine Revolution, signed a truce with Spain (the Pact of Biak-na-Bato) in December 1897. Under the terms of the truce, Aguinaldo and the revolutionary leadership agreed to lay down their arms and go into exile temporarily in Hong Kong in exchange for an indemnity of 1.7 million pesos. In May the following year, having secured American support, Aguinaldo returned to the Philippines on an American warship and continued his war of independence against Spain. On May 24, he announced the formation of an autocratic government. Then, on June 12, he made a declaration of independence and assumed the presidency. Together with revolutionary forces around the country, he launched a major offensive against Spain. By the end of 1898 the revolutionaries had effectively liberated the area from Luzon to the Visayas. On January 23, 1899, Aguinaldo promulgated a new constitution in the town of Malolos in the Province of Bulacan and established the First Philippine Republic.

Just before the declaration of the republic in December 1898, however, the Americans, on whom the Filipino revolutionaries had depended for support, concluded a peace treaty with Spain in Paris. In exchange for an indemnity of US$20 million, America gained the former Spanish colonies of the Philippines, Guam and Puerto Rico. President McKinley then announced America's intention to govern the Philippines by proclaiming the policy of Benevolent Assimilation. America had declared war against Spain in support of Cuban independence little more than half a year before the conclusion of the Treaty of Paris in April 1898. In May, America's Asiatic Squadron had entered Manila Bay and destroyed the Spanish fleet. Then, while waiting for army reinforcements to arrive, it captured Manila in a bloodless surrender and quickly established military control over the entire Philippines. Peace negotiations with Spain opened in Paris in September. They concluded in December with the signing of a peace treaty and the cession of the Philippines to the United States.

The new government of the Philippine Republic under General Aguinaldo was established amidst tensions with the United States. As I mentioned briefly in the opening section of this chapter, the Philippine-American War broke out just two weeks later, on December 4, 1899, following American provocations at the San Juan River Bridge where a soldier fired gunshots.

The American forces, boasting the latest weapons and equipment, had captured the revolutionary government's capital in Malolos, Bulacan Province, by the end of March and quickly established control over the entire archipelago. For two years after the fall of Malolos, General Aguinaldo continued to wage a guerilla war against the Americans while appealing to other leaders throughout the country for support. He was eventually captured in Palanan in the Sierra Madre Mountains at the end of March 1901 (Ikehata 1977: 73–84).[3]

Aguinaldo and 200 riflemen under his command entered the Cordillera Mountains from Ilocos Province on the west coast while fleeing from Malolos. They arrived in Banaue on December 7, 1899, while making their way to Ifugao Province via Bontoc. They remained in the village for almost two weeks before continuing eastward, making their way down the mountains towards the Cagayan Valley. As they had almost no food, while they were in the highlands the villagers sold them sweet potatoes, which were relatively abundant, at low cost. Aguinaldo's company also asked for rice and chicken, but the villagers generally refused because they did not have enough in reserve for themselves. There were exceptions, however, and some people did sell rice and chicken to the soldiers, but they were disappointed with the low prices they received and became even more reluctant to sell. Somewhat reluctantly, Aguinaldo's men then forcibly confiscated rice and chickens from the villagers, for which they faced a major backlash and were dubbed 'chicken thieves'. Sensing the villagers' frustration and hostility, Aguinaldo observed, 'America is not our only enemy. The locals are also against us and Banaue is a dangerous place for us.' Indeed, just after they left Banaue, the detachment guarding the rear of Aguinaldo's company was ambushed. A number lost their heads and rifles were also taken (Jenista 1987: 14).

In stark contrast, when 300 members of the American 33rd Infantry Regiment arrived in Banaue on December 25, 1899, in pursuit of General Aguinaldo, they wore uniforms, were well disciplined and carried their own provisions. When they procured rice and chicken from the villagers they paid for them handsomely, to the great surprise of the villagers. The

---

3 On the history of popular resistance, often dismissed as banditry, that broke out again and again in different parts of the Philippines following appeals by General Aguinaldo or in the name of Philippine independence and liberation, see Ileto (1979: 261–330).

regiment remained in Banaue for only two days, but they left a strong impression on the locals. 'The Kastilas took *palay* [rice] and chickens, Miliyu took *palay* and chickens, the *infantilia* paid for *palay* and chickens– good prices!' (Jenista 1987: 15).[4]

At the beginning of American colonization, Ifugao was part of Nueva Vizcaya Province. In 1905, however, Jeff Gallman, an American army officer, was installed as governor and Ifugao became independent. Apart from the first few years, when Gallman was active in pacifying the region by force, the American administration of the Cordillera generally proceeded smoothly. Especially in Ifugao, the American governors were able to build trust and maintain relatively friendly relations with both ordinary Ifugaos and their leaders. The Ifugaos show their love and respect for the American governors by referring to them with the honorific title 'Apo' in their reminiscences. The term 'Apo' generally means 'ancestor', but it is also used as an honorary title for grandfathers, elders, ancestral spirits and the Christian God (Apo Dios). The use of this honorific form of address shows that although the American governors were rulers who exercised military and political power, they were also able to play the role of patron, respecting and protecting the people and culture of Ifugao.

In provinces of the Cordillera outside of Ifugao, American governors were appointed for the first ten or so years of the American colony. After that, they were quickly replaced by Filipino governors. By contrast, the four American governors who governed Ifugao each served for more than five years. Between them, they maintained a close relationship with the Ifugao people for nearly thirty years.[5] Jenista (1987) conducted detailed research on the history of relations between the Ifugao and the local face of

---

4 It goes without saying that the Ifugaos did not immediately abandon their usual tactics of hiding temporarily when the American military first came into the area and then launching counter-attacks. While the Americans left a favorable impression on the residents of Banaue, when a company of American troops left Banaue in pursuit of General Aguinaldo, their cook, who was feeling unwell and lagging behind the others, was ambushed and lost his head to a band of Ifugao warriors (Jenista 1987: 16).

5 In other parts of the northern Cordillera and among other tribes, governors served short terms and the position was not monopolized by Americans. In Bontoc, until the end of the Leonard Wood administration in 1927, there were ten governors, of whom five were American. In Apayao, there were three American governors out of a total of nine, while in Kalinga there were three American governors out of a total of six (Jenista 1987: 198, 261).

the American colonial government based on oral histories collected from more than 100 people, as well as from documentary sources. He captured the characteristic relationship between the two sides by giving his book the title *The White Apos* (Jenista 1987). According to this account, the cultural values each side held dear were much more similar than either of them realized. This satisfied both sides of the relationship and allowed them to co-exist. Both Americans and Ifugaos valued individual displays of courage and fighting spirit highly. Furthermore, the American justice system, with its notion of 'playing fair and square', was easy to understand and therefore accepted by the Ifugaos. After the initial battles, both sides were able to draw satisfaction from the fact that 'we had a good fight' (Jenista 1987: viii–ix).[6]

---

6 However, the conflict between Ifugao warriors and American punitive expeditions was not a direct fight. As they had done when Spanish expeditionary forces entered their territory, the Ifugaos avoided direct confrontation and hid in the forests. When they saw an opening, they would attack. The following example is typical. Even after Banaue and the surrounding villages had been pacified and submitted to American rule, the farther village of Cambulo, deep in the mountains, defied the pacification campaign and even carried out headhunting raids in revenge against villages that cooperated in American attacks. In 1907 three young men from Cambulo entered the Bangaan district, where they attacked a man by the name of Ngatan and cut off his head before returning home in triumph. Ngatan's relatives reported the murder to the American governor, Apo Gallman, and asked him to punish the offenders. When Gallman and his subordinates set out for Cambulo to carry out their mission, the villagers as usual went into hiding in the forest.

Only a young man named Hangcha remained at home. He had been intensely jealous of the attention the three successful headhunters had received from the Cambulo girls and wanted to demonstrate his valor. When Gallman's column arrived at a point on the other side of a deep gorge that commanded a view of Hangcha's home, Hangcha stood on the stone paving outside his house, let out a war cry and began performing a war dance. With all the Ifugaos looking on from their hiding places, Gallman aimed his rifle across the valley and shot Hangcha in the forehead. Hangcha instantly fell to the ground dead. Gallman then addressed the villagers hiding in the forest. He announced in a loud voice that he would leave the matter at that, without destroying their village, but demanded that Ngatan's head be returned to him. The next day, the head was returned.

The Cambulo placed the blame for the incident not on Gallman, but on Ngatan's relatives whom they mocked as women for asking Gallman to resolve the blood feud (Jenista 1987: 65–7).

Indeed, to take a broad view of relations between American colonial governments, their local administrators and military personnel, and the colonized peoples of Southeast Asia, the Americans enjoyed much friendlier relations with minority hill-dwellers in almost every nation in which they operated than they did with the ethnic majority lowlanders, with whom their relationships were always tense. If we consider the case of the Chin, Kachin, Naga and Wa peoples of the Burmese high country under British rule, their overall society, culture and economy, and their lifestyle and relations with the outside world, and if we swap America for Britain and the Ifugao for the Chin and Kachin, there would be very little need to change anything else in most accounts. The Burmese highlanders and the Ifugaos both conducted headhunting raids in small groups against their neighbors and against lowlanders. Their dogged resistance to pacification campaigns by colonial administrations, their customary practices of judging truth or falsehood by holding the hand in hot water, their beliefs in various spirits, their ceremonies for appeasing the spirits (performed for the ancestors and tutelary deities in order to ask for favor or ward off evil), their customs of displaying skulls of sacrificial animals on the walls of their homes, and freedom of sexual relations prior to marriage in the young women's huts and young men's huts were all common to the two peoples. Moreover, both American and British administrators and military personnel saw these highland minorities as 'noble savages' who had not been polluted by civilization. Apart from headhunting, they respected their traditional customs and culture and strove to be their guardians and protectors (Jenista 1987: 243–6).

The same can be said of the highland minorities of Laos or Vietnam under the French or of the relationship between Charles Brooke, the White Rajah of North Borneo, and the Iban. From the latter half of the nineteenth century until the early twentieth, in the colonies of Southeast Asia there was general antagonism between lowlanders and highlanders and they regarded one another with contempt. In the context of this antagonistic relationship, rulers and colonizers felt more affinity for the highlanders and appointed themselves their sympathizers, protectors and wardens. The lowland peoples had a high culture derived from their historical experiences of the rise and fall of empires and their history of trade and intercourse with outsiders and they followed great world religions such as Islam and Buddhism. As a result, in their speech and conduct and in their communication style, they could compete on an even playing field or even surpass the cultural level of the colonizers. For their European and American rulers, this meant they could never let down their guard. By comparison, the highland and mountain minorities, with their modest ways of life, their simple forms of social organization, and their straightforward speech and action were relatively easy for the European and American colonists to understand and to communicate with (Jenista 1987: 246–9).

When compared with other Western powers, the characteristic feature of American colonial rule was its initial trumpeting of Benevolent Assimilation as a just cause. The Americans took the position that while the Philippines was not yet able to stand on its own as a nation-state, independence was not far off and America must help instruct and lead its colony towards it. America's desire to protect and to provide proper guidance to the ethnic minorities of the northern mountains was particularly strong. It was Dean Worcester, first Secretary of the Interior from 1901 until 1913, who set America's basic attitude and policy towards the highland minorities. He was filled with the spirit of the age that was encapsulated in the British poet Rudyard Kipling's 1899 poem, 'The White Man's Burden'. Like Kipling, he was a paternalist who believed that colonial rule and intervention was essentially benevolent and necessary (Jenista 1987: 240–1).

Kipling's poem, which opens with the call to 'Take up the White Man's burden/Send forth the best ye breed', goes on to explain that the purpose of colonialism is to serve 'your new-caught, sullen peoples/Half devil and half child'. For the United States, the 'half devil and half child' for whom the white man ought to assume responsibility was not the elite Christian lowlander whom the Spanish had already converted. It was the highlanders of the northern mountains – who resisted the lowlanders and the Spanish colonial government, kept their ancient customs, and carried out headhunting feuds with other villages and repeated attacks on the lowland villages – whom the American colonizer must educate and civilize. However, despite the paternalistic nature of the ideas of the white man's burden, in the first few years of his administration, Worcester was resolute in his pursuit of pacification, using force against those villages that refused to submit. However, once a village had shown its allegiance to the colonial government and ceased raiding, he worked to build roads into the villages, construct schools, send in teachers and develop the education system. The period from 1910, when pacification had been accomplished and a stable order was established, until the beginning of the war between Japan and the United States is referred to in Ifugao as 'peacetime' (Jenista 1987: 89, 135–55).[7]

It was the governors described above, and known as the White Apos, who stood at the head of Ifugao government. They were the ones who came into contact with the local people and interacted with them on the colonial frontline. All four were military men and even after they became governor each retained his rank as a commanding officer in the Philippine Constabulary. All four displayed an exceptional attachment to Ifugao. They behaved as generous protectors because of their internalized sense of the white man's burden and their own personal relationships with the Ifugaos. By remaining in their posts for five or more years, they were able to learn the Ifugao language and share conversation and jokes with the villagers. Furthermore, they did not actively try to propagate the Christian faith. Instead, they hosted traditional Ifugao feasts known as *Cannyao* and drank the Ifugaos' homemade rice wine when invited to do so until they were completely drunk. This was in marked contrast to the Spanish expeditionary forces, who, even after they had pacified a village, would almost never sit down at the same table with Ifugaos and eat the same food (Jenista 1987: 197–203).

The White Apos not only drank with the Ifugao men and ate from the same bowl, they maintained friendly relations with Ifugao women and frequently took them as local wives. It was not only the top provincial governors such as Gallman and Dosser who took Ifugao women as local wives – the officers and men of the Constabulary often did so too.[8] Most of the American soldiers who

---

7 The Ilongot who live in the mountains of Nueva Vizcaya, which borders Ifugao Province, and the Aeta who live in the mountains of Pinatubo in western Luzon also refer to the period of nearly half a century from the end of 'the period of Spanish rule' until the 'period of war' when the Japanese invaded not as 'the American period' but as *pistaimu* (peacetime).

8 The second governor, Gallman, had two Ifugao wives. The first was a woman from Banaue. About a year after she gave birth to his son, she returned to another Ifugao lover and Gallman took another local wife. The fourth governor, Dosser, when he first came to Ifugao as a commander in the Constabulary and long before he became governor, formed relationships with 'so many women [one contemporary] couldn't count the number'. Eventually, in 1911, he took a wife under Ifugao customary law from near the village of Banaue. They separated a little over a year later due to his wife's infidelity and Dosser later married other women at his future postings at Mayoyao and Banaue. His relationship with the first ended naturally when he was transferred, while the second ended when his wife died suddenly of influenza (Jenista 1987: 208–15).

were sent to the Philippines were single young men. They were forced to sign a pledge that they would not marry unless they were either promoted to the rank of captain or granted special permission by the head of the Constabulary. However, when posted deep in the interior far from towns such as Manila and Baguio that were filled with Americans, neither prying eyes nor rumor could touch them and they enjoyed a degree of freedom. In this context it was not uncommon for a soldier to rent a house near the garrison and house his wife or mistress there. He could then visit from time to time while still living in the barracks. This practice was not limited to soldiers. Some men who were sent to Ifugao as teachers, such as Barton (who penned numerous essays and ethnographies) and Beyer, stayed in the region for a long time and married Ifugao women. Of these, only Beyer had a church wedding and formalized the marriage under American law.

Based on the records alone, at least fourteen American men maintained close personal relationships with a combined total of twenty-three Ifugao women. Out of these relationships, eight babies were born, of whom four died in infancy and four lived to adulthood. It is not clear why the number of births was so low. The mixed-blood children who were the product of these relationships received tertiary educations and attained high positions in Philippine society. One of them, Gallman's son, was adopted by an Ifugao leader. At the Constitutional Convention of 1935 he represented Ifugao and later became a professor of history at Saint Louis University in Baguio. Another, Alfredo Cappleman, received no support from his biological father, but became a politician and was elected provincial governor immediately after the war (Jenista 1987: 219–25).

From the provincial governors known as Apos to the regular soldiers, American relationships with Ifugao women (other than Beyer's) were based on Ifugao customary law alone. Therefore, few continued for long, either because one of the parties had a change of heart or because the man received a transfer. Nevertheless, despite the cultural differences between the American men and Ifugao women, Jenista found that both parties tended to see their relationships positively even after separating. For the Ifugao women, the Americans were wealthy and could provide financial support. They valued sexual relations and affection highly, while the burden of house work, such as preparing food and weaving clothes, was light. The experience of marriage to an American man gave them a social position just below that of an American, which was an advantage later when they remarried. In Ifugao culture, women were permitted freedom of sexual relations in the young women's huts prior to marriage. Divorce and remarriage were also relatively easy to achieve. For these reasons, marriage to and separation from American males had no particular downside for Ifugao women (Jenista 1987: 221–2).

In this section I have summarized the background and day-to-day reality of the American government of Ifugao that began in the early 1900s, based primarily on Jenista's account. As Jenista concludes, the White Apos' protective attitude towards the Ifugaos resulted from their curiosity about and sympathy and compassion for the Ifugao culture and people and the friendships between individual Americans and Ifugaos, especially intimate relations with Ifugao women. This gave the Ifugaos a positive impression of the Americans and engendered a friendly attitude towards them (Jenista 1987: 228). I have also noted in my own research the very positive regard in which the Ifugaos hold America and the Americans.

General Yamashita and the Asia-Pacific War

The Japanese military lost many men in the Philippines. In some ways the Battle of the Philippines typifies the fortunes of Japan's armed forces during the Asia-Pacific War. Following an initial victory, the conflict progressed through a number of stages, resulting in defeat with massive casualties. This is a perfect microcosm of the Asia-Pacific War as a whole. In the final two months of the battle, the Japanese armed forces holed up in Ifugao, where their presence had long-lasting after effects.

Ifugao has a deep connection with Japan. As I explained in Chapter 2, Lopez Nauyac, along with other Ifugao elders, have frequently told me about their experiences while hiding deep within the mountains after fleeing from Japanese troops (see also 'War memories' later in this chapter). Young people are also familiar with the Ifugao experience during the war, having heard about it from their parents and grandparents. When I first went to Ifugao and began listening to the villagers' stories, I realized that they had misunderstood my intentions. They thought that I had come looking for the legendary Yamashita treasure (gold, silver, precious metals and other treasures that were believed to have been brought to the mountains of Ifugao and buried there by General Yamashita) and this rumor also spread to neighboring villages.

Among all the battlegrounds of the Asia-Pacific War, from China to Southeast Asian and the Pacific Islands, the Philippines is unique for the huge number of Japanese who died there. Approximately 630,000 soldiers and sailors of the Imperial Japanese Army and Navy participated in the campaign in the Philippines. According to surveys carried out by the former Ministry of Health and Welfare in 1964, 498,600 of them died (including 12,000 who died after the war had ended due to starvation and disease). This gives a casualty rate of nearly 80 percent and exceeds the number who died along the entire Chinese front, including Hong Kong.[9] It was the largest number of casualties from any single battleground, accounting for approximately a quarter of all Japanese servicemen who died in battle during the Asia-Pacific War. Of those who died in the Philippines, the majority, or 293,549 casualties, or 50 percent of the Japanese armed forces' total war dead in the Philippines, died in Luzon and the surrounding ocean. By comparison, according to Philippine government sources, of the then total Philippine population of 16 million, the war produced 1.1 million victims, including civilians (Nakano 2005).

The reason for these huge losses, as I explained in the introduction to this chapter, was Japan's total defeat in the Battle of Leyte Gulf (October 1944), the most strategic battle in the defense of the Philippines. The defeat meant Japan lost control of both the sea and the air. The army also rushed into a decisive land battle with America's Army of the Philippines without adequate preparation. They had no means to replenish their supplies of food or ammunition, leaving them little choice but to wage a war of attrition in order to buy time for the preparation of defenses on the Japanese mainland. The land war in the Philippines began as it ended in a defensive war for which Japan's military was almost completely untrained. The number who died from starvation and disease far outweighed those who died on the battlefield (Murao 1992: 12–14).

The tragedy of the battle is encapsulated in the person of General Yamashita Tomoyuki. General Yamashita's victories in the invasion of Malaya and Singapore at the start of the war had earned him the sobriquet 'Tiger of Malaya'. Just before the Battle of Leyte Gulf, he took up a new post in Manila as commander of the Philippines Area Army (Fourteenth Army Division), charged with defending the Philippines. He suffered a crushing defeat in the land war on Leyte Island that lasted for a little over two months. After that, he fought an extended war of resistance in northern

---

9 In 1948 figures, the number given is 476,776 (Murao 1992: 248).

Luzon that was characterized by continuous retreats (Murao 1992: 14). The main Japanese army force under Yamashita's command built a final holdout in Ifugao. There they dug themselves in and waited for the final showdown. The Municipality of Hungduan, where I carried out my fieldwork, was at the center of this struggle. In this section and the next I review the final year of the war in Ifugao with a focus on General Yamashita.

Yamashita is famous for having forced Lieutenant-General Percival, the British Army's General Officer Commanding Malaya, to surrender unconditionally in Singapore on February 15, 1942. On September 26, 1944, he assumed command of the Philippines Area Army and arrived in Manila on October 6. Yamashita was dispatched to fight a decisive battle with the United States armed forces in the Philippines that was to decide Japan's fate.

Ten days after Yamashita's arrival in the Philippines, America began its amphibious invasion of Leyte Island. Early in the morning of October 17, the American fleet massed in Leyte Gulf. The following day, they commenced ground operations and, on the afternoon of October 20, took the city of Tacloban with little resistance. General Douglas MacArthur landed with the Third Army, wading up to his knees through the surf, famously fulfilling a promise he had made two years earlier when he was forced to retreat from the Philippines: 'I shall return.' On the Japanese side, on October 19 the Army General Staff Office in the Imperial General Headquarters resolved to proceed with Operation Shō (Victory) One (a combined army–navy operation against the Allied forces in the Philippines). As part of this plan, the army made its fateful change of plan to engage the enemy in a decisive land battle on Leyte. Previously, the Japanese army's strategy had been the logical plan to only engage the American forces in Luzon and to make their final stand there. However, following the Formosa Air Battle, which took place before the Battle of Leyte, incorrect reports reached the Imperial General Headquarters from the front. Reports of 'a great victory that completely destroyed the American fleet including ten aircraft carriers' led the Imperial General Headquarters to make a wrong move without understanding the real situation on the ground.

The Japanese navy lost four aircraft carriers, three battleships, six heavy cruisers, four light cruisers, one submarine, 500 aircraft and 10,000 men in the Battle of Leyte Gulf, with the remainder of the fleet also suffering heavy damage. The combined fleet was left devastated, having lost almost all its military might. The Japanese forces completely lost control over the sea and the air. It was during this naval battle that the Kamikaze Special Attack Force launched its first attack on October 25 under orders from Vice-Admiral Ōnishi Takijirō, commander of the First Air Fleet. Even so, the Battle of Leyte Gulf was initially reported as a 'great victory'. Following this second inaccurate report, the Imperial General Headquarters decided to pursue a land battle on Leyte and deployed all available troops and materials.

In the records compiled by the former War History Office (now the National Institute for Defense Studies in the Ministry of Defense), the steps leading up to this decision are recorded simply as follows.

> General Yamashita took up his post just ten days before the enemy invaded Leyte Gulf. He assumed his command after having confirmed with the Imperial General Headquarters that the 'land war would be restricted to Luzon'.
> At the end of October, the Imperial Japanese Navy's Naval Air Group launched an all-out assault, seeking a decisive battle in the Philippines Sea. The Army Section of the Imperial General Headquarters decided, based on the aforementioned false reports, that Japan's decisive victory in the Formosa Air Battle meant a pitched land battle on Leyte would be possible. They were already in the process of changing their existing strategy and ordering a land battle on Leyte when they heard that a great victory had been achieved at the Battle of the Philippine Sea. They then ordered that preparations be made for a land war on the island. From the end of October, the progress of the Battle of Leyte began to go against the hopes of the Imperial General Headquarters, but they continued to insist that the decisive battle be fought there. (War History Office 1970: Introduction)

Despite opposition from the staff officers of the Fourteenth Area Army, Marshal Terauchi, Commander of the Southern Expeditionary Army Group, 'scolded' Yamashita and ordered him to follow orders from the Imperial General Headquarters. Within two months, the outcome of the Battle of Leyte Gulf was decided. As victory in a conventional battle was now impossible, on December 25 Yamashita ordered his remaining troops on Leyte to 'keep fighting independently, maintain a protracted resistance'. The order to continue the struggle without any assistance from outside meant, in effect, the abandonment of Leyte. On the same day MacArthur, who had been promoted to General of the Army five days earlier, claimed victory and an end to hostilities on Leyte.

The Japanese retreat to Ifugao

After the decisive defeat in the Battle of Leyte Gulf, the Japanese fought a protracted war of attrition from three strategic positions in the mountain areas – east of Manila, west of Clark Air Base and in northern Luzon (around Baguio and in the Salacsac-Balete region). The main Japanese force began withdrawing to these three positions from Manila in the middle of February. From late February to March 1945, approximately 20,000 Japanese soldiers, most of whom were members of the Manila Naval Defense Force, fought a ferocious urban engagement with the American invaders that continued for nearly one month and killed thousands of civilians.

Yamashita and the main force of the Japanese troops who had retreated from Manila took up a position in Baguio on January 12, 1945. American forces continued to launch strikes on Baguio, which fell on April 24 after three months of fighting. Yamashita then decided to fight a war of attrition against the Americans in order to defend the grain-producing region of the Cagayan Valley and retreated from Baguio to Cagayan (Takagi 1985; Ogawa 1978: 157–65, 176–84). The Sierra Madre Mountains tower over the Cagayan Valley to the east, while the Cordillera Mountains lie to the west. The two ranges join together in the province of Nueva Vizcaya to the south, creating a U-shaped strategic position in the region. However, the American strategy was to attack the Balete Pass directly from Manila in the south. The pass occupies a strategic position on the highway that links Manila with the Cagayan Valley from south to north. With air support, the Americans widened the existing track up the steep slope towards the pass to create a road suitable for motor vehicles. Confronting the American operation, with its dependence on masses of bulldozers and tanks, the Japanese hid themselves in caves and foxholes. Despite a lack of equipment, ammunition and food, they continued to launch assaults at close range. By the end of May, after four months of bitter fighting, the region between the Salacsac and Balete passes was under American control (Ogawa 1978: 197–236).

On May 15, when the fall of Balete Pass seemed inevitable, Yamashita moved via Bambang to Kiangan, the entrance to the Ifugao mountains. Kiangan is located in a basin surrounded on all sides by deep mountains. Even here, though, Yamashita's forces could find no refuge and were subjected to aerial bombardment by the Americans. On June 17 he shifted to the hamlet of Bakdan and then a week later, on June 23, to the even more remote hamlet of Habangan along the Asin River. This was where Yamashita built his last stand, which was intended to serve as the base of operations for a protracted resistance and bring to an end his many retreats. At around this time, the United States Army's 37th Infantry Division, which was moving northward to attack Balete Pass from the south, made contact with the 11th Airborne Division, which had made a parachute drop near Aparri to the north and was making its way south. The Americans had now established absolute supremacy over the main connection between Aparri and San Jose and the major road linking Baguio with Bontoc.

The Japanese forces that had retreated to the depths of the mountains of Ifugao Province were encircled by four United States Army divisions. On the following day, June 28, General MacArthur declared an end to major combat operations on Luzon:

> our northern and southern columns have joined forces, securing the entire length of the Cagayan Valley, heart of northern Luzon...Battered enemy remnants have been driven into the rugged mountain ranges to the east and west cut off from all sources of supply. Except for isolated operations this closes the major phases of the Northern Luzon Campaign, one of the most savage and bitterly fought in American history.

As far as General MacArthur was concerned, all that remained was a mopping-up operation. However, at that time the Japanese army still had a force of 5,000 men who had built defensive encampments from the upper reaches of the Asin River in Ifugao Province to Mount Pulag. They occupied an area spanning fifty kilometers from east to west and eighty kilometers from south to north, where they planned to conduct a protracted resistance. The purpose of the operation was to delay the 100,000 American soldiers who had surrounded them for as long as possible and thereby delay the invasion of the Japanese mainland (Murao 1992: 209–12).

However, while they intended to conduct a war of attrition, it was all that the various Japanese divisions engaged in the campaign could do to survive in the face of food shortages and the spread of disease. The memoirs of Mutō Akira (1952, 1981: 311–410), chief of staff of the Fourteenth Area Army, and Kurihara Yoshihisa (1950), a staff officer, give detailed accounts of the retreat of General Yamashita and his staff and their days in the jungle, as well as their strategic plans and the battles that took place.

Top left: A small Japanese NGO (CACEPPI) in partnership with the Philippine NGO Philippine Rural Reconstruction Movement (PRRM) built a mini hydroelectric generator in Abatan, near Wangwang. The father of the NGO's founder and chief secretary Aikawa Tamizo was sent to the Philippines as a Japanese language teacher and fled Manila along with the withdrawing Japanese army before dying in Abatan. When Aikawa visited the area to pray for his father, the villagers appealed to him, saying they needed electricity to improve their living standards. He founded the NGO in 1998. A PRRM British volunteer, who is married to an Ifugao woman, installs the mini-hydro generator. This second-hand generator frequently broke down and after about one year it became difficult to keep it going. (March 2, 2000)

Top right: Balete Pass (also called Dalton Pass), site of a fierce battle between American and Japanese forces from March to June 1945. The arch over the road downhill from the monument on the left indicates the border between the provinces of Nueva Vizcaya on the left (northern side) and Nueva Ecija on the right (southern side). (June 4, 2008)

Bottom right: Orlando indicating Nabigihan in Wangwang, Hungduan, where General Yamashita hid out. (March 16, 2006)

Of the Japanese residents in the Philippines who were traveling with the Japanese army, more than half died during the course of the evacuation, such as at the massacre at Lamut River (where stranded evacuees who were unable to cross due to flooding were killed indiscriminately by American bombs and aircraft-mounted machinegun fire). Nevertheless, nearly a thousand managed to escape from Kiangan with the soldiers up into the mountains. These civilians were not necessarily traveling with the Japanese troops by choice but were forced to do so, having been ordered to evacuate from Manila and Baguio by the military authorities. In spite of this, they did not receive food or other assistance from the army and therefore had an even worse experience of the evacuation (Murao 1992: 128–74).

War memories

For the Japanese soldiers, Ifugao was a living hell where they suffered from starvation and rampant malaria and dysentery. Military histories and personal memoirs contain detailed accounts of what transpired in the mountains of northern Luzon. For example, in 'The end of the *Shobu* (warrior's spirit) Group' of Ogawa Tetsurō's *Hokubu Luzon jikyū sen* (Protracted war in northern Luzon, 1978: Chapter 10, 165–6), he writes:

> In the camp, the biggest problem we Japanese faced was not enemy attack but lack of food and diseases such as malaria and amoebic dysentery. With 50,000 Japanese entering the region without even the hope of supplies being able to reach them from the outside, the result was a foregone conclusion. We left the natives' rice storehouses alone in the beginning in an attempt to maintain good relations with them but they were eventually emptied to feed the starving Japanese. We stripped the slopes of their [sweet potato] in no time. In addition, the virulent malaria that ran rampant in the environs of the Asin River and dysentery took the lives of the Japanese with terrifying speed. Lack of salt also contributed to the deaths.
>
> ...when we heard the occasional sound of a rifle or pistol shot or the explosion of a hand grenade from this or that valley or forest, we knew it meant that one of our fellow countrymen had killed himself in despair at starvation and disease but few of us felt any reaction. Basic standards of morality had broken down so far that it was nothing for one person to steal from another in order to live and we Japanese would mug and shoot one another in order

to secure food. In the worst cases, some people even ate the flesh of the dead. The valley truly was a living hell.

When Hungduan was targeted by enemy mortars and napalm attacks, the road from Hungduan to Tukkang became the road to hell. On the slopes of the valley, in its forests and copses, the Japanese who huddled in the natives' huts or among the rocks were like hungry ghosts, lacking both food and medicine. During the day they cowered in terror at the sound of enemy shells and at night they lay awake, plagued by an ever-growing number of lice. They passed their days in despair.[10]

The Ifugaos, too, were emaciated by food shortages, starvation, malaria and dysentery and many lost their lives. At first, when the huge number of Japanese soldiers invaded their lands, the occasional soldier might trade salt and matches for rice and yams, but in most cases they stole food from the

---

10 In two sections titled 'The Valley of Hell' and 'The limits of starvation', Shishikura (1980: 290) also describes the situation in Hungduan and Tukkang just prior to the Japanese defeat:

> You had to close your eyes when you saw the terrible sight in the jungle slopes on either side and below the narrow Tukkang road. In the drizzling rain the corpses of those who had fallen by the wayside lay in heaps on the ground. Every one of them was crawling with innumerable huge flies, as big as wasps. They were the corpses of people who had collapsed from want of strength while wandering around in search of food.
>
> Some lay with their chests blown open in what appeared to be suicide by hand grenade. Others had already been reduced to piles of bones while still wrapped in their ragged clothes. Some had died with their eyes wide open, staring at the sky. Some had shot themselves, using their feet to pull the trigger. Some were baring their teeth between swollen purple lips while others clasped family photographs, their hands like their bodies already succumbing to rigor mortis beneath their sodden blankets. Among the bodies were four or five where the flesh from their thighs had been carved off.
>
> Those who were close to death lacked the strength even to chase away the flies that gathered about them. They simply batted at the air while fire ants that had already caught the scent of death climbed in and out of their ears and nostrils.

See also the detailed accounts in 'Ashin kakoku, kikoku shūshū' (Asin valley, Devil frown, Chapter 12) and 'Saigo no Saku' (The last means, Chapter 13) in Ichiki Chiaki's (1999: 187–213) *Ashin: kaisō no hitō sen* (Asin valley, the Philippine war in memories) and Okada Umeko's (1980: 35–99) 'Ashin no midori yo, arigatō' (The green in Asin valley, Thank you).

empty homes and plots of the villagers who had hidden in the mountains. Towards the end, plots that had been harvested once were harvested again and even the smallest sweet potato was found and eaten. The people of Ifugao, who lost even their seed rice and the last roots of their sweet potatoes, ran out of food while they hid in the mountains. Weakened by dysentery and fever, many of them died.

Each year, the Hungduan government issues the Hungduan Municipal Profile. At the beginning of the publication is a simple statement detailing the municipality's history and current circumstances. The part dedicated to history is always the same. If one opens the publication from any given year, it is divided into the period of Spanish rule, the period of American rule and the creation of the municipality after the war. The section on the Japanese occupation reads:

> Hungduan was the center of warfare during the last stages of world war II. The mighty Japanese Imperial Army led by Tomoyuki Yamashita entrenched themselves at the vicinity of Mount Napulawan. To flush them out, the combined American and Filipino forces used bombs leading to the immense destruction of the rice terraces, Irrigation canals and massive evacuation of the people.
>
> The population of more than 14,000 inhabitants was reduced to around 3,540 after the war, many of whom died of hunger and diseases. (Municipality of Hungduan n.d.)

This dramatic population decline was not necessarily due to mortality alone but is also thought to include people who evacuated the municipality. The stories that village elders told me about the nearly three months of Japanese occupation of Hungduan Municipality are all very similar. When the Japanese came, the rice in the terraces was almost ready to harvest. While they were able to harvest some, the majority remained unharvested when the villagers fled into the mountains. There they suffered from hunger, cold and diarrhea, grew ill and lost family members, friends and acquaintances. The houses in the village were occupied by Japanese soldiers who burned the planks from the walls of their huts for cooking. As a result, they witnessed the strange sight of their huts with only roofs and structural beams remaining. They looked like a crop of mushrooms from the hiding places far away. None of the villagers witnessed Japanese

Top: Orlando and a municipal official standing below the summit of Mount Napulawan. The upper reaches of the mountain below the summit are covered in mossy forest. The trees growing densely near the summit are stunted. (March 7, 2003)

Bottom: A cutting that leads from the hill country of Ifugao into the mountains. In the distance is the bridge over the Ifugao River. Crossing the bridge takes you to Banaue via Lagawe. Turning left before the bridge takes you to Kiangan. (March 7, 2004)

soldiers eating the dead, as in the account above, but a number reported having seen corpses where the rump had been sliced off (for example, conversation with Bandao Atolba, March 12, 1999).

Angelina Gano, who was born in Hapao at the end of the war in October 1943 and spent her childhood there and worked in the village as a teacher, spoke about the war experiences that her parents had often shared with her. When Lopez Nauyac started his residents' association to reforest the mountain slopes (see Chapter 5), she agreed with the idea in principle and became a key member and treasurer of the group. However, she later left the group when Nauyac failed to produce every receipt for all his materials and living expenses, which she saw as unaccounted expenditure.

> As the war drew to an end, General Yamashita escaped to Hungduan and built his camp on the slope known as Nabigihan in Wangwang. His troops spread out and deployed themselves at various locations around Mount Napulawan. General Yamashita probably also evacuated from Nabigihan towards Mount Napulawan in the end.
>
> When the Japanese soldiers came the Americans followed hot on their heels. They bombarded Hungduan heavily from Lagawe and Piwon over the mountain using mortars. The houses and rice terraces of Patpat (located halfway up the mountainside facing just in the direction of Lagawe) were severely damaged by direct hits from mortars. There were also attacks across the mountains from Pigot in Bontoc. Hapao, too, was exposed to heavy shelling from the south and west. From time to time an airplane would fly through the valley, dropping bombs and firing its machineguns.
>
> The walls of the rice terraces were damaged in these attacks. Sediment that was dislodged from the crumbling terraces blocked up the canals. After the war we couldn't go back to cultivating the rice terraces straight away because no water was available for irrigation. There weren't enough hands to repair the terraces. If the terraces are not flooded, they dry out and cracks form. Then, if there is heavy rain, water seeps into the cracks and the walls of the terraces crumble away. Even when the war was over, they were in a perilous state for a long time. That's why we couldn't cultivate rice in the terraces straight away, even when peace came. For quite some time we had to live on the [sweet potatoes] that we grew in the swiddens.
>
> The Japanese soldiers started to arrive in great numbers around the time of the rice harvest, so it must have been May or June. The villagers were

afraid of the Japanese soldiers, so they fled to the mountains and took refuge there. While they were in the mountains, they were not killed by the Japanese soldiers directly, but many people died of starvation and disease. Malaria and dysentery were rife. Dysentery reduced me to skin and bones and my mother though that I might die. Fortunately, she always kept me warm. She wrapped me in a blanket and nursed me carefully and so I made it through.

(Angelina Gano (interview with author), March 1, 2007, at her home in Hapao)

Nauyac told me about similar experiences on a number of occasions. He was eight or nine years old at the time. When he fled into the mountain forests with his parents, an American shell landed nearby and exploded. A small projectile, perhaps a piece of rock or a shell fragment, was sent flying by the explosion and hit him in the middle of his forehead. He still bears a trace of the crescent-shaped scar it left there. In the following extract, he speaks about living in hiding in the mountains when the Japanese army came to Hapao.

> When I was born at Patpat, my uncle Lubo-ong came back from Baguio and gave me his boss's name, Reynaldo Lopez. He worked for Mr. Lopez's family, who owned a building along the Session Road, the main street in Baguio. That's the reason why they call me Lopez. While I was a boy, I often played with peers in the river. At the age of three I got a G-string and that became the only clothing of mine. I still clearly remember the day when I was in the river playing with peers, the strong current took away my G-string. After that I had to spend days naked as before.
>
> One day in June, one villager came to the field from the village, shouting 'Japanese soldiers are coming, Japanese soldiers are coming.' It was around five or six o'clock and he told that he saw some hundred Japanese soldiers crossing the bridge in the neighboring village. My mother called me and my brother to run away to the forest. We only brought some cooked rice in a basket and blanket. We went up the mountain into the forest and waited for village men to arrive later. As I was naked, I felt very cold. My family was poor and had no money to buy another G-string or clothing. When my father and other men arrived, we ate rice slowly but not all in the basket. We left some for tomorrow's meals.
>
> In the following afternoon, someone called [out] that Japanese soldiers were coming, but they were still on the other side of the valley. They were

carrying many boxes, probably ammunition and some other important items. For two days we were in the forest hiding ourselves calmly. We did not cook during the daytime, and only in the evening we cooked carefully so that the fire and smoke did not catch the attention of Japanese soldiers.

On the third day at around three o'clock in the afternoon, there [was] a very big explosive sound. A bomb hit a rice terrace…and made a big hole. We ran into the forest to hide, and another bomb fell ahead of us. It crashed a rock into small pieces to spray around and one piece hit just on the center of my forehead. It was probably a cannonball we called bazooka.

We went further up the forest and arrived [at] a guerilla unit camp of Duweg. A few days later…news came that Japanese soldiers were approaching and we run away again. A cousin girl of mine became separated from us but my father went to search and [found] her after several hours. We proceeded to a *barangay*, Mungtay-aku, near the border between Bontoc, where was a mine run by Americans before. And we went further in the same day before night to the other side of the mountain, to Nungpipokan village of Bago people near Bontoc. Villagers were so kind enough to provide us, some 100 Hapao people, with houses to rest and food to eat.

The following day my brother suddenly died of severe diarrhea. At around four o'clock on the same day people began to run away with the alarming shout that Japanese soldiers are coming. But we did not leave because we did not yet finish burying my brother. At the final moment my father told us to run away immediately but he was left behind to complete the burial. We hurried, following Hapao people heading to Bontoc.

My mother was pregnant and my nephews Merel and Guinamay, and their mother, Kamey, were together with us. My father caught up with us several hours later. According to him, he was hiding near the burial place immediately and watched the movement of the Japanese soldiers. Four of them arrived and began to dig the grave after looking around for a moment. Probably they thought there was treasure or something valuable buried. As it was desecration of the dead, my father and uncle got very [furious] and wanted to attack [the] soldiers to kill [them]. After this incident they came back immediately and encountered other Japanese soldiers unexpectedly. Soldiers fired several shots against them and we heard the gunfire echo, but fortunately they were saved without being hit by bullets.

We arrived at one of [the] villages of Bago people, but most…had already evacuated and many houses were vacant. Those who still stayed behind in the village were very kind to us. It was because we had [a] peace pact with them. The following day they presented a big chunk of meat to elder Diklihong, who was a peace-pact holder on our side.

Around that time our food…was almost gone, but fortunately we found a swidden field near rice terraces where sweet potato was planted. Some were big enough, probably weighing nearly two kilograms. We ate them for breakfast and dinner. Except for sweet potato, there was also plenty [of] chayote-bearing fruit. These crops really saved us from hunger. After spending a week or so there, we came back to Hungduan, first near to Luboong village and then to Bokiawan village. On the way back home we saw many corpses of Japanese soldiers as well as Ifugaos.

During that time American planes came into the sky of Hungduan and dropped many bombs. At the same time helicopters also flew over [the] Panique area on a hill at the outskirts of Hapao and dropped boxes of food and daily goods. Panique was the headquarter for the guerilla unit. After a week a plane flew over to Hungduan and dropped not bombs but many flyers notifying that General Yamashita surrendered finally. He entrenched himself deep in the forest of Mount Napulawan. As the mountain top is always covered with white cloud, it is called Napulawan, which means white and pure. General Yamashita walked down on foot, down to Kiangan, and attended the surrender ceremony there. The war ended with his formal surrender.

Finally, we could come back to Hapao, and I to Patpat. Soon after, my mother gave birth to a premature baby girl and the baby died immediately after. My mother also died after two days. My father wept quietly, but I could not stop… crying in [a] loud voice.

That was all I experienced during the evacuation period in the war. The war was meaningless, just causing death to many people, Ifugaos, Filipinos, Japanese and also Americans, regardless, soldiers or civilians. For all victims of the war I want to build this international peace park and to ask [for] support and collaboration from Japan and America. (Lopez Nauyac (interview with author), March 15, 1998, at his home-cum-office in Hapao, with additional information from later interviews)

Teofilo Gano, who is believed to be the most powerful shaman in Hapao, is even older than Nauyac. He was nineteen when the Japanese soldiers came. From the beginning of the war he took part in the guerilla forces resisting the Japanese. However, as he had no weapons, his activities were limited to monitoring the movements of the Japanese and reporting them to the Americans.

> I was born here [Hapao] on May 14, 1923. I joined the guerillas as soon as the war began, in January 1942. The command center (*quartel*, 'headquarters') was in Panique [in a flat area 100 meters above the road that runs through the village]. Captain Alfred Bunno from Hapao was our commanding officer. Although I said we were guerillas, our only weapon was a *bolo* [woodsman's hatchet], so we didn't fight the Japanese directly. I lived in Hapao until January 1945. For about a year after the war began, Japanese teachers would come to Hapao from time to time. They taught Japanese at the school.
>
> In April 1945 our guerilla unit moved to Kinayat, a village in the municipality of Cervantes in Ilocos Sur. I stayed in a camp in the hills above the village for four months. Our unit was attached to A Company, 1st Battalion, 11th Infantry, North Luzon. Our unit was a part of the United States Armed Forces in the Far East and so I receive a full military pension.[11] We moved from Cervantes to Bisan Pass and then on to Tuguegarao. Then, on August 1, we returned to Luboong in Hungduan. At that time, the area between Luboong, Wangwang and Tinoc was still occupied by the Japanese. But the Americans were beginning to break through. Within about two weeks, they had made it as far as the guerilla headquarters in Panique.
>
> On August 16 or 17 an airplane arrived dropping masses of leaflets from the sky. They read 'Japan has surrendered. The war is over.' The airplanes came a couple more times dropping leaflets. About two weeks after the war ended, the Japanese forces gathered into groups. Some of them started walking towards Banaue. However, many more Japanese troops went down to Kiangan via Magok to surrender then went to Banaue.
>
> In November, I went to Ilagang in the Isabela Province. There were still some remnants of the Japanese soldiers hiding up in the mountains. We went to tell them to surrender because the war was over. Within two or three weeks, the Japanese soldiers came down from the mountains and surrendered without

---

11　In July 1941 the Commonwealth of the Philippines army merged with American forces stationed in the Philippines to form the United States Armed Forces in the Far East. They surrendered unconditionally to the Japanese in May 1942. However, some troops stationed in regional areas rejected the surrender and waged guerilla warfare from bases in the mountains.

Top: Nauyac and Teofilo the morning after an all-night ritual. (March 9, 2001)

Bottom: Teofilo relaxing at home. His grandchildren watch television on a set brought back from Australia as a gift by his eldest daughter, Norma, who migrated there to work as a nurse. (March 10, 2001)

Top: The 'Spider Web Terraces' of Poblacion, Hungduan. The valley extending from the terraces towards the top left corner forms the road that the main force of the Japanese Army took when they invaded from Kiangan and when they went back down the mountain to surrender. (March 15, 2002)

Middle, bottom: The Kiangan War Memorial Shrine and the Ifugao Museum. (October 3, 1998)

a fight. On November 20 the commander said, 'the war is over, you should all go home.' So the unit was disbanded and sixty-three of us jumped in the back of a truck and rode back to Ifugao. Some people got off at Lamut, Lagawe and Banaue. About thirty of us came back to Hungduan. (Teofilo Gano (interview with author), March 2, 2007, at his home in Hapao)

Conclusion

In this chapter I have explained how, since the era of Spanish rule, various forces from outside Ifugao have made numerous attempts to gain control over the region. In an interview with Nauyac that I reproduce in Chapter 5, he explains why the term 'global' is appropriate to describe a movement that is based in the mountains of Ifugao. He recalls the retreat of General Yamashita's troops to the region. Their intention was to fight one of the last major engagements of the Asia-Pacific War here. However, according to Nauyac, the spirit of Mount Napulawan assuaged their fighting samurai spirit and they abandoned their desire to fight. This brought about the end of the war and so the world peace that followed was born in this land. Nauyac also points out how tourists from all over the world have been enchanted by the World Heritage-listed rice terraces and travel to Ifugao to see them.

Although Nauyac rarely speaks of it, I have shown in this chapter how long before the war, when Ifugao was under Spanish rule, it was subject to continuous military interventions intended to punish and pacify the region. At first, the Spanish came in order to guarantee Spanish rule over the whole of the Philippines and later they came to protect the Tobacco Monopoly's profits from a major export commodity. Ifugao's distance from Manila and the difficulty of accessing the region meant that achieving control over it was a means for global powers, such as Spain and America, to demonstrate their political might and their intention to rule over the entire archipelago. Ifugao's refusal to submit during 350 years of Spanish colonial rule had the effect of inviting continuous attempts at military intervention. Then, after a period of American rule, the Japanese and then the CPP-NPA positioned their armed forces in Ifugao. Once again, this shows how Ifugao is a battleground where the ruling power of the age and its opponents fight it out. To put it in more abstract terms, Ifugao provides a place where two great powers came into contact with one another, a critical surface or, as I described it in Chapter 1, a contact zone. It is unique in the sense that it continues to be a place where major global frictions appear in a concentrated form.

In any case, since before the coming of the Spanish, in every village of Ifugao, no matter how remote, Chinese jars, earthenware and porcelain, Italian glass and beads, mother of pearl from the South Sea Islands and other products from the world beyond the sea have been passed down through the generations as precious luxuries. In this sense, it is clear that the Ifugao world is not isolated from the outside world. Indeed, this should go without saying. To summarize the outline of Ifugao history presented in this chapter in a single phrase, we would not say 'now, the mountains are global' but rather that 'now, in the past and from the past, the mountains have been global'.

Part II
Re-establishing the Connection between the Local and the Global

Kidlat shooting Nauyac narrating at a reforestation site in Hapao (from *Kidlat Tahimik: The Father of Independent Cinema, 2009 U.P. Gawad Plaridel Awardee*, a souvenir DVD-R)

5 The Praxis of Meaning in Lopez Nauyac's 'Global' Gaze

> The globe is like one human body, that a wound in any part
>   of the body is felt all over the body.
> The rivers are the arteries and veins of the earth,
> The waters are the blood of the earth,
> The stones and rocks are the bones of the earth,
> The earth is the flesh of the earth,
> The whole world is just one living planet of God.

This poem was composed by Lopez Nauyac, the key driver of the reforestation movement in Hapao. I first visited Hapao in March 1998 to stay with Nauyac at his home, a traditional Ifugao house, which also serves as the office for his 'Global' NGO. A copy of this poem, typed on rough paper, was pasted to the doorjamb. It captures precisely the worldview of a man who preaches reforestation and the importance of protecting the *pinugo* forests and rice terraces. In this chapter, I introduce Nauyac in his own words. By tracing his personal philosophy, I consider the ways in which he imbues his reforestation movement with meaning.

In cultural anthropology, participant observation is used 'to grasp the native's point of view, his relation to life [and] to realize his vision of the world' (Malinowski 1984[1922]: 25). As Geertz (1973: 452) explains, 'the culture of a people is an ensemble of texts, themselves ensembles, which the anthropologist strains to read over the shoulders of those to whom they properly belong'. Having understood how research subjects attribute meaning to and interpret their own activities, the anthropologist then adds his or her own interpretations and reflections. In Geertz's (1973: 9) words, this foundational methodology allows anthropologists to make 'our own constructions of other people's constructions of what they and their compatriots are up to'. However, while on the surface this approach posits the native as the protagonist of his or her own world, in reality it treats him or her as a native informant, whose real role is set to enable the anthropologist to understand, interpret, analyze and describe the culture. If the natives spoke about their own culture as the anthropologist did, from an objective or a relativist perspective, they were dismissed as Westernized natives who had lost their own intrinsic culture. Indeed, they were no longer regarded as authentically native.[1]

In other words, anthropology has taken culture to be the subconscious precursor that guides the natives in their various customs and practices simply because they are customs. Anthropological research becomes the depiction and interpretation of that culture. The people who live within a particular culture have been regarded as lacking an understanding of the true meaning of their culture as a whole and incapable of giving a clear account of it. For all intents and purposes, they have been regarded as incompetents, who are incapable of stewarding their own culture. Said's *Orientalism* (1978) opened the floodgates for a profound critique by native intellectuals of the distorted power relations that underpinned the development of the discipline of cultural anthropology.[2] For example, beginning with Hobsbawm and Ranger's (1983) *The Invention of Tradition*, Anderson's (1983) *Imagined Communities* and Sollors's (1989) *The Invention of Ethnicity* led to a growing understanding among scholars that concepts like tradition, ethnicity, the nation-state and primitive society were all created or invented at a certain point in modernity.

Within research on culture, this constructivist perspective has certainly been very effective as a critique of essentialism and orientalism and in undermining the power of the state and people in authority. However, when constructivist perspectives are turned on movements for indigenous rights, which depend upon unique historical experiences and cultural traditions, they often rob decolonization movements of their potential and momentum and serve the reactionary function of maintaining Western hegemony. This has provoked a backlash from the native side and been met with a blistering critique (see, for example, Tobin 1995: 162). Clifford and Marcus's (1986)

---

[1] Majima (2000: 460) finds a representative example of this attitude in Griaule's reply to objections raised by African members of the audience at a lecture titled 'True African Civilization', held in Geneva in 1951, when the anthropologist said, 'the civilized blacks...are no longer the blacks whom I study'.

[2] For further details, see the section 'Dentō no sōzōron no kansei arui wa hanbaku suru neitibu' (The 'invention of tradition' discourse as a trap or the native's rebuttal) in Shimizu (2003: 98–105).

The Praxis of Meaning   133

Top left: In the garden of the neighbor's house in Hapao, Nauyac sits in a stone chair that is used by elders. (March 10, 2001)

Top right: Nauyac with the author standing in front of a statue outside the entrance to Nauyac's newly built house in Danghai, in the hills on the outskirts of Lagawe. (February 27, 2007)

Bottom left, right: Nauyac and his grandchildren watering saplings they have planted in Burnham Park in the center of Baguio. (March 18 and 19, 2000)

Writing Culture triggered a critique of the way anthropologists represent the objects of their research and of ethnographic authority and initiated a process of reflection and a search for a new anthropology. I argue in the conclusion to this book that this problem cannot be resolved simply by reducing it to a question of writing style and that the way to deal with it lies outside the text, in the construction and maintenance of equal and reciprocal relationships between anthropologists and native peoples.

Whereas a kind of involution of the approach to research within anthropology is underway, outside of anthropology, native peoples have themselves begun to give their own accounts of what they do, imbuing it with their own meanings and talking freely about their own cultures. They are demanding that their voices be heard and their explanation be accepted to be able to give an account of themselves. What is beginning to emerge is what Sekimoto (1994) calls 'discoursing of culture' (explication), Ōta (1998) calls 'the objectification of culture' and I refer to as 'the foregrounding of culture' (Shimizu 1997). Nauyac is an eloquent exponent of the environmental conservation, cultural revival and social development projects that he is pursuing through the reforestation movement and of Ifugao culture, and he explains their significance. He demands to be given a hearing and, once heard, to receive a response from the inquirer. My approach in this chapter is to share some of the stories he has told me and to add my own understanding by way of explanation. In this sense, this chapter consists of 'my story about his story'. First, let's listen to his story.

Success in Baguio and the journey home

Lopez Nauyac was born in Hapao in 1938, according to the official municipal record. His father told him that he was born on July 25, 1936, but when he started school in Hapao for some reason his birthdate was recorded as 1938. After completing elementary school in the village, he lodged with relatives in Banaue, more than ten kilometers in a straight line from Hapao and almost double by the zig-zag sweeping road, where he completed high school (in the Philippine education system, six years of elementary school were followed by four years of high school until 2015, when the Association of Southeast Asian Nations (ASEAN) community was established and high school became six years). When he went home to Hapao at the weekends or during the holidays, he walked for six or seven hours along steep mountain paths across the high pass. When the holidays were over, he returned to Banaue via the same route. The road linking Banaue and Hapao that made the journey possible by jeepney was only completed in the mid-1960s. After graduating from high school, he went to Baguio, where he worked in woodcarving workshops and cabinetmaking factories to save some money. He attended university at night, but his money ran out and so he withdrew in the second year. Later he made a living manufacturing and selling his own woodcarvings and ornaments as souvenirs for tourists. He became a very popular figure and after four years as a councilman in the Asin Road Barangay in Baguio, where a large number of Ifugaos and other Cordillera indigenous peoples congregated, he became Barangay Captain in 1982 and served in the position until 1997.[3] In 1995 he was invited to the Malacañang Palace to receive an award as one of the 'most outstanding Barangay Captains in the Philippines', where President Fidel Ramos presented him with the certificate and a commemorative shield.

The *barangay* of Asin Road is located at the mid-western limits of the city, about thirty minutes by jeepney (shared jeep taxi, a common form of public transport in the Philippines) from Baguio's central marketplace. Artisan woodcarvers from all over Ifugao tend to congregate there. Most of them make their living carving wooden objects for sale to tourists as souvenirs and for export. According to the *Development Plan of Barangay Asin Road* (2000), compiled by the *barangay* council, Asin Road developed after interrelated Ibaloi families relocated there from their previous homes nearby at the beginning of the 1950s and built a number of houses. It was closer to the Dangwa bus route than their former dwelling place, so it was easier for them to travel to and from the city center. After that, Ifugaos and people from other ethnic groups followed their relatives and friends who had already moved to Asin Road and the population began to grow. The *barangay* occupies an area of 3.5 square kilometers, making it the second-largest *barangay* in Baguio. In 1996 there were 1,161 households containing 5,736 individuals.[4] In the early period from 1950 through to the 1960s, in

---

3 'Asin' in the name Asin Road Barangay means salt. The term *barangay* originally referred to boats used by migrants who came to the Philippines from across the sea in the pre-Spanish era. Today it has come to mean the smallest unit of government. It is equivalent to the Japanese designation *mura* (village) in a rural area or *chiku* (district) in a city or town. The next largest administrative unit is the municipality, equivalent to the Japanese rural *gun* (county) or urban *machi* (town).
4 According to the 2010 census, Asin Road is the second most populous *barangay* of the city of Baguio, registering 11,454 inhabitants. The population has been rapidly increasing.

addition to the indigenous Kankanay and Ibaloi migrants who came from the mountains near Baguio, a large number of Ifugaos also migrated there. There were so many Ifugaos that the area was initially known as Ifugao Village (*Development Plan of Barangay Asin Road* 2000: 9).

The distribution of ethnicity based on language most commonly spoken at home (based on data from 2000) is as follows: Ifugao (21.1 percent), Kankanay (18.4 percent), Ibaloi (17.2 percent), Ilocano (14.3 percent – lowlanders), Pangasinan (11.7 percent – lowlanders), Tagalog (10.9 percent – lowlanders), Visaya (6.4 percent – lowlanders). This shows the multiethnic, multilingual and multicultural nature of the area, but Ifugaos are still the largest group, making up more than 20 percent of the total. In terms of religion, different Christian denominations are represented in the *barangay*, the largest group being Catholic, at 30.3 percent, followed by Born Again Christian (14.0 percent), Baptist (11.4 percent), Iglesia Ni Christo (11.0 percent), Jehovah's Witness (10.3 percent), Uniting Church (7.0 percent), Anglican (6.1 percent), Pentecostal (5.6 percent) and others (4.1 percent). One characteristic feature of this religious makeup of the *barangay* is that while 85 percent of all Filipinos are Catholic, they do not constitute a majority in Asin Road and, instead, a number of protestant denominations live alongside one another.

In terms of occupation as of 1998, 43.9 percent of household heads are self-employed, making them the largest group. The remainder are office workers (7.9 percent), migrant workers (5.0 percent), teachers (1.8 percent), electricians (0.9 percent) and other (38.5 percent). Many of the self-employed are carpenters, stonemasons, farmers and woodcarvers. Of those who are not self-employed, 12.5 percent are permanent salary and wage workers, while 43.6 percent rely on irregular work.[5] It seems that many irregular workers in Asin Road are casual construction workers or woodcarvers working as subcontractors, meaning that, in reality, 'the wood carving industry is the main source of income for the people who live in this barangay' (*Development Plan of Barangay Asin Road* 2000: 53). Tourist guides refer to the *barangay* as the 'woodcarvers village' or similar designations. The woodcarving workshops also contain display areas and tourists frequent the *barangay* to see the woodcarvers at work

---

5 In terms of monthly income, 24.9 percent of households earn 3,000 pesos or less, 25.8 percent earn 3,000–5,500 pesos, 22.1 percent earn 5,500–7,500 pesos, 15.5 percent earn 7,500–9,500 pesos and 11.7 percent earn more than 9,500 pesos.

The Praxis of Meaning

Top: Asin Road *barangay*. The houses stand on the slope of a hill. (February 29, 2004)

Bottom: Woodcarvers' studio in Asin Road. Compared with Hapao, Asin Road has easy access and is close to transport links, meaning big statues made out of larger trees are easy to transport in and out. (March 19, 2000)

and to purchase souvenirs. Almost at the lowest downhill end of Asin Road is the BenCab (a national artist) Museum, which opened in 2009 and displays granary gods, lime containers, native implements, weapons and other outstanding examples of indigenous arts and crafts of the Cordilleras.

Nauyac became a young leader in the *barangay* in the 1970s. After serving as a councilman, he was captain for three consecutive terms. He is a devout Christian who launched a fundraising campaign while he was captain to build the Ave Maria Church in Asin Road, and when it was completed he decorated it with Ifugao carvings and handwoven fabrics. He invited Congressman Onorato Aquino and other politicians to the groundbreaking ceremony in April 1991, where he performed a traditional Ifugao festive dance dressed in an Ifugao loincloth, handwoven vest and headdress. At a ceremony to celebrate the completion of the church, he brushed aside the objections of the Belgian priest and sacrificed a pig and performed a traditional Ifugao rite to thank God. He has also been one of the central figures at the *Cannyao*, a festive rite of the highland indigenous peoples that has been held in the center of Baguio since the mid-1960s.

When Nauyac was invited as a leader of the Ifugao community to various events and ceremonies in Baguio, he dressed in traditional costume, with loincloth and spear, and danced in time to the beating of a gong in ritualistic performances that visibly demonstrate Ifugao culture. He has been the subject of strong criticism from young indigenous people and a section of the political left, who accuse him of showing off and commercializing Ifugao culture to ingratiate himself with those in power. However, having been born an Ifugao and lived as a woodcarver, he takes pride in revealing the symbols of his Ifugao heritage in front of visiting dignitaries, foreign tourists and lowland Filipinos. He wants Ifugao young people and children who see him to feel pride in themselves and recognize their Ifugao heritage, and he hopes that these displays will fill them with a strong desire to protect their culture.

Nauyac and all the indigenous people who have come to live in Baguio have adapted to city life while still maintaining very tight relationships with relatives who have remained in their native villages. Nauyac visited Hapao frequently when he lived in Baguio, sometimes for matters connected with his woodcarving business. These visits helped him to understand that the future of rice terrace cultivation and traditional woodcarving was by no means guaranteed. Feeling that he must do something about it, at the beginning of the 1990s he started to urge the woodcarvers and

Hapao villagers living in the Asin Road Barangay to plant trees. He began germinating seedlings of native species suitable for woodcarving in a nursery he built behind his home. He took the seedlings with him on his trips to Hapao and planted them or divided them among the villagers and asked them to do the planting for him. When he stepped down as Barangay Captain in 1997 – and with his four children grown up and able to support themselves – he took the opportunity to move from Baguio back to Hapao to focus exclusively on reforestation. In 1998 he left his wife at their home in Baguio to take care of the woodcarving and brokerage business and returned to Hapao alone to dedicate himself to the reforestation movement.

Nauyac explained his reasons for returning to Hapao and his passion for reforestation as follows (this account is compiled from a number of conversations at different times).

> It is thanks to the forests that the people of Hapao have been able to continue cultivating rice in the terraces and making carvings. Unfortunately, deforestation and the drying up of irrigation water are becoming serious

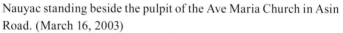

Nauyac standing beside the pulpit of the Ave Maria Church in Asin Road. (March 16, 2003)

problems. Trees suitable for carving are fast disappearing. If things continue as they are now, it will become even more difficult to grow rice in the terraces. The people of Hapao and Asin Road who rely on the manufacture and sale of woodcarvings might not have a job in the future. I myself have cut down the trees of the forest for woodcarving and damaged the forests. But when I look back, while I am deeply grateful to mother nature for providing me with the basis for my livelihood, I have come to reflect on the damage I have done and it pains me. I feel like I have injured my own body by my own hand. I need to heal these wounds and restore the forests so that I can live a tranquil life in Hapao and so I want to keep planting trees.

To explain Nauyac's work, the small Japanese NGO that supports his reforestation project produced a booklet, *Ang Bantay ng Mahiwagang Gubat* (*Guardian of the Enchanted Forest*), mainly for distribution to the elementary and high school students of Hungduan (1,500 words in Filipino, 500 words in English). The text was written by his eldest daughter, Emilia (local name Aginaya), based on what Nauyac told her. His second son, Wigan, provided the illustrations and Kidlat wrote a preface. As it is intended to be read by elementary school students, every effort was made to ensure the text is easy to read and understand. In this booklet, the circumstances leading up to Nauyac's epiphany about the need for reforestation are explained as follows.

> One night Mang [a respectful term of address used with the given name of a man] Lopez slept on the rooftop listening to the wind. He heard murmurings coming from a bunch of trees standing nearby.
>
> He understood what they were saying. He heard one tree say, 'These are days of peril. If we do not do anything, all will be lost. Our mountains will be barren.' Another tree spoke, 'No one hears our pleas…for thousands of years we chose guardians. We tasked these few men to help the forest but they stop when they are tired…Lately, no one has shown that Gift of Understanding.'
>
> In his amazement Mang Lopez listened silently. Gathering his courage, he asked them, 'What gift are you talking about?'
>
> The trees slowly approached Mang Lopez. An old tree spoke. 'After hundreds of years, at least someone can hear us. Ah, so long since the gift of understanding has manifested. He finally came home but now an old man.'
>
> Another concerned tree spoke, 'Old man, we have been looking for the gifted one, a man who understands the language of the forest. This man is

The Praxis of Meaning

supposed to be our guardian, our intercessor with the world. He shall watch over us so that man shall not abuse us. One who would tell stories so that we are taken care of. You have the gift, but are you willing to use it?'

'You have understood that the job ahead of you is hard. It will be full of sacrifices. It will not be easy, you have four tasks to do and you have only a short time.'

Mang Lopez replied, 'What are those task? And how short is the time?' The old tree spoke, 'First is Seed Gathering, second Seed Planting, third is the crucial part – Nurturing Season, and the last is Ritual of Harvest. These tasks are the cycle of life, are you willing to accept your duty as a guardian?'

'Yes...I sincerely accept the challenge. All I am asking is your guidance for this great task before me,' Mang Lopez replied.

Lopez Nauyac started to gather seeds. He would talk to the trees, asking their permission. They told him their secrets – where, when and how to gather their seeds. From the North to the South, he gathered seeds from different

A sign at the crossroads in Bagabag reads 'Welcome to the Gateway of the 8th Wonder of the World Banaue Rice Terraces'. (February 29, 2000)

kinds of trees like the Narra tree, Mahogany, Gmelina, Rosewood, Pine tree and other indigenous trees with the help of his family.

In the village some neighbors laughed at Lopez Nauyac, 'Crazy old man… talking to the seeds and trees? Why plant trees when there are still many trees around? Yes, Mang Lopez is just a dreamer.' Instead of helping, they went to Mang Ago's store and drank rice wine, gossiping about the old lover of trees.

Mang Lopez did not mind them. He went instead to his *pinugo* and planted seedlings ready for transfer in the watersheds.

One afternoon, his grandchildren and their friends came from school. They gathered around him and started asking questions. One child asked his grandfather, 'Lolo [grandfather], why are you planting trees?'

He told them, 'Listen very well and I will tell you why. Being a carver in my younger days, we have cut down many trees to carve and sell. I have a good woodcarving business. I hired many workers to help me cut trees. Many people like our products: visitors from foreign lands were interested so they ordered more. So more trees were cut down.'

…

'One time…I went to the lowlands…to find big trees to carve them into big statues. I entered the forest to look for trees and heard a different sound. It is like coming from a deeper part of the forest. I quickly came out from the place.

'As my companions started working, my head started to ache terribly and I felt very weak. I asked my workers to stop working so we can return back home because I could not bear the pain in my head.

'At home, I stayed in bed due to high fever and that night I had a bad dream. It is so real that it really frightened me. In that dream, I saw dead animals and plants. People are very weak, the land is barren, skeletal remains of animals are scattered on the ground. The sun is very hot, scorching my skin. I feel very hot.

'I woke up and saw that my pillow was drenched with my sweat. I stayed awake that night and it was in that time that I understood why I got sick. The dream woke me up to the reality of the future. It was a warning for me and my people.

'In those times I felt that something was not right. So in my last years as a community leader I started my campaign to plant trees. The trees called me to start planting so that you, my grandchildren, can live.' (Aginaya and Tahimik 2004a: 6–20)

It is important to recognize that, for Nauyac, the reforestation initiative is not based on the Western idea of reciprocity encapsulated in the phrase 'give and take', which has the sense of returning to the forests something that was taken, repaying the forests for supporting his livelihood or fulfilling his liability for having damaged them – this notion of reciprocity presumes a relationship between two free and independent subjects who enter into an exchange. Instead, for Nauyac, having grown up in the forest's embrace and received its blessings, he and the forest are inseparably connected. They share a symbiotic bond in which self and other have become one, which can be compared to the indivisible bond that exists between a nursing infant and its mother. Having cut down trees and wounded the forest, he feels the pain of having injured his alter ego, or a part of himself. Kidlat says that when Nauyac put this sense of a symbiotic bond and of unity with the forests and trees into words and deeds, he, himself, became clearly and fully aware of it for the first time. It is not that this was an entirely novel sensation. Kidlat says that he also must originally have had this awareness within himself but it was repressed, without his knowing, by the American-style education he received. Kidlat is drawn to the indigenous and wild understanding of nature that Nauyac describes and sees Nauyac as his spiritual guru.

In March 1998, when Nauyac packed up his things, put them into a jeepney and left Baguio to return to his home in Hapao, I was fortunate to be able to accompany him. On his journey home, Nauyac did not follow the usual route on the paved main road that is traversed by buses and cars and descends south to the lowlands and across Nueva Vizcaya from west to east before heading north on the Philippine-Japan Friendship Highway, turning off at Bagabag and heading northwest for Banaue. Instead, he deliberately chose to return via the mountain roads he had traveled in his youth.[6]

---

6 The usual route linking Baguio with Ifugao heads south on Kennon Road (Benguet Road) or descends to the west along Naguilian Road to La Union Province. After descending from the highlands to the south towards Manila for a while, it turns left at Urdaneta and heads east, crossing Nueva Ecija Province before joining the Philippine-Japan Friendship Highway, an arterial route that links Manila with Aparri in the far north of Luzon, at San Jose. After that the route to Ifugao is the same as the one from Manila, heading up to the north across Dalton Pass (Balete Pass) and entering Nueva Vizcaya, passing through Bayongbon and Solano and then turning left at the junction in Bagabag before heading to Banaue. The road from Baguio to Banaue is paved the whole way. Coaches to Banaue traverse this entire route and at night, when there is no traffic, it takes about seven or eight hours.

He left Baguio and crossed Benguet Province longitudinally, heading up to the mountains in the north. Entering Mountain Province and driving through Bontoc, he stayed on the mountain road as it climbed upward and after crossing the rocky pass he descended south to Banaue. In 1998 the road over the mountains past Bontoc was still unsurfaced and in terrible condition. In some places it was too narrow for two cars to pass each other. However, the surfacing of the road has since progressed and in 2015 the section from Baguio to Banaue via Bontoc was almost entirely paved. This has made life easier for the locals and also made it a popular course for tourists to take through the region. Jeepneys used to be the main form of public transport but around 2007 the progress in improving the road meant that minibuses started to make the journey on a daily basis.

We departed Baguio just after nine o'clock in the morning and arrived in Banaue a little after eight that evening. After spending the night at the home of a relative of Nauyac's, we arrived in Hapao the following morning. Nauyac chose the rough and winding road in order to seek inspiration from the vistas he would encounter on the journey home. They sparked pleasant memories of the past and he wanted to ruminate over each of them in order to strengthen his resolve to pursue reforestation with a view to his children's and grandchildren's future. Previously, when not on urgent business, he also traveled over the mountain road via Bontoc a number of times. But he was emphatic that after having decided to bring his life in Baguio to a close and stake his remaining years on the reforestation movement in Ifugao, this journey would be completely unlike his previous trips.

Throughout the long journey from Baguio through Bontoc and Banaue to Hapao, Nauyac stared out the window at the scenery. He explained that while he was looking outwards, he let his thoughts wander over everything that had gone into making him who he was today and recalling once again the meaning of his experience of modern history and that of the Ifugao people. As we drove along, he would sometimes stop the jeepney and share these reminiscences with me in a way that made them easy to understand. As we traversed the landscape, in Nauyac's mind's eye the journey served as an orientation for me to the Ifugao world. Personally, it was also a sentimental journey that made me recall the long journey that I had made in April 1977 by shared bus and jeepney from Baguio to Bontoc to Kalinga and then back to Bontoc and up to Ifugao. At that time I was a doctoral student staying in Baguio for three months and trying to find a suitable fieldwork site in the Cordillera Mountains. I

The Praxis of Meaning

Left: In front of Kidlat's home in Baguio near Burnham Park (see Chapter 6) loading a solar cooker, a farewell gift from Kidlat's younger brother-in-law, onto the jeepney. In the foreground, Kidlat records the scene with a digital video camera. (March 18, 1998). *Right*: Loading up seeds collected from native trees in and around Baguio just before leaving for Hapao. (March 18, 1998)

Left: Overlooking Bontoc (March 1977). *Right*: Lubo in the Tanudan River valley in Kalinga Province. (March 1977)

Rice terraces of Banaue and the Banaue Hotel. (March, 1977)

went on a number of short trips into the mountains in order to carry out preliminary studies. My first choice of field site was in the villages of the indigenous Kalinga people (such as Lubo) in the Tanudan valley of Kalinga Province. My second was Banaue, Ifugao, where I also stayed for a short time.⁷

The reason Nauyac left his successful brokerage and retail woodcarving business in Baguio to his wife, and a life in which he had made a name for himself, to return to his home village of Hapao was to restore the *pinugo* and common forests through reforestation and to revitalize the rice terraces he had abandoned (due to the damage to their irrigation canals) and to make them suitable for cultivation once again. He not only wanted to restore his own *pinugo* and rice terraces but to draw in his relatives and friends in Hapao and carry out a revival across the village as a whole. He hoped to recreate a proper Ifugao life for himself amid the *pinugo* forests and rice terraces. He wanted a secure economic future and a life of which the Ifugaos could feel proud and to restore a way of life that would win the respect of all.

His experiences as Barangay Captain in Asin Road, Baguio, and as president of the woodcarvers' association, where he had to interact and negotiate with non-Ifugao politicians, elected municipal officials, public servants, business people and tourists, had led him to develop a strong awareness of his origins and his cultural identity. He had been invited to the Malacañang Palace and presented with an award by the

---

7 I went to Lubo with a young student from a university in Baguio who was going home for a visit. Before I left, a number of soldiers had been killed when a Philippine Constabulary patrol was ambushed by the NPA on the mountain road between Tinglayan and Lubo, the same road taken by the bus. The Constabulary responded by conducting a search and attack operation. They came to Lubo during a festival and the atmosphere in the village was tense. At that time, President Marcos was planning to build an enormous dam on the great Chico River that flows through Kalinga Province, primarily for hydroelectricity. A large opposition movement developed and there were small-scale skirmishes and conflicts between the NPA guerillas, who were supporting the movement, and the Constabulary. Steve Magamnon, who is also from Lubo, studied cultural anthropology at the Sorbonne with support from missionaries. I decided not to go ahead with my fieldwork in Kalinga for a number of reasons, including my respect for an anthropologist who was from this particular village and a concern that we might end up competing with one another, as well as the difficult security situation. After a number of twists and turns, in October 1977 I began my research in the western foothills of Mount Pinatubo in the village of Kakilingan, looking at the society and culture of the Aeta, an Asian Negrito people.

Left: Nauyac the day after his return to Hapao. On the opposite side of the valley are the rice terraces of Patpat, where he was born and raised. (March 20, 1998)

Middle: Talking with the villagers underneath his office-cum-house. (March 20, 1998)

Right: Explaining the plan for reforestation to young leaders during a visit to Abatan the following day. (March 21, 1998)

Top: Nauyac teaching small groups how to construct a seedling nursery and raise seedlings at the back of his office-cum-house. (March 22, 1998)

Bottom: Kidlat recording the scene. (March 22, 1998)

president, and had traveled to the United Nations General Assembly in New York for the International Year of the World's Indigenous People in 1993 as an indigenous representative from the Philippines.[8] Through these interactions with people outside the Ifugao community and through having to negotiate and hold his own, he found by a circuitous route that he became even more conscious of the culture that embodies everything Ifugao.

From a young age he was recognized for his skills as an artisan and was able to make a living by producing and trading in woodcarvings. However, as he grew older, he developed age-related far-sightedness and could no longer perform detailed carving work. He also left the heavy work of rice terrace cultivation to a relative who worked the land as a tenant in exchange for half the crop. The best Nauyac could do was to lend a hand from time to time. Nevertheless, as I have already explained, he returned to Hapao to start the reforestation movement so that he could live within mother nature's gentle embrace surrounded by the forests and rice terraces. He also wanted to pass on this way of life intact to the next generation for them to continue. Since before the Asia-Pacific War, rice terrace cultivation and woodcarving, supplemented by swidden agriculture, have supported the way of life of the people of Hapao. Even now they form the basis of the livelihood for those who are too poor to continue their education past elementary school and therefore cannot get a salaried job or go overseas for work. Nauyac saw the need to restore the forests and plant trees for them, so that they too could have an abundant and secure future in Hapao.

Whenever Nauyac went back to the village from Baguio, he felt lighter and brighter, refreshed and happy. That is why he wanted to return and his desire was to live as his people had in the past, in a tranquil landscape amidst the forests and terraces. In order to realize this dream, in 1995 he

---

8 The Earth Saver Movement, an NGO with its offices in Manila, arranged the journey and Nauyac's stay in New York. In addition to one Ifugao and three Bontoc people from the northern mountains of Luzon, they also dispatched Aetas from Zambales in the mountains of western Luzon and indigenous people from Mindanao, for a total of fourteen indigenous representatives. Before their departure, they stayed in Manila for three days to exchange ideas and prepare. Nauyac was chosen for his reputation as Barangay Captain and because he was recommended by Kidlat. The president of the NGO was the wife of Senator Sonny Alvarez and the couple were friends of Kidlat.

had bought land in Boyyod, a *sitio* of Hapao, that was conveniently located along the road where the jeepneys pass. He was born in Patpat, high up on the mountainside across the river from Boyyod. If he wanted to get the villagers involved and advance the reforestation movement, then Patpat, which is about thirty minutes away via a mountain road that wends its way up the steeply terraced mountainside, was too far away from the main road linking Hungduan to Banaue. In 1996 he made further preparations for his return by purchasing a traditional Ifugao-style house from a relative in Patpat and having it moved to his land in Boyyod. He set it up as an office and residence. In the mid-1990s he stepped down as Barangay Captain of Asin Road, after having been in the position for three terms and after his four children were married and living their own lives. The burden of responsibility had lifted and his plans to return home began to solidify. Furthermore, as I explained in Chapter 2, the NPA guerillas who controlled Hungduan during the 1980s had withdrawn and peace had returned to the village. In the late 1980s and early 1990s, when he first began small-scale reforestation work with his relatives and friends, he was summoned by the local NPA commander on two occasions and interrogated about what he was trying to do and why.

In the next section, I share a number of stories Nauyac told me. I have copies of more than twenty long interviews (thirty minutes to two hours, mainly in English) tape-recorded at different times over a period of ten years and the content of these interviews frequently overlaps. I have deleted some of the overlapping sections and made some other small editorial changes.

Nauyac tells his story

Memory of business with Japan

> It was in 1970 when I started business with Japan. One afternoon at around two o'clock, a Japanese and a Filipina couple stopped by my shop and bought several carvings. They were Mr Sato but I forgot his name, and his wife, Cinaida, a Spanish *mestiza*. They lived in Manila running a business of secondhand refrigerators and other electric appliances, and a repair shop. They also had a travel agency. In the beginning their order was not so big, but little by little it was increasing.
>
> I went to Japan four times in the '70s for woodcarving business. The first time was to Flower Center, an amusement park in Gamagori City

in Aichi Prefecture, and I did a demonstration sale of woodcarvings and showed off Ifugao dances there. Ten to fifteen buses full with tourists came to the park almost every day. I also did demonstration sales at department stores in cities nearby. I was surprised and impressed to see how hard and long Japanese workers worked. They did not mind working overtime also, probably they could get extra income. For demonstration carving I needed wood, but I was prohibited from getting it from the forest by myself, that's why I had to buy material from lumber dealers. Almost all wood was imported from the Philippines. A piece of wood that cost 50 pesos in Japan was available in the Philippines at around five to eight pesos…I also had a chance to travel in Japan, and I was astonished to see all mountains were covered with thick forests. I understand that in order to protect forests, Japan imported necessary lumber from the Philippines.

While Nauyac was in Gamagori for the first time, he was approached by a Japanese gentleman who had stayed near Hapao at the end of the war as a young officer of General Yamashita's troop. He explained that he had a map of Yamashita's treasure and asked Nauyac to help him find the exact location. Half in doubt, Nauyac became interested in the excavation plan and made a tentative schedule for them to visit Hapao. Soon after, there came news that a golden Buddha and bars, part of Yamashita's treasure, had been found in a cave in Baguio and were later forcibly confiscated by law enforcers at the finder's house. The Japanese man and Nauyac became uneasy and abandoned the excavation plan.

> In 1974 I started business with Mr Matsushita and the order from him increased rapidly. I could provide several hundred…woodcarvings but could not produce more than that at my place, Asin Road Barangay. When I did not accept his order, he went to another place where carvers used machines. Of course, their products were poor quality…
>
> Thus business in Japan declined within a year. And around that time I met Kidlat, probably around 1978. In the beginning we did not meet so often, but his mother was my friend. She was a nature lover and worked at the City Botanical Garden as an advisor or a board member, planning and organizing special events for tourists. I built eight Ifugao traditional houses there for her, but they were ruined after several years due to lack of proper maintenance work. (March 20, 1998, at Nauyac's house)

Bond with ancestors by *pinugo* forest and rice terraces

Let us not think just for ourselves alone – what we are doing here will affect people in the entire world, entire globe. So, firstly, we Ifugao people here have inheritance of the forests, what we call *pinugo*, a private forest of each family. We want to expand that, we want to add and adopt other areas outside Ifugao, Mindoro, Mindanao and even Japan.

And terraces are really our inheritance from, and memorial of, our great- and great-grandfathers, all ancestors. So to abandon terraces means to discredit and dishonor them who built the terraces with their hard labor in succession for many generations. We have *baki* rituals, where we narrate all the names of generations. That is to remember, thank and honor them, and is a way to maintain the consciousness of being Ifugaos, and a way to connect us with our ancestors. That is a core of our culture, which makes our life different from others, lowlander Christians and foreigners. That's why they come here as tourists to see and appreciate our culture and terraces.

When the Pope came over to Baguio, he preached at Burnham Park, saying 'Worship God through your own culture', and I was very happy. And our people from Hapao living in Baguio…offered gifts to the Pope, woodcarvings. After the Vatican Council, the Church respects cultures, because God is in the culture. Who gave the culture to people? It's God! God gave cultures to Japanese, Indians and other people. God gave us all the means to survive and the means to worship Him. But as I said, it is through greed that one people wanted to dominate other people. Like Ispaniard, they came here to impose their own customs on people here. They had a hidden agenda to grab our land. You can see in the lowland wide haciendas once owned by Spaniards. But here in the Cordilleras they could not do that, because people here did not surrender to Ispaniard. They really wanted our land because there are lots of gold deposits here.

And they sold the Philippines to Americans, and then they declared that they owned whole mountain areas and everything you see on it. They imposed their system of land tilling and land here became national forests. We were deprived of our own land and were forced to become a second-class Filipino citizen, although rice terraces are much older than the government. We cannot have land title over land to register and are classified as occupants in the national forest reservation. As a result, we cannot avail [ourselves of] the banking system, because we have no land title for collateral to borrow money.

Now since our land is classified as forest reservation and a watershed for the lowland, we have the rights to demand subsidy for it for the purpose of reforestation and livelihood. We are supplying water sources for agricultural irrigation and electric generation for lowlanders. We are not benefited but only deprived, that's why we remain poor and are called cultural minorities, while they are always happy and proud. You can imagine how unjust this is! Last year [1998] the government celebrated the centennial of the Philippine Revolution and independence. We celebrated the centennial of under-bondage of foreign laws which are still imposed on us. (March 3, 1999, at Lopez's house/office)

A reason to plant trees

Nauyac visited Congressman Cappleman's house in Banaue at eight o'clock in the morning to petition for a donation to repair a broken girder in Hapao due to heavy rain and received 5,000 pesos. Then he began to explain his idea to establish an agroforest research center to study seedling methods for indigenous trees.

This is a joint project for the establishment of a global agroforest research center in Lamut, Ifugao, for the development and propagation of indigenous plants and trees especially that are in danger of extinction as materials for reforestation. And at the same time, it is the center for the training of all concerned people who want to know how to plant and to take care of forests. The budget is about five million pesos.

In my philosophy, there will be no end. God created the world, he saw it, and said it was good. If God sees it as good, God will not destroy the earth. What he is going to do is to renovate, because all created things will have to grow old, like human beings. So why now we have so many earthquakes? Yes, because like human beings, it also has rheumatism and all kind of diseases. The earth is also growing, but, like buildings, we can repent (rebuild), we can renovate, we can remodel. So...we have to cooperate with God, because I discovered an effective method in my experiments.

Why do *bangtinong*, very precious trees, not have much population, or do not have much seedlings to grow? I discovered that it had millions of seeds, even one tree has millions of seeds. But when these seeds drop on the ground, some are blown away by wind, some are drowned by water, and some are eaten by ants and insects. And then I discovered that when I got seeds and put them in a nice box, a seedbed, to take care of well, then they germinated. It was a

The Praxis of Meaning   *153*

breakthrough in our research. I discovered that God asked us to participate, because most seeds are just like human beings or animals. The moment a baby is born and there is no care, if no one takes care of a baby, surely it will die. So that is all just the same with seedlings. So we have to participate in His creation. That is why we must encourage and teach children how to care for trees and to love trees. That is my message when I am going to speak in schools. And I...expect [the school community] and schoolchildren to become a teammate of our nurseries.

Congressman Cappleman questioned Nauyac about the number of seedlings he had planted.

We have planted some, but not so many, because the location is limited in three *barangays*, Nungulunan, Ba-ang and Hapao. We have planted more than hundreds, thousands, for the last four years. The first planted ones are now as high as like this [raising his right hand over his head]. If you go into

Appealing to a legislator at the home of Congressman Benjamin B Cappleman in Banaue. (March 8, 2001)

Hungduan along the road, you will see the office of Global Forest, and in front of it you will see *bangtinong* trees and *Aguinaya* trees. *Aguinaya*…is a foreign tree, but I planted them here and gave them the name of my mother. Without my mother, I, Lopez, could not be here…I am the only son still alive, all the others died during and after the world war. My father died in 1965. So I have a *Nauyac* tree, also, by the name of my father. Because that is one incentive for people to plant trees, because they understand…trees and they want to respect parents, and they want to spearhead…planting. Because how do you understand academic or scientific names? That is foolish to call them unfamiliar names. We should rename them in Ifugao names so that people can understand and feel familiar. If they understand the name of trees and their products, then they will love and eagerly plant them. So soon I am going to make an exhibition place for seeds, collection of seeds and seedlings, and all products of wood. We have to put them in a museum to show the natural history of trees. I hope you, Congressman, understand and help us for our tree planting project. (March 8, 2001, at Congressman Cappleman's house)

A plan for a global peace park

Nauyac explained his plan to build a global peace park at Mount Napulawan to me when I first visited Hapao as follows, and he has since repeated this idea many times.

> When we [Kidlat and Nauyac] visited Hiroshima and Nagasaki in 1995 to commemorate the fiftieth anniversary of the atomic bombing, we were surprised to find how these two cities recovered…and developed. They are now modern cities [with] no traces of war damages. In our place, scars of the war [such as] damage to rice terraces are still there and fresh. That's why I wanted to [make] Hungduan a Global Peace Park in Asia, because that was the point of surrender of the Japanese army. The magical power of Mount Napulawan succeeded in convincing then General Tomoyuki Yamashita to surrender peacefully. He humbled himself in spite of being a Japanese warrior who commits suicide, *harakiri*. He chose to surrender in a humble way. The name of the mountain, Napulawan – *pulaw* means white in Ifugao, and white means clean, spotless, pure and peace – and whose magical power tamed a warrior's fierce mind…That's why Mount Napulawan, incidentally, became the point of surrender, and that ended the war.

Left top: *Bangtinong* tree at the entrance to the 'Global' office. The house with the large roof in the background is the general store next door. The 'Global' office is about five meters to the right of the general store, at the bottom of a set of ten stone steps. (March 13, 2001)

Left middle, left bottom: Commemorative plantings at the grave of a deceased friend. Almost all villagers are Christians. (March 6, 2000)

Right top: Nauyac happy to see how well the trees planted in the Hapao village commons are growing. (March 10, 2002)

Right bottom: Nauyac in full Ifugao dress holding saplings to plant at the grave of the deceased friend. (March 12, 2002)

If he had not surrendered, how many more lives might have been lost by the war, American, and especially Filipino and Japanese lives? So, to commemorate the magical power of Mount Napulawan and the birth of world peace, we have to build a peace park here. That is my program to be realized and I want… support from the world. For the first step of my plan, I have already begun tree planting by myself, but I want to get support from Japan and America. Because there must be no scar of the war on the land, scars are to be healed. All the land here should be covered with beautiful trees and green forests, which also serve the people here and maintain the environmental balance. All we need is massive reforestation.

Before, there were all beautiful terraces, but due to the neglect of irrigation since World War II, these terraces were being ruined. Because most of the families died in the war, and nobody attended the terraces. They died due to diseases and hunger. So, we want to put it back, we want to rehabilitate the terraces up to that point there, where the water is. If our irrigation will be rehabilitated…that is why we are asking funding from other countries to help us, because we cannot do it without such help. We are poor families…before, beautiful terraces reached up to the mountain. This is the highest point that was being stone-walled, terraces were built out of stone walls going up to the highest point there.

So how it would be nice, if it can be, this could be brought back to the glorious state of rice terraces. It is just a matter of one billion pesos, all those terraces will be rebuilt because we are going to do our best. This is the living heritage that we inherited from our great-great-grandfathers. Now with the modern equipment that we have, and now with the government that is coming in, and now that it is enlisted as UNESCO world heritage as a living treasure of culture, we should be able to receive some form of help, financial help, to rebuild these centuries-old rice terraces. It is possible, it is possible with asking the help of other foreign countries, more developed, like the United States, Japan, Australia and others, who can bring in help and we will bring back the glories of rice terraces. That is our plan, and that is why we are here working toward that goal.

Not only reforestation, but also livelihood programs such as agroforestry, fish culture, mushroom culture, honey culture and livestock production, I would like to introduce and promote here to enhance the living standard of the people. How much money do we need? Yes, it might be huge, but it's better to use the money for peace and life than for arms and war. Why don't we use the money to improve the life of the people here?

That is the project of our…Global Forest City Movement. Its main component is, as I told you, reforestation of the whole area and building an international peace park in Asia. We have to build and maintain a trail from Hungduan to the top of Mount Napulawan so that tourists would easily walk and enjoy the nature. We have to repair eroded parts and slippery parts, or to build a detour route. On some points along the trail, we will build sheds for rest and nurseries to raise seedlings. Visitors will get two or three seedlings with some donation and plant them on mountain slopes near the trail. We will help them to plant and take care of these planted trees. We will issue them a certificate of planting for the Peace Park with a thank you note. As our project is global, anybody from the whole world can come to Ifugao to participate in this tree-planting project.

As you came here and then have come to be directly involved in our project, you have to help me in polishing this idea and the plan and propagate it in Japan to get assistance for us there. To promote this project, I myself ran for the municipal mayor election of Hungduan, but lost with a narrow margin. (March 15, 1998, at Nauyac's house/office)

Nauyac also explained this idea and made a petition to politicians (mayors, governors and congressmen) in Ifugao whenever he could find a chance. In relation with this move, Congressman Solomon Chungalao introduced

Nauyac visiting the home of Congressman Solomon R Chungalao to petition for the construction of a Global Peace Park at Mount Napulawan. (March 9, 2002)

Bill No. 6,013, 'Building a Philippine–Japan Peace Park', to the Twelfth Congress in 2003. Chungalao visited Japan for several days with IKGS officer Tomita Kazuya to meet congressmen in Japan such as Ishiba Shigeru, the Minister of Defense, officers of JICA and funding agencies.

Cultural consciousness and identity: Ifugao as Christian

Let's go back to Nauyac's story.

> When I lived in Baguio, I promoted the *Cannyao* ritual festival there. It began in 1968 and lasted until 1996. All tribes in Cordillera, i.e. Kalingas, Apayaos, Bontocs, Benguets, Abras, and Ifugaos, had their *Cannyao* in common to communicate with God. I knew that it was the only means for people in Cordillera to come together peacefully for eating, drinking, dancing, instead of fighting and warring with each other.
>
> Every year we butchered many pigs at Barnham Park at the center of Baguio City, a maximum of nearly thirty heads. The park was filled with many people. It's much better to celebrate *Cannyao* together than going up to the mountains to join the NPA. One time the Bishop said that I was returning people back to the pagan way.[9] He thought I was destroying his fifty years of work for Christianity. But when the Pope came and said mass at Barnham Park, he said 'you can have your own cultural way to pray and serve for God.' I was very, very happy.
>
> Thanks to this kind of festival and occasion in Baguio, children became friends and intermarried, instead of tribal wars before in old days. That was actually my purpose of promoting *Cannyao*. So now, they do not condemn pagan ways to worship God, because for me it is God who gave to these people, for all the tribes, all the means to reach and worship God. Anyway, as for whatever differences we have, it's up to God to reconcile because…He knows much, much more than we.
>
> *Cannyao* was originally a ritual to butcher animals for God and pray for health of human beings and good harvest of crops. God would be much pleased if he might receive some offerings, much more than verbal praying… with no offering. It is just the same as Christian offerings at mass…

---

9   In answer to Kidlat's question, 'Which Bishop was that?', Nauyac said, 'It was Bishop Brages.'

Although living in a remote mountain village, Ifugao's cultural consciousness is strongly built on the villagers' daily practice as Christians.

Top: Old church building. (March 20, 1998)

Middle: A new building replaced the old one on the same spot, with donations from global networks, including the Hapao OFW communities in Hong Kong and Singapore. (March 12, 2006)

Bottom left: Relief of Ifugao musicians and dancers at the entrance.

Bottom right: The stained-glass window of the Holy Family in traditional Ifugao costume above the altar.

> Nobody can condemn pagan ways…because God is the one who created this world with so many different peoples with different languages and cultures. He…must want to be prayed and praised in different ways…We might get fed up if we have only one side dish at every meal, and this is the same for God, I am sure.
>
> What is good in offering animals, when you pray and butcher a chicken, you will check the color and condition of the bile. If it is good, that means God approves your plan to proceed. If the bile is not good, that means God does not approve. Then you have to wait for a few days, and you might repeat the process again. The Christian way is only praying and praying, not knowing the result of whether God approves or not. When we went to Japan, we butchered a chicken to know whether the plan is good or not. The result was good, but if it was bad, we had to postpone the plan.

I asked whether this God is a Christian God or Ifugao God, and whether this God is the same one he prays to before every meal.

> Christian God and Ifugao god *Kabunian* are the same one, with different names. Although I do not know the name of Japanese god,[10] different names of God such as *Jehovah*, *Kabunian*, *Apo Dios* and *Kami-sama* are all the same and the one. As different peoples have different cultures and languages, they have different names for the same god. Wherever you are and whatever language you use, you are just praying to the same god. He created this world with so many cultures and languages, because He wants to be prayed and praised with different languages, offerings and ritual ways. He loves all these peoples and listens to their prayers in different ways. (March 22, 1998, and March 9, 2001, at Nauyac's house/office)

The following, on rice terrace building and language differences, is narrated by Manuel Dumulag, March 11, 2006, at Angelina Gano's house in Hapao.

> As for differences of languages among Ifugao, I would like to add one [piece of] information. The same thing as the Tower of Babel also happened here in Ifugao. The people of Barangay Ba-ang built rice terraces along mountain slopes far up to the top, and then the people in Nungulunan also began to

---

10 I answered, 'Kami-sama'.

build terraces, and Barangay Bokiawan and also Barangay Hapao. They all believed that Ifugao god Kabunian would come down from the sky to this world following the terraces as a stairway. [The] original purpose of terraces was for Kabunian to use, not for rice cultivation.

When I read [the] Bible, I felt that the story of the Tower of Babel was very similar to our story. In Ifugao, when Kabunian actually came down from the sky, He said to the people, 'You competed [with] each other in building terraces farther up nearer to the sky. I will give you different languages so that you cannot understand each other and cannot boast [to] yourself nor envy each other.' Kabunian did not like the people to compete and boast…and that is the reason why Ifugaos have different languages.

Rice terrace cultivation, out migration and a visit to the United Nations

Our ancestors spent [their] lives only in and around the village, and seldom went out far away from the village. Only a few went to Baguio and it was after the war that many people went to Baguio, many worked as woodcarvers there. In [the] old days, there was no marriage with far-away villages. Not only with different tribes far away but also among Ifugaos there were fierce feuds. Even with Banaue we were hostile and could not go there easily. They were very brave and we might be attacked and killed there. Our ancestors had to live in this small world along the valley of Hapao River, and that's why they had to work very hard on rice terraces and swidden fields for their main livelihood.

After the war woodcarvings became commercialized and there were chances to work outside the village – for example, in Baguio. People realized that the world was much bigger, enough to find new places to live and new life ways to pursue. Some moved to neighboring provinces to practice shifting cultivation in wide and vacant forests. Accordingly, the number of mixed marriages with different tribes increased.

Those who did not move to other places were, in general, poor people, and the poorest families did not have…rice terraces. They do shifting cultivation to plant root crops such as sweet potato and taro for their staple food…I myself want to continue woodcarvings for cash income if UNESCO wants us to maintain rice terrace cultivation at Patpat, which I inherited from my father. It costs millions of pesos to maintain the irrigation channels through periodical cleanings and repairing. One channel (of the three) is not functioning because of landslides. As rice terraces are bonds connecting us with ancestors and have spiritual values for us, I really want to maintain it but cannot do all works necessary for it. I cannot repair the broken channel by myself because I am not strong enough and have no money. The harvest from my rice terraces is enough for only three months' consumption.

As you see and know well, rice terrace cultivation is really heavy work. That's why only those who do not receive higher education and cannot find employment jobs are working in the fields. School teachers and municipal office employees do not work in the fields because they have a monthly salary, a stable income. They let their relatives work in the fields as tenants. Though necessary works for rice terraces are many and heavy, like cultivating, repairing walls, cleaning channels, weeding, people do not reluctantly work in the fields because eating rice from your own rice field is a joy and pride of being Ifugaos. You feel that you are connected with ancestors who built and maintained terraces.

...I went to New York to join the celebration of the International Year for the World's Indigenous People, as an Ifugao representative, together with representatives from other areas in the Philippines, including Mindanao Muslims. I was chosen because my contribution to Asin Road community as a *barangay* captain was highly appreciated by the government. Our team from the Philippines took the position of 'indigenous people against modern civilization forced by the West.' We expressed our position by a stage performance. Long time ago, our ancestors lived near the forests mingling closely with animals. Human beings paid respect to animals and fully understood animals were indispensable for human beings. That's why they hunted game for food but never hunted during a breeding season. There were so many animals in the forests.

But one day, men in long pants and dressed up came with rifles. They declared that all lands belonged to them with proper titles in authentic documents. Natives in the Philippines had only spears and *bolos* and therefore could not fight against them fully armed with rifles. That was the colonization of the Philippine archipelago, and that's why foreigners could own big haciendas. Spaniards...sold out the Philippines to America with $20 million when they were defeated...at the end of the nineteenth century. Americans did the same, rule over the Philippines as Spaniards, grabbing the land from the people.

Although lowlanders easily surrendered, Ifugaos never gave up the fight against foreign invaders, and still continue the fight against unreasonable rule. The Philippines celebrated the centennial of the Philippine Revolution in 1998, but that was not true independence. Colonial rule has continued up to now, and foreign laws which were enacted without our consent govern us. We indigenous people are ranked as the second-class citizen while foreigners are treated with esteem. That is really funny, don't you think so?

For example, when you try to transport woodcarving products out of Ifugao, your truck might get stopped at check points along the national highway and products might get confiscated if you do not have special permits. Even though you have a good plan to develop community or private forests, DENR [Department of Environment and Natural Resources] always try to stop your plan. That is one reason why Ifugaos are still poor. Recently we can cut down trees and transport woodcarving products to outside Ifugao province if we obtain a *muyong* (a different term for *pinugo*) permit.[11] But people are not so active in planting trees and maintaining forests because they are afraid that the government might not recognize the ownership of *muyong* (private forest) and might do something unfavorable to them.

That is the reason why I organized…'Global Forest' and started a reforestation project with our own initiative and hands. Many villagers, including non-members of Global, understood the purpose and hoped [for] its success, and encouraged me to run for municipal mayor. I did, but failed by a narrow margin.[12] I named…Global Forest City Movement by my own idea,

---

11 A *muyong* permit is a certificate issued by the Department of Environment and Natural Resources that permits the transport and sale of woodcarvings made from timber harvested from a *muyong* (or *pinugo*, privately owned forest). To obtain a permit, the owner of the *muyong* applies to the department with a sworn statement that he or she will manage the forest appropriately. Under the Ramos administration, a proclamation prohibiting the felling of timber was issued in an attempt to clamp down on illegal harvesting. Without a *muyong* permit, the items can be seized at checkpoints set up along the national highway.

12 There was a Hungduan municipal election on May 11, 1998, soon after Nauyac's return from Baguio to Hapao. His friends and acquaintances strongly encouraged him to nominate for mayor, but he lost to the incumbent, Andres Dunuan, who was seeking a third term. The two candidates received 1,570 and 1,794 votes. Based on what Nauyac and his friends have told me about the causes of the defeat, it seems that Nauyac hesitated about whether or not to run and only made his decision on the day nominations closed, so his pre-election campaign was insufficient. The second reason was lack of funds. In spite of this, the fact that his friends persuaded him to run so soon after returning to Hapao and the large number of votes he received shows that the villagers expected that he would be able to bring in a major development project for them. Kidlat and the Sun Flower Co. (an artists' collective in Baguio chaired by Kidlat that also supports and

not by Kidlat's advice nor suggestion. It is because we live in a globalizing world that you came over here from Japan. Moreover, environmental issues are global matter and shared concerns of all human beings in this world. Producing oxygen forests are common property of human beings to survive. As I told you before, the purpose of the reforestation project here is to plant trees for Ifugaos, as well as Filipinos and all people on the earth. The second reason is to commemorate the end of the war and the birth of world peace exactly at this place in Ifugao. I want to appease the spirits of victims during the war, regardless of nationality, either Japanese or Ifugaos, with proper respect and rituals. (March 15, 2006, at Nungulunan elementary school after a tree-planting workshop)

Leveraging the past to build the future

Nauyac's explanations of the objectives and the significance of the reforestation movement to the villagers and to external funding bodies are of particular interest, both in terms of their content and the way he approaches them. As I explain in Chapter 4, the region of Mount Napulawan near Hapao was where the retreating Japanese army made its last stand and where General Yamashita eventually surrendered. Nauyac says that it was the spiritual power of the forests of Mount Napulawan that calmed Yamashita's ferocious spirit and placed him in a peaceful mood, leading him to accept the need to surrender. In fact, Yamashita's surrender also brought the war in the Philippines to an end and prevented the pointless waste of even more lives. Nauyac insists that this means Hapao and its surrounds are the birthplace of the postwar peace – in his own words, he said, 'World peace was born just here in Ifugao' (sometimes he said 'descended' or 'advented').

In pursuit of the Japanese army, the Americans attacked the area, dropping bombs and launching shells that damaged the rice terraces of Hapao in many places. Traces of this damage can still be seen today. A fragment of rock blown apart by an American shell struck Nauyac in the center of the forehead, leaving a deep scar. In 1945, fleeing from the Japanese troops, the villagers of Hapao were forced to abandon their homes

---

takes part in cultural activities in Hapao) opposed Nauyac nominating. When he did nominate, they issued a statement of neutrality, stating that they would not participate in the elections.

and take refuge deep in the mountains where they remained for about three months. During that time many died of starvation and disease and Nauyac lost his younger brother. Immediately after the war, his pregnant mother also died after miscarrying his younger sister. He explains the good fortune by which he and his father survived and by which he has continued to live a long life by saying that 'there is no doubt that God had some work for me to do, some significant work that I must accomplish. The reforestation movement is the mission He has given me.'

The Japanese soldiers who finally occupied Hapao after their long retreat took the foodstuffs belonging to the villagers, and the heavy American bombing that followed left substantial damage in terms of both life and property. The devastation of war remains visible in Hapao, both in the traces of rice terraces that collapsed and in the scar on Nauyac's forehead, and the villagers still find occasion to speak about their experiences of war. Nauyac says that it seems, however, that the Japanese and Americans have forgotten about the war. He wants to remind people of their history and for the Japanese and the Americans to feel a sense of responsibility for the crimes they committed and try sincerely to make amends. Having said that, he does not want an apology or compensation for the crimes of the past but reconciliation that opens towards the future through cooperation and for the two countries to put their energy into the pursuit of new projects. He hopes that by developing an awareness of their own history and by understanding that the enormous damage done to the people of Hapao was the price paid for peace, they will offer their support and cooperation to the reforestation movement that will provide a future for the children of the village.

In terms of Nauyac's relationship with Japan, it is worth noting that in the summer of 1995 he and Kidlat were invited to Japan by a Japanese NGO to commemorate fifty years since the dropping of the atomic bombs in Hiroshima and Nagasaki. For the ritual performance he would perform at the commemoration ceremonies, Nauyac reclaimed an unexploded 108-kilogram bomb from the bottom of the river that flows through Asin Road in Baguio. He spent several days sawing through it with a hacksaw to remove the warhead and made it into a peace bell. He took the bell with him to the peace park in Hiroshima on August 6 and to Nagasaki on August 9, where he rang it like a gong while intoning a prayer for peace. Then, wearing his Ifugao traditional costume (with spear, vest and headdress), he performed an Ifugao ritual for the repose of the souls of the dead.

Following his return from the pilgrimage to Hiroshima and Nagasaki, the next year he hung the bell from a small belfry on the roof of the Ave Maria Church in Asin Road that he had helped build as Barangay Captain. At the entrance to the church he hung a second cylindrical bell, which is made from the fuselage of the bomb, that is used to signal the commencement of mass and for the Angelus. Through his trip to Hiroshima and Nagasaki, Nauyac connected the unexploded bomb that the American military had dropped on Asin Road with the atomic bombs they dropped on Hiroshima and Nagasaki. However, unlike the atomic bombs, this bomb, having never killed anyone, was repurposed as a bell of peace and now it rings for the morning and evening mass and to chime the hours. The bell has been imbued with meaning as a link connecting different times, places and peoples: past, present and future; Hiroshima, Nagasaki and Baguio; and Americans, Japanese and Ifugaos. The bomb that became a bell is a symbol of the hope that war can be transformed into peace, and evil into good.

The journey that began by excavating the bell from the riverbed was recorded by Nauyac's collaborator Kidlat in his film *Our Bomb Mission to Hiroshima* (1995). It is also included as a dramatic episode in *Japanese Summers of a Filipino Fundoshi* (1996). In fact, it was Kidlat who asked that Nauyac be included in the trip to Japan, to which he had been invited through his personal network as an artist and cultural practitioner. The filmmaker paid for Nauyac's travel by economizing on his own travel expenses. He thereby turned the trip around, handing responsibility for the ideas and initiative for the trip to Nauyac and making the mission into a message from the indigenous people on the periphery of the world

who suffered from the bombs and shells of the American military at the same time as the Americans were bombing Hiroshima. Nauyac rose to Kidlat's expectations as a producer and filmmaker and expressed himself freely through his improvisational performance.

Nauyac takes his biblical diary and organizer, *365 Days with Lord, 1998: Liturgical Biblical Diary*, wherever he goes. He is a fervent Christian and opens the diary every night to receive inspiration. When I stayed at his home-cum-'Global' office in Hapao, he slept on his bed while I slept on the floor beside him. He always woke up during the night to urinate in an *arinola* (chamber pot). After that he would usually turn on the light and read the Bible for a while. He has a strong sense of his Christian faith and finds inspiration for his own work in the life of Jesus Christ. For example, although his relatives and friends back the reforestation movement and have cooperated with him at their own expense, not all villagers have been as eager to support him. When he first began, he got quite a few strange looks, but when funding for the project began arriving from Japan, malicious rumors started to circulate about where the money was going and the purposes for which it was being spent. Some people started criticizing him, saying that he was showing favoritism, misappropriating funds or lining his own pockets. When I asked him directly about these rumors, he often talked of how Jesus Christ was cursed by the Jews and crucified on the cross, showing that he was not the only person to have been misunderstood by the people of his homeland and his neighbors. Jesus Christ was misunderstood but he went to Jerusalem for the greater good in order to save the very people who failed to understand him.

A panoramic view of Patpat from the roadside near Orlando Mahiwo's house in Hobbong, Hapao. Kidlat's house is near the top of the terraces of the mountain on the right. The scattered houses and *pinugo* forests of Ba-ang are on the mountain on the left. The church is at the far left. (August 30, 2018, photo Yuri Chiba)

The life of Jesus Christ is the guide for Nauyac's own life and a source of inspiration. But he also has a strong sense of himself as an Ifugao. The evidence for this is that he still holds to Ifugao traditional notions of the soul and of the spirits of the ancestors and takes an active part in rituals connected with these ideas in all kinds of venues. In his heart there is no contradiction between being a fervent Christian and being an indigenous Ifugao. He has reconciled the two so that they can exist side by side. To live as an Ifugao and as a Christian seems natural to him and completely noncontradictory. He insists that everything in this world was made by God and the fact that there are many different peoples, culture and languages in the world is because that is how God made the world. God made the world this way because He wished to be praised in many different ways by people in different languages and by means of different rites and offerings. The many different varieties of flowers, birds, bugs and beasts color our world and lend it vitality and beauty, pleasing the human eye and gladdening the heart. If there was only one ethnicity, one language and one culture among all of humankind, the world would be very dull and this would be contrary to God's wishes. Nauyac argues that the Ifugaos were also made by God and God wants to be praised in the Ifugao language in the Ifugao way. Nauyac does not explain all of this consistently from beginning to end. He tends to share his thoughts abruptly as they come to him from time to time, sometimes using metaphors to aid understanding.

Nauyac also says that just as it is written in the Bible that the Jews sacrificed goats and sheep to God, so in Ifugao, where it is easier to raise pigs, they sacrifice pigs. The purpose of sacrifice is, however, exactly the same as it was for the Jews in the Bible. In the language of Israel, God was originally referred to as Jehovah and in English he is called God. In Ifugao, they call the same God *Kabunian*. In this sense, when Ifugaos practice their traditional religion, they worship the same God as the Christians, just with different words and in a different way. There is therefore no need to throw out the Ifugao way of worship. Instead, Nauyac strongly argues that it is important for Ifugaos to maintain and celebrate their traditions.

Nauyac's explanation constitutes a complete refutation of the way the Ifugaos were positioned as 'heathens' (during the American occupation they were widely described using the term 'pagan', with all its disparaging connotations) who were latecomers to modernity and who only became Christians long after the lowlanders had done so (when, after having repelled the Spanish punitive forces, they finally accepted American colonial rule). The claim that Ifugao traditional rituals, while differing on the surface from the way the lowland Christian Filipino majority worships, actually have the same content (and that this difference is in accordance with God's will) amounts to a claim that the lowlanders and the Ifugaos are equal before God. It is not that the Ifugaos were late in accepting the symbol of modernity and enlightenment that is the light of Christ. Rather, they worshipped the same God by a different route, and their acceptance, thanks to the Spanish and the Americans, of the religion known as Catholicism is simply the convergence of two paths that stem from the same root.

As I have already mentioned, Nauyac named the residents association he created for his reforestation movement the Ifugao Global Forest City Movement. He explained his reasons for this name as follows (this is an edited account based on a number of things he said at different times).

Nauyac in the seed-raising nursery behind his home-cum-'Global' office preparing the germinated seedlings of native trees for planting by repotting them into small plastic bags. The remains of a scar can be seen on his forehead. (March 6, 2000)

It is 'Global' because this is where Japan and the United States finally concluded their all-out war and the decisive turning point between war and peace was reached. All that is global is condensed here. Additionally, today foreign tourists come from all over the world as far as Banaue. I want them to come a little bit further and see the spectacular sight of the rice terraces and *pinugo* forests of Hapao, which are even more beautiful than those of Banaue, and for them to stay the night here and relax. I would like the villagers to build a hotel or open bed and breakfasts to facilitate this. Tourists would not only bring money and create employment but provide an opportunity for the villagers to reconfirm how wonderful it is to be an Ifugao and feel pride in themselves. Hapao is global, because its past and its future are connected to the wider world.

Nauyac also explains that the reason he calls this remote mountain village a 'forest city' is because he wants to pack the mountains of Hapao with great trees, just as the forest of buildings fills the city. He does not want Hapao to be a closed space but one that is open to outsiders so that they can come and go freely and easily. The figurative comparison of the densely growing trees with buildings and of the tree-covered village with a city recognizes the positive image that the villagers have of the city and turns it upside down, effectively communicating a fresh and positive feeling about the vision of the future that he wants to create through the reforestation movement.

He calls 'Global' a movement rather than a project because he does not want reforestation to be planned and implemented from above by governments and NGOs, but for the villagers themselves to understand his dreams and ideals and to be convinced of the benefit they will bring to themselves and to the next generation. It is important to Nauyac that the villagers take an active part in the movement. Even if they lack money, what is important is their own independence and self-help. If the movement does not draw in the whole village, it will be a failure. He explains that his experience as Barangay Captain in Asin Road taught him that taking the initiative and leading by example, rather than just using words, gives people faith and gets them to join in.[13]

---

13 I have asked Nauyac why he thinks his 'Global' movement, apart from a few sympathizers from the village's wealthier strata, is mainly made up of his relatives and personal friends and has not become a large movement that draws in the whole village. Nauyac responded by saying that the majority of the villagers

The Praxis of Meaning 171

Top: Steeple and bell of the Ave Maria Church in Asin Road (constructed from an unexploded shell casing).

Bottom: This bell was made from fuselage of the same unexploded bomb. It is used to announce mass, meetings and other occasions. (March 16, 2000)

Right at the beginning of my research in 1998, Nauyac made his position clear by saying, 'that's why I don't just want you [Shimizu] to look at us coolly as an objective researcher, I did not welcome you here just to do that.' He appealed to me insistently, saying:

> if you will take an interest in what we are trying to do and if you agree with it, then I want you to take on the position of Japanese representative for 'Global' and do your best to contribute to our cause. Tell JICA and other NGOs in Japan about our movement. Do whatever is in your power to help us raise the funds for our movement.

In Chapter 9 I explain how I became deeply involved in his movement after receiving this request.

Nauyac, with his unshakeable identity as both a Christian and an indigenous Ifugao and with a firm commitment to local history, works to connect the past with the present and the local with the global, to involve the villagers and to gain supporters for his movement both domestically and abroad, in what can only be described as an attempt to open up the local within a global network. It is a manifestation of the fervent search of an indigenous Ifugao who lives in the contemporary world to secure a legitimate place in it and to enrich his people both economically and culturally while maintaining pride in his ethnicity. Nauyac continually appeals to the villagers about the importance of becoming conscious of their history and culture and of maintaining it so that they do not forget that they are Ifugaos or lose their pride in their identity. He is also very conscious that this is an effective way to gain the sympathy of well-meaning people in the outside world and to gather support and interest for his work.

Nauyac's praxis as an indigenous intellectual and cultural practitioner, like that of other intellectuals and activists, objectifies culture and mobilizes it as a resource. In March 2002, together with Kidlat, he hosted the Indigenous Arts and Culture Festival. During the festival, the pair made

---

> are poor and consumed by their day-to-day lives and lack the time or the energy to participate as volunteers in 'Global' activities. His friendship and kindred networks in Hapao overlap in complex ways and there are also a number of loosely formed cliques. The people of Hapao do not always band together for a common cause. Nevertheless, in their daily lives the cracks between these cliques almost never show on the surface or turn into open conflict.

an installation work by displaying Ifugao woodcarvings and handwoven fabrics in a roofed open area next to the 'Global' office and draping them over the walls of other houses along the road. They also had some of Kidlat's artist friends from Baguio spend a week in Kidlat's house making paintings. The following year and the year after they repeated the event on a smaller, more condensed scale but the year after that there was no money left to hold it again.

For Nauyac, the reforestation movement in Hapao is both purpose and testimony to his return to his beloved hometown. It is a concrete attempt to restore tradition and return the landscape to its former glory so as to make the rice terraces serve as a foundation both for the villagers' subsistence and for a meaningful life, as well as to secure an ongoing supply of wood for the woodcarving industry that is such an important source of income. The strategy he has pursued to achieve these goals connects what appear at first glance to be unrelated places, incidents and standpoints, searching out and creating new meaning and significance. He connects the strengthening of a traditional livelihood in the rice terraces and *pinugo* forests with the deep anxiety and concern about environmental conservation held by artists from Baguio and an NGO in Hyōgo, Japan. Conscious of the good-hearted people who live in Japan and the United States, he implies that Hapao was the birthplace of world peace after the war. In his attempt to preserve and improve a lifeworld based on the rice terraces and *pinugo* forests, he looks to the past while trying to leverage it for the future.

Nauyac connects the attempt to strengthen the foundations that support the lifestyle and identity that the Ifugaos inherited from the ancestors with economic development, foreign tourism, and ethnic and cultural awakening. He positions this work as a powerful trigger or catalyst to enable the Ifugaos to continue to maintain their ethnic identity and pride both now and into the future. His is an attempt to anticipate the future by restoring the landscape of the past and remembering the history of war.

Defensive and offensive strategies in the midst of globalization

Nauyac fully understands the advantages and disadvantages of globalization. Significantly, while he remains vigilant, he chooses to ride the wave, responding to globalization proactively and putting it to use. At the end of the Second World War, the remote mountain village of Hapao was already embroiled in the turmoil of globalization. More than half a century later any attempt to escape from globalization by hiding out in the mountains of Ifugao is an impossible dream. Recognizing this, Nauyac well understands that to use Hapao, where the Japanese army and Communist guerillas holed up, as a stronghold to resist and oppose globalization would be anachronistic.

In the sense that Nauyac's strategy to preserve the basis for the Ifugao way of life and survival involves protecting the rice terraces, planting forests and maintaining traditional culture, it is an entrenched defensive strategy. At the same time, however, by actively working to expand his network outside Ifugao and even outside the Philippines, it can also be seen as a dispersed offensive strategy. While on the one hand he seeks to maintain and promote traditional culture with an awareness of the connection with the ancestors, on the other he calls on individuals, NGOs and international aid agencies to take an interest in Hapao's past and present and in the reforestation movement and to link up with them. The name Ifugao Global Forest City Movement encapsulates the clear-eyed recognition that Hapao is situated within a wider global network. It also shows his understanding of Hapao's modern history. The name is also strategic in that it is takes the existence of an overseas audience (individuals with an interest in indigenous movements or who are concerned about environmental problems) into account and sends them a message. One could say that Nauyac recognizes that he is not so much living in an age of globalization as living in one of the many globalized worlds that are already broadly connected on a global scale.

For Nauyac, globalization refers to the situation where the way of life of the people who live in the remote mountains is directly supported by the movement of people who have a global reach. It is influenced by them and in turn influences them. In this context, the name Ifugao Global Forest City Movement deliberately attempts to activate these transnational connections in order to clear the way for his people's way of life and their children's future. One aspect of this understanding and praxis is underpinned by Nauyac's personal experiences as an artisan woodcarver who made his living as a broker and salesman and profited by exporting most of his wares overseas, and also as an indigenous *barangay* captain who entertained VIP visitors from Manila and abroad.

When Nauyac became president of the committee to build the Ave Maria Church, he worked hard to raise money. The committee received donations from locals and subscribers in Baguio but was also greatly helped by donations from church organizations overseas. He had business partners in

The Praxis of Meaning

Top: Kidlat making a welcome speech at the Indigenous Arts and Culture Festival he and Nauyac organized in Hapao. The two people sitting on his right in Ifugao dress are artists who joined the festival from Baguio. On the far left is Kidlat's second son Kawayan. (June 15, 2002)

Bottom: Village elders dancing at the festival. On the right is the *monbaki* Teofilo Gano. (June 15, 2002)

his woodcarving business and supporters and organizations related to his church activities overseas and was well aware of the support this network provided. His experiences during several trips to Japan and to New York also seem to be factors in his development of a global consciousness.

However, Nauyac is not just a rare individual with a unique personal history and neither are his ideas or his movement exceptional. Rather, just as each municipality in Ifugao has revived a major traditional festival, what Nauyac is trying to achieve through 'Global' clearly shows the character of contemporary indigenous movements in northern Luzon more generally. Nauyac and other cultural revival leaders have adopted a position of strategic essentialism and placed ethnic identity at the core of their attempts to revive and strengthen traditional culture. At the same time, at the festivals and rituals where they display this cultural essentialism, they are conscious of their audience, particularly of the eyes and cameras of foreign tourists and reporters. When sending messages through the media, they typically imagine an outsider at the other end of the communication.

When addressing the Philippine national government, the mass media, and domestic and foreign NGOs, these leaders argue that they ought to be accorded the appropriate respect and be given a place in Philippine society as Filipino citizens who are equal to the majority lowlanders, but they also have their own unique culture and pride as indigenous people. When engaging with the mainstream of Philippine society, as well as demanding their rights as citizens, they also ask for special consideration as indigenous peoples. When addressing local and international NGOs, they ask for solidarity and moral support, as well as grants and aid for specific projects. In dealing with these indigenous peoples' movements, NGOs in the Philippines and abroad have developed close working relationships with local organizations, particularly with their leaders, and have also started to implement support programs for participatory economic and social development and environmental conservation. Rather than trying to support them through a well-intentioned but top-down approach from outside and from above, these NGOs find collaborators, partners and partner organizations among local people and develop and implement projects while respecting their local partners' initiative. This has become an essential precondition when applying for project funding or for running an NGO. In order for foreign NGOs to carry out development assistance smoothly and effectively, and in order to gain legitimacy for their intervention, they must develop a cooperative relationship with local NGOs and Peoples

The Praxis of Meaning

Organizations. This means that both sides need each other and make use of one another, building an equal relationship based on mutual interdependence. In Chapter 9, I discuss the genesis of the relationship between 'Global' and a Japanese NGO, how it developed and my own role in all of this.[14]

Using Kidlat's video camera, Orlando (Nauyac's nephew) records his own mother and Kidlat chewing betel nut. (March 22, 1998)

---

14 In 2003, after Nauyac moved his home-base and activities from Hapao to Danghai on the outskirts of Lagawe, I stayed with his nephew Orlando (see Chapter 8), who built a new house on Nauyac's land in Hapao at around the same time. Orlando belongs to the poor strata in the village that make their living working the rice terraces as tenant farmers for their relatives or by laboring on public works projects and from other irregular forms of employment. He was able to build a three-roomed house (currently unfinished) because he is Nauyac's nephew and lived next to Nauyac's old house in Patpat and devoted himself to the 'Global' movement as a volunteer. Most of the money to build the house was provided by his younger brother and sister, who supported him when they went to work in Taiwan. In the living room of his house, there is a television and video player that his sister brought back when she returned from Taiwan in 2005 for a visit. I was able to watch scenes of the *Tungoh* (traditional festival) from 2006 and 2007 on the video player because Orlando used a video camera Kidlat loaned him to record two-hour long films of each event.

Kidlat Tahimik understands and supports Nauyac's reforestation and cultural revival movement. More importantly, he is a collaborator who makes documentaries recording the movement. After studying in America and working in Paris, he decided to stop 'being a good little Third World boy' who was happy to get a pat on the head from the white man. He returned to Baguio and followed Nauyac on his return to Hapao to start the reforestation movement. He established a base there and now splits his time between Baguio and Hapao. He is not simply trying to escape from modernization and Westernization but to 'unlearn' his own identity and create a basis from which to fight against the tide of globalization through his cultural work, waging a guerilla war in the cultural sphere. Recognizing the reality that he cannot escape from the wave of globalization, Nauyac goes along for the ride while trying to revive traditional culture. Kidlat, on the other hand, sees the penetration of American mass culture and crass commercialism as the core of globalization. He tries to send a message of warning not to be swallowed by that wave.

6 Memories of Overdevelopment
Kidlat Tahimik's 'Circumnavigation of the World'

Kidlat Tahimik made his explosive directorial debut on the world film scene with his self-produced *Perfumed Nightmare* (1977), in which he also played the lead role. He went on to make his allegorical critique of modernity, *Turumba* (1981), and *Why is Yellow at the Middle of the Rainbow?* (1994), a documentary about his family's daily life in its historical and social context. For nearly twenty years Kidlat has also been filming Nauyac's single-minded devotion to the reforestation movement in Hapao and has made more than five documentary films about it.[1]

As I explain later, Kidlat Tahimik is not the director's birth name but a Tagalog word meaning 'silent lightning'. Through an analysis of his life and work, I introduce his earnest yet humor-filled quest to remake himself as an indigenous and authentic Filipino, after having been forced to develop amid the aftereffects of the American colonial policy of Benevolent Assimilation and having over-adapted to it through his education in English. In a televised interview, Kidlat and his life were summed up succinctly in the phrase 'from a global citizen to [an] indigenous culture advocate, from Eric de Guia to Kidlat Tahimik' (Bloomberg TV Philippines 2016).

When Kidlat's debut work was screened in San Francisco, Francis Ford Coppola happened to be in the audience. He lavished praise on the film, acquired the rights and arranged to introduce it to American audiences as a Zoetrope Studios distribution. A critical essay by Frederic Jameson (1992) focused further attention and praise on the film. Christopher Pavsek's (2013) recent study, *The Utopia of Film*, also includes Kidlat's work, alongside that of Jean-Luc Godard and Alexander Kluge, praising him as one of three directors whose work deserves a special mention in the history of film. In 2015 Kidlat was awarded the Caligari Film Prize at the Berlin International Film Festival for his latest edited digest of more than thirty

---

1 Kidlat kindly read through the draft of Chapters 6 and 7 to provide corrections, additional information, constructive comments and suggestions.

years of footage, *Balikbayan #1: Memories of Overdevelopment Redux III*, bringing the director once more into the spotlight.

Jameson's and Pavsek's analytical studies of Kidlat's work are both minutely argued and draw on extensive theoretical literature. However, they consider the films only as texts and their argument is mostly limited to the content of the films and their cinematography and dialogue (primarily that spoken by Kidlat), and they place them in the context of Western thought, film history and academic film studies. They show little interest in the broader context that lies beyond the images and dialogue, such as Kidlat's life course and the details of Philippine history, politics and culture. Filipino cultural critics and film researchers have severely criticized their work on these points (San Juan Jr. 2000; Tolentino 1996, 2001). For example, Tolentino (1996: 113) makes the following critique of Jameson's account:

> Jameson's engaging discourse could not escape reifying the conventions of marginalization and disenfranchisement. His attempt to provide a cognitive mapping of a 'Third World' text has not reached the desired destination.
>
> Jameson's construction of a 'Third World' reconstitutes the 'First World/Third World' dichotomy. This note examines Jameson's construction of Kidlat Tahimik's text in the postmodern context, or as a 'First World' representation of a 'Third World' text.

Jameson's and Pavsek's frame of reference, and that of other Western scholars and critics, is located in a thoroughly Western intellectual tradition and they rely heavily upon philosophers and scholars in the genealogy of Marxist thought. They read too much into Kidlat's work or read it backwards, as a criticism of the modern world that was produced or brought about by Western modernity. While they talk about Kidlat's work, they are blinded by the bright lights of the thinkers they cite. When I first began my fieldwork in Ifugao, I spoke with Kidlat about Jameson's essay. I told him that, speaking plainly, I found it almost impenetrable and was unsure what it meant. When I asked him if Jameson's analysis had truly captured what it was that he wanted to say, Kidlat replied jokingly, 'Re-reading Jameson's chapter on me, I still can't understand his post-modernism analysis. But that's OK, I am flattered he ends his book on *Perfumed Nightmare*. After all, that's his business, isn't it?' As I listened to this reply I felt myself start to relax. I came to like Kidlat even more and my interest in him grew. I realized that, for Jameson, who is a cultural critic, and Pavsek, who is a film critic and scholar, the value of a cinematic work is entirely contained within the text but that for me, as an anthropologist, the context must be considered alongside it. Indeed, it is even more important than the text.

Based on this understanding, I discuss Kidlat's life course and the chain of events that brought his films into being. I look at the light these texts might shed on their context and, conversely, how their context might inform our reading of the texts. To put it another way, I cross-reference the history, politics and cultural context of the Philippines with Kidlat's work and his way of being in the world. If my approach in this book has any originality at all when compared with the many scholarly and critical works that have already been written about Kidlat, it is in considering his filmography and career against the prevailing historical circumstances in the Philippines and, in particular, by focusing on Kidlat's pursuit of the Ifugao indigenous intellectual Lopez Nauyac.

Jameson and Pavsek have also overlooked the fact that an important objective of Kidlat's films is to deliver a message to the next generation of young people who will carry the future of the Philippines. They are not simply a critique of Western modernity and capitalism. Kidlat receives invitations to international symposia and seminars on experimental and alternative film abroad but at the same time gladly accepts invitations to take classes and give seminar presentations at universities in the Philippines, where he screens his films and speaks about them passionately. He uses his films as a pretext to talk about the work of Nauyac, the Ifugao sage.

Nauyac had already appeared in a number of important scenes in *Why is Yellow at the Middle of the Rainbow?* and is a fully-fledged character role in *Balikbayan #1*. The following scene from the end of the *Rainbow* film, where Nauyac is introduced in the concluding remarks, is typical. This scene recurs again and again as a central motif in his subsequent documentaries. In the scene, Kidlat and his son Kidlat Senior look on as Nauyac the Third World blacksmith uses a hammer to temper and shape red-hot old car parts, including a spring coil and a metal chassis, into woodcarving chisels. As they watch, Kidlat speaks the following dialogue to his son Kidlat Sr.

> Ok Kidlat, when you finish at university, you might consider enrolling with Maestro Lopez Nauyac. OK, you might not get a master's degree in bridge making, but there's a chance you might discover some hidden bridge that will reconnect us with the spirit of the land. Yeah, just check out Maestro Lopez.

Before he starts speaking, the song '*Manong Pawikan*' (Grandpa Sea Turtle), performed by Joey Ayala, a musician based in Davao City, Mindanao, with a deep concern about environmental issues and a respect for ethnic cultures, begins playing quietly in the background. Kidlat has a deep regard for the technique of bricolage, whereby people reuse waste items from everyday life as raw materials to make new useful items that have no relation to their previous use. He weaves this technique subtly into his first film through the character of the jeepney driver. The jeepney is a public transport vehicle common in the Philippines that is reconstructed out of old jeep parts. At the end of the Asia-Pacific War, large numbers of military jeeps were simply left behind. These old jeeps have been reincarnated as public transport jeepneys. In his second film *Sinong Lumikha ng Yo-yo? Sinong Lumikha ng Moon Buggy?* (Who Invented the Yo-yo? Who Invented the Moon Buggy) (1977–81), a spacecraft made from junk serves as a metaphor for the importance of recycling bricolage.

Nauyac's reforestation movement, which I discuss in the previous chapter, the stories he tells about the past traditions, and the vision of the future that underpins his movement are not for Kidlat merely raw materials for filmmaking. Nauyac is Kidlat's 'guru' and 'soul brother', a source of ideas and inspiration that assists him to reshape his identity. The mid-1970s when Kidlat made *Perfumed Nightmare* were a period of transition for the director. He came to reject the version of himself that he had created while bearing the Spanish name Eric de Guia as a Western-educated student. He felt that he had been brainwashed by American-style education and culture and absorbed an American sensibility and way of thinking right down to the very marrow of his bones in the earlier part of his life. The latter part of his life has become an earnest attempt to liberate the true cultural self that was suppressed in this process and to recreate himself anew with precolonial strengths. Nauyac is an essential spiritual guide in Kidlat's rebirth as a true Filipino. He is also a comrade who, through the reforestation and cultural revival movements, is trying to change things to make a better tomorrow for his children.

Nauyac's timely interventions are an eternal spring that motivates and informs Kidlat's reconstruction of his identity and his recognition and reclamation of Filipino-style emotions, concepts and philosophy. At the same time, Nauyac's reforestation movement, his ritual performances and his other non-Westernized activities provide Kidlat, as a documentary filmmaker, with a critique of the invasion of Western modernity and the postcolonial situation in an authentic indigenous voice, as well as a valuable source of exotic images. Nauyac is also a teacher who facilitates Kidlat's 'unlearning' and a living embodiment of the Filipino worldview and philosophy that Kidlat wants to communicate to the younger generation and to his audiences around the world. Kidlat and Nauyac are comrades in the cultural and social movement to strengthen indigenous identities and improve their social position as indigenous Cordillerans (who are looked down upon by Christianized lowlanders). They respect one another, work together and make use of one another. In this chapter and the next, I consider the possibilities and problems of Kidlat's cultural practice, with its strong essentialist hue. I discuss one pole of the global-local connection – that is, the cooperation between a global cultural practitioner and a local native intellectual – and discuss a number of examples of their work.

The fetters of colonial rule

Kidlat's first film, *Perfumed Nightmare*, is a semi-documentary allegorical drama. It opens with Kidlat driving a jeepney slowly across a small bridge surrounded by green trees that leads to a village. Next there are three repetitions of a scene in which Kidlat walks across that same bridge pulling a jeepney behind him. In the first, he walks across pulling a child's small red toy jeepney, thirty centimeters long, tied to a string. In the voiceover he reminisces about how he first tried to cross the bridge by himself when he was three years old. The next time he crosses, he pulls a larger toy jeepney, about sixty centimeters in length. Finally, he crosses while pulling a full-sized jeepney behind him. Each time he stops in the middle of the bridge and declares forcefully, 'I am Kidlat Tahimik. I choose my vehicle and I can cross any bridge.' In each of these scenes he wears the same T-shirt with lateral stripes.

By declaring himself to be Kidlat in the middle of the bridge he expresses resolutely his rejection of the persona of Eric de Guia. The three repetitions recall the disciple Peter's three denials of Jesus, which Jesus had prophesied on the Mount of Olives.[2] It is also a powerful declaration of his continuing

---

2 In the Garden of Gethsemane, before Jesus went to pray, he prophesied to Peter that, 'this very night, before the cock crows, you will disown me three times'. Later that night, after Jesus was betrayed by Judas and arrested, three bystanders said that Peter was one of the people who was with Jesus and three times he denied

aspiration to begin a new life as Kidlat Tahimik from this point onward. The symbol or metaphor of a bridge connecting two worlds and of walking across that bridge towards the world of freedom as a means of declaring one's intention appears again and again in Kidlat's later films. For example, in *Why is Yellow at the Middle of the Rainbow?* there is a scene where Nauyac explains how the bridge from Hapao that crosses the swift-flowing stream on the way up to the hamlet of Patpat was built using traditional techniques without machines.

Referring to himself as Kidlat is also a declaration. It symbolizes a turning point in the director's real life – when his eldest son was born in 1975 during the making of the film, he named him Kidlat. When he finished his film in 1977, by naming himself Kidlat after his son, he assumed his directorial pseudonym Kidlat Tahimik (or 'Quiet Lightning'). When the need arises to differentiate between the father and son, he reverses the usual generational order by calling his son, who received the name first, Kidlat Senior, while he becomes Kidlat Junior. Since he first began to refer to himself as Kidlat, the director has attempted to make interventions that overturn the strictures of everyday life and common sense and shake up the rigid organization of the world. From that time, he has pushed his decolonized name 'Kidlat' not only in the director's credit but also as his name in daily life. Furthermore, on June 12, 1998, he filed a petition with the court in Baguio asking for recognition of his change of name from Eric de Guia to Kidlat Tahimik Junior on the basis that 'he could not bear to continue using an American and Spanish-derived given name that symbolizes the humiliation of colonization'. He filed the petition exactly 100 years to the day when General Emilio Aguinaldo, the leader of the Philippine Revolution, issued the declaration of independence on June 12, 1898. Filing the petition with the court was

---

it, saying, 'I don't know what you are talking about.' Then the cock crowed and Peter remembered Jesus's words and wept bitterly (Matthew 26:31–75). After that, Peter strove to unite Jesus's followers in Jerusalem and went on a journey to proselytize about him. He was eventually martyred as part of Nero's suppression of the Christians in Rome. Incidentally, Kidlat later became an admirer of Tibetan Buddhism and in February 1997 he shaved his head and received a Buddhist initiation at a monastery in Kathmandu. After that he traveled to Kathmandu almost every year for some years to continue his training.

a very Kidlat-style commemoration of 100 years of independence.[3] At the same time, renouncing his Spanish-derived name was also a declaration of independence, a symbolic demonstration of his own autonomy and independence from colonial culture.

Kidlat was born on October 3, 1942, the first son of an upper middle-class family in the highland city of Baguio, a city in northern Luzon that was built in the early part of the twentieth century when the Philippines became an American colony. During the first part of his life he received the English-

Kidlat crossing the bridge for the third time while pulling a real jeepney behind him. Kidlat narrates the scene, saying, 'today I am still trying to make that final crossing to freedom'.

---

3 The court in Baguio initially accepted Kidlat's petition to change his name to Kidlat Tahimik. However, the public prosecutor appealed the decision on the grounds that rejecting its Spanish origins was not among six legitimate legal reasons to change one's name, and Kidlat lost the case. He could have brought the case to the Supreme Court within ten days but failed to do so because his lawyer had a traffic accident and could not work. Regardless of the court decision, he continues to use the name Kidlat Tahimik and intends to continue doing so. Only his mother and two younger sisters still call him Eric.

language education of a child of the Filipino elite. He obtained his Master of Business Administration degree from the Wharton School of the University of Pennsylvania and found a job as a consultant with the Organisation for Economic Co-operation and Development (OECD) in Paris. His was a smooth journey through life. However, since the mid-1970s his way of life has been in complete contrast with his earlier years. He became a hippie drop-out and then a free-spirited artist and cultural practitioner. This has been a conscious practice of dissolving and reconstructing the everyday, fixed self and liberating his inner indigenous self, allowing it to bloom so that he can become a true Filipino.[4]

---

4 The reason I discuss Kidlat and his work in such detail over two chapters is that his realization about his identity and his attempt to live differently are deeply related to my examination of my own identity and my own attempt to reconstruct it. I was born and raised in a dormitory facility for people who had been repatriated from the continent. The facility was located less than two kilometers from the United States naval base at Yokosuka. I grew up around the so-called *pan-pan* girls (bar hostesses) who serviced United States military personnel and *only-san* (a woman who became the lover or mistress of a single American soldier). In Yokosuka the only people who could speak English were these women and a few interpreters. In my child's mind, I regarded them all with a very complicated feeling of envy mingled with contempt. When I think about it now, these feelings were not so much my own as they were a reflection of the attitudes of my parents and the other adults around me. The closer one got to the Americans, the greater one's income and the easier it was to procure high-end luxury items such as Western liquor, cigarettes and chocolates. This was a source of envy and therefore produced a violent opposite reaction of fake stoicism from those who were unable to obtain these goods. The attitude was, 'for a true Japanese it is better not to suck up to the Americans but to maintain one's integrity, not speak English and stay as far away from them as possible'.

However, while my parents and the other adults around me implanted in me their fear of the occupying forces, their antipathy towards them and their desire to stay out of their way, I was attracted to the image of America that we saw on television in family dramas and in films and music from across the sea. Either way, America had an inordinately large presence in our lives. I grew up with this strangely ambivalent feeling of love and hatred for the United States, which continues to this day. For further reflections on the distorted development of the self that occurred in Yokosuka, see my paper on former Prime Minister Koizumi Junichiro and Yamaguchi Momoe (Shimizu 2011).

As someone who has been studying the Philippines for more than thirty-five years, I also want to demonstrate that it is possible to understand the relationship between the Philippines and Japan in a manner that breaks from the view that has been commonly accepted until now. The two countries are typically considered as being at opposite poles to one another within Asia as successful and unsuccessful

According to Kidlat, the earlier part of his life was a process of over-education and assimilation to the values and aesthetic sense of the Spanish and, even more so, of the American colonizers of the Philippines. He became a model student and overly conformed to these values and sensibilities. The latter part of his life then involved a process of decolonization of the soul, a peeling off of the imprints of that education one by one, giving them up and liberating the true self that was suppressed by that education (in his words, 'the *sariling duwende* (or inner playful *espirit*) that lay dormant inside'). In order to recreate his true self as a Filipino, Kidlat has been guided by Lopez Nauyac and has immersed himself in the cultural and spiritual world of the Ifugaos.

Kidlat's acute awareness of the way his own subjectivity has been constructed through having incorporated the West into the core of his being (a result of the colonial domination of the Philippines by Spain and America and the Catholic and English-language education he received) is by no means exceptional. For example, Kidlat's realization resonates with a story relayed by Liza Go, a Filipino woman who formerly lived in Japan, who makes the following observations from a diasporic perspective (that of a people who have been driven from their homeland and scattered across the globe):

> Colonial rule not only brought us economic, political and cultural subordination. For us, our identity as a nation is still 'only just beginning'. Today more than ever we are in the present-continuous tense on our way to becoming Filipinos... We have questioned the slave mentality that lies within us. We ask ourselves

> examples of the development of a modern nation-state. However, I am absolutely certain that in reality their formation under the imposing shadow of the United States makes them similar. They are half siblings with different mothers (sociocultural backgrounds) who share the United States as a father. For Filipinos, America's colonial rule during the first half of the twentieth century is an experience that they cannot forget even if they want to. For Japanese, on the other hand, the fact that during the seven-year rule and occupation after the unconditional surrender, authorities under MacArthur's General Head Quarters, through a skillful censorship regime, carved out Japanese morale and value in the American way is almost completely forgotten, though it ought not to be. I am drawn to Kidlat because I feel a sense of similarity and solidarity with his realization that his self was formed under America's shadow, his discomfort about his own nation and society, and his quest to reconstruct himself. I am planning in my next project to make a comparative study of the American experience in Japan and the Philippines.

many questions. To what extent have we internalized the logic of the colonizer? What impact does this have on our daily lives? (Go and Jung 1999: 14–17)

The psychological and existential angst of the middle and wealthy classes who have received their higher education in English and use it with dexterity is a theme much beloved by important Filipino novelists writing in English such as Francisco Sionil José, Nick Joaquin and NVM González. Their awareness of the fragility of the Filipino identity and the essential uncertainty and insecurity of their existence as Filipinos stimulates the search for that identity and gives it its significance. As Kajiwara Kageaki (1994: 12) elaborates with reference to Kidlat, 'the double-bind of acceptance of and subordination to Western culture, this state of discord between fortune and misfortune [means] the road to self-discovery has been the eternal quest of the Filipino intellectual right up until the present day'. In this sense, Kidlat shares in the troubles of the Filipino middle- and upper-class intellectuals who think, speak and write in English and he very consciously and sharply expresses the process of these struggles in his way of life and in his cultural work.

In the final repetition of the scene from *Perfumed Nightmare* discussed above, Kidlat proclaims, 'I am Kidlat Tahimik. I choose my vehicle and I can cross all bridges.' The image on the screen then suddenly changes to an image of daily life in the village. The young Kidlat is sleeping in his bed in an ordinary bamboo house. The English-language broadcast Voice of America plays from a transistor radio next to his head. As if called by the voice from America, Kidlat awakes. A poster of a white, blonde Miss Universe is stuck to the wall over the head of his bed. The seductive voice of America penetrates directly into even this completely ordinary rural village. However, another poster is fixed to the wall next to this one. It shows the historical evolution of the Philippine national flag from its origins as the banner of the Katipunan, the secret revolutionary society that led the nineteenth-century Philippine Revolution that began on August 30, 1896. On one side is the glamour of America and on the other is the flag that represents the Philippine nationalism that was championed by the Katipunan leaders of the war of independence against Spain and later the United States. Apart from these two posters, the walls of this almost empty little room are bare. The scene makes a symbolic display of the symbiosis between the mind drowning in the 'perfume' of American glamour and the mind that revolts against it, as well as the conflict and latent opposition that exists between the two.

Taking advantage of the opportunity provided by the outbreak of war between the United States and Spain over the question of Cuban independence (February 1898), the United States intervened in the Philippine struggle for independence from Spain. After defeating the Spanish, the United States signed the Treaty of Paris in December of that year and obtained the Philippines from Spain in exchange for an indemnity of $20 million. President McKinley made his proclamation of Benevolent Assimilation, in which he promised to enact a moderate and generous assimilation policy unlike that of Spanish tyranny. A memorable scene deals with these events in one of Kidlat's masterpieces, *Why is Yellow at the Middle of the Rainbow?* While Kidlat's son is studying this history in elementary school, he asks his father about the meaning of the word 'assimilation'. In doing so, however, he misspeaks, saying instead, 'What is benevolent assassination?' Kidlat was intrigued by this. He saw the mistake based on the similar spelling of 'assimilation' and 'assassination' as an example of a child's unclouded perception that sees into the nature of things expressed subconsciously through a verbal slip. In other words, Kidlat saw his son as accurately expressing the fact that his own English-language education and rejection of the values and way of life of a Filipino constitutes the murder of the soul.

Baguio, where Kidlat was born and raised, is a relatively new city that was built in the highlands at the beginning of the American colonial period. It was a hill station/sanitarium retreat from the intense heat of Manila. Therefore, unlike in other Philippine cities, the sense of American cultural hegemony is much stronger than that of Spanish heritage. This is symbolized by the American military base Camp John Hay. The camp was named after the thirty-seventh United States Secretary of State who served from 1898 to 1905 under presidents William McKinley and Theodore Roosevelt. It was Hay who negotiated the Treaty of Paris and proposed the American policy that led to the proclamation of Benevolent Assimilation.

One story in the seven-part *Why is Yellow at the Middle of the Rainbow?* (each part of the film is given the title of a color representing the political situation at that time) that comes after the People Power Revolution (February 1986), which toppled the Marcos dictatorship and saw Corazon Aquino elected to the presidency, is titled, 'We Are Colonial Red White and Blue'. It is followed by another, 'We Are Dis-harmonious Disney-color'. A total of seven coup attempts were led by young officers during Aquino's presidency. In opposing these attempts, she became more and more dependent on her defense secretary, General Fidel V Ramos, and the political and military power of the United States. Kidlat gently explains to his son that their awakening from the dream of the People Power Revolution and the betrayal of the expectations that people had invested in it was not merely the result of a military power game but had a deeper cause in the cultural uprooting of the Filipino people: 'War as a way of life connects best whenever a people are dis-anchored, disconnected, disoriented, de-colored by that avalanche of alien values which have no inner link to the land. Ask John Hay, he knows what I am talking about.'

The origins of the Philippines as a name for a definite geographical territory originates with the Spanish explorers who arrived in the archipelago in the latter part of the sixteenth century and named it Las Islas Filipinas after the Spanish prince Philip (later Philip II, King of Spain). The notion of a '*Filipino*' is even newer and came into use along with the awakening of ethnic consciousness in the late nineteenth century. At that time, the term 'Filipino' was used to differentiate a person of Spanish descent born in the Philippines (*insulares*) from one born on the Spanish mainland on the Iberian Peninsula (*peninsulares*). However, the economic development brought about by the opening up of the port of Manila to free trade (1834) and the completion of the Suez Canal (1869) meant that by the latter part of the nineteenth century, people of mixed race (mestizos, mostly people of mixed Chinese or native 'Indio' heritage) and native elites who had obtained economic power began to use the term. Eventually it took on its current meaning.

In other words, the Philippines, which gained a definite colonial border under Spanish rule, lacked a common ancient civilization or shared cultural heritage that might have united the peoples within that border together as a single ethnic group. The subjective sense of being a Filipino was nurtured by the resistance to Spanish and American colonial rule, the Japanese military occupation and American neocolonialism after the Second World War. The historian Renato Constantino (1975: 10) points out that, sadly, four 'liberations' have brought tragedy to the Filipino people:

> First came the Spaniards who 'liberated' them from the 'enslavement of the devil,' next came the Americans who 'liberated' them from the Spanish oppression, then the Japanese who 'liberated' them from American

imperialism, then the Americans again who 'liberated' them from the Japanese fascists. After every 'liberation' they found their country occupied by foreign 'benefactors.'

This sense of the past as liberation betrayed or as a setback has given Filipinos an acute feeling of dispossession in the present, a feeling that something important has been taken from them. This recognition that the Philippines today is not what it should be drives people to hope for and to attempt to restore what should have been. However, the Philippines had no ancient kingdom or unifying civilization before colonization, nor has there ever been a true liberation from colonialism. Therefore, the past can provide no glimmering light to give hope and pride to the current generation. The bright moment in Philippine history of the Philippine Revolution at the end of the nineteenth century was followed almost immediately by American provocation and military intervention and by the Philippine-American War, but when the Filipinos lost the war the dream of the republic was in tatters. The search for liberation, to finally realize the 'unfinished revolution', continues to this day. Society as it should be is conceptualized not in the past but by looking towards the future, where the frustrated revolution, the stolen liberation, can be reclaimed. The call to action to realize this conception fascinates people and mobilizes them to act.

This approach, the continuous search for a Filipino identity as part of the ongoing struggle to complete the unfinished revolution, was shared by both former president Marcos, who maintained a developmentalist dictatorship through martial law from the beginning of the 1970s through to the 1980s, and his bitter critic, the historian Renato Constantino, the opinion leader of the left-liberal forces. An acute sense of incompleteness and consciousness of ongoing deprivation stems from the failure (due to the domination and oppression of foreign powers) to realize the integral Philippine society that should have been and the true Filipino identity. This continues to produce a discourse and a movement to complete the unfinished revolution and to achieve true independence and liberation (Ileto 1993; Shimizu 1998: 187–92).

This feeling also underlies the language of the peasant farmers of Central Luzon who participated in the *Hukbalahap* Rebellion, which sought land reform in the 1950s. Kerkvliet (1977: 269) concludes his masterful ethnography *The Huk Rebellion* with the following words: 'A tenant farmer and veteran of the peasant movement eloquently summarized the sentiments of many others: "No strike, no demonstration, no rebellion fails. Protest against injustice always succeeds".' It is the conviction that everyday resistance and occasional rebellions are milestones along the way to a future liberation that is inevitable but which, without this daily practice of resistance, will never come.

Kidlat's search and his daily cultural and political practice is directly connected with the genealogy of decolonial thought and the movement towards decolonization by Filipino elites who aspire to the unfinished revolution. At the same time, it has its roots in a quotidian politics demanding justice and equality and recognition for the legitimate rights of the common people and the peasants, the day-to-day currents of class struggle. Nevertheless, as Kidlat has often said to me, the major difference between him and other Filipino intellectuals and activists is his firm belief that although indigenous people are often seen as exotic – yet are looked down upon as a backward people who have yet to receive the good news of Christ's gospel or the benefits of civilization – it is actually the highland people who have resisted colonization and maintained their unique indigenous culture. Kidlat says that by learning from their sensibilities and worldview, we can begin to become authentic Filipinos.

Most Filipinos (lowland Christians), including intellectuals, have no interest in the lifestyles of the indigenous peoples or in the potential of their culture. When they do think of them, it is often with prejudice and contempt. However, even this may be related to the incredible American influence on the Philippines and its absorption of both the culture and historical consciousness of America. After all, when Europeans settled America, the pioneers drove out and massacred the Native Americans who were living in the 'New World' that they had 'discovered' and then consigned the memory of that dispossession to oblivion.

The first man to circumnavigate the globe

The Portuguese explorer Ferdinand Magellan is said to have been the first person to circumnavigate the globe. However, before Magellan could arrive in the Spice Islands (present day Maluku Islands) by the east-to-west route, he died fighting a band under the command of Lapu-Lapu, the chieftain of Mactan Island off the east coast of Cebu City on Cebu Island in the Philippines (April 27, 1521). When the last ship finally returned home on September 6, 1522, after a difficult three-year voyage, Magellan's party, which had departed Spain on September 2, 1519, with a crew of 237 and a fleet of five ships, had been reduced to eighteen survivors and one ship, the *Victoria* (Masuda 1993).

The man who is credited to have circumnavigated the world successfully for *this* Spanish-sponsored expedition was Juan Sebastián Elcano, captain of the *Victoria*. However, it was Magellan who had planned the journey, fought for the idea against his detractors and managed, by the force of his conviction, to make the expedition a reality. Before circumnavigating the globe, Magellan had been part of a 1509 Portuguese military expedition to Malacca but he had yet to travel the remaining 900 kilometers between Cebu and Malacca. Elcano's personal completion of the voyage was the natural outcome of Magellan's logistical planning. The credit for the first circumnavigation of the globe is therefore accorded to Magellan's expedition (Masuda 1993: 257).

Kidlat's unending refrain is that neither Magellan nor Elcano was the first to circumnavigate the globe but Enrique de Malacca, who accompanied Magellan. Magellan acquired Enrique as a slave (most probably at the early stages of the siege by the Portuguese in 1511), baptized him with a Christian name, Enrique (in honor of Prince Henry the Navigator), and took him back to Seville and converted him to Christianity. He was the only Asian in Magellan's fleet (Suzuki 1997: 19). When the fleet arrived at Limasawa Island, off the southern tip of Leyte Island in the Visayas, Enrique served as an interpreter for negotiations with the local chief. Enrique's interpreting was also of great assistance in the baptism of the king and queen of Cebu Island and the conversion of 800 residents. According to Kidlat, the fact that Enrique and the islanders were able to understand one another is important because they belonged to the same cultural-linguistic world.

Having journeyed from Malacca to Portugal and, after his master changed allegiance to Spain, sailed from Sevilla westward over the Atlantic and then a torturous ninety-nine days crossing the Pacific, by fate Enrique returned to the same island where he had learned to speak Cebuano. To Kidlat *this linguistic circumstance* makes him possibly the first person to successfully circumnavigate the globe.[5] In fact, the diary of the voyage

---

5 For a detailed account of the Malay World, its breadth and its lifeworld, see Reid (1988). There are those who conjecture that because Enrique was unable to communicate in the local language when Magellan's fleet docked at Homonhon Island, off the southern coast of Samar, for several days before arriving at

(written by Italian chronicler Antonio Pigafetta and published in 1523, *The First Voyage Around the World*) gives clearer nuances that each island had its own linguistic variations: upon landing in Limasawa, the first island in the archipelago, Enrique could not communicate with the islanders (whose language we today call Waray). But a week later he could communicate with the natives of Cebu Island, where he spoke/understood Cebuano, the island's language (today called Bisaya). These linguistic details in the official chronicles of the first circumnavigation are the basis of Kidlat's film *Balikbayan #1*.

Furthermore, Kidlat maintains that after Magellan was killed on the seashore at Mactan Island, the wounded Enrique was sent back to negotiate for the retrieval of the body of the Captain-General. Enrique returned and reported that the enemies had a change of heart, with an invitation to a banquet – which resulted in a massacre of twenty-four Spaniards when the party turned bloody. Hereafter Enrique had stopped serving as interpreter. Soon after, Enrique disappeared and did not return to the fleet. From the Spanish point of view, the incident was proof of Enrique's negligence and betrayal. Pigafetta's diary entry, in hindsight, was that 'the interpreter has returned more cunning than we had thought...'

From Enrique's point of view, however, it may have been a form of first resistance to and revenge against the Spanish, who had dominated him as a slave. From Kidlat's point of view, Enrique had been a faithful friend to Magellan (who wrote in his last will that on the day of his death, the slave would become a free man). But when Magellan's brother-in-law took over as admiral of the fleet after Magellan's death, he ordered Enrique to go back to Spain to continue being the slave of his sister Beatrice, Magellan's widow. Until that point, he had maintained a pretense of obedience but perhaps in the end he was able to achieve his own purpose by coming to an understanding with the king of Cebu. Furthermore, if looked at from the perspective of contemporary Filipinos, like the earlier battle with Lapu-Lapu, the incident was a harbinger of subsequent resistance to and counter-offensive against Spanish colonial rule.[6]

    Limasawa Island and Cebu Island, he must have originally been a Cebuano who was captured by Islamic raiders and taken to Malacca, where he was sold and purchased by Magellan (Harper 2003).

  6 In Luneta Park (also known as Rizal Park) in the center of Manila a bust of Lapu-Lapu is included among those of around thirty Philippine national heroes that

Top: Kidlat standing in front of the Lapu-Lapu Stature, Mactan Island (photo: Kidlat Tahimik, year unknown).

Bottom: Enrique (Kidlat) and Magellan (inexplicably having a bath) meeting with Lapu-Lapu on the shore at Mactan Island. *From Balikbayan, Memories of Overdevelopment* (1980–2007, provisional version).

surround the pond in the middle of the park. Furthermore, the largest monument in the park is the Lapu Lapu Monument (otherwise known as the Sentinel of Freedom), a statue of Lapu-Lapu that was donated by a South Korean group. The pedestal of the statue of Lapu-Lapu at the Lapu-Lapu Shrine on Mactan Island is engraved with the following inscription in praise of the chief: 'Here on 27 April 1521 Lapulapu and his men repulsed the Spanish invaders, killing their leader Ferdinand Magellan. Thus Lapulapu became the first Filipino to have repelled European aggression.' The passage celebrates Filipino nationalism but,

It is Kidlat's dearest wish to make a film about the tale of Enrique and it has become his lifework. He had begun work on the project in 1982 and, like *Why is Yellow at the Middle of the Rainbow?*, he has added new versions of the project over time, re-editing parts of the film and transforming it over and over again. The latest version is *Balikbayan #1: Memories of Overdevelopment Redux III* (2015), but he continues to work on the film and re-edit it to this day (finishing *Redux VI* at press-time). It has an open-ended plot that extends into the future.[7] Furthermore, he says that much of the documentary footage he has collected while following Nauyac's activities with the reforestation movement will probably be re-edited to become a central story in the film. He uses the passive voice when he speaks about re-editing the film because, although he is the editor, he does not take a subjective and logical approach to unifying the structure of the film as a whole. Instead, he allows himself to be guided by inspiration or, as he puts it, by the cosmic vibrations, and surrenders to the story that the images dictate while he edits.

In the opening scene, a young Kidlat, wearing a loincloth, walks along a narrow path in the forest. A gnarled tree root, to be used in woodcarving, is slung over his shoulder. His own voice narrates the scene, saying, 'Our film begins after the circumnavigation of the globe. Enrique, the slave of Magellan, but now a free man, returned home in his native village.' Next comes a scene in which Enrique (played by Kidlat) hides up in the trees, hunting a wild boar. He flicks his yo-yo down to hit it in the forehead. He then explains, 'Yo-yo was not a toy for Enrique. Yo-yo was...an original Filipinos' jungle weapon.' The narrative voiceover continues to explain that

---

as discussed earlier, the notion of a Filipino as it is currently understood only emerged in the late nineteenth century. Before that, there was no overarching name for the ethnic groups that lived in the region called Las Islas Filipinas and spoke perhaps more than 100 different languages. Nor was there any consciousness of their being a single nation. This is an example of how the discourse of nationalism is produced through the erasure and obfuscation of the past and the creation of a new narrative (Tokoro 1999: 72–6).

7 *Balikbayan* (returning home) is used today to refer to Filipinos who return home after working abroad. The government's official view is that these migrant workers are 'contemporary heroes' who contribute to the national economy by earning foreign currency. For most people, the term carries the sense of a person who comes home in triumph laden with gifts. By making this the title of the film, Kidlat communicates the idea that Enrique was a pioneer who embodies the Filipino migrant worker experience of hardship and triumphal return.

because Enrique is a native of Ifugao who cannot read or write, he recreates his memories of circumnavigating the globe through woodcarvings. The visuals show carvings of various shapes located in and around his house. Kidlat identifies himself with the Enrique who circumnavigated the globe as he plays him in the film. Through the placement of the wooden statues all around the garden of his home, he also identifies Enrique with the Ifugaos.

The word *Balikbayan* in the film's title means a person who returns to his or her home. Today it specifically means a person who has come back to the Philippines after having worked abroad. According to Kidlat, Enrique is both the first man to have circumnavigated the globe and the first Filipino migrant worker. This idea is highly suggestive when considered together with the fact that about one in ten villagers in Hapao today travel abroad for work. It also assists us in thinking about globalization from the margins and from the grassroots. The collaboration between Nauyac and Kidlat on the production of this semi-documentary film continues to this day. Kidlat says that the final version, which will incorporate some of his ever-increasing amount of footage, may not be completed until 2021, 500 years after Enrique circumnavigated the globe. Provisional versions of the work continue to proliferate, meaning that even Kidlat is not certain what the final version will eventually look like. His current view is that the narrative of the final version will likely incorporate the films he has made about Enrique thus far and the *Orbit 50* documentary he made about his own low-budget trip around the world to celebrate his fiftieth birthday (fifty orbits around the sun) by planting a circle of trees around the world to commemorate 500 years since Enrique's great voyage.[8]

---

8 However, nearly forty years have passed since he first began filming with this work in mind. Even if he re-edits all the footage he has collected thus far, the actors have all aged. The man who played Magellan (a German baker who lived in Baguio) has died. He is therefore considering a final scene where the voyagers who circumnavigated the globe nearly 500 years ago are reincarnated and come back together once more to meet at the flower festival in Baguio. In order to facilitate this reunion, the scene in which the descendants of Magellan visit the descendants of Enrique who live in an Ifugao village is very important. Kidlat's second son plays the part of Magellan's descendant. He is the one who has inherited the most from his mother Katrin's German blood and he looks exactly like the first Magellan in terms of both his great stature and his bearded face. I spent a week in Baguio at the end of August 2017 and watched the latest version of the film with Kidlat at his home and met him almost every day for interviews in which he explained what he was trying to do.

When Kidlat turned fifty in 1992 he managed to get a free round-the-world airline ticket – to plant a tree in each place he stopped. Next to each sapling he placed a thirty-centimeter wooden American Indian statue carved by Nauyac to 'protect' each tree and did a ritual dance dressed in a loincloth. Kidlat had planned to return thirty years later, when they have become large trees, to film the ring of fully-grown trees as a tribute to the 1521 circumnavigator during the quincentenary in 2021. By departing from the Philippines, where Magellan met his end, and traveling around the world with a wooden Indian statue from a marginal territory far removed from Spain towards the center of the world in America and Europe, Kidlat's plan was to leave the footprints of an indigenous Filipino (the loincloth-wearing Kidlat) step by step. In doing so he hopes to remind us of the fact that the honor attributed to Magellan for circumnavigating the globe actually belongs to Enrique. It is a symbolic demonstration of his quiet counter-offensive against Western domination.

Kidlat's undertaking coincidentally serves as a metaphor for the out-migration of Hapao villagers to work in twenty-seven countries (the result of the ongoing process of globalization I explain in more detail in Chapter 8). Since the Philippines was first colonized by Spain during the Legazpi expedition (1564–1572) after Magellan's arrival, the Ifugaos have always had to maintain a defensive posture in order to defend their way of life against outside forces. However, in the sense that the contemporary wave of globalization means they must travel all over the world for work (except for Africa and South America, where, up to now, there are no Hapao villagers) and fight many bitter struggles to secure a place for themselves there and have a better life, they are now sallying forth in a more offensive strategy.

Kidlat is fascinated by Enrique because he deserves the honor for being the first person to circumnavigate the globe. He also sees Enrique as an adviser and spiritual guru to Magellan as he navigated unknown waters and as a pioneer in the resistance against the vanguard of colonialism. Also, Enrique's personal history of leaving Magellan's fleet after circumnavigating the globe closely resembles Kidlat's own. Kidlat made his second film, *Who Invented the Yo-yo? Who Invented the Moon Buggy?* (1977–81) based on the idea that both these discoveries were made by Filipinos. The film is set deep in the German countryside. The Filipino protagonist, played by Kidlat, wants to be the first person to play yo-yo on the moon. He gathers together the local children, teaches them about the wonders of the yo-yo and lectures them on astronomy. The dialogue is in English. One day the

Virgin Mary (Our Lady of Perpetual Sorrow), who lives on the moon, comes down to earth to pay a visit to Kidlat and asks him why he is always playing yo-yo. Kidlat replies, 'playing the yo-yo helps me think'. This image of the moon and the Virgin Mary was inspired by a real statue of the Virgin Mary with one foot on the moon that the director saw at an artists' commune in Germany where he once lived.

The protagonist in the film builds a rocket from a tin bathtub, a rubber hose, a wok and other bits of trash to travel to the moon. A kiddie cart becomes a lunar rover. When it finally comes time to depart, a helmeted Kidlat lights the engine, which is made from an iron pot and uses onions for fuel, and covers his ears. Suddenly the film switches to a hand-drawn animation of the rocket flying up into the blue sky, leaving nothing behind but white smoke. The animation is in the style of naive art, with its simple touch and air of innocence. The soundtrack features the excited voices of a broadcast of a real National Aeronautics and Space Administration (NASA) rocket launch.[9] As in his open-ended lifework *Balikbayan #1: Memories of Overdevelopment Redux III*, Kidlat's awareness of himself as a Filipino and his pride in that identity made him notice the hitherto unacknowledged Filipino inventions like the yo-yo and the moon buggy. It is an innocent, charming and witty film in which he portrays his development of a proud Filipino identity as he began to dissolve his colonized self and reconstruct anew after dropping out of an elite-directed career to join a German artists' commune.

An honor student in an American-style education system

Let us go over the details of Kidlat's origins once again. The city of Baguio, where he was born and raised, was built in the highlands 1,500 meters above sea level at the beginning of American colonial rule in the Philippines in the early 1900s. The city spreads out across undulating hills. It is a beautiful place with a mild climate where pockets of remnant pine forest dot the hillsides and bougainvillea flowers bloom prolifically. For this reason, it has many chalets and hotels where the wealthy from Manila

---

9 I had the opportunity to watch this version of the film during a retrospective screening of Kidlat's work at the Fukuoka Asian Art Museum in February 2003. Later I also received a DVD copy from Kidlat. For an overview of several works by Kidlat, including *Perfumed Nightmare, Turumba, Takedera Mon Amour* and *Why is Yellow at the Middle of the Rainbow?*, see Yomota 1993.

come for summer retreats. It is also home to many indigenous highlanders, and domestic and foreign tourists flock there in great numbers. Until 1992, when all American forces were withdrawn from the Philippines following the expiration of the Military Bases Agreement between the United States and the Philippines and their failure to reach a replacement agreement, the enormous military base of Camp John Hay was situated on a hill near the center of the city. It is a city with an atmosphere unlike any other, where the shadow of America's enormous power, the elegant enclaves of Filipino elite society, a rich natural environment and the culture of the indigenous people come together (Reed 1976). The landscape of Kidlat's birth and childhood was a melting pot where the American, the artificial and the modern co-existed with indigenous and holistic lifestyles. It seems reasonable to conclude that Kidlat's decidedly hybrid sensibilities emerged from just such an atmosphere.

Kidlat's mother, Virginia Oteyza-De Guia, was born and raised in Baguio. Her father studied forestry at Yale University as one of the first generation of scholarship students sent to the United States by the American colonial administration. On his return he formulated a master plan for forestry administration and came to be known as the 'Father of Philippine Forestry'. When Kidlat was born, his grandfather had already passed away but his mother says that she inherited the aspirations of her forest-loving father, leading to her own interest in the revegetation of Baguio and her work for environmental conservation. It also passed down to Kidlat and is one reason for his sympathy with Nauyac's *pinugo* or traditional watershed rehabilitation movement.

Kidlat's mother studied in the law faculty of the University of the Philippines. While she was a student, she was an awarded actress in the dramatic club of 1935. She campaigned in the 1937 women's suffrage movement – securing the right for women to vote in the general elections. She was also president of the University of the Philippines Women's Club and the Portia Society of women law students. In an open debate at the university in 1938, she defeated a brilliant young law student, Ferdinand Marcos, who would later become president. Although, soon after, Marcos passed the national bar examination with the highest-ever score and went on to become a persistent 'winner' in life, he could recount that he experienced being upstaged by a feisty female coed.

After graduating, Virginia returned home to Baguio to prepare for the law exam. In 1941 she was declared by President Manuel Roxas as the

Memories of Overdevelopment

first woman to be elected to the city council and after the war she was appointed acting mayor of Baguio (thereby becoming the first female mayor in Philippine history). When the Philippine Republic was established on July 4, 1946, she lowered the Stars and Stripes from the US colonial government flagpole and raised the Philippine flag of the newly independent nation. I interviewed her at her home in Baguio a number of times in the early 2000s. At that time, she was in her late eighties but she remained an extremely active Baguio notable and a columnist for the local newspaper. Kidlat's late father was a native of Laguna Province, an engineer and an architect who made his fortune working in the real estate industry in Baguio (Delgado-Yulo 1998).

After graduating from the Saint Louis University Boys High School in Baguio, Kidlat entered the engineering faculty of the University of the Philippines in 1958. Finding he had little interest in science, he transferred to the Speech and Drama department in the College of Arts and Letters. As a theater student, he was elected an accidental president of the University

Kidlat's mother beat Marcos at an oratorical tilt held at the University of the Philippines. (*Philippine Collegian*, the official student publication of the University of the Philippines, 1938)

Student Government, 1962–63 (a student position reserved mostly for law or business students). As the highest student official, he met regularly with the president of the university to discuss student issues. When foreign dignitaries such as Indonesian President Sukarno, Queen Beatrix of the Netherlands, and Prince Akihito and Princess Michiko of Japan visited the university, he took part in official welcoming parties as the student representative and also met privately with them. Prominent members of his student constituency included Jose Maria Sison, who would later become the founder and leader of the Maoist-influenced Communist Party of the Philippines (which led the protracted armed revolt against President Marcos's martial law regime), as well as other future political players, such as Boy Morales (who was to become a powerful strategist in Marcos's Cabinet), Miriam Defensor (later elected a senator), and Christian and Winnie Monsod (leaders in the anti-Marcos People Power revolt that evicted the dictator). At that time, Kidlat's dream was influenced by student politics such that he came to believe he might one day end up president of the Philippines. Becoming president of the student union was the perfect first step that put him on this career path.[10]

After graduation he obtained a scholarship to attend the Wharton School at the University of Pennsylvania, one of America's most distinguished business schools. At Wharton he was chair of the International Students Association and vice-president of the Wharton Graduate Student Government. He received his Master of Business Administration (MBA) degree in 1968. The theme of his master's thesis was the debt problems of the developing nations, but his opening paragraphs lacked the usual survey of the existing economic literature and instead focused almost entirely on Shakespeare's *The Merchant of Venice*. In the play, as the deadline for repayment of Bassanio's debt to Shylock draws near, the boat carrying his cargo is caught in a storm and he loses his property, putting him in a tight fix. Kidlat compares Bassanio's difficulties with the economic stagnation experienced by the debtor nations and their inability to repay their debts.

---

10 This description of Kidlat's life and his career trajectory as a filmmaker is based primarily on Tahimik (1997), de Guia (1997, 2005) and Yamashita (2001, 2002), as well as numerous interviews conducted with Kidlat over more than twenty years in various places including Hapao and Uhaj in Ifugao Province, Baguio, Manila, Tokyo, Fukuoka, Kyoto and Sannan-cho in Hyōgo Prefecture.

Already we can see his deviation from the discipline of economics and his inclination towards theatre and performance.

Kidlat returned to his alma mater for a brief period as a research fellow in the IEDR (Institute for Economic Development Research), before securing a position with the OECD in Paris, where he published comparative studies on fertilizer distribution systems in Third World countries. (Later, Kidlat realized his monographs on the supply of chemical fertilizers were used in the first global popularization of genetically modified hybrid rice varieties – known today as the Green Revolution. He regretted this by tearing up his Wharton diploma – a step to becoming an artist.) During his time as president of the student association at the Wharton School, Kidlat became friends with a quiet man from France. This friend was from an aristocratic family that owned a chateau on the outskirts of Paris and he introduced Kidlat to the high society of the French aristocracy, where he passed his days in Paris happily in the cocktail circuit of this glamorous world. He

Kidlat chatting with Princess Michiko as a student representative during an official welcome at the University of the Philippines (standing on Princess Michiko's left). (January 1961, photo: Kidlat)

had a splendid record that followed the seamless life course of which many Filipinos dream.

However, Kidlat began to feel that his elite and luxurious lifestyle was merely an affectation and that he was suppressing the 'true self' that lay within. When he began working at the OECD in December 1968, the general strike in France and widespread protests by workers, students and citizens against de Gaulle, known as *Les Evenements de Mai '68*, had just begun to subside. It had been a year in which protests raised fundamental questions about existing authorities and power structures. Arriving in Paris nearly six months after the general strike, he found a strange atmosphere in which the reverberations of the uprising continued to waft through the air amid a feeling of despondency and emptiness. Perhaps this prepared the way for him to question his elite lifestyle as an international official, reject it and transform himself.

On one occasion, Kidlat told me about an experience he had soon after arriving in Paris, when he encountered a violent confrontation in the streets during a May 1st Labor Day demonstration between students and workers and the riot police. As he photographed the melee on the streets, he framed his lens on the balcony above the riot as a bourgeois woman wrapped in her white gown, like an elegant Madonna, gazed down nonchalantly on the streets below. She displayed not a hint of either curiosity or fear. He was struck by the way this scene vividly displayed the distance between the class of the rich up in the sky and the students and workers being kicked by the riot police in the streets below and the real contradictions that existed between them. He found the contrast dramatic and hurriedly stepped back to reframe his photograph. Suddenly he was struck hard from behind the neck by a gorilla-sized policeman's truncheon and fell to the ground. He was taken directly to the police van, where the small lieutenant slowly exposed his film to the sunlight. Kidlat saw his master shot of the aristocratic woman in a white gown fading into an infinite sea of whiteness. The destroyed film was draped around his neck like a dog collar while he was subjected to harsh interrogation. He suddenly understood to which side his black-haired dark-skinned body belonged, despite having an MBA from an American university and a position at the OECD.

On another occasion in 1970 he performed in the play *Gallows Humor* with the OECD's amateur theatre group. As the only Asian, he could not be cast in a 'normal' white male role. Instead, he was cast by the director to play a special visitor in the prison cell of the man condemned to be hanged.

Kidlat the brown-skinned economist could play the role of Death – provided his face was painted death-white. As an actor, he rendered his lines with artistic flair. This aroused a deep feeling of cultural contradiction – feeling an acute sense of alienation and displacement in the white man's world of the OECD. When he was painted with thick white make-up in order to cover or negate the dark color of his face and body, he felt suffocated and oppressed. His mind was awhirl. In order to refresh himself, he took two months off in the summer and worked on a farm in Norway, where he passed his time pitching hay in the morning and typing a theater play in the afternoon.

By 1972 the discomfort of his life as an international bureaucrat led Kidlat to tear up his MBA, give away his tailor-made haute couture suits to his friends working in the kitchen of a Philippine restaurant, and resign from his economic consultant job. He began to re-word the acronym 'MBA' – that glaring testament to his successful life that guaranteed a stable future. Instead, he naughtily played with new meanings for MBA such as *Mababangong Bangugot ng America* (Perfumed Nightmare of America), or *Mababangong Bangugot ng Aliw-Wood* (Perfumed Nightmare of Holly/ Pleasure wood)[11] or McKinley's Benevolent Assimilation. The MBA was proof of the way his self had formed through the American-style English-language education he had received and to which he had over-adapted. Each of these alternative readings makes the acronym a symbolic reminder that not only he, but the Philippines as a whole, has been subjected to American colonial rule and continues to submit to American cultural hegemony.

Tearing up his diploma (the burning of his bridges) is an easy thing. But to survive during his transition from economist to artist required a sabbatical period to fine-tune his play. This would have to be financially supported by a quick windfall. Kidlat saw the opportunity by selling official souvenirs to the 1972 Olympic Games as his bridge to freedom. In the lead up to the 1972 Munich Olympics, Kidlat expected to make a profit of US$4,000–5,000 via a final MBA venture exporting 25,000 Olympic mascot souvenirs. The Olympic Committee approved his cute mascot Waldi (a nickname for a dachshund) made from translucent shells (used for old windows before glass become available) fished out from the Province of Capiz in the Philippines. However, the infamous typhoon

---

11 This word is a neologism made by combining the first part of the word 'Hollywood' with the similarly pronounced Filipino word '*aliw*' (amusement, enjoyment).

Gloria that battered the Philippines with rain for forty days delayed his shipment from leaving port and it did not arrive in time for the Olympic opening ceremony. Furthermore, when a terrorist attack targeting Israeli athletes was launched during the games by extremist elements of the Black September organization, the celebratory mood quickly evaporated. The well-selling Capiz shell mascots faced a depressed market in the second half of the games. Re-orders for the Waldis were cancelled. This left 8,000 of his 25,000 mascots unsold. The dream of instant profits from the two ventures and dedicating himself to finishing his play in seclusion at the farm in Norway came to naught. He felt a sense of déjà vu, as if the Shakespearean episode concerning Bassanio he had cited in his master's dissertation had come to life.

In desperation he loaded the thousands of remaining Waldi souvenirs into the jeepney he had imported with them from the Philippines and began a nomadic life, selling the mascots on streets from Paris to Rome, Oslo, Stockholm, London and Cannes. His MBA proved to be no help at all in selling the souvenirs after the frenzy of the Olympics was over. Returning to Paris, he spread out an Ifugao handmade cotton blanket on the street next to the Sorbonne. A former OECD colleague found him there wearing an Aztec poncho and selling the Waldis. He helped Kidlat sell the remaining Waldis at a Christmas charity sale alongside the usual Oxfam (an NGO based in the United Kingdom) Christmas cards. Thanks to this colleague, he was somehow able to offload most of the mascots and pay back his debts. Straight after the Olympic fiasco, in the autumn of 1972, Kidlat was so bankrupt he could not afford his apartment in Munich. He moved to an art commune, where he met Katrin Mueller, an art student from Munich, and they married five years later. (In *Perfumed Nightmare* there is a scene in which a pregnant Katrin becomes intimate with Kidlat, accompanied by the humorous explanation, 'Oh funny, the baby looked a little bit like me.') They joined a vegetarian artists' commune and, other than when they were traveling, made it their home.

'Unlearning' to decolonize the soul

Kidlat believes that this long journey, in which he lived as a jeepney driver-cum-street seller, awakened the *Bathala na Duwende*, that playful, creative *espirit* inside him, and it started to assert the local storyteller's voice in him. A direct translation of *Bathala na* refers to a Filipino proactive optimism when confronted with a risky situation. It means 'Let it be – as Bathala (God) wills it to be'. Or leave it to the cosmos (similar to 'Trust the Force' in *Star Wars*). The *Duwende* is an inner spirit that energizes us, our playful soul energy that trusts in a benevolent cosmos. Kidlat often uses this cultural strength of Filipinos interchangeably with '*indio*-genius *dwende*'. According to Kidlat, Filipinos who are unschooled all have such a creative spirit inside them, until over-Westernized rationality kills this intuitive strength. The term *indio*-genius is a neologism made by combining the terms 'indio' and 'genius' (to sound like indigenous). This is not just wordplay but a tactical move to show that the word 'indigenous' contains the idea of the 'indio' as genius.

The over-educated Kidlat needed to undergo a process of intentional unlearning, a conscious attempt to liberate the in-dwelling gnome or soul within that he had inadvertently suppressed. It was therefore essential to choose to live a lifestyle that was the exact opposite in every respect to the over-efficient, high-paced life he lived while on the elite course. This meant putting in perspective, dissimilating and rejecting the sensibilities and modes of thought that he had gladly assimilated through his education and development but which were preventing him from feeling or thinking in any other way – then, through a process of unlearning, to acquire a new sensibility and way of thinking to create a new self.

In general, when the term *Bathala na* (fatalistic attitude towards life, with connotations of 'whatever happens, happens') is emphasized as an important value in the Philippines, it carries with it a negative connotation. *Bathala na* is understood to mean an approach to life that is based on a realization of one's own powerlessness and therefore resignation. An alternative understanding is that it means trusting one's fate to heaven and throwing oneself into the fray, come what may.[12] However, according

---

12 For example, Nakagawa (1986: 70) gives a fairly typical explanation of *Bathala na*: 'one of the reasons given for saying that Filipinos are easygoing is the attitude known as *Bathala na*. It is an expression of fatalistic resignation, that whatever happens it does not matter.' In other words:
>grit. Sink or swim. The word *Bathala* means responsibility and na means already or no longer. In other words, come what may, never mind. It is a word that shows the fairly infamous attitude of the Filipinos. It relates to fatalism and desperation but some claim a positive meaning for it as an expression of bravery. (Nakagawa 1986: 66)

Virgilio Enriquez, whose work in establishing a new psychology of liberation I explain later in this chapter, criticized head-on these Western-style explanations

to Kidlat, this attitude is the result of the feeling of powerlessness that originates with being forced to serve foreign masters under colonialism. This experience distorted and diminished the original meaning of *Bathala na*, which is optimistic and positive. *Bathala na* was originally a forward-looking maxim that encouraged living to the fullest, just as a child who depends completely on the maternal love that keeps it safe is able to live with absolute faith in the power of life. In other words, it is a primordial value or power that makes it possible to face whatever life throws up with the maximum of improvisation and creativity based on a feeling of being held by divine grace. This allows one to maintain a feeling of humility and complete faith in divine providence.

The indigenous highlanders who, until recently, did not receive higher education (which Kidlat believes causes Filipinos to submit to colonial rule) still possess the ingenuity and creativity of the original *Bathala na*. However, even in those who have been educated, *Bathala na* has not been completely obliterated. Without realizing it, all Filipinos have it living within them. For the elites, whose bodies and sensibilities have been cast in the Western mold through colonialist education, they must first destroy the framework or cage in which they are imprisoned if they are to return to their true Filipino selves. Kidlat says that, for him, the trip he made around Europe to sell the mass of remaining Waldi mascots on the street provided him with this experience of unlearning. It might therefore be called a rite of passage for his rebirth.

Liberating and reconstructing the true self

It is not Kidlat's forceful documentation and critique in his writings and films of the residue and scars of the colonial past that I find so interesting. Rather, what drew me to him was his praxis, his concrete attempt to remake himself as a true Filipino in body and spirit based on his acute awareness that this history is part of his flesh and blood. It is

---

of *Bathala na*. He rejected this understanding of *Bathala na*, with its nuance of the escapism of an uneducated people or of accepting fate due to one's powerlessness. Instead, he argued strongly for an understanding of *Bathala na* as a form of backbone or fighting spirit that involves putting one's faith in the power of divine protection in the face of danger and looking forward boldly, even where the future is uncertain and unknown. For an overview of Enriquez's (1989, 1992) work and a reconsideration of Filipino values, see note 17 in this chapter.

in this attempt that he performs consciously, both in the public and in the private sphere, by connecting his private introspection in the pursuit of Filipino identity with his public cultural practice of representing his own Filipino-ness symbolically through film and installation works and expressing it through his theatrical performances. He does so in a manner that makes them difficult to separate his *real* life and his *reel* life.

Unlike many other anti-American intellectuals and artists, he never separates his public activity as an expressive artist from his own private life. Indeed, his private life is perhaps the more important of the two and he declares that before he is a filmmaker or any other role, he is a *tatay* (father) to his three sons.[13] This does not mean that he conceals his private life but, rather, the reverse. He records the little episodes of his family and

---

13 The film director Imaizumi Kōji, who assisted Kidlat with the final editing of *Why is Yellow at the Middle of the Rainbow?* in January 1993, described the Filipino director's personal life based on his own close observations as follows.

His wife Katrin lives in Manila where she is devoting all of her energies to her doctoral thesis on Filipino indigenous psychology... In the morning Kidlat does tai chi with his third son Kabunian. After giving him breakfast, he takes him to childcare. Then he goes to meetings of the parent–teacher association for his second and third sons, meetings for the cultural festival, meetings of the Art Guild, meetings of the neighbourhood association and assemblies calling for peace negotiations with the anti-government militias. He meets with visitors from Manila or abroad, conducts screenings of his films, takes a sick friend to hospital in Manila or goes to meet his homesick second son, a journey that takes three hours. Once a week he gives a lecture at the University of the Philippines in Manila and from time to time he asks his students to come to Baguio for residential workshops. He accepts requests to write articles and on top of all of this if he cannot send a fax due to the daily four-hour blackouts he makes international phone calls. At night he gives Kabunian his dinner and puts him to bed. After all this, I just couldn't mention 'film editing' to the tired and unfocussed Kidlat. When I look at his daily life like this, I realize that everyday life means having so many things to do...His films are a product of this way of life. (Imaizumi 1994: 19–20)

Kidlat's three sons' names all take the first letter of his wife Katrin's name, Kidlat (lightning), Kawayan (bamboo) and Kabunian (the name of an Ifugao god). The KKK that comes from lining up the first letter of the names is an acronym for the revolutionary secret society that led the Philippine Revolution at the end of the nineteenth century, the Kataastaasan Kagalanggalang Katipunan ng mga Anak ng Bayan. The names contain the poignant feeling of Kidlat's contemporary search for the decolonization of the soul. His three sons, unlike many Filipino

friends' daily lives with his video camera as if he was jotting in a notebook or journal. In doing so he looks like a beginner who has got hold of a video camera for the first time and is fascinated with recording anything and everything. He takes a relaxed approach to filming, recording whatever takes his interest at that moment and then putting it aside. Then, when he is making a film on a particular theme, he edits the film by selecting frames that have meaning within a particular sequence.

To facilitate this, he carries his video camera with him wherever he goes in a carryall that hangs from his shoulders. Whenever he attends small functions or events, he sports the secondhand 16-millimeter Bolex that was his favorite camera for more than twenty years. In 1995, the last film labs closed and it became difficult to obtain film for this camera and develop it locally. Since then he has used a Sony digital video camera and has edited the film with a Macintosh computer and tech-support from his eldest son Kidlat Sr., a media artist. The incidental events of everyday life are potential material for his cinematic expression. This means that in his everyday life – that is, aspects of his private life he is subconsciously expressing himself semi-performatively on the understanding that these moments may eventually be incorporated into his cinematic work and be noticed by his audience. Kidlat is his own cameraman but he often passes the camera to a friend or to one of his sons and thereby becomes simultaneously the recorded and the performer. In the same way, his sons are major characters in his documentaries and, as a result of being filmed, have come to be half-conscious performers.[14]

---

    upper- and middle-class children who study in the United States or Europe, all live and study in the Philippines.
14 This is one reason that such great kindness and warmth underlies all his films. He has a great love of film and by expressing himself through the medium of film, the great symbol of modern cultural production, he shows that he is not necessarily entirely opposed to modernity. In *Perfumed Nightmare* and *Turumba*, which have both been portrayed as critiques of modernity, the tone is warm and gentle. While looking at modernity critically with eyes wide open and portraying it with a feeling of loss for the halcyon days of a world that has been/is being lost, he never attributes blame. This might be a result of his boundless conviction that the knowledge and sensibilities that are the roots of his Filipino identity have not been erased but merely covered over.

Top: Kidlat dancing at a wedding of Orland Mahiwo in Abatan, Hungduan. His wife, Katrin, records the scene.
Bottom: Kabunian joins his father in the dance. (March 14, 2004)

This style of combining everyday life and filmmaking bore fruit as the wonderful film, *Why is Yellow at the Middle of the Rainbow?* For example, in the second scene of the film, Kidlat's five-year-old son (Kidlat Sr.) says, 'My father is afraid the next typhoon might bring our house down. Hopefully we go down in slow motion...that may even be fun.' Although he is a child, he has already developed an internalized cinematic sense. In other words, for him 'the world manifests in segments as in film' (Hara 1994: 8). Furthermore, this opening scene responds to a message in *Perfumed Nightmare*, 'When the typhoon blows off its cocoon, the butterfly embraces the sun.' At the same time, it hints at the way his sons' development and the future of the Philippines will constitute the story of this three-hour film. The story unfolds with major upheavals during and after Marcos's administration, including the assassination of Senator Benigno Aquino (1983), which signaled the beginning of the end of President Marcos's developmentalist dictatorship; the People Power Revolution (1986), which saw the senator's wife, Corazon Aquino, assume the presidency; the numerous military coups that tried to topple the female president (1986–89); plus natural catastrophes like the Baguio earthquake of 1990 and the eruption of Mount Pinatubo, the largest eruption in the twentieth century (1991). In this sense, *Why is Yellow at the Middle of the Rainbow?* is a length of tapestry woven from the warp of family life and the weft of social upheaval. Furthermore, while Kidlat weaves each stage, he re-edits the film, adding new scenes to the base of his older works as the children grow and society changes. The vivid works that result are an experimental attempt to transform his earlier work and allow it to replicate autonomously, based on his reinterpretation of Philippine society.[15]

Because the appearance of his family's daily life is performed and constructed in this way, Kidlat deliberately tries to downplay any cultural Westernization in his regular life in order to affirm and strengthen his identity as a Filipino. For example, he does not drink Coca Cola or eat McDonald's. He does not wear fashionable clothes such as suits or jeans that restrict the body. He usually wears baggy work pants purchased in Japan that are worn by construction workers there, as well as steeplejacks

---

15 Kidlat showed the 1989, 1991 and 1993 versions of *Why is Yellow at the Middle of the Rainbow?* at the first and third biennial Yamagata International Documentary Film Festival.

and T-shirts. If it is cold he favors the warm clothes he purchased in Kathmandu. He does not cut his hair and wears it long, down to his waist.[16] He does not carry a mobile phone or wear a wristwatch and does not worry about keeping time. He does not concern himself with making elaborate plans and preparations or sticking to strict timetables. He does not celebrate Christmas Day with gifts and instead gives his children a Happy Rizal Day present five days later on December 30. José Rizal is a Filipino national hero who was sentenced to execution by firing squad for treason on that day in 1898, at the end of the Spanish colonial period. It is a public holiday in the Philippines. He refers to his own birthdays as 'Orbit Days'. In other ways, too, he makes a habit of deliberately breaking with the common sense and conventions of mainstream Philippine society (de Guia 1997: vol. 2, 25).

Orbit Day celebrates one revolution of the earth around the sun over the course of 365 days and its return to the place it occupied in the cosmos on the day of his birth. This also reaffirms the fact that it is the rotation of the earth on its axis and its revolution around the sun that separates night from day and gives us the change of seasons. It reminds us that our own lives are connected to and influenced by the movement of the earth within the cosmos. To anchor himself with the movement of the universe, or what he calls the cosmic vibrations, and live in harmony with it is his philosophy of life. For Kidlat, the universe is the fountainhead from which we can obtain deeper meaning and value in our lives and thereby reawaken from the nightmare emanating from over-modernization and commercialism. It is the indigenous peoples who pay the greatest attention to the movement of the cosmos and live their lives in sympathy with it.

These habits are a conscious defense against the insidious assimilation to the incorporation of the sense of taste, of beauty, and of time, space and the body and of the disciplining and structuring of consciousness in accordance with European and, particularly, American values. They are also a means of rejecting those values and a form of resistance to them. By means of these defensive strategies, he maintains that it is possible to liberate the self from the invisible fetters induced by the imprinting of education and the mass

---

16 However, after becoming a monk at a temple in Kathmandu in Nepal in February 1998, he kept his head shaved for some years. After that he began growing his hair out once again.

media, thereby escaping the echo-chamber of colonial thought, creating one's true self anew, as a Filipino. At the same time, his consciousness of the importance of theatre and performance demonstrates his connection with mainstream Filipino middle- and upper-class cultural traditions.

An indigenous way of life

In looking to the culture of the indigenous people of the northern mountains for examples and hints to help him 'smash the outer shell' (cocoon) of his identity as a subject of cultural colonization and liberate his true self (the *indio*-genius *dwende*), his approach is inspired by that of Dr Virgilio Enriquez (1942–1994), who challenged the Western psychology methodologies applied to Filipinos. Enriquez was a professor in the Psychology Department in the College of Social Science and Philosophy of the University of the Philippines. Known as the 'Father of Filipino Indigenous Psychology', Enriquez had already severely criticized the approach to Filipino society and Filipino psychology that was imported from the United States in the 1970s. In its place he advocated for the establishment of a new psychology and social science that would deepen Filipino self-understanding. Instead of using English-language textbooks (previously, textbooks imported from the United States had been used unchanged) and English-language academic terminology to analyze the Filipino psyche, as was then common, he used the Filipino language to refine his concepts and perform his analysis. Where possible, he also published his essays and textbooks in the native language.

Enriquez advocated for and developed a *Sikolohiyang Pilipino* (Filipino Psychology) that aimed to decolonize the psyche. He aimed for the Filipino creation of a psychology that would awaken and liberate Filipinos. Unlike existing psychology that sought to forcibly apply theories and terminologies forged within Western culture to Filipinos, he analyzed the language used by ordinary people and by developing insights into the meaning-world they created through their use of this language, he tried to understand the psychology of the people as a whole. Enriquez called the explicit use of this methodology of returning to the people and adopting an indigenous orientation 'Indigenous Psychology'. The people whom he considered to be indigenous were the majority Filipino lowland Christians, particularly commoners, such as peasants and the urban poor, who had not received a higher education.

Enriquez stated that the purpose of the movement for a Filipino Psychology was, first, to refuse and to resist any psychology that rigidified the colonial mindset of Filipinos; second, to oppose the industrial psychology that was developed in the advanced industrial societies and therefore only adapted to the conditions of those societies and, instead, to develop a psychology of everyday life; and, finally, to refuse an elite-oriented psychology that exploited the masses and to aim for a psychology of liberation. He called on individual researchers to immerse themselves among the people, to live in their villages and to work among them (Enriquez 1992: 26–7).[17] Enriquez's aspiration and the movement he founded continues to this day as the *Pambansang Samahan sa Sikolohiya* (National Association of Psychology), where the research program he began continues to develop and become more and more sophisticated.

Like Kidlat, Enriquez had studied in the United States. In 1966 he entered the graduate school of Northwestern University after receiving a scholarship from the Rockefeller Foundation and he received his doctorate in 1971. Upon returning to the Philippines, he took a teaching position in the Psychology Department of the University of the Philippines and began to focus on the study of the Filipino language. In 1982 he received

---

17 In *From Colonial to Liberation Psychology*, Enriquez (1992) criticized the analysis of the 'Filipino personality' and Filipino values in the writings of Frank Lynch and other non-Filipino researchers writing in English. These writers stressed the importance of the 'triangle of *hiya*' (shame), *utang no loob* (gratitude) and *pakikisama* (concession) to support their contention about the importance of smooth interpersonal relations to Filipinos. He argued that this analysis, which was promoted by colonial social science, was mistaken and that these were just one category of values and ought to be grouped together as 'accommodative values'.

He argued that there was another category of 'confrontative values' that included *Bathala na* (decisiveness), *Lakas ng Loob* (power, indignation/guts) and *Pakikibaka* (clash), which were the opposite of the accommodative values. Enriquez therefore denounced the America-oriented scholars who over-emphasized accommodative values and either deprecated or ignored the other values, thereby helping to create an image of the Filipino that was, at worst, obsequious and, at best, cheerful, sociable and hospitable (Enriquez 1992: 64–5).

For a detailed account of Enriquez's 'liberation psychology' and the Filipino psychology movement, see Shimizu (1998b: 176–83). Kidlat's wife, Katrin de Guia, who wrote a doctoral thesis on six Filipino artists, including Kidlat, that pondered the origins of their creative practice, also received advice and inspiration from Enriquez, who was her doctoral supervisor until his death.

a second doctorate from the Filipino language department of the same university. Enriquez was born and raised in the city of Bocaue in Bulacan Province, which borders Metro Manila to the north. As Tagalog was his mother tongue, he spoke Filipino in a soothing tone that was easy on the ear. However, he studied the language in order to deepen his understanding of it, to gain insight into the depth of its inner world and to expand its potential as a mode of expression.[18] In studying the Filipino language in order to unlearn American-style psychology, he was motivated by almost the same aspirations as Kidlat when he apprenticed himself to Nauyac in order to learn about the Ifugao culture and worldview.

Kidlat's wife motivated Kidlat's awareness of Enriquez's revolutionary research. She studied in the psychology department at the University of the Philippines and under Enriquez's supervision she obtained her doctorate. Her dissertation, 'Filipino artists as culture bearers' (de Guia 1997) was published in a revised form as *Kapwa, the Self in the Other: World Views and Lifestyles of Filipino Cultural-Bearers* (de Guia 2005). In the book she searches for the source of the creative inspiration of six Filipino artists. In her consideration of Kidlat's work, she combines her attached insider-view as his partner with the objective detachment of a researcher.

For both Enriquez and Kidlat, the awareness of and aspiration towards indigenousness is the first step towards achieving the cultural liberation, first, of the self and then of society and the nation. However, the concrete image of the indigenous in Enriquez's mind was the people who live in his hometown of Bocaue – in particular, the peasants who live in the nearby agricultural villages. He built a psychological field station in one of those villages, where he trained his students and carried out his research. If we were to sum up the essence of the Filipino psychology Enriquez aspires to in a single keyword, it would be 'indigenous'. He includes in this term the lowland Christians who make up 90 percent of the total population, the majority of Philippine society.

However, while the term 'indigenous' in Enriquez's books *Indigenous Psychology and National Consciousness* (1989) and *Indigenous Psychology*

---

18 Filipino is the national language of the Philippines. The main body of the language is made up of Tagalog, which is spoken in Manila and Central Luzon, combined with words of foreign origin and neologisms. The constitution contains the aspiration that the language 'shall be further developed and enriched'. The relationship between Tagalog and Filipino can be compared with the relationship between the language spoken in Tokyo and its environs and standard Japanese.

(1990) refers to the lowland Christians, for Kidlat it is the highlanders (such as the Ifugaos) who have retained their unique culture and are therefore the true indigenous. Like Enriquez, Kidlat is a member of the majority lowland society but he believes that an unwavering indigenousness is latent within him. He is convinced that because it is merely covered over by the brainwashing induced by his submission to an English-language education, if his inner self can break out of the invisible cocoon-like shell that is gently wrapped around it, then he can restore his true indigenousness.

When the Philippine Congress enacted the Indigenous Peoples' Rights Act of 1997, the entitlement to land rights and other rights stems not from precedence, in the sense of having lived in a place the longest, but from the idea of an indigenous people's having lived in a place continuously since 'time immemorial'.[19] As Kubota and Nobayashi (in Kubota 2009: 12) point out, in various contexts throughout the world, the small number of people who proclaim themselves to be indigenous share a common understanding that they 'possess an original and indigenous culture and a way of life that has been there from the very start'. This observation is unexceptional in the case of the Philippines and of the Ifugaos. However, in Japan the term 'indigenous people' has been translated as *senjūmin* and this is the term that has entered common use. The Ainu people of Hokkaido are said to be a representative example of *senjūmin*. The term is a compound based on the word *senjū*, which has a strong nuance of 'the people who settled here first'. It implies an understanding of indigenousness based on having settled in a place before any other group.

The groups who are based in Hapao and the other Ifugao villages and towns typically emphasize their indigenousness as the foundation of their cultural activities and their political and social movements, and in their petitions and claims for rights. Advocacy NGO groups in Manila and Baguio that work for indigenous peoples often hold seminars intended to strengthen indigenous consciousness. The staff of these groups not only come to

---

19 This is followed by the phrase, 'on account of their descent from the populations which inhabited the country, at the time of conquest or colonization, or at the time of inroads of non-indigenous religions and cultures'. Taken literally, this means that the lowland Christians who make up the vast majority of the population and were forcibly converted during Spanish colonization can also be considered to be indigenous. However, the majority lowland Christians are not included among the indigenous peoples, neither in legal terms nor in terms of actual usage or policy.

Banaue, but also about once or twice a year to Hapao, in order to hold oneday seminars. During these seminars and in their own self-consciousness, Ifugaos rarely think about their indigenousness in terms of a comparison between themselves and other ethnic groups and about 'who was here first'. Instead, it is the tangible heritage of the rice terraces that stretch out in front of their eyes that gives them a very strong sense of being connected directly to the ancestors who built them, a notion of indigenousness that goes back to the mythical beginning of time. The people of Ifugao, at least for the duration of the Spanish colonial period, were not conquered by any external governing authority. Nor have they lost their land to any other ethnic group that came afterwards. They are proud of having fought boldly against Spain and hung onto their land tenaciously. In the case of the American colonization, they were not defeated militarily but gave up their weapons and submitted to having their territory incorporated in response to friendly persuasion and a policy of appeasement. They believe that they have continued to hang on to their land, particularly to the rice terraces and forests that provide the basis for their way of life.

Therefore, for Nauyac and for the other villagers, their sense of indigenousness is not one of precedence over a conquering ruler or some other people who usurped their land. Rather, it is a palpable sense of the direct connection between themselves, living in the present, and the ancestors, who built the rice terraces immemorially long ago. The rice terraces that form the backdrop to their daily lives are the intermediary that serves to validate that connection in a physical form. It was Lopez Nauyac's awareness of and advocacy for his own indigenousness (Kidlat calls him the 'philosopher of the forest') that came to serve as a guide for Kidlat Tahimik, a member of lowland Filipino society's super-elite, in his struggle to reconstruct himself as a true Filipino. The foundation of Nauyac's indigenousness is not in proclaiming that his people settled here first, but in his love for the place where he was born and his devotion to local culture. This is what Kidlat responds to and from which he derives inspiration. This is what resonates with Kidlat's conviction that he, too, can be indigenous.

The *senjūmin* movements of the past half century have mainly been led by the children and grandchildren of indigenous people in the United States, New Zealand, Australia and Latin America who were forced off their homelands, massacred and deprived of their lands (or defrauded of them by means of treaties) by immigrants from Europe. These countries are known as settler societies in that the colonists who came later now make up the

Left: Kidlat giving a welcome speech at the opening ceremony of the Third *Kapwa* Conference 'The Knowledge of Indigenous People in the Academe', an event he and his wife Katrin organized almost single-handedly. On his left sits Native American leader Dennis Banks (one of the indigenous leaders at the Wounded Knee occupation in 1973). Nauyac's face can be seen in the background between Kidlat and Dennis. (June 27, 2012, photo: Himaru Yoshihiko)

Right: Kidlat dancing at the closing celebration. (June 30, 2012)

Top: Press conference following the opening ceremony. On Kidlat's right are Nauyac, Dennis Banks and Ainu leader Kayano Shirō. (June 27, 2012, photo: Himaru Yoshihiko)

Bottom: Kidlat making a speech at the closing ceremony. On his right is the face of the *monbaki* Teofilo Gano from Hapao. (July 1, 2012)

vast majority. For movements that seek the restoration of land rights in this context, the sense of having come before (*senjū*) that is implied by the term 'indigenous' is an important one. It is appropriate in such cases to translate the term into Japanese as *senjūmin*. Furthermore, most 'indigenous' movements have developed from the demand for rights to land and resources and for the respect and social position that is their due. Hall and Fenelon (2009: 139–41) argue that the struggles of Canada's First Nations and the native nations in the United States are over sovereignty; those of the Mexican Zapatistas and the Miskito of Nicaragua, the Kurds of Iraq and the Aymara of Bolivia are for autonomy; while those of the Adivasi peoples of India, most of the *pueblos indigenas* of Latin America and the Zulu of South Africa are for minority group status.[20]

In the Philippines, 330 years of Spanish colonial rule and fifty years of American colonial rule did not result in colonists from the West becoming a majority. In terms of language, while a small number of elites became conversant in Spanish and English, the majority of the people continued to use the language of their region or ethnic group. In March 1998 there was a referendum on whether to create a Cordillera autonomous region that would include the six provinces and Baguio City of northern Luzon, where indigenous people make up more than half the population (Abra, Apayao, Benguet, Ifugao, Kalinga, and Mountain Province), but it failed by a large majority. Only in Apayao Province did the votes in favor of the proposal

---

20 According to Shimizu Akitoshi (2008b), the Declaration on the Rights of Indigenous Peoples that was adopted by the General Assembly of the United Nations in 2007 is an innovative document for anthropology and the concept of 'indigenous peoples' is one to which the discipline must pay particular attention. This is because the declaration defines indigenous peoples as a people in international law. In other words, it defines them as collective subjects with the right to self-determination and recognizes them as 'ideally, having sovereignty equivalent to that of the nation-state in which they currently reside.' In the vocabulary of states, the people who were previously referred to as native(s), aborigine(s) or indigene(s) were seen as having to be 'assimilated' or 'integrated' for the sake of 'progress'. In practice, they became objects of 'ethnic and cultural extermination'. The recognition of these people (or of their children and grandchildren) as a 'people' in a legal sense 'contains elements that might destroy the structure of states that were built on the exclusion of indigenous people'. In other words, the designation of 'indigenous people' as equal sovereign subjects existing within states could constitute a major challenge to the foundations of the existence of the state.

outnumber those against. This suggests that it is by no means certain that what the indigenous people who live in the highlands are seeking is political autonomy.

Traveling film, or strategic naive film as cultural critique

Returning once again to Kidlat, by adopting *Bathala na* as a basic position for his way of life and his filmmaking, he consciously prioritizes the liberation of the *indio*-genius *dwende* that lies dormant within. This is why his filmmaking is almost entirely unscripted and proceeds by improvising whatever is taking place in that moment. In his later works he has done away with a screenplay entirely. Kidlat has a broad beginning, middle and end of his storyline – not a detailed script, as required in commercial filmmaking. He simply turns his camera on anything in his daily life that he finds interesting. He cannot foresee in that moment the kind of film that the scene will fit into. However, these individual scenes, which he shoots whenever something strikes his interest, eventually come together as a complete work. Even though they are a mishmash of unrelated miscellaneous episodes, he edits them into meaningful sequences by choosing scenes that share organic connection based around a particular theme or group of themes welded together by a focused narration track. Kidlat has faith that by enjoying to the full the occasional events and happenings that occur along his path towards a better future and the liberation and reconstruction of his self, the footage he records will eventually reach provisional completion as a single film. The sequences are often discontinuous, but his technique makes the best of this by allowing discontinuity to stimulate the poetic imagination, which ultimately leads to the expression of a rich content. The stories do not necessarily develop in chronological time. Instead, by moving freely and easily across space and time the audience can come along with him to enjoy the leaps and bounds of a creativity and expansive freedom that is unbounded by the real world.

Kidlat's attitude to film production is to place complete faith in the philosophy of *Bathala na* and of the power of the cosmos to arrange the world such that it will assume a desirable form. He declares:

> The co-director in my films is the cosmos. I don't work alone, I work together with the cosmos. Whatever this means for people, for me it means '*BAHALA NA*' – Leave it to the cosmos…*Bahala na* is an ancient pre-Filipino gift. To

me, it means you put your best energies, your best inputs (intelligence, sweat, muscle power), your best heart, into any endeavor (*Todo Bigay*). The rest you resign to the Cosmic Will. (de Guia 1997: vol. 2, 59)

He explains his editing process as follows.

The way I make my films is like collecting images; it's like making a stained glass window. You collect colored…glass over years. Today I may find a broken beer bottle, tomorrow I may find a 7-UP bottle. I'll have all these in a box and may find a pattern: if I like a landscape or profile, I pursue that and I finish the film by shooting [the last sequences to fill up] any holes that are still missing in the stained glass mosaic…Maybe I'm just an accumulator of images and sounds and then I make *tagpi-tagpi* [patching up] and sew them together…I just work with images and I put my sounds on and then I put a flow of things and start juggling the sequences back and forth. I don't try to find surrealist images even in the way it happened in 'Perfumed Nightmare.' I was a madman when I was making that film and still am. I sometimes wonder how certain elements enter the film. (San Juan Jr. 2000: 272)

As I mentioned above, although Kidlat studied engineering when he first went to university, he ended up majoring in theatre (Speech and Drama). He has never received a systematic education in film. While living in the German artists' commune after quitting his job at the OECD, he learned the art of film production by apprenticing himself with film students doing their diploma films and watching friends who worked in film, such as the director Warner Herzog. He developed his own style through a process of trial and error. His debut work *Perfumed Nightmare* (1977) won the International Federation of Film Critics Award at the Berlin International Film Festival that year. It also received enthusiastic praise from Francis Ford Coppola and, thanks to his support, gained worldwide distribution.[21]

---

21 When Kidlat made *Perfumed Nightmare*, he had never seen a film directed by Coppola. He first met him at the Cannes Film Festival in 1983. Until that point, the two of them had walked completely opposite paths as filmmakers (Coppola directed big-budget Hollywood blockbusters, Kidlat self-produced *Perfumed Nightmare* with a tiny budget of US$10,000) but their paths did cross in an unexpected way. Pagsanjan, where Coppola shot *Apocalypse Now* (1979, production cost US$310 million), is less than 100 kilometers from Balian, where Kidlat shot *Perfumed Nightmare*. Furthermore, the people of the independent

Apart from screenings at university seminars and the like, Kidlat has few opportunities to show his films in the Philippines and they are more frequently screened abroad.[22]

Kidlat with Nauyac in his editing studio, located in a building owned by his mother on Session Road in the center of Baguio. (March 14, 1998)

    kingdom that Colonel Kurtz creates in the film in the jungles of Vietnam were played by 150 Ifugao extras (Coppola 1995).
22 His films are rarely seen in the Philippines. On the rare occasion when they are screened, the audience comprises middle- and upper-class intellectual elites (Tolentino 2001). In 1994 he received the Lifetime Achievement Award from the Film Academy of the Philippines, but his films only had two single screenings at a commercial venue in the Philippines for a general audience – the first time as part of a special program, *Pelikula at Lipunan* (Film and Society), curated by Nic de Ocampo at the SM City Mall in Manila and on a post-midnight television broadcast for the 100th Anniversary of Cinema on Channel 2, and the following year in a retrospective at the SM City Mall in Manila and on television on Channel 2. On July 22–24, 1996, a special program titled 'Kidlat, Ngayon! Memories of Overdevelopment: A Retrospective of Films by Kidlat Tahimik', in which almost

Moreover, he is not only director but producer, screenwriter, cinematographer, editor and production tasker for his films. He does all the work by himself and frequently appears as the main actor.[23] When he is performing in his films, he explains the basic scenario and frame structure to a friend and then hands over the camera. In his own words he is like the player of a Yamaha 'One Man Band Organ'. He opposes the Fordist division of labor in Hollywood film production and, as an artist, he continues to explore the potential of 'handmade' films (Tahimik 1997: 14). This method is both intentional antithesis of the Hollywood style and a product of desperation because he lacks the funds to produce films any other way and therefore has to do everything himself. In *Why is Yellow at the Middle of the Rainbow?*, his son asks innocently, 'What means Third World?' Kidlat explains to him gently, 'Third World is a way of solving problems.' His is a Third World filmmaking technique, a praxis of bricolage that uses whatever materials are available to achieve its goal.

Kidlat explains that in Hollywood filmmaking, the destination and the route of the journey are predetermined. This is 'full-tank-cum-credit-card' movie making as opposed to his 'cups-of-gas' filmmaking, in which he proceeds little by little towards an unknown destination, doing what he can on an ad hoc basis given the resources available. In other words, he does whatever is possible with the funds (or rather, the very little money) that he has at hand. Because the Hollywood approach depends on a third person for big-time funding, the funder becomes the real director (the commander-in-chief). Film production is restricted by time constraints, leading to a rush to finish by the fixed deadline. This, Kidlat says, is surrendering the movie creativity to the *time-is-money*-dictator. (He is quick to attribute the 'Time is Money' slogan to Benjamin Franklin, who founded the university where Kidlat got his MBA.) It is as if the director is wearing a straitjacket and cannot shoot the film freely. This kind of cinema production is better described not as filmmaking but as 'fillmaking'.

---

his entire existing oeuvre was shown, was held at the University of the Philippines Film Center (Yamashita 2002: 33).
23 As well as acting in the central roles in his own films and regularly appearing as interviewer or supporting actor in documentaries centered on Lopez Nauyac, Kidlat has made cameo appearances in films by other directors, such as Marilou Diaz-Abaya's *Joze Rizal* (1998) and Imaizumi Kōji's *Abon: chiisana ie* (ABONG/ Small home) (2003).

Kidlat came up with the term 'fillmaking' through a typographical error he made while preparing for a 1987 writer's conference on World Narratives for filmmakers and writers at Duke University. He was invited as one of three filmmakers to expound on film as the contemporary narrative. He was instructed to submit a manuscript suitable for publication in order to receive the funding. Usually at conferences he speaks from the heart, without reading from a prepared script. While rushing to type the paper, he made a typographical error, misspelling the word 'fill' for 'film', therefore referring to Hollywood fillmaking. He interpreted this as a cosmic error – a kind of revelation that appropriately expressed the reality of commercial movies on the assembly line (just to *fill* up the grocery shelves). He therefore used it in the title of his paper, 'Cups-of-gas filmmaking vs. full tank-cum-credit-card fillmaking' (Tahimik 1986). He has used it ever since as a keyword when criticizing the film industry (Tahimik 1987: 1–4, 1997: 15, 37–8).

In *Perfumed Nightmare* he plays the lead role of a jeepney driver. In *Turumba* his wife plays the role of a foreign buyer who purchases large quantities of local handicrafts, a character that symbolizes the coming of commercialism to the village. In *Why is Yellow at the Middle of the Rainbow?*, his three sons play major roles. This film is a kind of home video that documents their growing up over a period of more than ten years. In all his films, his friends and ordinary villagers appear, as well as his family. He does not use professional actors to whom he would have to pay a high fee. He also gets film suppliers to sell him their expired film stocks at a lower price.[24] He says that Hollywood cinema and the Philippine cinema that has been influenced by it are made to sell tickets to an audience that salivates (like Pavlov's dogs) from the mere smell of sex and violence. This is just 'fillmaking', mass-production on a factory assembly line in accordance with a set formula. Kidlat's filmmaking, on the other hand, is a kind of 'filmmaking as voyage' or 'traveling film'.

Perfumed Nightmare was a 'traveling film' in two senses. The film's hero, the rustic jeepney driver played by Kidlat, is an admirer of Wernher

---

24 He also uses an old editing machine that he keeps in a room in an old building owned by his mother on Baguio's main street, Session Road. He shuts himself away there to edit his work. While he does not have a regular job, as the scion of a notable Baguio family, he is certainly not poor. He owns an apartment with a number of rooms in the UP Village residential area of Quezon City and lives off the rental income from this apartment.

von Braun, the director of NASA's space exploration program that won the race to land on the moon. He organizes the village children into a von Braun fan club, of which he is the president. He dreams that one day he too will travel to the promised land of America and become the first Filipino astronaut. However, a strange coincidence leads him to be taken to Paris by an American who made his fortune selling bubblegum vending machines. When he arrives at Charles de Gaulle Airport in Paris, he is flabbergasted by its moving walkway and captivated by the modernist beauty of the cube-like elevated corridor tunnels (which he calls bridges) that link the buildings together. However, when Kidlat befriends an old cheese-and-eggs vendor selling from her street-cart and her fellow street-vendors are evicted by the construction of an enormous supermarket, he begins to have doubts about the kind of 'progress' that is brought about by modernization. He then recognizes the desolate spectacle created by modernity's material civilization and the reality of daily life in it. His adoration turns to disillusionment and he begins to understand the cultural strengths of his forefathers and the possibilities this offers. He turns down an invitation from the American businessman to fly to the United States on a Concord (a symbol of the peak of capitalism and modernization). After he has traveled across space and time to modern France from the non-modern Philippines, the film ends with the suggestion that he should return once again to the non-modern Philippines. This is the first sense in which it is a 'traveling film'.

This plot places the film at risk of becoming a hackneyed road movie. The first half of the film is a travelogue that allows its Western audience the thrill of peeping into the exotic charm of the primitive Philippine countryside. As if to whet the appetite of a Western audience, the film includes a scene where the young men of the village are circumcised. This is a rite of passage that facilitates and acknowledges the transition from childhood to adulthood by means of an individualized initiation through a painful ritual. But it is also the turning point after which a child becomes a full member of the village community. Pavsek (2013: 114) notes that for both Theodor Adorno (a German philosopher) and Kidlat, 'bodily pain is the result of oppression, but also the necessary, indeed utopian, reminder that oppression must be eliminated'; furthermore, 'the experience of pain has an anticipatory function as a presentiment of a future without it, and to relieve human beings of that experience is to foreclose the anticipation of that future, and for that matter possibly any future'. He thereby places the circumcision scene in relation to the more general problem of oppression in the context of contemporary critical thought.

The latter half of the film is Kidlat's European travelogue. However, there is an ever-present danger of what might be called reverse orientalism, in which the reality captured in the film will be reduced to the usual stereotypical images and thereby ultimately strengthen these stereotypes. Kidlat skillfully avoids this dilemma by shooting the film in the vein of a family movie. In souvenir photographs of family and friends, the photographer and the photographed frequently change places and later enjoy viewing the finished product together. In *Perfumed Nightmare*, too, Kidlat is on the side of the observer as director and as cameraman but at the same time he is on the side of the observed as the main actor. This is best demonstrated in a scene in which he visits a photographic studio to obtain a passport photograph for his trip to Paris. When he receives the prints from the studio, they include pictures of Kidlat pulling all kinds of faces for the camera. For the children who crowd around him, these over-the-top expressions resemble the strange faces of a coquet or of a comedian trying to attract and amuse his audience. The children roll around laughing at the finished photographs of Kidlat (in a way that appears completely natural and unremarkable). They draw on the photographs and turn his face into that of a smiling dog. One of them says to a nearby dog, 'hey, you, smile for your passport photo' and covers its mouth with his hands, forcing it into a snarling grin to great bursts of laughter. The children enjoy the scene of Kidlat playing the comedian and gather around to enjoy making jokes at his expense.

The amateur actors from the village who appear in Kidlat's films are not only portrayed through his camera – when his films are finished, they invariably become his audience, watching and critiquing them together in the village. They inevitably laugh at seeing Kidlat living/performing his daily life in their familiar village and becoming bewildered amid the exotic spectacle of Paris, and they cheer along while enjoying the films. In other words, he is conscious of the gaze of the villagers who will both perform in his films and later appreciate them as an audience. He incorporates this awareness into the content of his films.

The cozy home movie charm that permeates the entire film, the naturalism and amateurishness of the acting by the villagers-turned-actors, as well as their intimate relationship with Kidlat, are all connected to the fact that his films are underpinned by real life. The village that provides the setting for *Perfumed Nightmare* was his father's hometown in Laguna Province south of Manila. Not only does he have many relatives there, but on March 22, 1963, a memorial to Kidlat's deceased younger brother was erected in the local school yard.[25] In a desperate attempt to reduce the production costs for his film, he had little choice but to play the role of the protagonist himself, to stage the film in his home village, and to use his relatives and acquaintances among the villagers as actors. This resulted in a blurring of the lines, reversing and mingling the relationship between recording/being recorded and watching/being watched.

Kidlat's films have never been commercial films produced on the assumption that they will be shown to general audiences at cinemas in the city. His first films were aimed at Western audiences and later at Filipino university students, intellectuals and cultural practitioners and an audience in Japan. At times he has made films with international funding bodies (for example, *Banal Kahoy* (Holy Wood) (2002), which received funding from Japan Foundation) or international film festivals in mind. Nevertheless, he makes few concessions to his Western or Filipino audiences and has little patience for allowing them to gawk at an 'exotic' way of life of the Filipino villagers from their comfort zone on the outside. The reality in his images is not adapted to fit stereotypical images for easy consumption. Instead, he reproduces stereotypical images and then disrupts them by exposing them to reality. He asks his Western audiences to look at the world anew from over the shoulders of the villagers who are watching the films in which they have acted, and to align their gaze with them. He demands that they look at the life of the Filipino villagers with neither the bias and contempt nor the distance that derives from applying Western common sense and values. Similarly, he asks them to look on the streets of France and Germany from the perspective of the Filipino villagers who sympathize with Kidlat. The second sense in which Kidlat's works are 'traveling films' stems from this demand that the audience shifts its position of gaze to the Filipino perspective. It is this subtle invitation to shift from the Western to

---

25 Kidlat's younger brother died young, when his plane crashed while flying over the Indian Ocean on his way to Greece to take part in the World Jamboree representing the Boy Scouts of the Philippines. The family donated all the indemnity money offered by the airline to erect a village school named in his memory, Victor Oteyza Deguia Elementary School. Since then, Kidlat's whole family has traveled to their 'home village' on the anniversary of his brother's death to hold a memorial mass.

the Filipino, from development and modernity to stasis and non-modernity, that draws the audience in and makes his films so fascinating.[26]

This film calls on the audience to come along for the ride with its jeepney driver protagonist. Even before he goes to Paris, Kidlat-as-jeepney-driver has been making the round trip between the village (tradition) and the city (modernity) over the bridge on the outskirts of the village each day. The village is already directly connected to modernity and integrated into it. However, the film does not paint a simple opposition between the exotic, mythical, non-modern local customs of the Philippines and the West's First World modernity. After all, the protagonist is himself obsessed by his dream of space travel – an activity that incorporates all the wonders of modern science – and dubs himself the president of the von Braun fan club.

Through the medium of bricolage that makes use of the dexterity of 'traditional' handicrafts, the villagers' way of life is already under the influence of the civilization created by Western technology. While they make use of the things of this technological civilization, they practice another way into a modernity that differs from that of the West. This is symbolized by the jeepneys that serve as a form of public transport for the common people. At the end of the Second World War, large numbers of American military jeep engines and chassis were left behind. Skilled workers took these parts and rebuilt them to make the jeepney, turning the detritus of war into a form of public transport.[27] In other words, they have rearranged the modernity that

---

26 Jameson (1992: 204) admires the way Kidlat avoids the danger of falling into the style of a hackneyed travel movie:
> not by metamorphosis into the great Western spatial image (as, say, in Antonioni's notorious documentary on China), but rather by regression to some first and more primal level of the first forms of photography, the family snapshot or the home movie, the wonderment of sheer reproduction and recognition...Kidlat's aesthetic project rejoins a whole range of Western avant-garde or experimental projects in which the home movie, the non-professional, non-institutional use of the camera, symbolically becomes the Utopian escape from commercial reification.

The bricolage technique of filmmaking and the quality that Jameson recognized through his keen insight into Kidlat's debut work is developed to its fullest extent later in *Why is Yellow at the Middle of the Rainbow?*

27 Today, second-hand Japanese engines have replaced American ones and the jeepneys are put together using all kinds of salvaged parts. The chassis of a jeepney is painted with designs and artworks that express the owners' tastes and opinions and adorned with flags, statues and other ornaments. The passengers ride in the back, on long benches built on either side.

was forced upon them to create a new modernity for their own convenience and on their own terms. As a director and a cultural practitioner and as a father, Kidlat's aim is not to contrast modernity and non-modernity but, rather, having received that which has been offered (or sometimes imposed) by modernity, to adapt it by means of an improvisational and creative imagination so as to make it work for his way of life.

Naivety as political strategy

After becoming the first person to circumnavigate the globe as part of Magellan's crew, Enrique de Malacca returned to his homeland and betrayed his Spanish captors, thereby escaping from slavery and liberating himself. Similarly, Kidlat traveled from Baguio to Manila and then from Philadelphia on the east coast of the United States to Paris and Berlin before completing his own circumnavigation of the world via India, Nepal and Japan. After this he began to challenge Western hegemony and to engage in an ongoing practice of self-liberation. In the beginning, he criticized the infiltration of Western cultural and economic influence and created films rich in allegory. Later, his actual practice and performance of daily life, his recording of it first on film and later in digital, and his use of this footage as the raw material to create a finished work while locked away in his editing studio have become his ongoing political practice as an artist in the cultural arena.[28]

---

28 In order to unlearn his old self in mind and body, Kidlat keeps his distance from American values and aesthetic sensibilities, but he does not completely reject American culture and society, nor its university system. He does not go out of his way to reject invitations to spend time at American universities as a visiting professor. When he is invited to an international symposium, he will deliver a presentation or performance, but slightly sidestep the organizers' intentions and expectations. In 1984 he spent one year as an artist in residence at the East-West Center at the University of Hawai'i. In 1990 he was a visiting professor in an independent film production course at San Francisco State University.

As mentioned above, his mother and two sisters call him by his old name of Eric. His older sister, Genie, was professor in the School of Economics at the University of the Philippines Baguio. Her three sons studied in the United States and remained there. When she retired in 2004, she went to live with one of them in Chicago. His younger sister, Patricia, lived with her husband, a Swede who works for an international aid organization, and their two daughters in Baguio until their two daughters were university age. They now live part-time in Sweden while their daughters work in England and South Africa.

Memories of Overdevelopment 231

Over time, the content of his political messages and the style of the films he uses to communicate them have changed again and again, from *Perfumed Nightmare* and *Why is Yellow at the Middle of the Rainbow?* to *Banal Kahoy* (Holy Wood) (2002) and *BUBONG! Roofs of the World, UNITE!* (2006). While reflecting his own bodily and spiritual journey, the films, too, continue on their own global and cosmic journey after they are made. If the theme of *Perfumed Nightmare* was his fascination with modern Western civilization and his disillusionment with it, then his third film, *Turumba* (1981–83), portrays through the eyes of a boy the way Western civilization is expressed in the equivalence of value under capitalism. When this logic infiltrates the rural villages, the effigies and decorations that were originally made for the *Turumba* festival become commodities that splinter the rich and diverse world of communal social relations. The mood

Video jacket for *Turumba*.

created throughout the film by the repetition of its simple and gentle theme song and the purity of the young boy's gaze, together with the unfolding of its simple narrative, enhances the powerful sense of yearning that the film produces for what has been lost through the penetration of capitalism.

As I mentioned above, the making of Kidlat's second film, *Who Invented the Yo-yo? Who Invented the Moon Buggy?* was based on the idea that the yo-yo was originally a weapon used by Filipino hunters and that the moon buggy that humankind first used to walk on the surface of the moon was also designed by a Filipino-American. Where skepticism and critique of Western cultural hegemony and economic dominance were the theme of his first and third films, his second film reminds us of the creativity of the Filipinos and arouses a sense of pride and self-awareness in being Filipino. Of these three films, only the last film, *Turumba*, at least in theory, was based on a prepared screenplay. However, during filming Kidlat made full use of the naturalistic and improvised flow of the performance and dialogue of his amateur actors. In this sense, in the home movie quality of his early works, he was already producing films that simply record the real and allow the audience to recognize it anew. Since *Takedera Mon Amour* (1987–89), he has made conscious and deliberate use of this technique. The provisional results of this work came together in *Why is Yellow at the Middle of the Rainbow?*

His use of amateurs as actors, including himself, his family and friends and people from the villages, give the films an impression of aimlessness that may well be called strategic naivety. They make us feel that there is a separate domain where Western cultural hegemony has not yet been fully realized and that another world that can serve as a focus of resistance to that hegemony already exists. In his later period, he no longer writes even a broad treatment in advance. Instead, living in tune with the cosmic vibrations, dealing with the prevailing social conditions and reacting to current events have all become the material for a video diary. As a result, however, his lifestyle and activities, which have now become the raw material for his films, have become half-performative as Kidlat and those around him are already aware that they may well appear in one of his films. The borderline between life and performance has become blurred. He captures this world, in which truth and fiction are indistinguishable, on film and recreates it in the editing studio. In doing so, the films reflect a reality that is trapped within the fetters of history and power politics, while also serving as fantastic metaphors that poke fun at the seemingly rigid and unchangeable yoke of reality, break it down and problematize it.

As a shaman inspired by the cosmos and as a trickster who breaks down Western hegemony, Kidlat's unaffected, simple and sincere way of life and filmmaking function as a sophisticated political strategy.

7 The Politics of Representation
Culture as a Resource

As I discuss in the previous chapter, literary scholar and cultural critic Frederic Jameson (1992) has written an erudite critique of Kidlat's work as a contemporary form of cultural-political praxis. However, Jameson fails to detect one of the important messages contained within Kidlat's films – the director's reconstruction of his own colonized sensibilities and mode of thought – and makes no mention of these issues in his essay.[1] Western critics, like Jameson, understand Kidlat's work as a challenge or provocation, an expression of skepticism towards Western modernity, or even of modernity itself, and as a critique of it from the place of the non-modern. This is how they position and consume his work. However, for Kidlat the more pressing question is the problematization of the particular historical processes that made him and that made Philippine society. By

---

1 Two Filipino critics who have commented on Jameson's essay have praised the analysis as a whole but also point out the fundamental defect that it completely ignores the social and historical background of the Philippines. They reject the intellectual hegemony Jameson maintains despite his misunderstanding of the context of Kidlat's work. Of particular importance is Jameson's neglect of the historical importance of the San Juan River Bridge. The second is his failure to understand the significance of the village's protective saint, San Marco (St Mark the Evangelist). The first film, *Perfumed Nightmare* (1975–77), was made during the martial law period (1972–81) when President Marcos entrenched his despotic and oppressive regime, with the military and financial support of the United States standing in the background (see, for example, Bonner 1987). Jameson suggests that the film avoids criticizing the Marcos dictatorship directly, but for a Filipino audience the film's criticism of contemporary politics and of the Marcos regime is abundantly clear. With its wealth of references to American political and cultural hegemony, the film is no less significant today. Jameson's understanding of the jeepney factory as a reference to a non-modern and genial world of handicraft artisanship has also been criticized for its failure to recognize the reality of jeepney production, with its low wages and hard physical labor, leading to a complete misinterpretation (San Juan Jr. 2000; Tolentino 2001).

exploring how these histories, even now, continue to act as a fetter and by confronting and reflecting on these histories, he hopes to overcome them and to find a way to liberate himself, Philippine society and the Filipino people.

His films are a record of a daily life that is motivated by the search for his own liberation and freedom. His later documentaries record Nauyac's reforestation and cultural revival movement and serve as a record of the words and deeds of the man who has become Kidlat's mentor and has shown him firsthand how to liberate himself. He entrusts Nauyac, as a native intellectual, to make his subtle critique of Western modernity and present an alternative worldview and a way of life that can serve in its place. It is characteristic of Kidlat's films that the critique of Western modernity is not direct and aggressive but is made gently and softly through their overall tone. While taking pleasure and interest in the process of opening himself up and liberating himself, Kidlat goes about his daily life, half-performatively, in front of the camera. The two Kidlats, the one performing his daily life and the film director who asks the people around him to film him (and who later edits the footage), exist side by side within him, without any particular contradiction. Nauyac, too, both leads his reforestation and cultural revival movement and stands in front of the camera, explaining the significance of what he is doing and imbuing it with meaning. In this sense, he is a co-conspirator with the same intention as Kidlat. Together they are a conspiracy of two.

While playing the hero of his debut work, *Perfumed Nightmare*, Kidlat wears his hair in the mop top style made famous by The Beatles, a seemingly minor detail that could be easily overlooked. At first glance, the haircut appears to offer further proof of the main character's enchantment with and acceptance of Western youth popular culture, as embodied by The Beatles, and of his willing surrender to the seductive Voice of America radio broadcasts. When I saw the film in 1982, that is how I interpreted it. However, when I asked Kidlat about it later, he said that this is a traditional haircut for Ifugao men that is known as the *bunot*. It is worth noting that the hero wears an Ifugao hairstyle in a film that portrays his basic worldview and outlook on life so directly, because it clearly demonstrates his affinity with and admiration for the Ifugaos, who embody all that is uniquely Filipino, un-colonized and indigenous.

Previously, in German director Werner Herzog's film *The Enigma of Kaspar Hauser* (1974), Kidlat had appeared as an indigenous chieftain

The Politics of Representation

from northern Luzon whose role was to continue quietly playing the nose flute to sound the alarm lest his people be destroyed. It is said that Herzog decided to include this scene after having been inspired by a conversation with Kidlat. In this role, where Kidlat performs as an indigenous man mourning the loss of traditional culture and appealing for its preservation, we can see in a condensed form the basic pattern of the latter part of his life.

Remembering history

The bridge at the entrance to the village that appears in the first scene of *Perfumed Nightmare* spatially connects the village (traditional society) and the city (the modern world) that coexist, and simultaneously connects the past and the present in time. Of the two, it is perhaps the latter historical

Kidlat's collage and article in the *Philippine Daily Inquirer*. In the collage, Kidlat holds his bamboo camera at the ready while standing on a bamboo model of the San Juan River Bridge. He is adopting the position of an indigenous person observing and recording the Philippine-American War. (February 16, 1992)

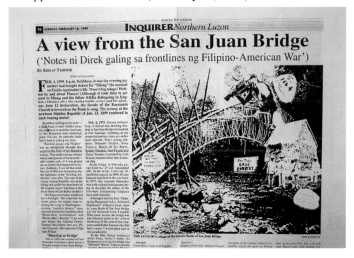

connection, symbolized by the bridge, that speaks most directly to the theme of Kidlat's reconstruction of the self and to the message contained in the film. The bridge to the village is a metonymy that recalls the memory of the San Juan River Bridge on the outskirts of Manila, the starting point for the Philippine-American War. After its victory against Spain and its acquisition of the Philippines, the United States immediately sent reinforcements to the archipelago to intervene in the Philippine Revolution. There they bided their time, waiting for the right moment to attack. On the night of February 4, 1899, a three-person American patrol stationed at the bridge happened upon a small number of Philippine Revolutionary Army soldiers and attacked them. This incident served as the trigger for Lieutenant General Arthur MacArthur Jr. (father of Douglas MacArthur, the Supreme Commander who governed Japan during the postwar occupation) to order an all-out assault on the Philippine Revolutionary Army. The Philippine-American War had begun.

The bridge serves as a reminder of the origin of all the historical processes that have shaped both the Philippines and Kidlat himself, the events at the beginning of the history of the remaking of Philippine society and culture under the overwhelming influence of the United States. In remembrance of the 100-year anniversary of the American provocation at the San Juan River Bridge, Kidlat wrote an essay, 'A view from the San Juan Bridge' (*Notes ni Direk galing sa frontlines ng Filipino-American War*), which, together with a collage image he had made, appeared in the February 16, 1999, edition of the *Philippine Daily Inquirer*, where it took up almost an entire page. In the essay, Kidlat makes the following observations as he looked back on the making of *Perfumed Nightmare*.

> 'Shooting [at] Bridge'
> Feb. 4, 1899 saw a sentry of First Nebraska Volunteers shoot down a Filipino soldier at San Juan Bridge. *Palibhasa,* the centennial of that spark of the Filipino-American War, happened as Mama and I were watching the Aguinaldo [the leader of Philippine Revolution and the first president] play – 100 years later, to the hour...
>
> Feb. 4, 1975. *Parang kahapon lang* [As if it was only yesterday] – I filmed that shooting incident at San Juan Bridge on location at Fort Santiago...At the bridge, a Nebraska private fired his 45 cal. Springfield rifle. At the bride, I shot my 16-mm Bolex camera. In 1899, Private Grayson had fired at the war front. In 1975, this wannabe filmmaker was the cultural battleground, trying to decipher the nature of the love-hate relationship Filipinos have with America.

Although I shot my film *Mababangong Bangungot* (a.k.a. Perfumed Nightmare) without a script, *alam ko, yung* [I know, that the] Battle of San Juan Bridge was the historical event I needed. With poetic license, the bridge was that reference point in the *cultural awakening* of the central film character called Kidlat Tahimik (this film hero's name, I would adapt later as my pseudonym.) (Tahimik 1999: 16)

In *Perfumed Nightmare*, Kidlat happens across an American businessman who is to take him to the United States.[2] Before he leaves, his mother hands him the wooden sculpture of a horse that she has carved from the stock of a rifle that belonged to his late father, who was shot by an American soldier.

Mother: So Kidlat, you go with an Americano. You are like your father, fascinated by the white man's smiles.

Kidlat: Do not worry, mama. I will become rich in America and I will take you away from here.

Mother: Your father was a happy coachman. He always sang as he worked. One day a smiling stranger gave him a rifle, the bridge to freedom, your vehicle to freedom. 'We will help you with your revolution against Spanish tyrants', said a smiling Americano. Your father stopped singing. Before end of the revolution, the days of Ispaniard were numbers. When the Ispaniard surrendered, your father sang again. As he sang a sweet song of victory, Americans were buying us in Paris. Your singing father tried to enter liberated Manila at San Juan Bridge, he was stopped by an American sentry.

---

2 In the first part of the film, we are suddenly transported to the scene of a camp at the World Scout Jamboree. When the American representative returns to Manila, he hires Kidlat to take him in his jeepney. When they arrive in Manila, the man asks Kidlat to accompany him to the United States with the jeepney and work for his company there. Kidlat accepts the invitation, thrilled at the prospect of traveling to the United States. However, before going to the United States they spend some time in Paris, where Kidlat has the job of replenishing the bubblegum in the street vending machines belonging to the American businessman. The story of Kidlat's growing disillusionment with modern civilization in the latter part of the film takes place in Paris rather than the United States because Kidlat started making films while he was still in Paris and this part of the film is a work of bricolage that makes use of the footage he accumulated during that time.

It was his last song. From the butt of your father's rifle, I carved this horse. 'Killed for trespassing on US military property' was the military report attached to his corpse. For $12 million [actually, $20 million], we became U.S. military property.

Kaya, a bamboo craftsman (with a big butterfly tattoo on his chest): Yes, Kidlat, for $12 million they bought your soul and mind. That was the official military version of your father's death. The fact was suppressed to hide our true strength. Kidlat, it's time [for] you to know the truth. I was there and I saw it all happen. [Scene flashback to the San Juan Bridge scene, February 4, 1899] He did not need his rifle. *Tapos na revolution,tapos na! Pannalo kami, panalo kami*! *Tapos na revolution*! (The revolution was over! We won!)

Your father took a deep breath, [and then] he blew with a fury that was stronger than the wind of Amok mountain, Kidlat. He killed more Americans…before they finally stopped your father. Kidlat, when the typhoon blows off its cocoon, the butterfly embraces the sun. The sleeping typhoon must learn to blow again.

The end of the film becomes a reply to this highly metaphorical episode. Having finished his business in Paris, the American businessman says to Kidlat:

There are many VIPs [very important people] in town, and you will meet them at my farewell party tomorrow, men more godly than your Wernher von Braun. Right after the party we will fly to America on Concorde. You will be the first Filipino to fly supersonic. Tomorrow, Kidlat, tomorrow you shall be with me in paradise!

However, having learned during his stay in Paris that the modernity proudly shown him by the businessman is actually a 'perfumed nightmare', Kidlat declines to accompany him. He then forces his way into a masquerade party where the world's power elite are celebrating the completion of an enormous supermarket that was built after the street-sellers who previously occupied the site were chased out. With a powerful puff of air, he blows down part of the building and sends it and the gathered elites flying far away. With the carved horse made from the rifle stock belonging to his late father, who stood up to fight for the revolution he believed in, mounted like an emblem on the bonnet of his jeepney, he drives through the ruined buildings of Paris that he toppled with his breath (in reality, probably an area being demolished for redevelopment). The scene is shot on a diagonal from behind the jeepney, with the carved wooden horse filling the right-hand side of the screen. The horse becomes the master of the screen, speeding gallantly onward. Kidlat's voiceover comes in over the top:

> This is the last will and testament of Kidlat Tahimik, and declaration of independence. I, Kidlat Tahimik, of my own free will, hereby resign as president of Wernher von Braun Club and relinquish all rights and duties as president and founder of the club, and furthermore I totally resign my membership from the club. This resignation is absolute irrevocable and effective now...I am Kidlat Tahimik. I choose my vehicle, I choose my bridge.

Kaya's narration follows repeatedly, 'When the typhoon blows off its cocoon, the butterfly embraces the sun.'

Next, Kidlat climbs into the dome of a huge chimney resembling a space shuttle that has been left on a construction site, finding, to his surprise, that a family of three could easily live in there. Straight away

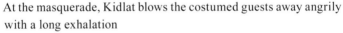

At the masquerade, Kidlat blows the costumed guests away angrily with a long exhalation

he fills the part of the dome that serves as the engine by blowing into it with a rubber hose and the chimney takes off and flies away. It lands in his hometown in the Philippines and the film ends with a scene of the setting sun in Balian village.

Perfumed Nightmare was released in 1977, the same year as George Lucas's first *Star Wars* film. *Star Wars* provided a tangible image of modernity, progress, and the development of science and technology as the means to build a bridge to the stars and to extend human activity across the universe. By contrast, Kidlat has made it his life's work to build a bridge to the true self that lies within.

Jameson is not the only critic to have written favorably about *Perfumed Nightmare*. Wim Wenders (1977), Werner Herzog (1978) and Susan Sontag (1980) (in Tahimik 1997: 54–5) have used words such as 'primitive style', 'formula-free spontaneity' and 'innocence' to describe the peculiar charm of Kidlat's films.[3] However, there is a fundamental difference between his 'primitive' style and that of the school of Western painting known as 'primitivism'. The primitivists were a school of artists who had received formal art training but who, after mastering orthodox techniques, made a deliberate attempt to escape from their strictures.[4] Kidlat's films,

---

3 *New York Times* film critic Vincent Canby (1981, in Tahimik 1997) points out that, as a complete work of art, film necessarily involves a high degree of technical manipulation and that, therefore, a truly naive or primitive film production, like a primitive nuclear physics, is a contradiction in terms. He nevertheless considers Kidlat's work to be one of the rare successful examples where primitivism and modern techniques coexist without leading to a rupture or contradiction.

4 The celebrated Nobel Prize-winning Japanese author Ōe Kenzaburō also saw *Perfumed Nightmare* when it was shown at the Third World Culture conference at Duke University. It left a deep impression on him – he called Kidlat 'a kind of Kurosawa of the Philippines' – and he observed that both directors open windows to the world, the only difference being that Kurosawa's films opened inward to the Japanese soul while Kidlat's open outwards to the cosmos (Tahimik 1997: 15–16).

In fact, there is a detailed portrait of the leader of a theatre movement group from the Philippines by the name of Cos in Chapter Six of Ōe's novel *An Echo of Heaven* (2001), which was inspired by his meeting with Kidlat. The name Cos is an abbreviation. The man's real name is a Tagalog one meaning 'cosmic will', but the novel explains that the abbreviated English translation has become his nickname. Episodes from *Perfumed Nightmare* and Kidlat's real life experiences are joined together to construct a mysterious and fascinating character. (Yomota Inuhiko kindly pointed out to me that Ōe had included Kidlat in one of his novels and I was able to follow this up.)

on the other hand, are 'primitive' and 'innocent' because he has never formally studied the techniques and grammar of film.

As I explain in the previous chapter, Kidlat learned how to make films not in the classroom but by watching his film director friends as they worked in the artists' commune and he acquired his skills through trial and error. When Kidlat repudiated the self that had been over-educated in the Western system and quit his job at the OECD, he decided to start a new life. Having done so, he felt that he should learn the technique of filmmaking as pre-modern artisans learned their craft – by watching masters at work or following model examples, copying them to learn the techniques and then, having mastered them, by putting them to use freely in accordance with his own nature. Even without imitating established Western techniques like a

The horse emblem on the bonnet of Kidlat's jeepney, carved from the butt of a rifle belonging to his father who was killed during the Philippine-American War, promenades through the ruins of Paris.

monkey,[5] he believes in the self-organizing power of the cosmos. He has a simple yet unshakeable faith in his in-dwelling *Bahala na Dwende* and its ability to respond directly to the cosmos. If he liberates that *dwende* and puts it in charge, then the work will come together of its own accord (Kidlat 1997: 54)

However, this approach is also a sophisticated political strategy that Kidlat chose deliberately and consciously. Kidlat learned firsthand from experiences such as his appearance in the play *Gallows Humor* that he can never become, nor will he ever win recognition as, a Westerner with full membership, no matter how diligently he tries to imitate one. He knows this from the bottom of his heart. If, no matter how hard he tries to play the role of a performing monkey and imitate the West, he will always be locked out as that monkey, then his first task is to stop trying to earn praise by performing the role of a clever little monkey. He also realized that questioning and disrupting the Western ethnocentrism that clearly divides the human (Western = modern) from the monkey (Filipino = non-modern, probably the author myself) – and the framework of classification, regulation and systematization that supports it (which also serves as a mechanism of exclusion) – is an effective Third World cultural strategy. This is the strategy he decided to pursue. As the Third World has already been incorporated within the First World, he tries to launch a counter-attack in the arena of film in which both worlds share the modern techniques and refined style of expression, but he uses a handmade technique that defies Western expectations and appears at first glance to be a bricolage of his own way of doing things (a style that he decided on himself, a free technique). In the following sections, I consider his pursuit of this strategy in a number of individual films.

A home movie reflecting contemporary social upheaval

Kidlat uses the primitive and naive film production techniques for which he received high praise in *Perfumed Nightmare* even more consciously in *Why is Yellow at the Middle of the Rainbow?*, which is also a traveling film,

---

5 Though Kidlat does not use the word monkey, I use the word following a popular Japanese saying, '*saru-mane*' (monkey-style learning by imitating an example without any critical thought), just to emphasize the mode of non-reflexive style of learning. Among G7 countries, there is no monkey living except in Japan, where a monkey is very close and familiar to the people as a mirror image of human beings.

even more so than *Perfumed Nightmare*. As the director recognizes, of all his films, this is the most auto-biographical, a warm and personal film-diary documentary. It is a compilation of episodes featuring the parent–child bond in a range of daily interactions. In the background are the events that shaped Filipino society. There are scenes that seem like he just recorded his children being cute, while others are recreations of real events.

In this sense, to a pure documentarian who believes simply and unquestioningly that only the plain facts ought to be recorded, the film is a kind of challenge or protest from a documentary filmmaker who is also an artist. In other words, 'it is a film that pushes against the boundaries that define documentary film' (Hara 1994). Even more importantly, this filmic record, which begins at the time when his eldest son Kidlat Senior was five years old and covers nearly fourteen years of his three sons growing

A pamphlet from the Japanese release of *Why is Yellow at the Middle of the Rainbow?* (Cinematrix 1994)

up, simultaneously holds up a mirror to the political situation that rocked the Filipino society surrounding Kidlat's family. It is both a personal film diary and a documentary or commentary on the broader political situation from the perspective of daily life, and of how the political situation enters into that life. The individual, the family and the regional community, Filipino society, the global political situation and even the movements of the earth itself (volcanic eruptions, earthquakes, typhoons) all mingle together, responding to one another and coming together to form a complete whole. *Why is Yellow at the Middle of the Rainbow?* truly shows the wide world in which Kidlat's family live in all of its breadth. To borrow Hara Masato's (1994) words, it is 'a film where footage taken from everyday life self-replicates' and becomes 'a mirror held up to the cosmos'.

The year 1981, when the film begins, was the year when the martial law and curfew, which had been in place since 1972, was lifted in order to welcome and celebrate the visit by Pope John Paul II to the Philippines. The tense and oppressive atmosphere of society was tentatively cast away, but it was also the period when the developmentalism of the Marcos regime began to collapse under the impact of the second oil shock (a sudden increase in the price of oil that started with the Iranian Revolution of 1979). In August 1983 Benigno Aquino Jr. (Ninoy) was assassinated at Manila International Airport (renamed Ninoy Aquino Airport after his wife, Corazon, became president after the People Power Revolution in 1986) when he returned from three years' exile in Boston, the United States, shot in the back of the head from behind by one of the soldiers who accompanied him as he walked down the jet bridge from his China Airlines flight.

Aquino had been a former senator and Marcos's greatest rival. When martial law was declared, Aquino was arrested and imprisoned on charges of murder, subversion and possession of illegal firearms. In 1977 he was sentenced to death. However, the regime was unable to execute the popular Aquino and in 1980 he was given permission to travel to the United States on humanitarian grounds to receive heart bypass surgery (but also to receive political asylum) and went into exile. After successful surgery, he remained in Boston, where he lived an active life. However, with kidney trouble taking the sheen off the leadership of the strongman Marcos, Aquino became the only person with the potential to replace him as president. The fact that an influential politician who had left his comfortable life in exile with his family and risked his life for the sake of his native land and people could be assassinated in broad daylight before his feet even touched the ground of the mother country triggered a powerful shockwave and changed the political situation in the Philippines overnight. The assassination was the trigger that brought the citizens of Metro Manila, who had previously stayed out of politics, suddenly into the streets to hold mass rally after mass rally. The season of fervent politics had arrived. At the peak of the movement, the snap presidential election was set for February 7, 1986, with strong pressure from the United States, and the following People Power Revolution (February 21–25) led to Corazon Aquino's installation as president.

Why is Yellow at the Middle of the Rainbow? follows these events as they unfolded, painting a vivid picture of the upheaval of Filipino politics and society through the interlacing of documentary and news footage. We see the spectacular scene of welcome for Aquino's return from exile, with yellow cloths and handkerchiefs wrapped around street lights and trees all around the airport and lining both sides of the route from the airport to the center of town. This bold expression of welcome drew on the lyrics of the popular American song 'Tie a Yellow Ribbon Round the Old Oak Tree.' After the assassination, the color became the symbol of the movement against Marcos.

After Ninoy Aquino was assassinated, his wife Corazon Aquino always wore black in mourning for more than a year, and when she announced her candidacy for the presidency she took to always wearing yellow, the symbolic color of compassion for and solidarity with Ninoy, as well as anger and objection to Marcos.

'I am Furious Yellow', the subtitle of the final (1994) version of *Why is Yellow at the Middle of the Rainbow?*, pays homage to the collective citizen consciousness that manifested like a momentary dream in the Philippines as a result of the successful People Power Revolution. This symbolic color captured the mood of the times, the anger at the Marcos dictatorship and the aspirations for a democratic society even more than the wife of a national hero did. Kidlat skillfully portrayed the atmosphere and the mood of this period through his editing of the film, which combines home movie with documentary.

The achievements of the People Power Revolution, symbolized by Corazon Aquino's inauguration, created a 'democratic space' that enabled social reform in a context of freedom of speech and debate. It was assumed that a 'rainbow coalition' made up of a broad alliance of conservative, moderate and liberal forces would bring all its power to bear on the construction of a better society to replace Marcos's despotism. However, the newly reopened parliament watered down the poor peasants' longed-for Comprehensive

Agrarian Reform Law. Repeated coup attempts (seven times) against Corazon Aquino's government created social instability, which in turn entrenched economic stagnation. In July 1990 a huge earthquake struck Kidlat's hometown of Baguio. The five-star Hyatt Terraces Hotel collapsed, and the earthquake left 1,648 dead and caused 40 billion pesos damage. The euphoria created by the 'revolution' quickly faded away.

In June 1991 Mount Pinatubo in western Luzon erupted in the largest volcanic eruption of the twentieth century. The ash and debris that fell over the five surrounding provinces dealt a devastating blow to agriculture. The eruption caused serious economic damage, but it also had unanticipated political effects, ultimately leading to the complete withdrawal of all United States military bases.[6] The Philippines was also battered by Super Typhoon *Trining* (104 people missing or dead, damage totaling 3.5 billion pesos (US$77 million)) in October 1991, followed in quick succession by Super Typhoon *Uring* (6,357 missing or dead, damage totaling 6.5 billion pesos (US$143 million)) in November that year. In 1992 chronic electricity shortages worsened, with almost daily blackouts lasting for several hours and, in some areas, for more than ten hours. Amid these setbacks and a sense of disillusionment in the pursuit of economic growth, Kidlat trained his camera on the indigenous people living in the mountains of northern Luzon around Baguio. He rediscovered them continuing to maintain their simple way of life despite economic failure, political instability and natural disasters. Once

---

6 After the huge eruption, Clark Air Base, which sat at the eastern foot of the mountain, was covered in a layer of volcanic ash 50–60 centimeters thick. To remove the ash and rebuild the base would have been very expensive. At that time, negotiations to extend the lease of the base were nearing completion. However, the United States demanded a reduction in the rent equal to the cost of the clean-up, while the Philippine side demanded that, on the contrary, in a time of disaster the United States ought to make allowances. The two sides became locked in opposition and negotiations on the compensation that would have to be paid by the United States stalled. The Philippine side made major concessions and the governments of the two countries ultimately reached a consensus, but the Philippine Senate rejected the treaty to extend the loan. Apprehensive about the economic shock that the withdrawal of the United States military might have, President Aquino planned to hold a national referendum to nullify the Senate's decision, but she was unsuccessful. As a result, the United States military bases, which were the source and the symbol of the constraints placed on the Philippines from the beginning of the twentieth century by its special relationship with the United States, were removed. With the spell of American power broken, the Philippines was forced to find a new place for itself within Asia.

again, he detected in them an enormous hope, as was vividly shown in the 'Indio-genius Brown' version.

Why is Yellow at the Middle of the Rainbow? combines a number of earlier versions of the film that had been edited and released at different times. Each of these earlier versions vividly and honestly portrays the prevailing atmosphere and feelings of the people of the Philippines – their anger, hope, dreams and disillusionment – during different periods of social crisis and renewal. The earlier versions were each given the title of a color that expressed the political situation and social atmosphere at the time they were released. The individual sections are 'I Am Frivolous Green' (1981–83), 'I Am Furious Yellow' (1983–86), 'I Am Curious Pink' (1986–89), 'We Are Colonial Red, White and Blue' (unknown), 'We Are Dis-harmonious Disney-color' (unknown), 'We Are Disastrous Gray' (1991), 'We Are Powerless Black' (1992), 'Indio-genius Brown' (1993) and 'Epilogue' (1994). They premiered at the first, second and third Yamagata International Documentary Film Festival in 1989, 1991 and 1993, where they received an enthusiastic reception from audiences. The self-replication of the work about once every two to three years ultimately resulted in the three-hour long documentary *Why is Yellow at the Middle of the Rainbow?* They are eyewitness reports from a filmmaker living in the midst of the maelstrom of this significant period in the contemporary history of the Philippines (the search for a grounded nationalism and national liberation from Marcos's developmentalist dictatorship via a peaceful democratic revolution).

The most recent version in terms of production years, 'Indio-genius Brown', which provides the final scene for *Why is Yellow at the Middle of the Rainbow?*, poses a question and a challenge about the future of the Philippines after the complete withdrawal of United States troops. It is a candid declaration of Kidlat's keen recognition that the simple era in which anyone who was anti-American could be a patriot had come to an end. It was no longer possible to affirm one's position just by criticizing the outsider and it therefore became necessary for Filipinos to look for the foundations of their own identity within the Philippines, on the ground beneath their feet. In the 'Epilogue', Kidlat speaks to his eldest son:

> OK Kidlat, when you finish at the university you might consider enrolling with Maestro Lopez Nauyac. OK you may not get a master's degree in bridge making but there's a chance you might discover some hidden bridge that will reconnect us with the spirit of the land. Yeah, just check out Maestro Lopez.

The metaphor or image of a bridge connecting two worlds, which appeared in the opening scene of *Perfumed Nightmare*, is also emphasized here. Maestro Lopez, from whom the son (and the director himself) ought to learn, continues working devotedly at his bricolage making a *bolo* (knife) as he hammers away at the red-hot coil spring from a car.

In analyzing this scene, it is important to note Kidlat's attempts to reverse or overturn the meanings buried in the landscape of Monument Valley in the United States, which was used as a location in John Ford's *Stagecoach* and other films in the Western cowboy genre. The film begins with a scene of Kidlat walking towards John Ford's Point in Monument Valley, which overlaps the border between southern Utah and northern Arizona in the American West. At the end of the film, just before Nauyac appears, another scene features John Ford's Point, this time covered in a thin layer of snow. In *Orbit 50: Letters to My 3 Sons* (1992) (the 'Orbit 50' of the title refers to his fiftieth journey around the son – in other words, Kidlat's fiftieth birthday), a short film in which Kidlat travels around the world, Kidlat wears an Ifugao loincloth while placing an Ifugao carving of an American Indian and planting a tree with this same location in the background. Before I had a chance to get a detailed explanation of the meaning of this scene from Kidlat myself, Yomota Inuhiko met with the director at the 1993 Yamagata International Documentary Film Festival and learned about his 'curious project' to commemorate the 500-year anniversary of Magellan's circumnavigation of the globe:

> There will probably be grand ceremonies and commemorations for Magellan in Spain. But in the Philippines, where Magellan met his end, we are too poor to hold any kind of commemoration. [Kidlat] Tahimik told me that he would make up for this lapse by placing carved wooden American Indian statues all over the world and planting a sapling next to each one. In twenty-seven years I may no longer be alive, but the saplings will have grown into great trees, towering over my wooden statues and shading them gently. (Yomota 1993: 796)

To celebrate his fiftieth birthday, Kidlat made a low-budget round-the-world trip to carry out his plan. It was a demonstration intended to add to the tale that it was not Magellan but Enrique de Malacca who, regardless of whether he was a Sumatran or from Ifugao (see previous chapter), was the first to successfully circumnavigate the world. In Chapter 3 I discuss in more detail

Kidlat's second son Kawayan learning from Ifugao carpenters while they build a new house next to Kidlat's old one in Patpat (*top*) and his third son Kabunian (*bottom*). (March 15, 2004)

the relationship between this voyage, contemporary globalization and the transformation of the Ifugao villagers' way of life.

Everyday resistance and negotiation in the cultural arena

A pioneer of independent and alternative film

As Kidlat himself acknowledges, he is not a political person in the usual sense of the word. That is to say, although he readily attended demonstrations and political rallies during the Marcos dictatorship, he is not directly involved in political campaigns or social movements. He is not a member of a political party or group and, in that sense, he does not maintain a clear political position. He does not participate in the politics that are fought over during elections for the national and municipal parliaments or the executive. Nor does he make petitions or get involved in lobbying or left-wing party politics. Nevertheless, he is very conscious of the politics of the cultural arena and he does not demur from actively intervening. Indeed, he sees the cultural arena as having a particular importance as the site of struggles and negotiations over everyday politics and he continues to be an activist in this arena.

He is aware that just by living their daily lives, he and his children are impacted both directly and indirectly by the rule of the politically and economically powerful. He sees culture as connecting daily life and everyday consciousness with the political. In other words, he sees that it is through the so-called cultural arena, in particular, that politics tries to insert itself into daily life. A lahar is a deluge of mud in which ash, sand and other debris left on the mountainside after a volcanic eruption is suddenly washed down following torrential rains. After the eruption of Mount Pinatubo in 1991, every wet season for nearly ten years triggered lahars that caused major damage to areas downstream. Because of this, the word 'lahar' implies an overwhelming force that washes away, inundates and overturns the foundation of one's way of life and provides a concrete image of this process. Even if he cannot completely escape from the cultural lahar symbolized by Hollywood cinema, Kidlat's way of life is disciplined by his resistance to being swept away and drowned in it. Rather than indulging in the excesses of Western culture, he searches for and tries to create joy and richness in his daily life. This has become the style of his political struggle. The praxis of his daily life is a conscious negotiation with

The Politics of Representation

Top: Young people bring a *karaoke* set and have some fun underneath Nauyac's office-cum-home. (March 14, 2004)

Middle: In the same location, sometimes groups of women also weave cloth. (March 10, 2000)

Bottom: A parabolic antenna to receive satellite broadcasts on the roof of Sanchago's house. He is the owner of the general store located next to Nauyac's house. The Patpat area with several houses and rice terraces can be seen on the other side of the valley. (March 6, 2003)

Western, particularly American, hegemony in the cultural arena. Recording this praxis is his primary motivation for making films.

In the 1990s the villagers of Hapao started borrowing masses of Hollywood movies from the video rental store in Banaue and watched them enthusiastically. This is one example of the way American culture descends like a lahar. Another is how, from the beginning of the 2000s, a small number of wealthy households installed parabolic antennas and it became easy to watch more than 100 channels via satellite. As they grew richer by working overseas, the villagers brought back televisions, videos and cameras as souvenirs or sent back money that enabled the villagers to purchase these items.

Kidlat is concerned that the penetration of American culture will lead to rapid changes in both the villagers' way of life and in their hearts and minds. Previously, in *Perfumed Nightmare*, Kidlat clearly saw the villagers as a simulacrum of himself, with their ears keenly attuned to the Voice of America radio broadcasts and transfixed by the perfume of American progress and modernization. Not only the villagers, but most Filipinos as well, are intoxicated by dreams of America's perfumed nightmare. However, Kidlat believes that the Ifugaos can still apply their unique 'culture' as a brake (his important concept for culture) and continue to live authentically without losing themselves to the seduction of the perfumed nightmare. Kidlat therefore encourages the Ifugaos to maintain their traditions and culture, make ready for the lahar and be on their guard against it so as to avoid being swallowed whole.

For Kidlat, traditional culture can provide Filipinos with the power to resist the onslaught of globalization and hold their ground. However, he does not provide a clear definition of what that culture actually is. Rather, he equivocates by calling it 'that which acts as a brake' against their being 'bewitched' or 'swallowed up' and forgetting who they are. Alternatively, he talks of that which creates discomfort or frustration with Western culture, that which encourages hesitation and reflection rather than a willing accepting and embrace of the lahar. If we must define it, from the point of view of strategic essentialism traditional culture is a way of life that is based on a traditional value system and worldview (De Guia 1994: 15).

Kidlat says that 'in the Philippines, we are the victims of cultural genocide'. He tries to sound the alarm by lamenting that 'although we were not murdered outright like the American Indians were, instead our life-force is being sapped from us slowly by soft drinks and fast food shops, and by the popular music that we hear everyday from the radio'. The sorrow Kidlat feels at a colonization that manifests itself through cultural genocide is dismissed by some Western intellectuals with trendy comments about 'nostalgia for the present' (Jameson's words referred to and discussed by Appadurai 2004: 29–30). There is a deep gulf between the two and the real meaning of Kidlat's bitter struggle is almost completely lost on Western cultural critics.[7]

As Kidlat repeats again and again, the Filipino majority, known as the lowland Christians, largely submitted to Spanish colonization. After the

---

7 For example, in discussing popular music Appadurai (2004) says that in the Philippines today, American popular songs are even more widely disseminated and popular than they are in the United States. Furthermore, the Philippine versions are far more faithful to the original than are contemporary American renditions:
> An entire nation seems to have learned to mimic Kenny Rogers and the Lennon sisters, like a vast Asian Motown chorus...not only are there more Filipinos singing perfect renditions of some American songs (often from the American past) than there are Americans doing so, there is also, of course, the fact that the rest of their lives is not in complete synchrony with the referential world that first gave birth to these songs. In a further globalizing twist on what Frederic Jameson has recently called 'nostalgia for the present', these Filipinos look back to a world they have never lost. (Appadurai 2004: 29–30)

The perversion of looking back to a past that never was, as in a dream – the bittersweet nostalgia for something for which no concrete experience that could give rise to it ever was, an empty world where the signifier floats freely without a referent – is a phantom created by submission to education and enlightenment under American colonial rule. It might also be described as an optical illusion produced by the commercialism that sells like a charm the mass culture of Hollywood films, popular songs and fast food.

With these thoughts in mind, when the clothing retailer Benetton asked Kidlat's second son Kawayan to be a model, the request was refused on the basis that his modeling would be 'a commercialization of the colonial mentality that whiteness is beautiful and would strengthen and reproduce that mentality'. Of Kidlat's three sons, Kawayan is the one who looks the most like his mother, a handsome blonde standing at more than 180 centimeters tall. After studying at the national Philippine High School for the Arts at the National Arts Center, Mount Makiling, he was selected for an exhibition for young up-and-coming artists at the Lopez Museum at just twenty years of age and has continued to achieve brilliant successes as an artist. When he was a child, he spent time with his mother in Germany during the summer holidays, so as well as speaking fluent English, he understands German. Yet despite this superficial appearance, inside he has a strong sense of himself as a Filipino and in his daily life in Baguio he speaks with his fellow artists in the Filipino language.

Philippine-American War, the United States policy of Benevolent Assimilation brought American-style education to brainwash the people. They thereby came to accept American things and to desire them for themselves. The intellectuals who received their higher education in broken English were the worst affected. As I have already explained, having been educated after Philippine independence, Kidlat is bitterly aware that he too has reproduced himself as a colonial subject. By contrast, the indigenous highlanders, whom the majority Filipinos despise, are the only people who retain their unique culture and are therefore able to continue their resistance to colonization by a foreign power. Kidlat thinks that the highlanders' retention of their own culture – that is, the maintenance and reinforcement of their fundamental identity and pride as indigenous and authentic Filipinos – is a political act of opposition to the brainwashing and coercion of the colonial forces.

In the struggle with American hegemony in the cultural arena, the lowland Christians are in a much weaker position than the indigenous people. Indeed, they have already lost. Therefore, Kidlat, in contrast to the widely accepted idea in Filipino society that the 'backward and undeveloped' indigenous people ought to be educated and instructed in American fashion, thinks that it is actually the lowland Christians who need to have their eyes opened by indigenous culture so as to be liberated and saved. As I discuss in the previous chapter, Kidlat believes that in order to reconstruct a Filipino subjectivity and a true nationality, a process of 'unlearning' by means of indigenous culture is essential. In practice, as we saw in the abovementioned final scene of *Why is Yellow at the Middle of the Rainbow?*, Kidlat regularly tells his sons to learn Ifugao knowledge and skills.

For Kidlat, the indigenous *bahag* (loincloth) is the most representative expression of indigenous culture as a form of resistance against foreign influence. His film *Bahag Ko, Mahal Ko* (Japanese Summers of a Filipino *Fundoshi [loincloth]*) (1996) asks the question, 'why did the Igorots (the indigenous people who live in the Cordilleras) become ashamed of wearing the loincloth and (comparing them with those of white people) of their own bodies?' The film sends a message that there is no need to be ashamed and that the indigenous ought to hold onto their traditions and their bodies and have pride in themselves. The film records a visit by a group of four Ifugao woodcarvers led by Nauyac to the Takedera Temple in Hannō city, Saitama Prefecture, Japan, in August 1996. The previous year, an old Japanese cypress that stood in the grounds of the temple toppled over when it was struck by lightning. The Ifugaos carve the fallen tree into a totem pole featuring motifs of Ifugao gods. In the final scene, during a send-off party at the end of their two-week stay, everyone is in high spirits and gets up to dance. Along with the Ifugao men, the temple priest removes his clothes and joins the circle of dancers wearing only his loincloth.

Kidlat also wears a loincloth in this film. Furthermore, when he spends time in the Ifugao village of Hapao, or when attending special functions, he always wears a loincloth. When he is overseas attending events such as the seminar at Duke University or other symposia and international conferences on video ethnography and documentary film, when it is his turn to present he always does a performance wearing only his loincloth, as if to poke fun at the abstruse talks delivered by the other presenters. He gets bored with the repetitive and impenetrable presentations and debates on film and representation. Instead of giving a similar presentation himself, he takes off his clothes and presents himself wearing only a loincloth and carrying a handmade bamboo video camera on his shoulder. He moves around the participants as they sit in their seats and sticks the

Kidlat helping to plant rice in front of his house while wearing his loincloth. (March 5, 2004)

camera in their faces. He has conducted similar performances during screenings and lectures in Tokyo, Yamagata, Fukuoka and Kyoto. He is convinced that these performances are more interesting and have more impact on the audience and the other presenters.

His performances stem from his keen sense of the power relations that exist between the observer, who does the representing, and the observed, who is represented. By turning his bamboo model camera on the presenters (with their argumentative and eloquent narratives about representation) and the audience members, occasionally getting right up in their faces, he forces them into the position of the person who is being filmed. By putting them in an uncomfortable position where they lose their personal space, the exact opposite of their usual positionality, he confuses and silences them. This overturns the subject-object position. As the camera turns on them, the participants are forced from their active and subjective position of standing on a podium delivering their pet theories, or watching and decoding films in their own way, into the passive position of the object, who is silently recorded. The performance places the attendees in the position of the indigenous people who are being spoken about at the conference but who are rarely present themselves. Using the body and gesture, rather than words, he stimulates the development of an awareness that to speak of the indigenous and to be indigenous are two radically divergent things. The meaning encapsulated in the bamboo camera is his stance of 'looking at reality from an indigenous perspective and communicating what is in their hearts' (I have heard Kidlat say this many times and he also emphasized this at the Fukuoka Prize forum on September 15, 2012).

Since his presentation at the Duke University conference, he has continued to repeat this simple yet powerful performance. When I invited him to a series of symposia, film screenings and lectures on his work at Kyushu University and the Fukuoka Asian Art Museum in February 2003, he conducted this loincloth performance at both venues. Kidlat also presented at a session I organized at the Thirteenth Kyoto University International Symposium on 'New Horizons of Academic Visual-Media Practices' in December 2009. On this occasion he also carried out a loincloth performance. He appeared on stage with great ceremony, dressed in the formal cap and gown that students wear to receive their doctoral degrees. He stood calmly videoing his Japanese co-performer, who played the role of an indigenous person doing a dance. However, in

The Politics of Representation

Top: At an international symposium on experimental film practice at Kyoto University, Kidlat wears a cap and gown as a symbol of academic authority while filming a native (indigenous Japanese) played by his friend.

Middle: Throwing off his cap and gown, he reveals his loincloth underneath. Carrying a bamboo video camera, he dances in time to the gong played by the Japanese co-performer who also put off his *kimono*.

Bottom: Even after the performative interpretation of his life on stage is over, Kidlat continues to perform. Posing as an indigenous person, he 'records' a statue of the classic image of Marilyn Monroe clutching at her skirt while steam from the subway below lifts it up (carved by a friend from Hapao), a symbol of modernity.

the middle of the performance he removed his cap and gown and placed the video camera to one side, dancing in his loincloth in tune to a gong played by the other performer. Then, after dancing freely for a period of time, he assumed the role of an indigenous person dressed in a loincloth and, in full command of his bamboo model camera, turned the lens on the audience, who were previously the observers. He shifted his positionality from that of the observer/recorder to the observed/recorded and then devised an about face, reversing his social position to stare back at the observers and turn the camera on them. It was a dynamic performance of the inversion of relations of power.

It was also a concise performative recreation of his own life course, which I detail in the previous chapter. In the first half of his life Kidlat was on the side of those gazing on the Third World as he tried to help it. In the latter part of his life he dropped out and, in addition to being the recorder, he put himself in the position of the recorded. Going further, he consciously adopted a position of staring back at/filming back at the Euro-American First World. The performance summarized the forty-year history of his own metamorphosis, of the process of his dissolution and reconstruction of the self in search of liberation. Nevertheless, with the end of the Cold War (1989) and the collapse of the Soviet Union (1991), the division of the world into First, Second and Third worlds has lost its meaning. This means his questioning has become less a protest against the First World from the Third World and more of a warning about the penetration of American mass culture that has accompanied globalization and an attempt to preserve a distinct culture.

His performances and films have been seen mainly by Western and Japanese audiences. In the Philippines his audience is limited to a handful of intellectuals and the students he teaches as an adjunct professor at the University of the Philippines and Ateneo de Manila University and some other universities. The funding for his films has also come from abroad: from a German television station for *Turumba*, the Japan Foundation for *Takedera Mon Amour* and *Banal Kahoy* (Holy Wood), and the Aichi Arts Center for *Japanese Summers of a Filipino Fundoshi*.[8] As these examples

---

8 Having said that, his reuse of existing footage and the fact that the film and footage he shot using these grants are also diverted for use in later films means there is not always a one-to-one relationship between a particular film and a particular grant.

suggest, since self-producing *Perfumed Nightmare* and winning the Caligari Film Prize at the 1977 Berlin International Film Festival, he has tended to receive his funding from Western and Japanese sources and it is reasonable to conclude that he has been making films with a Western and Japanese audience in mind in the first instance.

Nevertheless, Kidlat insists that no matter the source of his funding, he wants the message in his films to be seen above all by other Filipinos. Regardless of his intentions, however, because his works are completely out of keeping with the Hollywood style, he has had few opportunities to screen them at home. He knows that he is a Don Quixote tilting at windmills, but he believes that the meaning of his solo fight and the ideas he has incorporated into his films will one day be understood by young Filipino filmmakers. He says that his dream is that his films will stimulate and encourage these young filmmakers and that they will start to focus more clearly on making fascinating films that are rich in political nuances and opinions. He knows to realize this dream he may have to place his hopes on the next generation or even the generation after that. Nevertheless, he says that somebody today has to plant the seed and this is his task. He has spoken with me about this animatedly many times, both at his homes in Baguio and Hapao and while traveling together by bus, since we became reacquainted ten years ago in 1997.

It is certainly the case that within the Philippines, very few people have been able to see his films at the theatre in real time, and this remains the case today. To redress this, he donated land near Session Road in the center of Baguio to build a cinematheque attached to an art space that was constructed for him and his fellow artists. The walls, floors and seats in the cinematheque are all constructed from wood and each seat is designed differently in the image of an Ifugao woodcarving, making the space into a work of Kidlat's expressive art. A column resembling a totem pole beside the screen is carved with the image of Enrique de Malacca standing on the shoulders of Magellan and looking off into the far distance. Even this cinematheque, however, has limited opportunities for Kidlat to screen his films. However, he takes the long-term view, hoping that many children and young people of the next generation will become an audience for his films in the cinemas and universities of Manila, Baguio and Cebu and he firmly believes that they will understand the ideas he has incorporated into them. In fact, the Cinemalaya Philippine Independent Film Festival in Manila since

2005 has changed the situation completely.⁹ A number of directors, who are mainly in their twenties and thirties, have started making low-budget self-produced and alternative films using digital video. Accompanying this has been a renewed interest in Kidlat's films and cultural work. Professor Nicanor G Tiongson of the University of the Philippines (film studies, theatre, political and cultural critique), who worked hard to get the Cinemalaya film festival off the ground, credits Kidlat as the father of independent and alternative cinema in the Philippines and says that he is the one who cleared the way for the great number of young talents who have appeared since 2000 (in a conversation we had while he was a visiting fellow at the Center for Southeast Asian Studies, Kyoto University, in 2010).

The organization of a number of retrospectives of Kidlat's work exemplifies the recent reassessment of his work and the attention it has received thanks to the flowering of independent and alternative cinema. At the third MOV International Digital Film Festival in October 2008, five of Kidlat's films, including *BUBONG! Roofs of the World, UNITE!*, were shown in one screening program under the title 'VIDEO-PALARO: The Video Diaries of Kidlat Tahimik' at Robinsons Galleria in Manila, as well as Bacolod City, Dumaguete City and Iloilo in the Visayas. Over a period of fifteen days from January 12, 2009, the University of the Philippines Film Institute showed almost his entire oeuvre.

In June 2009 he also received the University of the Philippines Gawad Plaridel prize from the College of Mass Communication.¹⁰ He received the prize for his remarkable contribution to independent and alternative film production in the Philippines. The specific citations for the prize were, first,

---

9 Cinemalaya is a neologism that combines the word 'cinema' with the Filipino word '*malaya*' (freedom). Of the films that are submitted to the festival, the best are chosen to screen in the Main Theatre and Little Theatre of the Cultural Center of the Philippines over ten days in July. Of the films that are screened, the directors of the best films receive a prize of one million pesos (approximately two million yen) as a contribution to the production costs of their next film. The opportunity to show their films and to win prize money is a great attraction for young directors. Brillante Mendoza, who received the Best Director Award at the 2009 Cannes Film Festival for *Kinatay* (Butchered), got his start at Cinemalaya.

10 Gawad Plaridel was the pen name of Marcelo H del Pilar, the editor of the *La Solidaridad* newspaper and one of the leaders of the propaganda movement that sought reform and autonomy from Spanish rule. The recipient of the prize must be a person who believes in a democratic and progressive Philippines and in the role of a critical, cautious, free, independent and responsible media within it.

The Politics of Representation

Poster from a Kidlat Tahimik retrospective held at the UP Film Institute, January 12–15, 2009.

A nighttime performance at the pedestrian crossing on Baguio's busiest street, Session Road. (2002, photo by Kidlat Tahimik)

his excellence in the art and craft of cinema; second, his pioneering struggle to bring independent film production in the Philippines to the attention of audiences around the world; third, his courage in making and circulating his films completely independently of the commercial distribution system; and, fourth, his education and support of the next generation of young Filipino filmmakers, both through his films and his active involvement in forums, workshops and film festivals.

According to Professor Rolando B Tolentino, who was Dean of the College of Mass Communication at the time of the award, Kidlat's mind skillfully and easily navigates the complex entanglement of multiple problematics, including the global and the local, transnationalism and nationalism, (post)modernity and tradition, resulting in a kind of Third World cosmopolitanism. He praises the films, saying, 'Without a doubt, he is one of the foundational pillars in the most recent renaissance in Philippine cinema. While his contemporary co-directors, such as Lino Brocka, Ishmael Bernal and Mike De Leon negotiated between commercial and alternative cinemas, Kidlat remained entrenched in a conceptual independent art cinema' (Tolentino in College of Mass Communication 2009: 7). Another critic writes:

> Kidlat Tahimik is a coded film text unto himself. By appearing in his own film, he becomes the text that we need to unpack not only in terms of context but also all the way to the ideology which he tries to present to us. Most importantly, to actual academics, he becomes the very semiotic that we need to decipher. Kidlat is a…living meaning…because it's his life that he films…and by watching the film we begin to learn our history, our culture, and more than anything else, we begin to learn the very consciousness that informs us in the lives that we live. (De Ocampo in College of Mass Communications 2009: 29)[11]

---

11 In his interpretation of Kidlat's films, Campos (in College of Mass Communication 2009: 20–21) observes that the worlds of Kidlat's films are in marked contrast to the obscure and ambiguous imaginary worlds produced by many experimental filmmakers. As if he were following Eisenstein's montage method, the depth of Kidlat's meaningful worlds comes through directly, just as they are. Moreover, each individual frame is imbued with meaning and the synergies and discords between them continue to endlessly create new meanings. Unlike the simplistic self-expression that individualists tend to fall into, his films are instructive and empower the community. Unlike documentary films that stick too closely to a mundane reality, his films are reflective and mythological. A poetic truth becomes

Indigenous backlash

Whether he aims to defamiliarize Western audiences or hopes for the cultural and political awakening of the next generation of Filipinos, the cultural essentialism of Kidlat's representation of the core of Filipino cultural resistance to the lahar of Western and American culture (with the *bahag* and his images of it) have troubled some Ifugao and Igorot intellectuals and invited a backlash. For example, one such intellectual, Rowena Nakake, who studied at the University of the Philippines Baguio and returned to Hapao to get married at the end of the 1990s, and who works in the Hungduan municipal government, expressed her displeasure as follows:

> It may be a form of artistic expression but for most ordinary people, Kidlat's portrayals suggest that Ifugao people still wear loincloths and spend all of their time performing exotic rituals and dances. We are of the same Christian faith as the lowlanders and while aspects of our lifestyle and our beliefs may differ from theirs, we share much more in common with them. In spite of this, Kidlat emphasizes only the differences and if he is not careful then he is likely to only encourage a biased view of us by the lowlanders.[12]

Another indigenous person from Sagada (a village near Bontoc), Jovanni Reyes, a member of staff with the Save the Ifugao Terraces Movement NGO that works for sustainable development and the conservation of the rice terraces, told me in no uncertain terms when I first began my research that he does not need Kidlat to lecture the people not to be embarrassed by his loincloth. He himself is not ashamed of it and during special rituals and other events he wears a loincloth at the appropriate time and place. But as Filipinos, in daily life outside of particular rituals, Ifugaos may

---

important. In contrast to Mike De Leon's psychological films, which gleam with a razor-like sharpness, Kidlat's are an unpredictable bricolage where anything is possible. Unlike the stories of poverty that emerge from the social realist and tragic films of Lino Brocka and Brillante Mendoza, Kidlat's works are comedies full of humor and a feeling of exultation.

12 Using the loincloth as a cultural representation of Filipino identity and resistance also clearly runs the risk of excluding women. In the graphic diary style of Kidlat's early works, his three children, who appear as the main actors, are all boys and in his later works Nauyac is the main protagonist. Even if it is unintentional, the whiff of androcentrism might be the weak point of Kidlat's work.

wear jeans and sneakers and have the right to live as the lowlanders do. In Kidlat's films about indigenous people, the loincloth appears outside its appropriate context, just to attract the gaze of a curious audience. The reason indigenous people dance in their loincloths is to bring the hearts and minds of the circle of dancers at a festival or other occasion together as one, so that they can experience a feeling of spiritual fulfilment, togetherness and joy. However, in Kidlat's films this spirituality and sense of unity is not communicated appropriately. He shows an imitation of the outward appearance and ignores the spirituality. This man criticized Kidlat severely, saying that he is not an Ifugao but an outsider after all and that there are major problems with his arbitrary representation of indigenous culture through the loincloth in terms of the 'representability, legitimacy and the acceptability of the content of his films'.

In Kidlat's basic strategy of everyday political struggle and negotiation in the cultural arena, he uses performance and film to disrupt and defamiliarize Westernized common sense and the hegemony that supports it. However, his first consideration is not to aggressively attack the West but to film scenes from his own life journey towards freeing himself, sometimes poking fun at himself and thereby unsettling existing notions. We could call this a kind of trickster critique by his other self, of the self that received a high level of education in English and absorbed a Western intellect and sensibility. To borrow an expression used in the Philippines, he smiles ironically at the self that unknowingly became a 'banana' (yellow on the outside but white on the inside) and then suddenly laughs it off. It is a device for liberating the in-dwelling *indio*-genius *dwende* that is shuttered inside him. He invites the viewer to look at familiar scenes in a different way and, having acquired a new imaginary, to look at it from a different perspective, thereby creating an opening through which to remake the world in a different way. His films and his performances are catalysts for revolutionizing and transforming the world. He intends them to act as a kind of shock therapy or a tonic to incite Filipinos to wake up and change their consciousness in order to attain true freedom.

Precisely because he cannot imitate Western tactics for Western audiences, he emphasizes indigenous culture, and the loincloth in particular, as an 'other' to Western culture. However, even if his 'strategic essentialism' is an effective strategy when directed towards Filipino lowlander elites and intellectuals (in terms of achieving his objective of provocation and transformation through defamiliarization), it does raise the question of how much he understands his own positionality and the relationships of power that pertain to his representations when looked at from the indigenous point of view.

Nevertheless, while he fully acknowledges these criticisms, he continues to collaborate with Nauyac, each wearing a loincloth, and to film Ifugao traditional costumes, rituals and events. This is because, as I explain in the previous chapter, he is convinced that within him lies an *indio*-genius *dwende* and that he too is an indigenous Filipino. Kidlat's praxis, which is sincere but can also come across as self-satisfied and comical, might appear to be that of a celebrity to anyone with some familiarity with his own personal history. Whatever he says about having dropped out of the elite course he previously trod as an official with an international organization, he has since received critical acclaim as an artist and cultural practitioner on the international stage and is the privileged son of a notable Baguio family. No matter how heartfelt his love and admiration for indigenous culture is and no matter how sincerely he might wish to be reborn as an indigenous person and change his way of life, his performances and documentaries of himself wearing a loincloth can come across as the intolerable joke of an elite or, even worse, as just a game by a member of the idle rich. Some young indigenous people, particularly those who have studied in Baguio and Metro Manila and taken on lowlander lifestyles and values, also have reservations about or are even repelled by Nauyac's wearing of the loincloth. It follows that not only Kidlat's but also Nauyac's loincloth performances and films run the risk of misusing or even perverting the image of indigenous peoples.

Of course, Kidlat can never really become a true Ifugao native and nor can he really defy his own elite status just because he wants to. Nevertheless, he is unlikely to stop filming and making movies. Responding to criticisms of his strategic essentialism as someone who is neither native nor a subaltern (a subordinate group that is subject to social oppression or political exclusion) is likely be a major issue for him now and into the future. To take Kidlat's point of view for a moment, strategic essentialism is always a double-edged sword. Whether it is wielded by Kidlat or by someone else, the possibility of making rights claims by emphasizing and demonstrating otherness necessarily carries with it the risk of becoming trapped within otherness. There is also the problem of representation, of who has the right to represent whom, and of legitimacy, of what ought to be represented in what way. Engaging in a debate on either of these questions does not seem particularly productive. Of course, Kidlat does not have that right to represent the other. However, native intellectuals who criticize Kidlat do not necessarily have the legitimate right to represent the villagers in Kidlat's or Nauyac's place.

In fact, acting in her capacity as a media and communications officer for the municipal government, the woman whose harsh criticism of Kidlat I mention above includes numerous pictures of men wearing traditional loincloths on pamphlets, the government website and in commemorative booklets produced to promote the revival of the traditional *Tungoh* festival. By doing so, she tries to excite captivating images of Hungduan as a place where people live with an exotic and dynamic traditional culture. If we adhere to an essentialist purity that says that only the indigenous have the right to speak of indigenous things and that they cannot be represented, there is a danger that those who are structurally pushed to the margins will be imprisoned within their existing positionality. If people who are in a weak position are the only ones who are allowed to speak for themselves, the result will be to strengthen and reproduce existing social divisions.

An authentic representation of indigenousness is likely to prove impossible. Hapao village is supported by the three core industries of traditional rice terrace and swidden agriculture, woodcarving for the tourist industry and migrant labor. It is no longer a homogeneous community. Traditional economic and social class divisions have been exacerbated and many villagers move to Asin Road Barangay in Baguio to lodge with relatives or obtain a university education. My friend of thirty years, Sylvano Mahiwo, who was born in Hapao, went to Japan to do his doctorate on Japan's cultural policy towards the Association of Southeast Asian Nations (ASEAN) and became a professor of international relations in the Asia Center at the University of the Philippines (he died in 2015).[13] As I have already mentioned and discuss further in the next chapter, well over 150 people from Hapao have migrated overseas for work over the past two decades. The quest to find a way to maintain tradition while entering into

---

13 At Tokyo University he studied international relations under Professor Hirano Kenichirō and in February 1991 he obtained his doctorate for a dissertation titled 'Postwar Japan's Human and Cultural Policy Towards the ASEAN'.

the modern world is different for each individual and everybody has to walk any number of different paths. The figure of today's 'real Ifugao' is fractured and uneven, even within a single individual, and as a result there is no single authentic figure.

It follows that an honest response to the criticism Kidlat has received from native intellectuals – that his representations are orientalist or essentialist – ought not try to produce a definitive representation of the real Ifugao, but nor should it be to abandon the attempt entirely. The answer probably lies somewhere in between – for example, by making films that incorporate the voices and perspectives of the people who are portrayed within them, as Kidlat has tried to do, and to do so even more consciously. Perhaps the style of filmmaking that Kidlat pursues in *Why is Yellow at the Middle of the Rainbow?*, which responds sincerely to criticism and changing circumstances from outside and reflects the process of responding through the editing of new versions, is also part of the answer – that is, to continue

Watching one of his works-in-progress on television with some of the villagers. After the viewing, Kidlat listens while they share their impressions of the film. Nauyac appears on the screen. (March 12, 2000)

to edit new versions as the situation develops, allowing the new work to be born out of a never-ending process of deconstruction that is always in progress and that can then become the basis for yet another work.

Praise for Ifugao culture and engagement in its renewal

Kidlat continues to record Nauyac up close and his attempts to make films from the provisional edits he produces from time to time has no end. For Kidlat, the camera is embedded as a part of his daily life. He also remains convinced that the Ifugaos are the people who have continued to maintain a true Filipino sensibility and worldview, and a culture and way of life of which they can be proud. This may seem at first to be an unreasonable expectation to place upon them, but Kidlat sees the Ifugaos as the only source of potential and salvation. Ifugao culture is the guiding star towards his own rebirth and Nauyac is the spiritual guide whose words and actions are a source of inspiration for Kidlat.

Having been born and raised in the city of Baguio in the heart of the highlands, the Ifugao people and their culture have been part of Kidlat's life since childhood. Since Kidlat returned from Europe, his mother's friend, Nauyac, has played an indispensable role in helping him to bring art together with daily life and politics, in his own personal transformation, and in clearing the way for a new social and cultural space in the Philippines. Nauyac is trying to secure his people's dignity and social status as an indigenous people by keeping and respecting the unique culture of the Ifugaos. He is not only Kidlat's soul guru, but his comrade and companion in the arts and culture movement. Kidlat asks Nauyac to stand in front of the camera and talk as an indigenous man about the preservation and revival of his culture or about the reforestation movement. At other times, they work together on a plan and carry it out together. Kidlat records all of this. Since making *Why is Yellow at the Middle of the Rainbow?*, taking the footage he has collected back to the editing studio, and cutting it up to create his filmic narratives as inspiration strikes him, has become an important pillar of Kidlat's practice.

Significantly, when Nauyac retired as *barangay* captain and returned to Hapao in 1998 to immerse himself in the movement to protect the natural environment of the forests and rice terraces, Kidlat bought a traditional Ifugao house and had it relocated to Patpat near Nauyac's family home. He stays there when events take him to Hapao and makes regular visits at

The Politics of Representation 271

other times too. In 2003, with the assistance of Ifugao carpenters, he built another traditional-style house beside it, with his sons also helping. He hopes to base himself there more permanently and dreams of passing his old age with the Ifugao villagers. Building this second house is part of his master plan to realize this dream. It is possible to see Kidlat's journey from

Left: Kidlat editing some of the footage he has collected at his studio in Baguio (March 14, 1998). He has been using digital video since the end of 1990s. He edits the digital footage on an Apple Mac. His eldest son, who is a journalist and video artist, is teaching him how to use the software.

Right top: The traditional house Kidlat bought and had relocated to Patpat to use as a home base in Hapao. The fabric hanging from the front of the house was made by his second son, Kawayan, who is an artist, and was inspired by his stay in Nepal. (October 3, 1998)

Right bottom: Inside the house, Kidlat carries out some maintenance on his Bolex 16mm camera while children look on with interest. (October 3, 1998)

Baguio to Manila and Philadelphia and then on to Paris, circumnavigating the world before returning to Baguio and sinking deeper into the Ifugao world, as a symbolic return to the womb, as an attempt at rebirth.[14]

Since Nauyac moved to Hapao from Baguio, Kidlat has had great sympathy with his passion for the reforestation movement and has become a powerful collaborator. When Nauyac returned to the village, he stopped by Kidlat's house near Burnham Park and received a solar cooker and other gifts before he departed. At about the same time, Kidlat successfully applied for funding from the Toyota Foundation in Japan through the Baguio artists' collective, Sun Flower Co., which he chairs, in order to support Nauyac's work from the sidelines. The US$14,300 funding enabled them to carry out a project in 1997 called 'Research on Traditional Forest Resource Management Practices Among Ifugao Wood Carvers: The Participatory Approach in Hapao' (Project Number 96-I-031). The project involved inviting village elders and young leaders to two workshops in the village to collect and disseminate traditional knowledge about forests and trees in the Hapao region. The funding also covered some of the costs for the construction and operation of a seedling nursery. The project employed Nauyac's second daughter, Vivian, who had worked as a live-in maid in Hong Kong for four years after graduating from the University of the Philippines Baguio, as the primary research assistant to collate, organize and record for future use the knowledge on forest and tree management obtained from the villagers.[15] The following year the project continued

---

14 However, late one night in February 2004, when the Hapao house was nearly complete, Kidlat's home in Baguio burned to the ground. Rebuilding his family home therefore became his priority. He put his plans for a secluded life in Hapao on hold and ultimately abandoned the idea of moving there completely. Instead he visits the village regularly at the New Year and for major events. Fortunately, although his family was asleep when the fire broke out, they were able to escape and there was no loss of life, but some of Kidlat's film footage, his family's art collection, and various documents and clippings were destroyed. When he rebuilt his home after the fire, he built a dwelling for himself and his wife, as well as separate dwellings for his three sons on a large piece of land. The design and interior of the dwellings accords with each occupant's own sense of style and they are all completely different. Rather than making detailed plans, they drew up a basic design and then explained directly to the builders their ideas for the compound and the various details.
15 After that, Vivian married a young Israeli she had met in Hong Kong. After selling accessories on the street in Japan for about six months, they went to Israel together and have lived there ever since.

under a slightly different name, 'Research on Knowledge Related to Traditional Participatory Forest Management Practices in Hapao,' after receiving a further US$9,200.[16]

As well as supporting Nauyac's reforestation movement from the sidelines, drawing on his own concerns as a filmmaker, Kidlat held regular practical workshops on camera operation and film techniques. He donated a digital video camera and film cartridges to the villagers and helped them to document and record their rituals. Almost as soon as the project had begun, it was featured in a full-page article in the *Inquirer*, a national newspaper, with accompanying photographs. The article concerned 'the vanishing of Filipino values' and discussed how Kidlat 'has taken it upon himself to put the camera into the hands of the tribals so that they may have the power to record their culture themselves' (Demetillo 1997). It contained a description of the workshops along with explanatory statements from Kidlat and a report on how the villagers enjoyed the workshops.

> Many nuances are lost in the outsider's daily lifestyle and rituals. 'For instance...when children are taught to ask permission from tree spirits to pass by their area, an outsider may not see that this may have an indirect bearing on forest management. Such respect for the inhabitants of the forest can already be a built-in mechanism which later on in adult life will act as a cultural "break mechanism" against rampant logging. Furthermore, a recording of daily lifestyle may be something convenience will not allow outsider researchers to do. Cordillera tribes are cultures of "oral traditions." Values embedded in folktales and epics are passed on through story-telling gathering around the family hearth or on occasions that collect the community together, such as harvest and weddings. Today, children spend the whole day in school and with homework at night, there is a breakaway from an old rhythm that allowed the passing on of old knowledge to new generations. Audio-visuals, properly assembled, can be looked at as today's surrogate tool of oral traditional transmission. These may not have the polish of National Geographic

---

16 At that time I happened to be a member of the selection committee for the Toyota Foundation's international aid grants. I advocated for Kidlat's application strongly. (In this sense, I have been deeply involved in Nauyac's reforestation movement in Hapao from its early stages.) The results of the two-year project were supposed to be submitted in the form of a report and a film record, but only a draft was submitted and so, technically, the report was never finalized.

documentaries, but they will have the feel of "home movie" intimacy closer to the old family warmth of story-telling by a dinner fire.'

Kidlat Tahimik hopes that the inevitable entry of technology can be used constructively rather than turning tribals of deeper wisdom into passive consumers of 'Hollywood mindsets' through cable television. (Demetillo 1997)

To concentrate on his work of using video to increase self-awareness of traditional culture among the villagers, Kidlat applied successfully to the Toyota Foundation again in 2003 and received US$14,300 for a project on 'Participatory Video Production for Indigenous Cultural Education' ('Indigenous Video-S.E.R.V.I.C.E. (Shoot, Edit and Replay Video for Indigenous Culture Education)). This project had the same goal as anthropologist Terence Turner's work with Britain's BBC. To support the self-empowerment of the Kayapó of the Brazilian Amazon, Turner provided them with the necessary knowledge, techniques and materials to make their own video recordings. Kidlat's was an attempt get the people of Hapao to take an interest in their own culture and, by focusing the lens of their cameras on the landscape of the village, its traditional rituals and the details of their daily lives, to make video diaries that serve as a starting point for cultural preservation and revival (for a detailed account, see Shimizu 2003: 166–8). Just as Kidlat is both recorder and recorded, the project actively supported the villagers to both record themselves and be recorded. The assumption was that if the villagers became familiar with the cameras and became confident in using them, it would awaken their interest in their own lifestyles and rituals, strengthening their awareness of their own unique culture. He wanted to help the Ifugaos to use the video cameras as effective weapons of the weak in order to think about what it means to be an Ifugao and as an opportunity to preserve their culture. If possible, he hopes to teach them more specialized editing skills and support them to deepen their ability to express themselves.

In addition to the activities discussed here, Kidlat has personally provided funds for repairs to the irrigation canals that direct water into the rice terraces and for Nauyac's reforestation movement. The footage of his support work for Nauyac has been edited and shown in films such as *Banal Kahoy*. The English title (literal translation) of this film, *Holy Wood*, evokes the idea of both a sacred tree and the capital of the cinematic world. Of course, it thereby conveys a critique of Hollywood film. (However, Kidlat says that this film is only a provisional version

The Politics of Representation 275

Top: Mathew Paduaon operating a borrowed video camera. (March 4, 2001)
Bottom: Atchin videoing her father, Orlando. (March 12, 2000)

that had to be completed as part of a report to the international body that provided the funds.)

Together with Nauyac, Kidlat has also worked hard to revive the *pun-nok* (tug-of-war), a traditional Hapao harvest ritual. Each year this ritual attracts a crowd of participants and is conducted with great fanfare. It frequently features in the newspaper and was incorporated into UNESCO's list of Intangible Cultural Heritage in 2015. The *pun-nok* is one of the harvest rituals that make up the agricultural rituals of the Ifugao agricultural calendar. In the 1970s, when the CPP-NPA seized control of the area, many people left and the ritual was suspended for more than ten years. Nauyac was passionate in working to revive the ritual and persuade the villagers of its importance and Kidlat provided the necessary funds. The *pun-nok* was originally conducted by villagers from both sides of the river that separates Hapao from Ba-ang as a ritual divination to determine which side would enjoy a bumper harvest the following year.

In Hapao the wealthiest households that own the largest amount of terraced land are referred to as *kadangyan*. Those with the second largest amount are *umonob* and those that have an average amount of terraced land are *maikatlo*. The large number of farming families who have less than the average amount of land are known as *maikappat* (Respicio 2015b: 108–9). The *tumon-ak* is the first person to carry out major agricultural work such as rice planting or harvesting. The *tumon-ak* may be either male or female and is chosen from among the eldest children of *kadangyan* families. He or she starts the agricultural work or ritual for the village on a day determined through divination by a *monbaki* (ritual specialist) with the assistance of the elders. To become the *tumon-ak*, the candidate must not only come from a family with the largest amount of terraced land but, importantly, be seen to be able to bring in a rich harvest for the village. If there is a major incident in the village or pests and disease continue to affect the crops, the *tumon-ak* may be changed (Respicio and Picache 2013: 10).

The *pun-nok* was revived at the end of the 1990s after the period of NPA rule. The villagers differ as to who first issued the call to revive the ritual. However, it is clearly related to the fact that the *Tungoh* was revived in Hungduan in the first half of the 1990s or, more precisely, to the growing interest in reviving traditional rituals. Nauyac responded to this interest and actively encouraged the villagers. Once it was revived, Kidlat provided money to feed all participants and some prize money for both winning and losing villages. According to an article by Pedro Florends on the *pun-nok* in the *Baguio Chronicle* in 2016, the revival took place in 1997 thanks to the support of Kidlat and Nauyac. Kumano Takeshi, who conducted a year's fieldwork focusing on religious practices in Ba-ang in the middle of 1990s, cautions that the religious significance of the *pun-nok* is being neglected and mentions Kidlat's involvement in the revival as a prize-money sponsor, which caused the secularization of this rite as a competitive game (Kumano 2007:92–3). As at the *Tungoh* that is organized by the Hungduan municipal government, men are expected to wear loincloths during the *pun-nok* and the bright red color of the loincloths adds to the festive atmosphere.

In addition to Kidlat's important role in the revival of the *pun-nok*, he also contributed indirectly to its inclusion on the UNESCO list of Intangible Cultural Heritage. The National Commission for Culture and the Arts became aware of the *pun-nok* thanks to Espiritu's article in the *Philippine Daily Inquirer* (September 5, 2012) that was accompanied by an attractive photograph. The article aroused strong interest from the commission and a team was rapidly dispatched to investigate. This confirmed that, along with the *huowah* rituals that are conducted over the preceding days, this agricultural ritual still had a meaningful function within the village community. Thanks to this report, preparations to submit the ritual for inclusion on the UNESCO list began rather hurriedly (Respicio and Picache

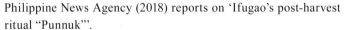

Philippine News Agency (2018) reports on 'Ifugao's post-harvest ritual "Punnuk"'.

2013). The *Inquirer* reporter was a friend of Kidlat's who was based in Baguio and learned about the ritual from him. The article made no mention of the fact that the *pun-nok* had been interrupted and then revived. Instead, it gave a tacit understanding that this was an authentic traditional ritual that had been passed down from the ancestors and still had deep roots in the community.

The revived *pun-nok* enables the villagers to enjoy the sense of community that manifests during an exceptional space and time, but thought has also been given to the way visitors and tourists from outside the village see it. Authenticity is emphasized through the red palette of the participants' dress, the rope made from rattan that is used for the contest, and the ancient lineage of prayers and chants that are intoned by the *monbaki* before the commencement of the ritual. At the video workshops organized by Kidlat in Hapao, his eldest son, the media artist Kidlat Senior, also took part as his father's assistant. He taught basic video camera skills, film technique and basic editing, recorded the revived *pun-nok* and produced a thirty-minute documentary, *Tribal Videos* (2001). In 2002 the film won the Discovery Channel's First Time Filmmakers Initiative.[17]

Mobilizing culture

So far in this book I have introduced the work of two individuals who eulogize and actively mobilize the culture of the indigenous Ifugao society of the Philippines. Ifugao culture is an important resource for Kidlat in two senses. First, in his project to reconstruct his own identity, Ifugao culture is the copybook that he feels he should do his best to imitate and follow. In this sense it is a resource containing fruitful activators and nutrients for his thinking. Second, as a filmmaker it is a source of messages that

---

17 The use of Sony video cameras to revalidate and reevaluate traditional culture is another example of the hybrid cultural strategy Kidlat has consistently adopted. The contradiction and conflict between his desire for and reaction against modern and Western things is symbolized by his use of film as an expressive medium. It can also be seen in his admiration and ambivalence regarding nativism and traditional culture and ways of thinking. This conflict remains unresolved. Rather than choosing between the two, he suspends his choice and tries to live in acceptance of this contradiction. Indeed, by his honest revelation of his own ambivalence, he embodies and problematizes the conflict that the Philippines as a nation and as a people have held within them since their inception (Yamashita 2001: 61).

relativize and critique the First World straight out of the Third World, rather than Kidlat having to speak that message himself. For his films it is also a resource in the sense that it is a treasure house of source materials that can become 'exotic' images in his films. Kidlat's mobilization of Ifugao culture in his documentary films about Nauyac's work have brought him praise and increased his reputation. Nauyac, too, has become the willing subject of Kidlat's films and in them he speaks about the importance of protecting traditional culture and the way of life of the Ifugaos, surrounded by the forests and rice terraces. He performs the role of an evangelist for the authentic Ifugao, who lives in harmony with nature and fears the gods. Off-screen, both as a leader in the indigenous community in Baguio from the 1970s to the mid-1990s and as the leader of the reforestation movement since his return to Hapao in 1998, Nauyac has continued to call on national and local governments and domestic and international NGOs to support social development. When appealing to these bodies, Nauyac actively attributes meaning to the history and culture of the Ifugaos, whose livelihoods are based on rice terrace farming. By doing so, he has secured funding, materials and technical assistance from governments and NGOs in the Philippines and Japan to support cultural revival, reforestation, the maintenance of community infrastructure and social development.

In this section, I consider the conscious and proactive work of Kidlat and Nauyac from the perspective of the mobilization of Ifugao culture. The notion of mobilizing cultural resources has attracted significant attention in Japan for more than ten years. In 2002 the Association for the Study of Cultural Resources was established. The association's founding statement made the following declaration: 'We possess ample cultural resources from the past and the present. We have a responsibility to effectively utilize our existing stock of cultural resources and to create new cultural resources that can be passed on to future generations' (Association for the Study of Cultural Resources 2002). The statement goes on to define the concept of a cultural resource as follows:

> we call the sum total of the valuable materials that give us clues to understand society and culture at a particular time, the body of cultural resources. The body of cultural resources is both material and immaterial. It includes buildings and cityscapes that cannot be contained within museums or repositories as well as traditional performing arts and rituals. (Association for the Study of Cultural Resources 2002)

The Association for the Study of Cultural Resources was established mainly by members of the Folklore Society of Japan. In recent years, however, there has been a growing interest in looking at culture as a resource within the discipline of cultural anthropology. For example, a group of researchers who specialize in cultural anthropology and ecological anthropology, a field best represented in the work of Uchibori Motomitsu, conducted a major research project on resources and human activity between 2002 and 2007.[18] I was involved in a working group on 'The Generation and Utilization of Cultural Resources', which was led by Yamashita Shinji. Responding to the well-known work of Pierre Bourdieu on cultural capital, Yamashita clearly explains the significance of analyzing culture not as capital, but as a resource (Yamashita 2007).

Yamashita (2007: 48) points out that 'the function or effect of culture exists under particular conditions and for a particular purpose. In other words, it "becomes a resource".' Therefore, it is the process of mobilizing the potential that lies latent within culture to perform some particular function or has some particular effect that needs to be investigated; that is, the means by which 'cultural becomes a resource' and the process of 'making culture a resource'. He emphasizes that rather than seeing culture in this process as the subconscious system that organizes the operation of everyday life, the topic with which anthropology has been concerned until now, we should see culture as something that 'appears when consciously manipulated and created as a resource and utilized to obtain a particular objective...In this sense, the mobilization of culture today occurs within the context of the three-sided relationship between the nation state, the global economy and the substantive communities in which people live' (Yamashita 2007: 48–9, 68).

Moriyama Takumi, another member of Yamashita's group, concisely compares the particular features of the concept of 'cultural resources' and the horizon that opens up when they become the focus of attention through a comparison with Bourdieu's cultural capital. According to Moriyama (2007), Bourdieu's cultural capital appears in three different

---

18 The official name of the project was MEXT Grant-in-Aid for Scientific Research on Innovative Areas 'Distribution and sharing of resources in symbolic and ecological systems: integrative model-building in anthropology'. The results were published in the seven-volume series *Shigen jinruigaku* (Anthropology of resources) by Kōbundō.

The Politics of Representation

states: an embodied state, an objectified state and an institutionalized state. In each case, 'time' is the critical factor. By thinking about time together with capital, '"cultural capital" can be defined as something that, having been accumulated, is preserved within the process of returning to itself as it accumulates over time, and within the temporal process of its inter-generational succession; and if possible proliferates quantitatively' (Moriyama 2007: 64). Moriyama explains that the concept of cultural capital 'is a conceptual apparatus for adding to phenomena related to social structure such as class formation and the reproduction of class over a given period of time and is therefore a structurally-oriented concept' (Moriyama 2007: 65). By comparison, Moriyama argues, the concept of cultural resources is action-oriented and therefore enables us to focus on the individual specificities of the mobilization and utilization of a 'resource'.

After explaining the advantages and potentialities of understanding culture as a resource, Moriyama conducts a detailed case study of the transfer of the corpse of Ranavalona III in French colonial Madagascar. In

The fourfold question of 'Who' in the 'Mobilization' of 'culture' (Moriyama 2007: 85)

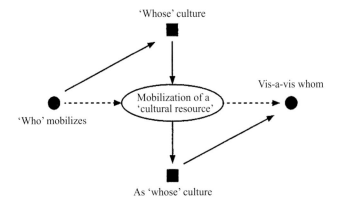

this study, he takes up the problem of the relationship between different actors in the mobilization of culture in terms of a 'politics of cultural resources'. According to Moriyama, it is the problem of the subject that needs to be considered in the dynamic moment of 'mobilization' of an activity-oriented 'cultural resource' – that is, the question of who 'mobilizes' a 'cultural resource'. In this regard, the main issue is the fourfold question of 'who': (1) 'who' mobilizes (2) 'whose' culture (3) as 'whose' culture (4) 'vis-a-vis whom' (Moriyama 2007: 85).

Moriyama's argument is both clear and convincing but he neglects the most important question with regard to the mobilization of culture. If, as Yamashita says, culture as a resource 'appears as something that is utilized for a particular purpose', and if the 'mobilization' of 'culture' is 'directed by an intention to influence another' (Moriyama 2007: 88), the question that needs to be asked is what is the purpose of mobilizing culture? Moriyama claims that looking at 'cultural resources' from the perspective of the active moment of 'mobilization' makes visible the relationship between individuals that lies beyond the relationship between people and culture. If that is the case, there needs to be an awareness of the direction in which the influence is exerted, or of its destination – in other words, of the ultimate purpose of the mobilization. As Moriyama suggests in the concluding subheading of his paper, 'Towards a politics of cultural mobilization', we have to ask, 'to what end and for whom?'

According to Imamura (2007), the original meaning of the term 'resource' has always carried a strong sense of a tool that is 'useful for something' and anything and everything that comes within the range of human activity (in its broadest sense, economic, cultural etc.) manifests as something with the potential to 'become' a resource (for a human being). Not only human beings but 'all living things take things from their environment that may be useful to their survival and "mobilize" them'; therefore, a resource 'can be defined as a state in which a latent potential has been realized, or, as a realized potential' (Imamura 2007: 13–14). Uchibori (2004: 9) defines 'resource' more concisely as 'an element of the environment that is utilized by organisms, including human beings, for their survival'.[19]

---

19 Imamura (2007) later abstracted even further from the concept of a resource. After arguing that 'a resource is nothing other than a thing that is of use to human beings, a helpful thing' (Imamura 2007: 357), he explains that originally a resource was: something that emerges from the origin of all usefulness and functions as a proxy for that origin (source)…in other words, the source as it is

Drawing on Imamura and Uchibori's discussion of resources, if we return to the question of the attempt to mobilize culture, we can see that the actor first becomes conscious of culture, then substantiates or objectifies it as an object and then through exhibiting, manipulating or taking advantage of it, tries to gain some benefit or have some effect. However, in practice actors do not mobilize culture in its entirety. Rather, they take some constitutive element and as they display or represent it, make a political claim, or push a commercial interest (such as tourism promotion), they imbue it with meaning. The culture that is mobilized in this way is, to borrow Imamura's words, a stand-in or generalization for all of the elements of culture that exist as a variety of potentialities. On the one hand culture is a 'hold-all' for all these elements (Imamura 2007: 359), while on the other are the people who are the intended object of the mobilizer's claims. To connect the two and to generate a meaning-function that will have the greatest commercial, artistic or political effect, those elements that the intended target of the mobilization will appreciate as having meaning or value for them, and that will act on them, will be selected and represented as culture.

This hold-all concept of culture overlaps almost completely with the definition of culture put forward by EB Tylor, who was the leading researcher at the time when evolutionary theory was the mainstream of research in anthropology ('that complex whole which includes knowledge, belief, art, morals, law, custom, and any other capabilities and habits acquired by man as a member of society' (Tylor 1871: 1)). However, opposed to this concept of capital 'C' Culture that had an affinity with evolutionary theory, the American anthropologists who followed Franz Boas saw culture not as a way of life or mode of action in and of itself, but as a framework for imbuing action with meaning or for synthesizing experience.

For example, Clifford Geertz (1973: 5) gave his famous definition as follows: 'believing, with Max Weber, that man is an animal suspended

---

cannot be of use to human life and so it is necessary to mobilize that origin as a resource. We call this a resource in the sense of 'a source that re-appears or is re-stored'. (Imamura 2007: 359–60)

Uchibori (2007: 18–19) accepted Imamura's idea and wrote:
a resource is originally an 'origin' or 'source' that precedes individual instances of its use by human beings. That is, unlike a source, the term emphasizes the aspect of a source as it is mobilized for human use...I want to see a resource as a tool for thinking about 'something that acts within human activity as well as offering some active power to human life'.

in webs of significance he himself has spun, I take culture to be those webs'. James Peacock's (2004: 7) definition of culture as 'the name that anthropologists give to the taken-for-granted but powerfully influential understandings and codes that are learned and shared by members of a group' makes a clear distinction between the use of the term in anthropology and its everyday use.[20]

On the clash between the general concept of culture and its use in the discipline of anthropology, Sekimoto Teruo's (1998b) concise outline is of relevance here. According to Sekimoto, there is nothing in this world that can only be referred to using the word 'culture'. All individual things that are referred to as culture inevitably have their own name. Therefore, 'culture is not a name for some particular thing. Instead, the use of the term culture to write or speak about something is a rhetorical device that procures a particular effect' (Sekimoto 1998b: 21). In other words, culture is an all-encompassing higher-order concept like resource. When the need arises, various individual things that each have their own name can be bandied about as specific manifestations of culture with some benefit or effect. However, the culture that Sekimoto refers to here is, in his own words, not 'culture as lived experience' but 'culture as narrative' (Sckimoto 1998b). In other words, it is not culture in itself but culture for another, consciously manipulated and spoken about in anticipation of some political or economic effect.

If both resources and culture first emerge when they become the focus of an utterance and if they contain some hidden potential to be utilized for a particular purpose, then in order to think about culture as a resource, as Moriyama and Yamashita argue, it is the process whereby culture is actualized, extolled and utilized as a resource that needs to be investigated – specifically, the ways in which it is talked about when it is put into words in a speech act and the ways in which someone explains its meaning or significance.

---

20 In their study of the conflict between the Native American Menominee people and white hunters and fishers over the conservation and utilization of biological resources in Wisconsin, Medin, Ross and Cox (2006: 11, 27–31) argue based on a detailed empirical study of the discord between the frames of meaning the two groups use to understand the natural environment and its biological resources. While basically following Geertz's definition of culture, they address the gap left by its static understanding and advocate for a cultural-consensus model that values the dynamic side of cultural processes and the distribution view of culture.

In conclusion, in the process whereby culture is mobilized as a resource, culture as it is lived in itself – that is, as the complex totality of human knowledge and mental practices that Tylor includes in his definition of the concept of culture – becomes the object, a storehouse or hold-all of potential resources. Apropos of this, we choose from among this totality that which we think has value or importance as our culture. By imbuing our choices with meaning through an elaborate rhetorical process, culture first materializes as a valued specific 'thing' or 'notion'. It also becomes something worth defending and developing. It follows that in order to protect and develop that which is materialized as culture, it is necessary to support the people who own that culture both psychically and financially.[21] The culture that modern anthropology has made the object of its study is the code that enables meaning to be imbued in resources and read off them. It follows that when culture is mobilized as a resource, Tylor's culture (a thing) is mobilized through Boas's culture (as a code of meaning). The two genealogies of definitions or ways of understanding culture actually coexist, functioning in mutual interdependence and supporting one another.

As I discuss in Chapter 5, when Nauyac explains the significance of reforestation to the villagers he first gives an economic reason; namely, as he has said on many occasions, we have to protect the terrace agriculture and woodcarving that are the basis of our means of subsistence. He also emphasizes the religious and cultural meaning of reforestation; we have to protect the rice terraces because they are permeated with the sweat of our ancestors' toil and their rituals of devotion. It is the ancestors who gave us our lives and the terraces are the concrete proof of the unbroken chain that stretches back to them over countless generations.

This explanation is enough to convince most of the villagers of the importance of reforestation. Indeed, rather than being convinced, they too live in the same world of meaning inhabited by Nauyac.

On the other hand, when he appeals to the government or NGOs in the Philippines, he does not only talk about the rice terraces in terms of the inestimable meaning they have for the Ifugaos. Above all, he emphasizes their value as a piece of cultural heritage that demonstrates the pride and

---

21 For a detailed account of the suffering of the Aetas after the eruption of Mount Pinatubo as an example of the process through which culture is selected, mobilized and spoken about in order to demand rights and recognition in indigenous revival and rights claims, see Shimizu (2003: 242–52).

dignity of the Philippines as a whole. When he addresses Japanese NGOs, he emphasizes that the rice terraces are a UNESCO World Heritage site, the fact that Ifugao was the destination for General Yamashita's final retreat at the end of the Asia-Pacific War and the wonders of the environmentally responsible way Ifugaos live in harmony with nature. In order to obtain the broadest base of support and cooperation for his reforestation movement, Nauyac consciously utilizes the language and rhetoric that speaks to his target audience and tugs on their heartstrings to obtain the best results. He is a collaborator and co-conspirator in Kidlat's work in the culture movement, in addition to his pursuit of reforestation and social development. He skillfully and persuasively uses the discourse of an activist and expounds eloquently and forcefully something he believes in from the bottom of his heart.

Betwixt two layers of contradiction and conflict

As I discuss in the previous chapter, since *Why is Yellow at the Middle of the Rainbow?* Kidlat has continued to maintain a close personal relationship with Nauyac. As a film director he has also continued to place him in the central role in his films, thereby targeting and objectifying him. However, the relationship between the two, as I repeatedly point out, is not necessarily a fixed relationship between a director giving instructions and an actor following them. Sometimes it is Nauyac who records Kidlat's loincloth performances. Furthermore, beginning with *Our Bomb Mission to Hiroshima* and *Japanese Summers of a Filipino Fundoshi*, Kidlat has taken sole responsibility for raising the funds and making the other necessary preparations to take Nauyac and a number of Hapao woodcarvers to Japan. When he was invited to the Fourth Echigo-Tsumari Art Field Triennale in July 2009, Kidlat took his third son, Kabunian, but he left Nauyac to select the rest of the team. Twelve Ifugao woodcarvers joined the troupe and spent three weeks on a plot of land in the rice terraces of Tōkamachi, reconstructing a traditional Ifugao house. In a sense, as well as being Nauyac's spiritual disciple in the reconstruction and liberation of his self, and a film director and artist who performs alongside him, Kidlat is also a kind of manager, a producer who draws Nauyac onto the stage and creates a place for him to express himself.

Once again, I stress the important point that the specific ideas and the overall concept for their various activities, and the meanings attributed

The Politics of Representation 287

to them, are left almost entirely to the sensibilities, ideas and initiative of Nauyac. It was Nauyac who first came up with the idea for the reforestation movement in Hapao and gave it the name 'Global'. He has conceptualized, guided and put into practice the movement's various activities. However, whenever he is holding a somewhat larger event, he tells Kidlat where and when it will be held and when they meet he explains the gist of what

Top left: Ifugao woodcarvers line up for a commemorative photograph at the opening ceremony of the Fourth Echigo-Tsumaari Art Field Triennale. Nauyac is second from the left in the front row, the next but one is Kabunian and the next but one after that is Kidlat.

Top right: During the Triennale, they wore traditional dress continuously. Here they are riding on a train dressed in their loincloths and wrap skirt.

Bottom left: The almost complete traditional house and totem pole.

Bottom right: Dancing at a social event.

(All four photographs July–August 2009, source: Hasegawa Tatsuo)

he is trying to do. On these occasions, Kidlat might suggest additions or changes that will give the event broader appeal for people from outside the village but he respects Nauyac's ideas and his overall concept. Kidlat always ensures that he gets himself there before the event and records documentary sequences from it. When he is filming, he is both directly and indirectly conscious of the likely audience for the finished work. Similarly, when Nauyac is speaking to the villagers and guests in attendance, he is always conscious of also appealing to the audience on the other side of the camera who will see the completed film.

When Kidlat turns the camera on Nauyac and asks him a direct question, Nauyac is aware that he is responding not only to Kidlat and the villagers but to an audience in Manila or even abroad. On these occasions, he speaks very clearly, explaining his ideas and his dreams or making a specific critique in what amounts to a kind of improvisational performance. You could say that Kidlat's camera skillfully and precisely draws out Nauyac's worldview, his ideas and his various pronouncements in the form of concrete episodes or claims. Kidlat plays the role of a midwife who holds up Nauyac's worldview and delivers it into the world. Furthermore, while they talk informally day to day before the camera is switched on, Kidlat listens to Nauyac's thoughts, asks questions, draws out what he is trying to say and sometimes even adds something of his own. The two bounce ideas off one another. In this sense, to repeat it again, they are both co-performers in and co-producers of the documentaries. They are also co-conspirators who deliberately aim to disrupt fixed understandings of the world and invite their audiences to see things in a different way. They share the same intention to rebuild society on the basis of new relationships.

As I explain in Chapter 6, Kidlat frequently switches places, from the recorder to the recorded, the observer to the observed and the narrator to the listener. In a conscious attempt to defamiliarize the audience's existing worldviews, he inverts the relationship between subject and object. The relationship between Kidlat and Nauyac began when Kidlat approached Nauyac as a guru from whom he could gain hints and guidance in the reconstruction and liberation of his self. However, as can be seen in their work to revive the *pun-nok*, as their friendship deepened they became comrades dedicated to cultural revival. In their conversations they endlessly trade questions and opinions, swapping places as in a game of catch, and seem to derive great enjoyment from this kind of brainstorming session. The fluidity of their daily lives, as in their films, suggests that remaining for too long in immobile, stable perspectives and stances is uncomfortable for them, if not taboo, and we can clearly identify their search for freedom and lightness.

Kidlat does try to resolve the double-layered contradiction or conflict that exists between his orientation towards and rejection of the modern and the Western that is symbolized by film as an expressive medium and its reverse, his orientation towards and vacillation over nativism, or the primitive culture and psyche. Rather than choosing between the two, he tries to live within the contradiction. By deliberately living this contradiction, he is able to embody within himself the conflict that the Philippine nation and people have been holding inside from the time they first emerged. As a cultural strategy, this deliberate surface-level inconstancy in his use of constructionism and essentialism for different purposes must be noted and subjected to careful consideration. Thinking outside the box and trying to disrupt existing common sense, the figure of Kidlat contriving to

Nauyac speaking in front of a television camera at the opening of a model traditional Ifugao village (*Tam-Awan* Village) in Banaue. He will stand in front of a camera given any opportunity, not just for Kidlat, and always speaks eloquently. (March 8, 2001)

defamiliarize the reality that we can see so clearly right before our eyes (with a joking and foolish playfulness that is nevertheless sincere) is connected with the psychic currents of the *pusong* (trickster) that has recurred again and again in the popular history of the Philippines.

Part III
Negotiating with Globalization

Kidlat with Dennis Banks, a co-founder and an activist of the American Indian Movement (AIM, organized in 1968), at the opening ceremony of the 3rd KAPWA International Conference in Baguio (June 27, 2012), courtesy of Yoshihiko Himaru.

8 Working Overseas and Reviving Tradition
Spreading Wings and Putting Down Roots

In Hapao today the villagers embrace migrant work as they struggle to strengthen and develop the foundations of their way of life. This suggests a shift from their entrenched defensive strategy, adopted to preserve their villages and rice terraces during the Spanish and American colonial periods, to an offensive strategy pursued by individuals leaving their villages to work in distant lands where they earn cash incomes. As a result of migrant work, the villagers' spatial consciousness is no longer limited to the village, municipal or provincial levels of the Ifugao world, or even to the Philippines, but has expanded beyond the seas to Asia, the Middle East, Europe, North America and Australia. Furthermore, as their spatial consciousness has expanded outward to the wide world, their realization of the chain that connects them to the ancestors who built up and protected the basis for their way of life has strengthened a historical consciousness that stretches back into the distant past. This was reinforced by the UNESCO World Heritage listing of the rice terraces in 1995 and the domestic and international attention this brought. Looking down on the world from a bird's-eye view, globalization has brought about an enormous movement of people and things and caused a 'compression of space and time'.

For people living out their lives at the grassroots, it has given rise to an expansion of the global scale of the space of their everyday lives and of their consciousness and an extension of their historical and temporal consciousness, both backwards to the past and forwards to the future. Globalization has also triggered a reflexive process, whereby people develop a strong concern with their own positionality within this expanded spatial and temporal horizon and an awareness of the variety and the extent of the network of connections that support it. One example is a collaborative project of 'Global' since 2000 with a small Japanese NGO (IKGS) in the countryside of Hyōgo prefecture, which I will introduce in Chapter 9 as a grassroots networking of small people crossing the national border.

Migrant workers from Hapao

When a banquet was held in Hapao to celebrate Father Bugatti's ordination in 1999, two mutual-aid societies for Hapao women living in Hong Kong sent donations. According to Eliza Madiwo, who was working in Hong Kong at the time and was active in establishing and running these organizations, the first of these societies was established in 1995. Of its thirty-five members, one was from Magok (in Tinoc), two were from Uhaj (Banaue), and five or six were from Nungulunan and other villages in Hungduan. The remaining twenty-seven or -eight were from Hapao. Almost all of them were working as live-in maids. They met every Sunday in Victoria Park, where they enjoyed chatting with one another and talking about their experiences. At Christmas and New Year, they would get together and throw a party. The names of the members of the two organizations were listed in a commemorative booklet that was compiled to celebrate the ordination. Between 1999 and 2000, the first group had sixteen committee members and forty-two ordinary members and the second had nine committee members and twenty-nine ordinary members. The latter included women who were born in Hapao but had since moved (or, at least, their parents and/or spouses had moved) to Baguio.

As the experiences of these women shows, over the past two decades the rapid spread of globalization has extended up into the high mountains of the Philippines, giving the villagers a chance to earn cash incomes by becoming migrant workers. As a result, their way of life and their consciousness is changing rapidly so that, at least on the surface, it is coming to resemble that of the lowland Christians. When they rebuild their homes with the money they earn through migrant work, they almost always adopt the basic style of lowland homes, with concrete block walls and tin roofs. At the same time, their identity as Ifugaos has been strengthened, a process that is driven by their surface-level assimilation to lowland culture. In order to reinforce these identities, municipal governments have been leading a revival of traditional Ifugao festivals on a grand scale. While rituals associated with the agricultural calendar have been in decline in most households, for weddings and funerals the situation is quite the reverse and large sums of money are expended on rituals and sacrificial feasts to accompany them.

Nauyac's neighbors who have become migrant workers

As I discuss in Chapter 3, the woodcarving industry is an important source of income for the people of Hapao. Many also move to Baguio, Manila and other cities in the Philippines to find work or migrate overseas. One early example of a migrant worker in Hapao is Joseph Nakake, who went to Saudi Arabia in 1984 and spent two years working as a furniture maker. Since the end of the 1980s, a growing number of women started going to Hong Kong or Singapore to work as live-in domestic helpers. I confirmed a total of 149 individual migrant workers in Hapao as of 2007, including those who were currently working overseas. Taking into account the probable existence of Hapao families who have a member working overseas and have themselves relocated to another prefecture and the likelihood of simple survey error, the total number of overseas migrant workers from Hapao is probably as much as 160 or 170. This is nearly 10 percent of the village's total population and closely mirrors the proportion of migrant workers for the Philippines as a

Joseph Nakake cradling his grandchild at a viewing platform next to his house overlooking the rice terraces of Hapao. (March 13, 2001)

whole. However, it is notable that there are no Hapao permanent migrants in the United States nor migrant workers in Japan (entertainers), both prominent destinations among the majority lowland Christians.

The 149 migrant workers I identified traveled to twenty-seven countries as of 2012. The most common destination was Taiwan (49), followed by Hong Kong (40), Singapore (14), Israel (12), Spain (11), Saudi Arabia (9), Canada (7), Germany (6), Australia (5), the United Kingdom (5), Kuwait (5), Bahrain (4), Lebanon (4), Libya (4), South Korea (4), Cyprus (2), United Arab Emirates (2), Middle East (country unknown, 2) and the United States (2, including 1 in Saipan). One migrant worker was identified in Ireland, Sweden, Italy, France, Abu Dhabi, Malaysia, Micronesia (Pohnpei) and the Caribbean (country unknown). The numbers given here total 194 because some migrant workers have been to two or three different countries. In some cases, migrant workers also return to the same country two or three times. Contracts for migrant workers in Hong Kong, Singapore and Taiwan generally last for two years. At the completion of the contract period, many of them return home for a few weeks' vacation before going overseas once again.

In terms of gender, 127 individuals (the overwhelming number of migrant workers) were female. There were only twenty-two males. The range of their occupations also relates to the gender balance of the migrant labor force as a whole. The vast majority are domestic helpers (93), followed by factory workers (31), live-in caregivers (15), nurses (9), ice carvers (4), waitresses (4), construction workers (3), furniture makers and cabinetmakers (3), carpenters (2), administrators (2) and civil engineers (2). There was also one forklift driver, one dental assistant, one security guard, an NGO social worker and a hotel receptionist. Of these, the job that characterizes the workers as Hapao villagers is carving: four migrant workers have used their woodcarving skills to carve ice sculptures, working in hotels in the United Kingdom, Italy and Dubai for a long time. No villagers have gone to Japan to work as entertainers, but some members of 'Global' have traveled to Japan to meet with Japanese support groups. Others have accompanied Kidlat to art festivals and similar events in groups ranging from just a few to about ten.

In Boyyod, where the 'Global' office that also serves as Nauyac's home is located, there are sixteen houses lined up along the road. Fifteen individuals from thirteen of these households have gone overseas for work. Below I briefly explain the circumstances that led each of them to work overseas. I interviewed them myself, without a translator. The languages used were English and Filipino.

Joseph Nakake (b. 1953). Born in Hapao, Joseph Nakake is the younger brother of the late Professor Sylvano Mahiwo of the University of the Philippines Asia Center (international relations).

> In 1982 I went to work in the Saudi Arabian capital Riyadh together with three other villagers from Hapao. While I was working as a woodcarver in a workshop in Baguio, I was approached by a recruiter who offered to arrange a job for me in Saudi Arabia. I thought this was quite strange because he knew that the worship of idols is strictly forbidden in Islam and suspected that as it was a desert country there would not be any materials suitable for woodcarving. However, the salary was US$450 per month (at that time, $1 was equal to 7.5 pesos) and there was…an additional $50 to cover…food, so while I still had my doubts, I decided to go. At first I was taken to a factory that manufactured aluminum doors and windows. Using gestures, I explained that I couldn't do this kind of work. Using some pieces of wood that I had brought with me, I explained that I could do woodcarving work. Then I began fixing and decorating wooden doors and furniture and fitting out the interiors of new buildings. After my three-year contract expired, I returned to Hapao. Then I took another three-year contract and went back to Saudi Arabia. However, the second time I ended up coming home after only eighteen months. Unlike the first contract, there was no salary increase upon signing the new contract and the work was harder. I used the 65,000 pesos I saved while working abroad to build the house where I now live. This house is the fruit of my hard work as a migrant worker. (Conversation with Joseph Nakake, July 24, 2009)

Richard Sikat (b. 1975), Joseph Nakake's son-in-law (the husband of his eldest daughter, Rowena).

> After graduating from the Baguio Colleges Foundation, Richard married Rowena, who is a University of the Philippines Baguio graduate, and came to Hapao to live. At first they lived with Joseph Nakake…but when their second child was born they moved into their own home, which was built on the same piece of land. Rowena got a job as a public relations officer with the Hungduan municipal government and Richard also found employment as a program facilitator with CECAP2 [Central Cordillera Agricultural Programme Phase 2]. However, when CECAP2 was wound up in 2003, he was made redundant. In addition to doing odd jobs, he looked after the housework and the children while his wife was working…in June 2009 he traveled to Saudi Arabia,

where he started working in the office at a construction site. An agency in Manila found the position for him…It charged a commission of 47,000 pesos [US$1,034; 1,000 peso was equivalent to US$22 at the time]. The repayments for the commission came out of his wages. His monthly salary was 22,000 pesos and there was free accommodation and food, so he earned enough to save. (Conversation with Richard's wife, Rowena Nakake, July 26, 2009)

Ben Melon (b. 1963), eldest son of Victor Melon, who is the janitor at the Hungduan municipal office and the second treasurer for 'Global'.

After getting married in 2006, Ben was living in Hapao with his wife, Adarna, who is originally from Lagawe, until she went to California to work as a domestic helper. In May 2009 Ben went to join his wife in California. Ben has a job in the Lagawe office of the Department of Environment and Natural Resources. He took six months' leave before leaving for the United States, but he is not sure whether he will return after that. If he finds a good job, then he will probably stay and the children might also go to America with him. (Conversation with Ben's father, Victor Melon, July 24, 2009)

Ranny Melon (b. 1974), wife of Randy Melon (b. 1973), Victor Melon's third son.

Ranny was working as a live-in domestic helper when she got married in 2005. returning to the Philippines temporarily, she married Randy and lived with him for two years. After that, she left the care of their baby to Randy and her father-in-law (Victor) and returned to Hong Kong in 2007. Randy has been a member of the Hapao village council (Cagwad) since 2008. (Conversation with Victor Melon, July 24, 2009)

Rosinda Melon-Tickque (b. 1977), second daughter of Victor Melon.

After marrying a man from Lagawe, Rosinda went to work in Israel as a carer for an elderly woman in December 2006. She returned to the Philippines for a vacation in December 2008 but after staying for about one month she went back to Israel, where she is still working. [According to her father, she is quite satisfied because she has Sundays off and her employer is kind. He was unsure of her exact monthly salary, but thought it was between US$700–800. She paid a commission of around 30,000 pesos to the broker who found her the job.] (Conversation with Victor Melon, July 24, 2009)

Joselyn Paduaon (b. 1969), third daughter of Mathew Paduaon, a rice cultivator and woodcarver who is a good old friend of Kidlat and an active member of 'Global'.

> I worked as a live-in domestic helper in Taiwan for one year between 1995 and 1996. My employer could speak a little English but he had a strong accent that I found very difficult to understand. My monthly salary was 13,000 Taiwan dollars. When I left for Taiwan I had two preschool age children. The children's grandparents, whose home is on the same block of land, looked after the children for me. When I returned from Taiwan, I had two more children, so I gave up any thought of going abroad for a second time. (Conversation with Joselyn Paduaon, July 24, 2009)

Paula Tayaban (b. 1964).

> After studying in a secretarial course at Baguio University for two years, I spent nearly a year working as a taxation officer at the Hungduan Municipality in

Paula Tayaban cradles her youngest child at home. (March 13, 2002)

1985. The municipal government was almost completely non-functional and I was paid on a monthly basis at a rate of 14 pesos per day so I quit after less than a year. In 1986 I went to Kuwait for two years, where I worked as a live-in domestic helper and babysitter. The salary was paid in Kuwaiti dinar at a rate of 2,500 dinar per month. This is far more than an elementary school teacher in Hapao gets. However, in order to get the job I had to pay a total of 20,000 pesos to the broker, including a 15,000 peso placement fee and a 5,000 peso processing fee. After my two-year contract expired I returned to Hapao and got married the following year. I had two children one after the other. Once the children had grown up a bit and no longer needed as much care, I went overseas once more to work in Taiwan from October 1994 until December 1997.

It was hard leaving the children, but I felt [I] had no choice because it was for my family's sake. The placement fee was 55,000 pesos. There was no processing fee because I handled everything myself. At first I worked as a domestic helper in Chiayi [Taiwan]. The contract was for one year, with a possible one-year extension but in the end I didn't renew. I had asked for a raise and was denied it, so I chose not to renew. After paying 20 percent tax on my monthly salary and about 2,000 pesos into an installment savings scheme, I was left with about 9,000 pesos in hand.

I decided to go to Taipei and became a TNT [an abbreviation of the Filipino phrase *Tago Ng Tago*, meaning to stay in hiding. It has come to mean working illegally abroad]. I found a good placement as a live-in domestic helper, but I did not want to be arrested as an illegal worker [so] I didn't go out into the city. I stayed at home most of the time. If I hadn't become a TNT and made a good salary, I would have been left with a debt after [my] migrant work and it would all have been for nothing because most of the first year's salary disappeared while paying back the debt incurred for the placement fee. While I was in Taipei, I counted seventeen other people from Hungduan working nearby. All of them were women and almost all were live-in domestic helpers. Only five worked in factories. If you work in a factory you have to pay for dormitory accommodation and food. You cannot save unless you work overtime. (Conversation with Paula Tayaban at her home, March 9, 1999)

Anneclare Gano (b. 1982), eldest daughter of Santiago Gano, who runs the general store next door to Nauyac's home and 'Global' office.

After graduating from a hotel and restaurant management course at the University of the Philippines Baguio, Anneclare worked for two years at a restaurant facing onto Baguio's Burnham Park. Despite her specialist knowledge, she received only 3,000 pesos per month and was treated like an intern. She grew tired of this and started working at a toy factory called TI-Texas. The base salary there was still only 7,000 pesos per month and there was constant overtime work. Some of her friends were also starting to get tired of the low wages and one by one they left to go and work overseas. She decided to give it a try and asked an agency in Manila to find her a position. In 2006 she got a two-year contract for a job as a kitchenhand in a restaurant in the Dubai airport. Food and board were included, and the monthly salary was 10,000 pesos. [Her mother speculated that the salary was probably on the low side because she had to pay 20,000 pesos for her flights and the employer had to pay a processing fee to the agency after she started working.] She only gets Sundays off and she gets tired because she has to stand all the time while working. She feels confined because all she does is go between the dormitory and the kitchen, so she doesn't like it but she has to make the best of it. (Conversation with her mother, Regina, July 24, 2009)

Juliever Himmiwat (b. 1979), eldest daughter of Peter Himmiwat, who makes his living as a rice farmer and from irregular jobs.

After graduating from the commerce faculty of Saint Louis University in Baguio, Juliever returned to Hapao and worked for two years as an administrator at the CECAP field office. The 12,000-peso monthly salary was good but after the two-year contract expired it was not renewed. After that she worked at the municipal government offices, but her salary was half that of her previous job at 6,000 pesos a month. She therefore decided to go overseas. In December 2006 she went with two friends to Dubai in the United Arab Emirates. They entered on a tourist visa and she paid the 30,000-peso air ticket and other expenses using her savings from her previous jobs. She found a job relatively easily and took a short trip over the border to Iran in order to secure a working visa. The workplace was a large breadmaking company and her salary was equivalent to about 15,000 pesos per month. After working there for two years she renewed her contract and returned home briefly. She was well thought of at work and for the second contract she received a major pay rise up to 50,000 pesos a month. Dubai is an open society and there are few restrictions related to Islamic law, so it was an easy place to live. The money is good but if she found a job with a reasonable salary back in the Philippines she would like to come home and work here. (Conversation with her mother, Fatima, July 25, 2009)

Jacquiline Himmiwat (b. 1981), second daughter of Peter Himmiwat.

After graduating from the engineering faculty of Saint Louis University in Baguio, [Jacquiline] started working at a construction site in Pasig in Metro Manila. Her monthly salary was 15,000 pesos. After that, she changed jobs twice and worked for a total of more than three years in Manila. She thought it was important to build her experience first. In May 2008 she went to Dubai and found a job on the construction site for the World Trade Centre. Her monthly salary was about 35,000 pesos. However, the impact of the Global Financial Crisis brought construction to a halt and she was laid off after just ten months. She was forced to return home for a month. Fortunately, just before leaving Dubai she secured a position with another company there. The monthly salary at the new company is 80,000 pesos. The two sisters, Juliever and Jacquiline, send remittances that enable the family to cover the tuition fees for their younger siblings while they are at university. (Conversation with her mother, Fatima, July 25, 2009)

Remedios Baguilat-Tupon (b. 1972).

After graduating from high school, I studied at a theological college in Ilocos Norte for two years before returning to Hapao. Before I was married, I went to Taiwan to work as a live-in domestic helper for two years from 1996 until 1998. An agency in Manila found me the position and I paid them a processing fee of 39,000 pesos. I borrowed 35,000 pesos from three relatives in Hapao and Hobbong. The interest payable was 6 percent per month so when I started working my first priority was to pay back all of the debt.

My monthly salary was 15,000 pesos. At the time, the Taiwan dollar and the Philippine peso were almost at parity. Of the 15,000 pesos, the equivalent of about 2,900 pesos was taken out for taxes [however, this was refunded when she returned home]. My employer took a further 2,000 pesos as part of an installment savings plan. Of the remaining 10,000 pesos, I dedicated 8,000 to repay my debt during the first six months. That left me with 2,000 pesos but I saved most of that too and sent it back to the village to support my parents and siblings with their living expenses. After repaying the debt, my older brother said he wanted to start a business, so I loaned him 30,000 pesos. However, the business failed and the money was never returned. In the end, I had 30,000 pesos left and so I lent it to a friend with a *sangla* loan (a rental agreement involving an interest-free loan with a rice terrace as guarantee. In lieu of interest, the creditor receives the right to cultivate the terrace until the loan is repaid.) She needed the money to pay the broker for a job overseas. The rice terraces I gained in return were quite large, so I was able to secure enough rice to just about feed a family of four for a year. Before I made the loan, I asked my brothers [to] work the land as my tenants in exchange for half the harvest. After four years the money was repaid, so I lost the right to the terrace but I was able to build the house I currently live in with the money. This house is the fruit of my working overseas. I am the fifth of seven children. Three have moved to Baguio and three remain in Hapao. One died young in an accident. In 2004 I got married and had children. I am currently pregnant with my third child. (Conversation with Remedios Baguilat-Tupon, July 25, 2009)

Gregorio Yog-yog (b. 1973), eldest son of Dimath Yog-yog (motorized tricycle driver), who lives next door but one, uphill from Nauyac's 'Global' office-cum-residence.

After graduating from the engineering faculty of the Baguio Colleges Foundation (now the University of the Cordilleras) Gregorio worked all over Baguio and other cities in Ifugao. His mother's (Dimath's wife) older sister went to work in Australia about twenty years ago as a nurse. There she married an Australian and became a citizen. His aunt helped him to go to Australia in 2000. For the first six months he attended an English-language college and after that he found a job as a forklift driver. He obtained permanent residency and has made Australia his home. [His father did not know how much he makes per month.] (Conversation with his father, Dimath, July 25, 2009)

Jacquilin Yog-yog (b. 1980), second daughter of Dimath Yog-yog.

After graduating from the nursing course at the Pines City College in Baguio, [Jacquilin] passed the national certification exam and worked for two years to gain experience. After that, her older brother helped her to go to Australia in 2004. At first, she obtained a trainee visa. In the morning she studied for four hours in an English-language program and in the afternoon she was able to work legally. After completing the English-language course, she got a job in a hospital and obtained her working visa. Her older brother loaned her the money for the flights to Australia and her first two years of living expenses, so now she is working to pay it back. (Conversation with her father, Dimath, July 25, 2009)

Joan Ab-abulon (b. 1979).

> Joan graduated from the English course in the education faculty at a university in Santiago, Isabela Province, but got married during her fourth year and after graduation she became a housewife. In March 2008 she got her first job overseas as a live-in domestic helper in Lebanon, where she does the housework and looks after the children. At first she struggled with the unfamiliar food but she got used to it and is happy there now. When she started she was only given the family's leftovers to eat but now she eats together with the family at the table. She has only received half of her salary so far, but she will receive the balance when she completes her contract. The only problem is that her employer hates it when she talks with the other Filipino housekeepers in the neighborhood and would prefer her never to even meet with them. Apparently, their previous housekeeper discussed the family's private affairs quite freely with the other Filipino housekeepers and was fired before she had completed her contract. An agency in Manila found her the position. She is repaying the 30,000-peso processing fee over time out of her 10,000-peso monthly salary. Her husband borrowed the money from his siblings, so she is not sure what the interest rate is. [In the beginning she and her husband lived in Hapao and Joan's parents looked after the three children (their grandchildren).] Then her husband Oscar found a job in Potia, Ifugao, where his parents live, and moved there with the children. Now they live with his parents. (Conversation with her mother, Pasita Ab-abulon, July 25, 2009)

Gemma Biahon (b. 1981), eldest daughter of Pedro and Rosita Biahon, who live next door to Nauyac on the downhill side. Pedro owns a jeepney but works at a hotel in Baguio and his eldest son drives the jeepney, making the round trip between Hapao and Lagawe via Banaue each day. Rosita is the village's only broker for the woodcarvers who have *muyong* resource permits (permission to harvest timber in one's own private forest).

> I graduated from the dentistry course at Baguio's Pines City College in 2004. While I was working at a dental clinic in Pasay in Metro Manila, a broker came in one day and said that they were looking for someone to work in a dental center in Saudi Arabia. My boss encouraged me to take it, saying that it would be a good opportunity for me, so I decided to go. I really wanted to go to Israel, where they pay really well. I thought I would be happy to work even as a caregiver if it was in Israel. But the processing fee you have to pay the broker in

order to go to Israel is high and it takes time to get the paperwork together, so I decided not to let my first opportunity to work overseas pass me by. In the end it took about a month because everything went through rather smoothly and I was able to travel to Saudi Arabia in November 2006. The agency handled all of the paperwork and their fee together with the cost of the air ticket came up to the equivalent of about one month's wages. The base wage was 2,000 riyal and there was another 500 riyal from various allowances, so the total was 2,500 riyal. One riyal is equivalent to about 12 or 13 pesos. There were three dentists at the center from Jordan, Syria and Egypt and each had an assistant. I was an assistant and communicated with the dentists in English. They spoke Arabic among themselves. I fell in love with a man from Benguet whom I met in Saudi Arabia. On July 4, 2009, we were granted forty-five days contract-renewal leave and we returned home together. [On July 27 they had a civil wedding at the municipal office and went back to their home for a celebration]. (Conversation with Gemma Biahon, July 25, 2009)

A couple exchange vows at a civil wedding before Mayor Pablo M Cuyahon Sr. (July 27, 2009)

Jane Caligayan Mahiwo (b. 1981), wife of Orlando Mahiwo, nephew and right-hand man of Nauyac.

> In January 2009, Jane started working as a live-in domestic helper in Taitung in Taiwan, leaving the care of the children to Orlando and Grace, Orlando's first wife's daughter. Her monthly salary was equivalent to 20,000 pesos. However, her after-tax income in the first six months was about 17,000 pesos after 3,000 pesos was deducted for taxes and health insurance. The cost of making the journey, including a 95,000-peso processing fee leveled by the agency in Manila and a training seminar in Manila run by the Technical Education and Skills Development Authority (including tuition, round trip ticket to Manila and accommodation) came to a total of 130,000 pesos. As she didn't have that much cash she borrowed about 70,000 pesos from six sources including friends, relatives, acquaintances and a cooperative association. The interest and loan conditions differ for each source. Her relatives and close friends are not charging her interest. However, the private lender and other individuals who have lent her money on the same basis charge 10 percent per month. The cooperative association charges an annual rate of 16 percent, but the first eighteen months' interest was deducted from the initial loan. (Conversation with Jane's stepdaughter, Grace, July 29, 2009)

Orlando Mahiwo and his younger siblings

As the case studies above indicate, in Hapao it is predominantly women who travel overseas for work. Men tend to stay at home and tend the rice terraces, work as woodcarvers and perform irregular casual work in construction and similar jobs. Nevertheless, many men live and work temporarily in camps near the forests in the neighboring provinces of Nueva Vizcaya and Isabela, where they go in search of raw materials for woodcarving. They also work in larger cities such as Baguio and Manila. Even without going overseas, the men frequently leave the village for work. Both the women and men of Hapao are highly mobile. In order to provide a point of comparison with the migrant workers discussed above, here I present the story of Orlando Mahiwo, the husband of Jane, whom I discussed above. I will also explain how his younger siblings went to work in Taiwan to help pay for Orlando's children's school fees.

Orlando Mahiwo (b. 1966).

I was born in 1966 in Patpat hamlet on the other side of the valley from Hapao, just like my uncle Nauyac. I completed elementary school. Until I remarried, to Jane from Abatan in March 2004, I lived with my three children in my parents' house in Patpat. In 2005 I borrowed a corner of Nauyac's land in Boyyod to build a house and then I moved there. I was able to borrow some of Nauyac's land because I have been volunteering to help him with the 'Global' reforestation movement and have become his right-hand man.

I borrowed the money to build the house from my younger brother and sister, who worked abroad in Taiwan. I have never worked overseas myself. For two or three years after I finished elementary school, I helped my father in his rice terraces and swiddens and did some woodcarving. In 1982 I started working at a woodcarving and cabinetmaking workshop in Manila called Global Mix that was managed by my uncle. He is also from Hapao but had left to live in Manila. There were about fifty Ifugaos working in the factory.

Hapao woodcarvers harvesting large street tree acacias in Lagawe using chainsaws. (March 11, 2003)

I worked in some other factories operated by the same company in Angeles, Pampanga Province, and elsewhere. I also worked at an oyster farm in Cavite. I worked for Global Mix for more than ten years, but I only made 100 pesos per day in take-home pay and I had no plan for the future. A while after I came to Manila I married Marilyn Bella, a woman from Camarines Norte (in the Bicol region of southern Luzon) who was working in a textile factory. We had three children, including Grace, her daughter from another marriage and our own two children, one boy and one girl. It was difficult to raise them in Manila, so we returned to Ifugao. Soon after we returned to Ifugao in 1992, Marilyn went to work in a factory in Taiwan for two years. When her contract finished and she returned to the Philippines, she did not come back to Ifugao but went straight back to her parents' home in Camarines Norte. She went from there to Hong Kong to work as a live-in domestic helper. The next time she returned, she still did not come back to Ifugao but went straight back overseas to Taiwan to work in a factory. In the beginning she sent money back for the children but after a while she stopped. She even stopped contacting us.

After returning to Hapao I lived in my parents' house in Patpat and worked as a tenant farmer for my relatives, dividing the harvest with them fifty-fifty. I worked on road maintenance gangs as a day laborer to earn some cash. It is not enough to cover the school fees for the three children, so my younger brother Tito and my younger sister Juliette kindly support[ed] us by sending us money they earned working in factories in Taiwan. The reason Juliette went to Taiwan in 1994 in the first place was that my ex-wife broke off all contact with us and stopped sending us money and we were struggling to make ends meet…Juliette graduated from a nursing school in Bayombong, Nueva Vizcaya. She got her midwifery license and was working in the hospital in Hungduan. However, she only made 200 pesos a day and she did not have a full-time position. She started thinking about going overseas to work and went with a friend to an agency in Manila to see about a job. She applied for a post in Libya and received a tentative job offer, but because she only had one year's experience in a hospital and the minimum requirement was two-years' experience, she was unsuccessful. If she had been able to go to Libya with her friend, then she probably would have made more money.

She decided to go to Taiwan, where it was easy to get a job in an area unrelated to nursing. She went back to Taiwan four times for three years at a time, working there for nearly twelve years. However, each time was for a completely different employer and at a different factory. That is to say, each time she went, she changed her name. She applied for a visa and entered the

Top: Orlando Mahiwo and his mother standing in front of the house built by their cousin, Sylvano Mahiwo, a professor at the University of the Philippines. (March 13, 2002)

Bottom: Orlando and Jane dancing at their wedding ceremony in Jane's home village of Abatan. (March 13, 2003)

country under a different name. In 1994, when she first left, she worked for a monthly salary of 14,000 Taiwan dollars at a doorknob factory. The rest of the time she worked making computer motherboards or performing product inspections. Her monthly salary was between 15,000 and 17,000 Taiwan dollars. Up until August 2002, the dormitory, food and medical expenses were free but after that they started to deduct these expenses from her pay. The basic wage was not enough to allow her to save, so she forced herself to accept doing overtime and made more money that way. Rather than taking eight-hour shifts, she took the longer twelve-hour shifts and did overtime every day. Juliette got engaged to a man from Manila whom she met during her final stay in Taiwan in February 2007, just before she came home. As soon as she returned, the man and his parents and relatives came to Hapao…and we slaughtered a pig and held a proper engagement party. After that, she went to Manila to live with him.

My younger brother Tito also worked in a factory in Taiwan on two occasions for three years at a time. Now he is at a woodworking shop in Capas in the Province of Tarlac. The manager is a man from Patpat. Working here in the Philippines, he only makes enough for his own needs and so he has not yet married. (Conversation with Orlando, March 2, 2007)

Migrant workers from three influential Hapao families

So far, I have discussed migrant workers from the Boyyod area of Hapao, where the 'Global' office is located, but Boyyod is not remarkable nor exceptional but rather average. I now discuss a number of migrant workers from some of Hapao's most influential families.

Gloria Bumangabang (b. 1962), wife of Hilario T Bumangabang, mayor of Hungduan for six years from July 2001 until June 2007.

> I spent a total of ten years and two months working overseas, both before and after marrying Hilario. I went overseas to work for the first time after I had to withdraw from university in my second year when my scholarship money ran out. At first I worked for two years and three months as a live-in domestic helper and nanny in Abu Dhabi between 1983 and 1985. I found the job through a Manila-based agency when they sent a recruiter to Banaue. The agency charged a processing fee of 5,000 pesos and my monthly salary was equivalent to 3,000 pesos. As I had to look after children, I did not get any time off. However, I accompanied the family on a car trip to Syria, Jordan and Saudi Arabia and enjoyed seeing so many different places.

My second position was in Kuwait from 1987 to 1989, where I worked as a live-in domestic helper in the home of a Lebanese family. My monthly salary was equivalent to 3,500 pesos. In 1990 I went to Hong Kong, where I worked for eighteen months in the home of a doctor, mostly caring for the doctor's elderly parents. In 1991 I returned home and got married and then stayed in Hapao for five years. I had children and was very happy but for the sake of my children's future I went overseas for work once more. It was tough and I was very sad to leave the children but I stuck at it. In 1996 I went to Taiwan, where I worked for four-and-a-half years as a carer. The money I earned as a migrant worker before I got married paid for my mother's medical bills and to educate my nieces and nephews. It was not for me. I think that the special quality of Ifugaos like myself is that we are patient and hard workers. That's why the employers are so happy to have us. (Conversation with Gloria in her home in Hobbong, July 26, 2009)

Elisa B Madiwo (b. 1958).

I was born at Camp 6 in Baguio but a few months later moved back to Hapao with my parents. In 1982 I graduated from the University of the Philippines Baguio with my teaching degree. I started working right away as a substitute

Elisa in front of a statue of the Virgin Mary in her garden at home. (March 13, 2002)

teacher at the elementary school in Hapao. The following year, 1983, I became a full-time teacher and was dispatched to Batad in Banaue. The rice terraces there were beautiful but it was even further away than Banaue, a three-hour walk from the place where the jeepney dropped you off in the remote mountains. It takes about five or six hours to get to Batad from Hapao by jeepney. On top of that the pay was low, so that after two years I stopped working there. My two younger sisters were studying at university and I wanted to help them with their tuition. I worked in Singapore as a live-in domestic helper for an American couple. They were both lawyers and they had a one-year-old child. My job was to look after the children and do the housework. The two of them went back to New York after about one year. They said they wanted to take me with them to America, but I refused because it was too far from the Philippines. My salary was 370 Singapore dollars a month.

In 1986 I returned to the Philippines and immediately got a job back at the elementary school in Batad. The following year I took a number of courses at the University of the Philippines summer school. I wanted to get my master's degree in education. In 1989, after three years in Batad, I returned to the school in Hapao. I swapped positions with a teacher from Banaue who was teaching in Hapao. But the wages were still low, so in 1992 I went to Hong Kong to work as a domestic helper. The processing fee was about 30,000 pesos. I lived with a Chinese family from Guangdong who sold fish at the market. They were not particularly wealthy. The salary was 3,200 Hong Kong dollars. There were three children aged five, seven and nine. I slept in the same room as the children. It was difficult because neither the parents nor the children understood English. So I bought [a] cassette tape and a dictionary and learned enough Cantonese to make day-to-day life a little easier.

After two years working there I got two weeks' vacation and came home to the Philippines. Then I went back to Hong Kong in 1994 and this time I worked for a Chinese family from Singapore as a domestic helper. The husband worked for a newspaper and had a second job managing a bookshop. I was thrilled when I saw a book called *The Philippines: People Power* in the shop and felt proud to be a Filipino. My salary was 3,800 Hong Kong dollars. In this and the previous stay, when I was able to save a bit of money I would go to the Philippine National Bank and wire the money to my account in the Philippine National Bank in Lagawe.

In 1996 I went to Hong Kong for the third time. That time I didn't live in the home of my employer but in a dormitory-style apartment. I would go in to work at one house during the morning and do the cleaning and laundry and then go to another house in the afternoon and do the same sort of domestic chores. In 1997 Hong Kong was about to be handed back to China and one by one the best employers started leaving Hong Kong for America or Canada. That meant my actual wages went down and I wasn't able to make as much as the last time. Even so, I kept working there for two years. During that time there were numerous police raids on the apartment looking for visa overstayers. In 1998 I got two months' vacation. I was happy to come back to the Philippines but when I tried to go back to Hong Kong, it seems the employer had decided not to renew my contract and so the paperwork never got finalized. So I couldn't go to Hong Kong and while I was overseas my teaching license had lapsed.

In Hong Kong most Ifugaos would socialize in groups based on their regional dialect. Ifugaos only really got together in a big group for things like Christmas. Usually the people from Banaue would get together with others from Banaue and those from Hungduan with others from Hungduan. But I went to an evangelical church, so I made lots of friends with other Filipinos apart from the Ifugaos. During my third year in Hong Kong in 1995, I organized a group called the Hapao, Hungduan Organization OFW-Hongkong. We put Hungduan in the name, but almost all of the thirty-five founding members were from Hapao. Other than the people from Hapao, there were four or five from our neighboring village of Napulawan, one from Magok in Tinoc and two from Uhaj, Banaue. We used to get together in Victoria Park and bring sweets, talk about nothing in particular and share news. (Conversation with Elisa at her home in Hobbong, March 13, 2002)

Angelina Gano (b. 1943), whom I introduce in Chapter 4, told me the following story about herself and her ten children. I asked her to talk about her children's experiences as migrant workers, but she began by talking about local memories of the war. The account below is an edited version of our conversation.

I was born and raised in Hapao. My mother told me that around the time of the rice harvest in 1945 (June), a large number of Japanese soldiers who were retreating from Kiangan came to Hapao. They quickly took all of the crops so there was nothing left for us to eat. The villagers managed to survive by eating wild grasses like *rono* (a weed similar to Chinese silver grass) sprouts and other wild vegetables, but many people died of starvation or illness. She said that I also became skin and bones and looked like I would die.

In 1960 I entered Saint Mary's University in Bayombong and graduated in March 1963 with a bachelor's degree in elementary school education. I took summer classes and studied as hard as possible so that I could graduate in less than four years. Most of the teachers in the schools in Ifugao were [lowland] Ilocanos who had left their hometowns to teach, so they were all trying to find someone to take over from them as quickly as possible so they could return to their homes. That meant that I was lucky enough to find a job when I graduated and I started teaching in June. In September I married my husband, who was also a teacher. From then until I retired in June 2001, I kept working as a teacher. While I was working I had ten children and I stayed working while I raised them. My husband was also a teacher. He is a little older than me, so he retired about three years earlier.

All ten of my children grew up healthy and strong but in 2001 my second son David was killed when he became the victim of hazing by a group of senior offices and other troops while he was in training in the military. They were probably jealous because he had been given a chance at promotion sooner than the others in his cohort. In order to get the promotion, he had to undergo a period of intensive training. He was in training when he was targeted and beaten up. They held his arms open and his legs down and punched him repeatedly in the stomach. His organs swelled up inside him. He was taken to hospital for treatment but later he died. His older brother rushed to the hospital and managed to speak to him briefly, so we know who did it. But because it's the army nobody will come forth as a witness. We don't have the money to take it to court and so there was nothing we could do but cry ourselves to sleep. I believe that God will punish them for what they have done.

In terms of my children's experiences working overseas, my eldest daughter, Alicia Candelario [b. 1964], went to work in a factory in Taiwan for two years from 1990 to 1992. During that time, I looked after her three children for her. When she came back from Taiwan, she went to study at nursing school. Since graduating she has been working as a nurse at the Good News Hospital in Banaue. If she has the opportunity and the conditions are good, she would like to work in a hospital overseas.

My second daughter, Brigida Bacanog [b. 1967], now lives in Canada. She graduated from the nursing school of Saint Jude College in Manila and went straight to Canada. One of her teachers was already in Canada and was working as a nurse. The teacher said that the hospital there was short of nurses so the ten graduating students from her college who had the best results were put forward for the jobs. She was included in the ten, so she went to Canada, but with a Philippine qualification you cannot become a registered nurse there. So she worked as a kind of intern while she re-did her nursing studies and then obtained her Canadian certification. She is now a registered nurse and has Canadian citizenship.

My eldest son, Ciricano Gano Jr. [b. 1969], is a policeman in Banaue. His wife, Josephine, is working as a carer in Saudi Arabia. This is her fourth year working there. She is making arrangements to move to a hospital in London. Her three children live with their father and go to a private school in Banaue but on the weekends they come to stay in Hapao.

My second son, David, was killed while serving in the military, as I said earlier.

My third daughter, Elvira [b. 1975], worked abroad for about ten years. Now she is married to a Swede and lives in Sweden and she doesn't work. Her husband is an engineer with Canon Sweden and so they can live on his salary. Elvira graduated from a nursing school in Cabanatuan in 1994. After that she started working as a nurse at a hospital on a military base in Gamu, Isabela Province. After working there for two years she went to Libya in 1996, where she worked as a nurse for two years. Then she went to France for two years. In 2000 she went to Saipan and worked for four years. During that time she passed the [United States] board exam for nursing and also got her American

Angelina (center) resting by the roadside near Hapao. (March 12, 2000)

visa. She could have stayed working in Saipan or gone to the...mainland if she wanted to. But then she met her husband and they go married, so now she is a housewife and doesn't have to work.

My third son, Floyd [b. 1976], graduated from the Philippine Military Academy [PMA] in Baguio and now serves in the Presidential Security Guard.

My fourth daughter, Geraldine [b. 1978], studied commerce at Saint Louis University in Baguio. After graduating she went to Taiwan for work in 2000. After working at the Acer Computing factory for five years, she went to Israel at the beginning of last year, where she now works as a carer. Compared with the 50,000 pesos she paid to the agency when she went to Taiwan, going to Israel cost her 250,000 pesos. But the monthly salary is equal to 25,000 pesos, so if she works for one year she will be back where she started. It's a two-year contract with the possibility of renewal, so after she has paid back the money for the placement fee she should be able to make a good income. She works in the home of an elderly couple. The husband has a disability and needs some assistance but the wife is quite well, so Geraldine just helps her to care for her husband and with the housework. The couple have a daughter but she is married and lives elsewhere, so they treat her like a daughter. They even send us Christmas presents.

My fifth daughter, Hedeliza [b. 1980], graduated from a hotel and restaurant management course at the University of Baguio in 2001. While she was studying she trained in the Ritz Carlton in Singapore for six months. After graduating from university, she got a job at the Baguio Country Club and after that moved to another hotel. But now she has come home to Hapao and is getting ready to go to Canada with help from her sister Brigida. Brigida is working in Vancouver but Hedeliza will probably end up working in Montreal. She will work as a nurse at first, but she says she will look for a job in hotel or restaurant management so that she can make use of her knowledge and experience. Without a nursing certificate she will have to enter Canada as a caregiver and then look for a job that suits her where she can make a good income.

My sixth daughter, Imee [b. 1983], studied education at Saint Louis University in Baguio in 2003 and has her teaching license, but it is hard to find a job as a teacher and the wages are poor, so she went back to school again to become a nurse. She is currently in her second year of nursing at the Our Lady of Fatima University in Valenzuela, Metro Manila. In the future she plans to go overseas and work as a professional nurse.

My fourth son, Jayson [b. 1988], is currently in his second year studying nursing at the University of Baguio. He really wanted to join the military but he failed the exam to get into the PMA. His older brothers who were already in the military recommended that he study engineering for two years before entering the PMA because that way he would understand the lectures and do well on his exams. But he hates maths, so he gave up on entering the PMA and instead took the nursing course.

Imee and Jayson both say they want to work overseas once they have graduated. I never told them to go and work overseas but the wages in the Philippines are so low and it's just like all young people, they think things are better overseas. (Conversation with Angelina Gano, March 1, 2007)

Like Angelina, Hapao's most senior *monbaki*, Teofilo Gano, also began by talking about his experiences of the war as part of an anti-Japanese guerilla unit, which I discuss in Chapter 4. His eldest daughter and two sons went overseas for work and eventually emigrated permanently. Teofilo is both a *monbaki* and a devout Catholic. He always attends mass on Sunday and actively engages in sharing sessions (making confessions or talking about episodes from one's life), where he talks about his faith and his experiences. The following is an edited account of his narrative.

Teofilo Gano

In 1935 when I was twelve years old I received baptism from the Belgian priest Father Francis Lambrecht. At that time, he was based in Banaue and occasionally came to Hapao to say mass. When he came to Hapao he would bring bundles of used clothes as gifts and divide them up among the villagers. People came not only from Hapao but from the neighboring villages because they wanted those clothes. They would listen while he said mass and many of them were baptized. At that time, only a very few wealthy families had the money to buy clothes from the shop in Banaue. Usually people would pound tree bark to make it soft and then make clothes from the material. However, they would buy cloth for their loincloths from Banaue.

After the war ended we came back to the village. From January the next year, 1946, I went to Baguio to work as a woodcarver. There were a number of former American servicemen who were living in Baguio and running businesses there. Some Filipinos would help them or work for them. I came back to Hapao for a while and married Gupi from Ba-ang, the next village over. Together we went to Baguio once again. For the first two years I worked as hard as I could to save money.

In 1948 our eldest son Jose was born. After he was born my wife and child returned to Hapao to live. I worked as a woodcarver in Baguio and went back to the village only when it was time to prepare the terraces, plant the rice and sweet potatoes and for the harvest. We lived like that for about ten years.

About once every two years another child was born. All together we had eight children. But our eldest son, Jose, fell from a truck in 1975 and died, leaving two of his own children behind. By that time, I had already become a *monbaki*. I decided I wanted to become a *monbaki* when my third daughter Teresa had diarrhea when she was young and it looked like she might die. She was saved by a *monbaki*. The first *monbaki* I asked for help told me to prepare a chicken and wait for him. I cooked some rice and waited for him, but he never showed up. Then I went to ask another *monbaki* who lived in the hamlet of Panique and he came that night. After he prayed her diarrhea suddenly stopped. The next morning and then all day and night and into the next day there was no more diarrhea. On the third day her stools returned to normal. This made me believe in the power of the *monbaki* and made me want to become one too.

My eldest daughter, Norma, was born in 1951. In 1971 she went to Australia. Before that she completed a two-year nursing course in Baguio. In Australia she studied nursing again while she was working and passed her registration. After she graduated she got a job at a hospital right away. In 1974 she came home for a while and married her childhood friend Maliano Dunuan from Poblacion, Hungduan. The two of them returned to Australia. Dunuan also took a nursing course and got his qualifications. Norma has been living in Australia ever since. From time to time she comes home bearing gifts.

My second son, Henry, was born in 1953. He has been living in London since 1988. He withdrew from the university in Baguio in his second year and straight away he started working there as a woodcarver. He was recognized for his skill and was employed as a specialist carver making ice sculptures for the function center at the Hyatt Terraces Hotel. This was before the Baguio earthquake. After working at the Hyatt for five years he found a job as an ice carver in London through an agency. I helped him with some of the agency fees and travel costs. Once he was settled in…London, he took his family there to live with him.

My third son, Peter, was born in 1955. When Henry decided to move to London he asked Peter, who was working as a woodcarver, to come and learn the knack of ice carving. He gave him two or three months of intensive training and then Peter replaced his brother at the Hyatt Terraces. After working there for a year, Peter was lucky enough to find a job at a hotel in Kuwait. Fortunately, he moved before the Hyatt Hotel was destroyed in the Baguio earthquake in July 1990, but eight months after he arrived in Kuwait the Gulf War broke out. He had to come back to the Philippines and he came back to Hapao to live for a while. During that time, he got married and found a job as an ice sculptor at a hotel in Jeddah, Saudi Arabia. He worked there for two years and then came home for a while. Then Henry sponsored him to come to London and he has been living there since.

Top left: Teofilo conducting a ceremony as a main *monbaki*. (March 8, 2001)
Bottom left: The morning after an all-night ritual. (March 9, 2001)
Right: Teofilo speaking in church during mass. (March 4, 2001)

All of my four other daughters are married to men from Hungduan and, apart from one, who lives in La Union Province, they all live nearby. (Conversation with Teofilo Gano, at his house, March 1, 2007)

So far in this chapter I have reported on the experiences of migrant workers from sixteen households in Boyyod, where Nauyac's 'Global' office-cum-residence is located, and the households of Angelina Gano and Teofilo Gano, two influential individuals in Hapao who are active 'Global' members. When these accounts are looked at as a whole, we can see that there are three times as many women migrant workers (nineteen) as men (six). This reflects gender balance of migrant work in the village as a whole. Of the women, most were domestic helpers and caregivers. They have traveled all over the globe, principally to Taiwan and Hong Kong, as well as to the Middle East, Europe, the United States, Canada and Australia, among others. There is an overlap between the duties of a domestic helper and a caregiver, but where caring for older people has become an important occupation, using the terms 'caregiver' and 'caretaker' comes with a feeling of self-respect.

One characteristic of the migrant workers from Boyyod and the influential families from the better-off strata of the village is that many of their children have graduated from university nursing schools and therefore have the potential to go overseas as professional nurses. Nursing is considered to be a specialist profession that comes with a higher social position, a better salary and a definite career path. Like the lowland Christians, many high school students set their sights on becoming nurses. Once they enter nursing school, the stories they hear and the prodding they receive from their classmates makes them want to go overseas, where they can earn higher salaries. Norma, Teofilo Gano's eldest daughter, got the chance to go to Australia as early as 1971. After studying for a second time in a nursing course there, she was able to work as a registered nurse and gain permanent residency. However, she returned to Hapao in 1974 to marry her childhood friend and maintains her links with Hapao by bringing her children back to her hometown to visit her parents every two or three years.

Almost all the migrant workers depend upon specialist recruitment agencies to find overseas jobs and complete the necessary paperwork. Most of the villagers go to Baguio or Manila, where they ask an agency to process the paperwork for them. Recently, the number of agencies in Manila has dramatically increased. In some exceptional cases, where a sibling or someone else they know is already well-established overseas, they can ask them to sponsor them. Where an agency is engaged there are various processing fees and there is also the cost of a government-mandated 150-hour (three-week) preparatory training course, the cost of spending time in Manila to complete the course, and other costs that add up to several months' wages (usually equivalent to three to six months). A prospective migrant worker needs to have enough capital to cover these costs. In addition, if they have to pay for their own air tickets, the total cost of making the journey might come to six months' or a year's wages in the destination country.

Although household incomes in Hapao are higher than the average for Hungduan, few households have enough cash on hand to cover these costs. The usual practice is to borrow money from the village cooperative (at 16 percent interest per annum) or from relatives and friends (where the rate of interest varies depending on the lender and their degree of intimacy with the borrower and may be anything from zero to 20–30 percent per annum). Sometimes the borrower may be able to obtain a *sangla* loan by renting out rice terraces in exchange for cash. If the prospective migrant worker cannot raise enough money through these means, then he or she might borrow it from a lender in Banaue. In that case, the interest rate varies depending on

Henry, home from London for the 2008 *Tungoh* festival. He works as an artisan ice carver in a London hotel. (April 16, 2008)

both the lender's and the broker's relationship with borrower and ranges from a couple of percent per month up to 10 percent.

Israel stands out as a place where migrant work has been institutionalized. As Gemma Biahon explained, there are many positions for caregivers/domestic helpers and nurses and the wages are high (US$1,000–2,000). However, the costs and agency fees associated with making the trip to Israel are also high (20,000–25,000 pesos, approximately US$440–550) and a limited number of families are able to raise enough money. Generally speaking, not only in Israel but in any country or industry where the wages are good, the first year's wages will disappear to repay loans and the worker can only start saving in the second year.

Migrant workers (more than three-quarters of whom are women) send remittances from overseas or bring money back with them. They use it to help their younger siblings or nieces and nephews to pay tuition, as well as to pay for large traditional rituals for their ancestors or to hold celebrations, to renovate or build new houses or purchase prestige items such as rice terraces, televisions and DVD players. When buying DVDs, they prefer Hollywood action films, such as *Rambo*, to the Tagalog films produced in Manila. In this sense, migrant work embeds the villagers in the larger global economic system. Not only have households come to rely on migrant labor for their subsistence, it seems that the means of raising their prestige within the village and sources of pleasure and amusement are also now located overseas. The villagers are raising their standard of living while holding their own against the globalizing trend and going along for the ride.

The revival of the *Tungoh* festival

In Hapao, while migrant labor has become a conspicuous feature of village life since the 1990s, the villagers have also developed a stronger awareness of their traditional culture and their identity as Ifugaos. After the end of CPP-NPA control over the area at the beginning of the 1990s, the mayor of Hungduan felt that there was an urgent need to rebuild the villagers' way of life and their social structures. His efforts sparked a growing interest in Ifugao culture and identity. In 1992 the mayor took the initiative to improve the municipality's social and economic situation. The municipal government decided to hold a major festival in order to promote tourism and agriculture and to encourage an awareness of Ifugao traditional culture and pass it down to the next generation. Thus the *Tungoh* festival (a traditional rite) was reborn.

According to the explanation in the commemorative booklet produced for the festival each year and information I received from the villagers, *Tungoh* was originally held at the completion of rice planting or harvesting, and when the first rains announced the end of the dry season. It also referred to the period of rest that followed these rituals, when no work other than basic household chores were performed for two or three days.

According to Kumano (2007), who has undertaken fieldwork in the village of Ba-ang, which lies over the river on the other side of the valley from Hapao, the traditional *Tungoh* was held during the agricultural off-season, about three months after rice planting, when a bountiful harvest was assured and the villagers were waiting for the harvest. Its 'major feature was ritualistic games. The games were held because the agricultural work was done and as a manifestation of village-level communality' (Kumano 2007: 89). The *Tungoh* was also celebrated two weeks after the harvest. On both occasions the main events were tug-of-war (*pun-nok*) held across the river and *dopap* (wrestling standing on one leg). However, when the CPP guerillas took control of the area in the 1970s (see Chapter 4), the games were no longer held. Kumano (2007: 94, 96) explains that when the *Tungoh* was revived in 1992, it became 'a fiesta, the traditional games and contests were transformed and the consciousness of the festival as an agricultural ritual faded. There was an increasing secular emphasis on tourism development. Furthermore, when local politicians invited the prefectural governor and congress members, it became a political show.' He concludes that 'the *Tungoh* Festival initiated by the municipal mayor is a mix of the concern for tourism promotion of a man from Hapao and the pride of the Ifugaos'.

The revival of the *Tungoh* and its transformation into a spectacle (parades and performances in traditional dress and the games between different villages) can be seen as a contemporary 'reinvention of tradition' (Hobsbawm and Ranger 1983) with the clear intention not only to improve people's livelihoods through tourism promotion but, more importantly, to arouse and to strengthen their identities. However, what the municipal government did not do much was to revive the agricultural ritual of prayers and thanks for an abundant harvest that was held at particular times of the agricultural year. As Nakake (1997) points out, rituals, labor exchanges and communal work practices tied to the agricultural calendar have declined, like other traditional customary practices directly connected with the Ifugao way of life. Instead, the municipal government has focused on carrying out magnificent games where individual villages compete with one another in tug-of-war, arm-wrestling, *dopap* and bamboo pole climbing, and has guided the development of the festival and given it full backing. *Hudhud* chanting (of epics and eulogies), songs and dance displays are held before the audience and a panel of judges, as well as a marathon climb up to the summit of Mount Napulawan and back. These events are an attempt to increase the feeling of unity within each village by competing to see which village can outdo the others. At the same time, by celebrating together and having fun, the festival is an attempt to confirm and strengthen Hungduan's identity as a whole, by differentiating itself from other municipal festivals.

Because the *Tungoh* takes place in mid-April, when the Japanese academic year is just beginning, I was unable to attend for a long time. In October 2006 I left Kyushu University to take up a position at the Center for Southeast Asian Studies at Kyoto University, where my teaching load was lighter. In April 2008, ten years after my first visit to Hapao, I attended the *Tungoh* for the first time. Unfortunately, that year there was a major traffic accident near Diadi, Nueva Vizcaya, when the bus that links Hungduan with Maddela, Quirino, came off the road and fell into a deep ravine at a little after noon on April 11, just before the commencement of the *Tungoh*. Ten people died at the scene and another two died later in hospital. Half the victims, including municipal councilor Peter Pocapio, were from Hungduan. Another nineteen victims had serious injuries, which meant they had to spend a long time in hospital. Many people living in Maddela had moved there from Hungduan in search of agricultural land and more than half the victims were traveling between the two cities to visit relatives.

For a time, there was talk of canceling the *Tungoh* because of the incident, but in the end it was decided to scale it back and hold the festival over one day instead of three. The plaza and the basketball court next to the municipal government building were the main venues for the various events. Next to the arena, each of the nine *barangays* had built a traditional house and there they served *tapuy* (rice wine) to the prefectural governor and other regional government officials, journalists and foreign tourists. A few people got drunk and started some high-spirited dancing, but out of respect for those who had died in the accident, there was no enthusiastic sounding of the gong and the festive atmosphere was missing. In the afternoon, there was *hudhud* chanting, singing, dancing and ethnic games. When it came to the inter-village tug-of-war, some teams could not rustle up enough members and others failed to appear at all. In the end, the teams that competed were assembled from whoever was there.

Working Overseas and Reviving Tradition

Barangay teams enter the arena in front of the municipal office building for the *Tungoh* festival. (April 13, 2000, photo Rowena Nakake)

The reinvigorated *Tungoh* festival is held for three or four days on the third weekend of April each year with the objectives as follows:

- To strengthen appreciation and interest in the Ifugao culture especially in the aspect of arts such as indigenous songs, dances, games, architectural designs, among others, and rituals.
- To enhance the knowledge of the young generation regarding their cultural practices by encouraging them to observe and participate as well in the Tungoh activities.
- To facilitate good community relations, cooperation, unity and understanding among participants from the nine barangays.
- To promote tourism industry in the municipality. (Lacbawan 1999: 2–3)

While there are minor variations to the program each year, a key element is the marathon from the festival ground outside the municipal office building up to the summit of Mount Napulawan and back. On the second day, representatives from each *barangay* parade into the festival ground wearing traditional dress for the opening ceremony, followed by *tapuy* and syrup-making demonstrations and rituals to drive away evil spirits. In the afternoon the traditional games and contests are held. At night there is a 'Traditional Culture Evening' featuring traditional singing and dance contests. On the third day there are games such as inter-*barangay* basketball, volleyball, chess and badminton (for children under twelve). At night there is a colorful Miss Hungduan contest.

In the above quoted report, Lacbawan (1999: 4) concluded that 'After the celebration of the Tungoh…it could be said the festival was able to attain its objectives. As observed, it facilitated in general, a cultural awareness among the people of Hungduan especially to the young minds.' The successful revival of the *Tungoh* and its transformation into a spectacle to promote tourism and strengthen local identity was largely the result of the effort of long-serving Hungduan mayor Andres Dunuan Sr., with the material and moral support of the National Commission for Culture and the Arts. Hilario T Bumangabang, who was a municipal councilor when the *Tungoh* was revived in 1993 and later became mayor, explained the events leading up to the revival as follows.

> In 1993, when Andres Dunuan was mayor of Hungduan and I was a member of the municipal council, he spearheaded the decision to hold the *Tungoh* festival

Working Overseas and Reviving Tradition 327

Bamboo bole-climbing competition and arm wrestling. (April 18, 2004, photo Endō Mizuki)

every year on April 17. We had three goals. The first was to strengthen the tourism industry in Hungduan. The second goal was to revitalize our culture. At that time our culture was in danger of being lost and almost nobody was actively trying to preserve our traditional culture. We wanted everybody to understand that we couldn't just let our culture disappear. In addition, since the beginning of the 1990s, tourists started to visit Hungduan to see the rice terraces in greater numbers. One of the reasons for this was that the CPP-NPA guerila forces had been driven out and order was restored. Apparently, some of the people from the National Commission for Culture and the Arts (NCCA) who came from Manila to see the terraces thought that our culture was dying out. So we decided to make a plan to show them that our culture was still alive in a way that they could understand. We invited the chair of the NCCA to be our guest of honor at the first year of the revitalized *Tungoh*. The following year [1994], the NCCA gave us a 90,000-peso grant to bolster the *Tungoh* festival. The year after the grant was 75,000 pesos and it has slowly decreased since. Last year [2005] it was 25,000 pesos. We did not apply for this grant, it was the commissioners who offered it. In our original plan for the festival we didn't think about getting external funding. We wanted to do it by ourselves and each *barangay* paid their own way. The third goal was to change people's thinking, in particular to encourage our young people and give them a chance to consciously continue practicing our culture. We thought about what would get the children and school students excited about becoming involved.

Former mayor Andres Dunuan came up with most of the ideas...and it started with the unanimous support of the whole municipal council. Our former mayor was involved in the tourism industry himself, so he had a strong interest in tourism. He ran a guesthouse in Banaue called the Halfway Lodge. He was always chatting with the guests who stayed at the lodge. One of his regular guests worked in journalism. I'm not sure of his/her exact job but s/he had a strong interest in Ifugao culture [and] arranged things so that the first year's *Tungoh* was reported widely in the newspapers and the media. Before the *Tungoh* we (the municipal councilors and senior officials) went to Baguio to promote the festival and ask the media to come and report on it. Thanks to that, there were articles reporting on the festival including pictures in the *Inquirer*, the *Manila Times* and the *Philippine Star*. Of course, local papers the *Baguio Reporter* and the *Midland Courier* also gave us a good write-up. It was also featured in some magazines and the mayor told me it was reported in *Asiaweek* and *Time*.

Tug-of-war and dancing at the *Tungoh* festival. (April 16, 2008)

When I became mayor in 2001, we started holding a bigger Grand *Tungoh* every three years, to coincide with the end of the mayor's term of office, in addition to the annual festival. We also began to hold a number of rituals to revitalize our traditional culture during the Grand *Tungoh*. We wanted to show our hospitality to our guests from outside the municipality and to the tourists who come to the festival and get them excited. We also expanded participation in the festival beyond the *barangay* level groups to include local NGOs and other organizations. It is a traditional festival, but we also asked the church fathers to participate and to say mass at the opening ceremony. Our way of life combines our traditional culture and our Christian religion. That's why I say our tribe is retrieved/re-tribed. (Conversation with Hilario Bumangabang at his home in Hobbong, March 18, 2006)

While Hungduan was reviving its traditional rituals, in neighboring Kiangan to the southeast the *Gotad* festival was revived at about the same time. The revival in Kiangan was one of provincial governor Teddy Baguilat's feature policies and was implemented when he was elected mayor while still in his thirties, after three years serving on the municipal council (he served two consecutive three-year terms as mayor between 1995 and 2001). Baguilat began preparing for the festival as soon as he was elected and the following year (1996) he received a grant from the NCCA to hold the first *Gotad*. The content is similar to that of the *Tungoh*. Baguilat went on to be elected governor of Ifugao in 2001 (serving until 2004). After he failed to secure a second term, he partnered with International *Kudzu* Green Sannan (a small Japanese NGO that I discuss in the next chapter) as the director of Save the Ifugao Terraces Movement and gave his full support to implementing the JICA Partnership Program with 'Global'. Baguilat was re-elected governor in 2007 and in 2010 he was elected to represent Ifugao in the Congress of the Philippines.

Banaue, the launching pad for rice terrace tourism, was the first place in Ifugao to revive its traditional festivals. At the beginning of the 1980s, the surfacing of the road to Banaue was completed. When tourist coaches began running directly from Manila around that time in 1979, the *Imbayah* festival commenced. Originally the *Imbayah* festival was a celebration of the end of the rice harvest, when the *kadangyan*, the village's wealthy and influential families, would slaughter ten pigs and two buffalo as a sacrifice and lavish *bayah* on the villagers in a celebration that lasted

Top: *Imbayah* festival in Banaue.

Middle: Japanese 'Global' volunteers Okamoto Kiyoko and Kamijō Kozue dancing at the festival.

Bottom: Kidlat filming the dancing. (April 15, 2008)

for thirteen nights of singing and dancing. *Bayah*, the term from which the name of the festival is derived, is a cloudy rice wine brewed in large Chinese jars. Former Banaue mayor Adriano Apilis Jr. revived the *Imbayah* festival in 1979. According to his younger sister and chair of the Cordillera Tourism Council, Carmelita Mondiguing, 'we realized that due to booming tourism, the Ifugaos were beginning to forget their culture and traditions. The festival aims to remind them of the importance of preserving them' (Leprozo 2003).

Since then, the *Imbayah* festival has been held every three years and has increased in scale each time. When I attended the festival in 2008, it was held over four days, April 23–26. On the first day, the nineteen *barangays* each conduct parades and performances in the street. In the lead are people wearing loincloths made from tree bark who are followed by others wearing ever more sophisticated styles of traditional dress. In the middle of the festival, there is traditional singing, dancing, gong recitals, *hudhud* chanting, arm-wrestling, *dopap* wrestling, stilt-walking contests, rice polishing contests and more. One event that is very popular with the tourists is a race where contestants wear traditional dress while riding wooden handmade scooters down the mountain for forty kilometers from the rice terrace viewing platform to the city office in Poblacion. The race was added to the festival after the revival and has no connection with tradition. However, wooden two-wheeled skateboards and four-wheeled box-shaped vehicles were made by hand as children's toys in the past. In this sense, rather than a break with the past, the race can be seen as a kind of bricolage where the past is put to use for a different purpose.

In addition to the revivals in Kiangan and Banaue discussed above, other festivals held in 2003 were the *Kulpi* festival in Asipulo (April 22–24), the *Igkhumtad* festival in Mayoyao and Aguinaldo (April 24–26), and the *Gotad* festival in Lagawe and Hingyon (precise dates unknown). I was unable to confirm the exact details of these festivals but all seem to have been revived during the 1980s and 1990s.

Branching out and putting down roots

Hapao and the other *barangays* of Hungduan are located deep in the mountains and are remote even compared with the rest of Ifugao. Over the

A race from the viewing deck that overlooks the Banaue rice terraces down to the city on home-made wooden scooters has become a hit with tourists. (Photo Mike Smith)

past two decades, migrant workers from these remote mountain villages have gone overseas and international aid has arrived. Through these developments, life in the village has become ever more closely tied to spaces far beyond the border. As they have turned their minds towards and stepped out into the great world outside in their search for resources to sustain their way of life in the village, they have also begun to focus on aspects of their own culture that make visible their identity as Ifugaos in a concrete way. These include traditional rituals and games and the knowledge and techniques relevant to their way of life. They have begun holding grand events where they perform in ethnic dress, as we can see in the revival of the *Tungoh* festival. At the same time as they have begun to leave the village to work far away across the seas, they have begun to reaffirm and perform their own ethnic and cultural roots in a more visible way.

The villagers know that their individual and ethnic identities lie in the Ifugao way of life and culture. This culture is deeply rooted in and supported by their means of subsistence and in the landscapes centered on the rice terraces. It is therefore inextricably fused with the natural environment. This awareness has only been further strengthened by globalization. When a tree grows and spreads its foliage to shade the ground below, it also sends its roots deep into the earth. Similarly, as the villagers' networks expand across the world, they see even more clearly that their contemporary way of life also has deep roots in a continuing history that stretches back to the distant past. They are being led to reconfirm and even rediscover that their contemporary way of life is supported by their ancestors' toil in building and repairing the stone walls of the terraces over many generations and that the forests, water sources, paddies and soil, and the blessing of the gods contribute to maintaining their society. Rice terrace agriculture is a symbol of this.

Contrary to popular opinion, deepening globalization has not necessarily meant homogenization and the erasure of difference (Friedman 2006). Rather, as Roland Robertson (1997: 5) argues, the spread of particularism has produced global diversity. However, globalization also provides moments and pathways that enable the development of subjective connections that directly link these individualized and diversified regions. As I argue in more detail in the following chapter, it also makes them more aware of one another's differences and commonalities. Furthermore, attempts to strengthen cultural awareness, as can be seen in Nauyac's work or Hungduan's *Tungoh* festival, are not attempts to respond to globalization by escaping to ancient traditions, nor are they a reactionary backlash against it. Rather, a growing interest and pride in the authenticity and indigenousness of ethnic culture is quite the opposite. It is a necessary validation of the self that enables people to ride the currents of globalization proactively, by strengthening their foundations and making them more visible and self-conscious. These attempts can also be understood as a strategy to seek recognition as an other with a different but equal culture that is worthy of respect within what they now understand as a global arena.

What makes this strategy possible and has enabled so many Hapao villagers to become migrant workers is the system that exists in Filipino society for sending huge numbers of migrant workers out into the world. The rapid increase in Filipino migrant workers was encouraged under President Marcos's developmentalist dictatorship as an important means of obtaining foreign currency. The hope was that remittances would provide support to the national economy from the flank, in a context of uneven economic development. Specific measures were implemented to encourage migrant work from the mid-1970s. Following the assassination of Benigno Aquino Jr. in August 1983, the Philippine economy contracted severely and large numbers of people went overseas looking for work. Many Filipino lowlanders had to go overseas to find jobs in order to survive. As they did so, the number of recruitment agencies smoothing the way to work overseas increased in proportion. At both government and social levels, systems developed to support and encourage migrant labor. The Ifugaos were a little behind the lowlanders in their adoption of migrant work, but they are now making the most of the opportunities this system offers them.

The importance accorded to English-language education as a result of American colonial rule is another factor. English is taught alongside Filipino from the elementary school level and at the higher levels of education, lectures and tutorials are given in English. This means that most Filipinos are comfortable using English for everyday conversation and, even in Hapao, university graduates (and high school graduates to some extent) can read, write and speak English. Their confidence in their ability to speak English and their optimistic belief that English can be more or less understood all over the world makes it easier for individuals to travel abroad, as does the presence of other people from the same region or linguistic group and Filipino mutual aid and friendly societies in the destination country.

More than half the migrant workers from Hapao are from wealthy households and have a tertiary-level education. In other words, their education outside the village (and usually outside the prefecture) has connected them with one end of a global network. They seize the opportunity to work overseas, in locations that lie at the other end of that network. In one sense, migrant labor is a system whereby the advanced countries absorb high-quality labor power from the developing countries at a low cost. However, many of these workers are themselves highly educated and have gained detailed knowledge about working conditions abroad from their friends, relatives and acquaintances. Armed with this knowledge, they embrace the opportunity to work overseas as a chance to make a real improvement in the quality of the life that they have experienced up until now.

9 International Cooperation
From Entanglement to a Participatory Anthropology

When I conduct fieldwork in one place for an extended period of time, I usually develop close relationships with the people who make up that community, as I suspect most people would. I cannot devote myself entirely to observation like an invisible man. Sometimes this intimacy creeps up on me unnoticed while I am busy with my research. At other times it happens suddenly, when the shock of some incident or another makes me forget myself. Either way, whether I like it or not, Shimizu the anthropologist becomes entangled in the various problems and the webs of human relationships that are encountered in the field. Of course, it might be possible to always place the research above all else and to apply the brakes at this point, continuing to maintain some distance. In fact, many anthropologists make it a golden rule to treat the target (phenomena and people) of their research as an object, so as to guarantee the objectivity of their research and remain detached, observing the situation coolly. However, it is also possible to choose to accept becoming entangled in some incident or problem and to use the opportunity to make a deeper commitment to the field, treating the experiences and understandings that come from this 'insider' perspective as important in themselves. The anthropological methodology of participant observation already contains the potential for this kind of anthropology. If one pursues this potential, then the fields of committed anthropology and of the anthropology of response-ability/anthropology of engagement/anthropology of collaboration opens up.

As I mention earlier, my first fieldwork experience in the late 1970s was in the southwestern foothills of Mount Pinatubo in western Luzon. The June 1991 eruption of Mount Pinatubo, the worst volcanic eruption in the twentieth century, caused extensive damage to my former field site and this provided the occasion for me to make a deeper commitment to address the problems faced by people in the field.¹ My earlier book, *Funka no kodama* (Echoes of the Eruption) (Shimizu 2003), is an ethnography of the indigenous Aeta people who lived in the foothills of Mount Pinatubo and bore the worst effects of the eruption. It records their journey to rebuild their lives after the disaster. It is also a record of my own response, agonizing over each step as I was drawn into the maelstrom created by the eruption. At first I hesitated, fearing that if I became too involved in the field I would not be able to pursue my research. However, as I took part in one relief activity after another, I became more and more involved in disaster rehabilitation and reconstruction with the victims. In the beginning I was a passive participant entangled in the maelstrom. At some point, however, I elected to become actively involved. In this sense, my experience can be seen as a journey from passive involvement to active commitment. The book is also a record of my own awakening and transformation, and of the change in how I practice cultural anthropology. My experience of research in Hapao involved a more deliberate repeat of this movement from passive involvement to active commitment.

During the 1997 May holidays, I went to Baguio at my own expense. There I met with Kidlat and Nauyac and listened to them talk about their recent work. I became interested in what they were saying about Nauyac's reforestation movement. In March 1998 I went to Hapao for the first time to conduct preliminary research.² I spent about a week staying with Nauyac at his home-cum-'Global' office. One night we were drinking a little gin after dinner when he urged me to introduce him to a Japanese NGO that could partner with 'Global' and help him to procure funding from Japan. I felt I could not refuse him and so, upon my return to Manila, I hurried to the home of Tomita Kazuya in Zambales Province. Tomita was a personal friend and a field officer for International *Kudzu* Green Sannan (IKGS),

---

1 It is not so much that I chose to become involved as that I could not turn a blind eye after I had visited the site, met with my friends who were suffering after the disaster and learned of the severity of their predicament. While listening to the stories of my disheartened friends in the evacuation centers and the tent village, and again during the rainy season when they and their children and grandchildren were wasting away from diarrhea and losing their lives one after the other due to the spread of influenza and measles to which they had no immunity, I felt that I wanted to do something and that I must do something.
2 In April 1977, while I was looking for a suitable fieldwork site, I visited Banaue and a number of neighboring villages, but I never made it to Hungduan.

International Cooperation 339

Meeting Nauyac for the first time in Baguio.

Top: Talking about the seeds he has collected (native hardwood species that are ideal for carving). (May 2, 1997)

Bottom: Nauyac tending to the seedlings that have germinated in the nursery at the back of his house while Kidlat films him. (May 2, 1997)

a small Japanese NGO that conducted reforestation work using *kudzu*-vine (*Pueraria lobata*, arrowroot) in the southwest foothills of Mount Pinatubo (where I had conducted fieldwork in the late 1970s) after the volcanic eruption. On that occasion, IKGS made tentative enquiries about conducting a project in partnership with 'Global'. Fortunately, however, when I went back to ask Tomita about the project again the following year, he readily agreed. I immediately started offering materials and ideas to assist in writing the grant application.

The partnership between 'Global' and IKGS was successful in securing 86 million yen (about US$800,000) in funding over the seven years between 2001 and 2008 from five sources, including Japanese extra-governmental organizations and private foundations. With this funding it carried out reforestation work in Hapao and the surrounding region. One of the funding bodies was JICA (in 2003 JICA's status changed from that of a special public institution to an independent administrative institution). It is worth noting that this joint project was the first to receive funding under JICA's Partnership Program (Support Type), which provided 10 million yen (about US$90,000) in 2002–04. This was followed by 45 million yen (about US$410,000) in 2004–06 under the Partner Type program. The project featured regularly in JICA's newsletter and other publications and became a model for what the Partnership Program would look like in practice.

When the JICA–Kobe survey team first arrived in the village in March 2002 to conduct a feasibility study (to determine whether implementation was possible and whether it could reach the intended goals) for the JICA project, I was in Hapao doing fieldwork. As well as giving the team a warm welcome, I provided them with a detailed and favorable account of the state of affairs in the village and of the thinking behind the reforestation project. I later prepared a report as the head of the evaluation team at the conclusion of both the Support Type and Partner Type projects.[3] In this sense, just as Kidlat is both Nauyac's collaborator and a producer of documentary films about his work, for nearly ten years through every

---

3 In fact, the preparation of the drafts for these reports, which mainly involved compiling the details of the project, was undertaken in the case of the first project by JICA staff members Maeda Kuniko (JICA Domestic Operations, Partnership Program Division) and Ōi Akiko (JICA Hyōgo, Partnership Program Division), and for the second project by Kawada Fuji (JICA Hyōgo, Partnership Program Division, Ōi's successor in the role). I then added my overall evaluation of the project and made some corrections to the drafts.

year's visit I have been both a collaborator and archivist for the reforestation and social development projects pursued by Nauyac and Tomita. After becoming entangled in their work and then actively committed to it, I did everything in my power to assist them. At the same time, there was another me that continued to watch that process coolly and at times critically from a place of detachment. Having said that, it might be better to describe what happened by saying that I vacillated between attachment and detachment, questioning and worrying over what was happening, as I both committed myself and observed the process at the same time.

In this chapter, I discuss the grassroots international solidarity, exchanges and cooperation that took place between the reforestation and social development projects in Hapao, which I discuss in great detail elsewhere in this book, and IKGS, the NGO with its offices in Sannan in the Hikami District of Hyōgo Prefecture in Japan, which supported it.[4] They are both very small places deep in the mountains of the Philippines and Japan – you could say they are located in the nooks and crannies of the wider world. However, the creation of direct connections and exchanges between these villages has contributed to the revitalization of both regions. By looking at the way each organization has striven to create a rich and meaningful way of life that is rooted in a particular locality and place in the context of rapid globalization, we can examine the active engagement and embrace of globalization that takes place at the grassroots level.

As I touch on in Chapter One, Appadurai (1996) uses the term 'globalization' to refer to a world in which flows across national borders at a number of dimensions can no longer be accounted for under the old center–periphery or dominant–subordinate models, nor by the models of push-factors and pull-factors in migration theory (this is the idea that political, economic and social factors in the sender and receiver countries, such as the poverty of sender countries and job opportunities in receiver countries, causes people to migrate). As a result of these flows, the composition of definite constellations and structures (which Appadurai terms '-scapes') of ethnicity, media, technology, finance and ideas are neither autonomous nor complete within the frame of the nation-state. He argues that each scape forms under the influence of its own unique

---

4 On April 1, 1999, Sannan was merged with three neighboring municipalities into Sasayama City. This was the first merger to take place as part of 'the great Heisei merger'.

constraints and stimuli. At the same time, because scapes also function as variables, mutually mediating and limiting the movement of other scapes, they assume the form of a structure that is integrated and multi-layered but also divergent. Drawing on the definitions of Giddens (1990) and Appadurai (1996), I argue somewhat provocatively that in the case discussed in this book, mountain communities in both the Philippines and Japan that are living with the impact of rapid globalization have grabbed hold of the wave and ridden it towards a globalization from the hinterlands and from the margins. They are practicing in fragmentary form a popularly-led grassroots globalization.

Development strategy and forest management policy

The reforestation movement and livelihood improvement in Hapao and the international cooperation from Japan that supported it, as considered in this chapter, fall within the social development approach, which has received renewed attention in recent years within the framework of post-Second World War development theory. To summarize the development strategies that have been pursued since the Second World War, the first strategy adopted aimed to develop the national economy as a whole, with modern manufacturing industry as the main axis. It was thought that the poverty problem would be solved through the trickle-down effect, as the benefits of economic development permeated naturally through the social layers. Since the 1970s it has become clear that strategies that prioritize national economic development do not necessarily resolve the issue of poverty. As a result, strategies for development changed to take account of basic human needs. There were calls for a community development approach, which was tried out in practice.

However, the two oil shocks in the 1970s bankrupted developing countries. In the 1980s the implementation of structural adjustment policies in these countries under the guidance of the World Bank promoted cuts to government expenditure (small government) and privatization. As a result, the basic human needs approach took a large step backwards and living conditions for the poor and disadvantaged worsened. Criticisms directed towards these politics prompted reflection and led to an emphasis on social development as a more comprehensive approach that aimed at self-help and independence and the realization of social justice. A social development approach developed out of the methods of participatory development in the 1980s and the women-in-development perspective. It became mainstream in the 1990s and has come to stand next to economic development as one of the two pillars of development (JICA Research Institute 2003). This is symbolized by the adoption of a declaration at the World Summit for Social Development at Copenhagen in 1995 that stated that 'economic development, social development and environmental protection are interdependent and mutually reinforce one another' (JICA Research Institute 2003: 147–54; Edelman and Haugerud 2005: 5–10). The reforestation and environmental protection movement and attempts to revive tradition and improve livelihoods in Hapao happened to share the same overall goal expressed in the declaration for an interdependent and synergistic development that encompasses the economic, social (cultural) and environmental aspects of the villagers' way of life.

Reforestation policies wherein villagers would carry out afforestation and take responsibility for forest management under the leadership of their fellow villagers were adopted as a concrete means of triangulating economic development, social development and environmental protection. At the end of the 1980s, community-led reforestation and forest resource management, as well as sustainable utilization, were recognized as the most effective methods to protect forest environments in Southeast Asia (Vergara and Fernandez 1989; Poffenberger 1990; Ganguli 1995). The implementation of these policies has taken place against the background of the dramatic loss of three-quarters of southern Asia's forests, from 250 million hectares in 1900 to 60 million hectares by 1990. During that time, regional governments were not simply wringing their hands. They implemented various reforestation projects, principally packages that included technical assistance and loans. However, most of these programs failed. This led to growing interest in an alternative to the top-down approach where project implementation took place in accordance with directives from central governments. The bottom-up or decentralized approach involved communities becoming active participants in projects and even proposing and implementing them themselves. This became the mainstream approach for the conservation and utilization of forest resources (Poffenberger 1990).

In general terms, the approach to forest regeneration and protection in the Philippines since the 1980s has involved the government carrying out both integrated social forestry programs and contract reforestation programs side by side.[5] The Integrated Social Forestry Program commenced in 1982. This program granted land rights to people who were illegally cultivating public forests and grasslands on the condition that they grow trees on at least 20 percent of their agricultural land. This policy was the first participatory forestry management policy introduced in the Philippines. However, in reality the strongest aspect of the plan was as a substitute policy for land reform that could be carried out in public forest lands where private ownership was otherwise illegal.

When the Aquino administration came to power in 1986, the newly established Department of Environment and Natural Resources energetically canceled timber felling licenses granted during the Marcos period. At the same time, it implemented a Contract Reforestation Program that depended heavily on grants from Japan and other developed nations, as well as the Asian Development Bank. Under this program, reforestation was carried out using contractors who employed local residents as forestry workers. Contractors were obliged to carry out planting and three years of follow-up management and were paid a specified reforestation allowance for each stage in the process (clearing, soil preparation, planting and weeding). When the three-year contract period expired, the forests reverted to government ownership and a final reforestation payment was made depending on the success of the reforestation (measured by the survival rate of the saplings). Because the government provided employment opportunities to highland villagers under this program, contract reforestation was deemed a 'participatory' forestry policy. However, in reality the local villagers were just day laborers rather than self-motivated participants in afforestation. In most contract reforestation projects, the contractors were not locals but outsiders. Most failed due to bribery and corruption. According to Seki (2002: 22–25),

---

5 According to Inoue (1997), two possible strategies can be conceived for the appropriate management of tropical forests: 'complete industrialization' or 'reconstruction of the commons'. The first strategy aims at the 'full development of the market system', where villagers' private property rights to forests and upland meadows are guaranteed. The second strategy would be to aim for collective management of upland forests and fields by villages or other groups, based on institutional recognition of their previously customary communal property and management. In the case of Ifugao, the pinugo forests are held as private property by individuals or members of the same family but are also under the collective discipline of the village. It is interesting that their management practices are halfway between the two possibilities postulated by Inoue.

who conducted research on one such project in Central Luzon, nearly 90 percent of the afforested lands were left without a single surviving tree or were never planted out in the first place.

The lesson of the failure of the large-scale contract-based reforestation programs between the late 1980s and the early 1990s was that attempts that are based on a top-down and artificial division of forest lands 'not only lacked social legitimacy but failed completely in terms of both their environmental goal of greening barren areas to promote watershed protection functions and their forestry goal of supplying timber by cultivating planted forests' (Seki 2002: 28). To avoid these problems, new forestry management strategies were adopted based on respect for the existing use of forest and upland resources by local people in the Philippines. In particular, the Ramos administration's Executive Order No. 263 established Community-Based Forest Management (CBFM) as 'the national strategy to achieve sustainable forestry and social justice'. This changed the direction of forest policy in the Philippines from state-led resource management to community resource management (Seki 2002: 17, 28). As I discuss in Chapter 3, Ifugao already has a traditional system of private ownership (sometimes shared ownership by parents and children or between siblings) of the forests located uphill from the rice terraces. These *pinugo* forests are an integral part of the rice terrace landscape. This indigenous resource management system recognizes the rights and responsibilities of individual villagers to the forests, but it also involves the rest of the villagers in a system of collective regulation. In this sense, the Ifugaos were clearly ahead of their time. Moreover, Nauyac's 'Global' reforestation movement was very much in line with this major change in national forest policy.[6]

---

6 In applying CBFM, indigenous highlander society and settler lowland society are dealt with separately and CBFM guarantees two different types of ownership rights to forests and meadows. Indigenous communities are issued with a unique Certificate of Ancestral Domain Claim that ratifies the customary rights they enjoyed in the past without alteration. However, settler communities who mainly migrated up from the lowlands are issued with a CBFM. It is assumed that they do not have enough knowledge and experience to be able to protect and utilize the upland forests and meadows. In their case, local residents' associations with responsibility for forest management are organized under the Department of Environment and Natural Resources and are subject to government supervision and guidance.

Brosius, Tsing and Zerner (1998) were early to point out the risk of a confrontation between activists, organizations and NGOs in the developed world (who are concerned with environmental protection in the Third World) and another group who might be called advocates for environmental stewardship and who support local people. However, the community-based natural resource management approach makes it possible to both protect natural environments that are at great risk of destruction and provide social justice for the people who have historically lived in these environments. In order to realize this, Brosius, Tsing and Zerner (1998) argue that dialogue and cooperation are needed between the government planners, NGO staff and environmental movements who are trying to pursue these policies, and researchers who study Third World community development and environmental protection. The reason such cooperation is essential is that both groups have limitations and problems. The former often fail to take into account the historical and cultural background and the political forces at play. They have a tendency to provide abstract, unrealistic and generalized portrayals of the situation on the ground and to use terms such as 'community', 'rights', 'resources' and 'management' as a form of window dressing. This can result in proposals for projects and implementations that are not suited to the context. On the other hand, the latter have a tendency to fetishize their own distant and critical stance and to avoid expressing opinions about or attempting to solve specific problems or contribute to a constructive agenda. The issue of defining terms (ideas) is thereby reduced to a philosophical problem of essentialism and runs the risk of becoming removed from and evading the real problems that arise in the implementation process. In other words, while both camps talk about empowering people in the field, the former is in danger of falling into the trap of providing window dressing for the top-down model, while the latter can fall into the trap of 'view-from-nowhere criticism'. In order to avoid these unproductive traps, Brosius, Tsing and Zerner (1998: 159–60) advocate strongly for a dialogue between the two camps.

Four ethnographies of development in Ifugao

Development is a prominent theme in recent research on Ifugao and three ethnographies focusing on women in development are of particular interest. They are Milgram's (1997) *Crossover, Continuity and Change: Women's Production and Marketing of Crafts in the Upland Philippines*,

Kwiatkowski's (1998) *Struggling with Development: The Politics of Hunger and Gender in the Philippines*, and Hilhorst's (2003) *The Real World of NGOs: Discourses, Diversity and Development*. Each of these studies analyzes the interface between Ifugao society and external politic-economic systems, with a focus on women's livelihoods and economic activity.

Two researches on women in community-driven development

Milgram looked at the role of women in the production and sale of handmade fabrics, woodcarvings and woven baskets in the villages surrounding the tourist center of Banaue between December 1994 and September 1995 and at the kind of changes these activities brought about in women's social position. According to Milgram, in the production of hand-woven fabrics, weavers produced fabrics for both everyday and ritual use within the family, while simultaneously engaging in the production of fabrics for sale as commodities in the tourist industry. She also highlighted the fact that the women who produce the fabrics also control the entire production process. When designing hand-woven fabrics for sale as souvenirs, they catered to tourists' tastes while also attempting to insert their own aesthetic sensibilities.

While the women weavers were impacted by various external influences and constraints, through their own subjective choices they actively responded and skillfully adapted to the changes in their personal circumstances and the economic environment brought about by the penetration of tourism and commercialization (Milgram 1997: 165–8, 217–18). This was even clearer when she considered the manufacturing of carved wooden items, which some women have started to become involved in, and in finishing and sales, which are almost exclusively the domain of women. When women succeed in these areas and start turning a profit, their menfolk take on most of the housework in their place and the women begin to expand their activities, from production to sales. They may even expand further by purchasing sewing machines to make bags and shirts with their hand-woven fabrics, eventually accumulating some capital. In Banaue at least, the homogenous peasant society where people aim simply to survive is disappearing. The inequality that has accompanied the commercialization of handicraft production is not only visible across genders but in the class differential between those who have some access to capital for business and those who do not, between producers and brokers or merchants, and between the successful and unsuccessful merchants (Milgram 1997: 339–402).

Milgram's overall conclusion is that in the commercialization of handicraft production in Banaue, women have not necessarily been driven to the margins as they have in some parts of the Philippines and in other countries. She emphasizes that the industry has opened up a space for women to pursue brokerage and sales or sewing businesses, enabling them to raise their social status. The women's own words show that they have come to live as selective and subjective agents in the sphere of handicraft production. She also suggests that the establishment of cooperative associations for the production and sale of handicrafts would be an effective and necessary means of enabling this healthy development to continue now and into the future (Milgram 1997: 411–12).

Kwiatkowski, on the other hand, conducted a total of sixteen months of fieldwork in three Ifugao villages (she avoids specifying which ones), beginning with one year of primary research and following up with a number of supplementary trips between 1990 and 1993. Before that, from the end of 1984 to the beginning of 1987, she worked as a community health volunteer with the Peace Corps. Her experiences with the Peace Corp gave rise to misgivings about Western leadership in development projects and the Western value systems that are embedded in them. This led her to become an anthropologist and return to the same areas in which she had worked in order to carry out fieldwork and rethink and reevaluate her earlier work.

Kwiatkowski describes the implementation of development assistance in Ifugao, one of the seven poorest provinces in the Philippines, by international aid agencies, governments and NGOs. She focuses on the various medical projects that are intended to address poverty and malnutrition in Ifugao. Ironically, most of these projects delivered an existential shock that caused the decline of customary practices governing the division of food resources and sacrificial feasts that previously contributed to guaranteeing the nutrition of the poor. They have therefore had the opposite of their intended effect or failed completely (Kwiatkowski 1998: 28). The failure of Western development projects is due to the fact that they are forced upon local people based on a particular worldview. They ignore historical and institutional structures such as class, gender and other forms of disparity and inequality in the target society and are formulated by outsiders and implemented from above (Kwiatkowski 1998: 15). Furthermore, the Aquino government adopted these development and healthcare projects to combat, at the grassroots, the communist

NPA guerillas, who had a strong presence in the Cordillera Mountains of northern Luzon. The projects were therefore closely tied up with and complementary to military tactics associated with low-intensity conflict.[7] She points out that, as a consequence, these projects were introduced and carried out not from the humanitarian perspective of welfare or human rights but with distinct military and political objectives (Kwiatkowski 1998: 111).

According to Kwiatkowski, the root cause of the problems of poverty and malnourishment that plague Ifugao are problems of distribution resulting from social relations such as class stratification and gender inequality. Despite this, the approach taken by governments and international aid agencies targets the malnourished individual and concentrates exclusively on the individual body. These projects operate on the level of the body by teaching individuals about health and hygiene, giving nutritional supplements (drugs), weighing bodies and subjecting them to continual follow ups. Rather than looking at the fundamental problems of social power and distribution that cause poverty, they locate the problem in the individual or the family, particularly in the women who bear the primary responsibility for housework and raising children. Through this subtle shifting of blame, they force individual women to take on the responsibility for recognizing and coping with poverty (Kwiatkowski 1998: 298). It follows that the recent tendency to emphasize women's participation in development projects will still contribute nothing to solving the problem if the development projects themselves are unsuitable or even harmful (Kwiatkowski 1998: 293). She concludes that the real solution to poverty and malnutrition is to be found through the reform of unequal social structures. She argues that it is the development of social movements with roots in the community that has the real potential to create a better society and a better way of life (Kwiatkowski 1998: 303). When dealing with poverty, as with the issues of reforestation and environmental protection

---

7 The notion of 'low-intensity conflict' indicates an ongoing state of conflict that lies somewhere between war and peace. The term is generally used to refer to terrorism, guerilla warfare, and religious and ethnic conflict. In the Philippines in the 1980s, the military trained civil defense units without direct government involvement. The strategy was to use these units to prevent the NPA from expanding its sphere of influence.

discussed above, Kwiatkowski recognizes and emphasizes the importance of movements that are rooted in the community and led by the community.

While they both deal with the theme of development, Milgram and Kwiatkowski portray the lives of Ifugao women very differently. This stark contrast is the result of differences in their research subjects. Milgram focuses on Banaue, the center of tourism development in Ifugao. Her research looked at women with an entrepreneurial spirit who are actively pursuing their businesses, despite their small scale. By contrast, the women in Kwiatkowski's study probably live far from Banaue and have no links with tourism development. Furthermore, they live in conflict zones where minor skirmishes between the Philippine Constabulary and the CPP-NPA continue as part of an ongoing struggle for control on the ground. These regions are located deep in the mountains, where it is difficult for the police and military to maintain surveillance and where government services fail to reach. Anti-government forces have therefore based themselves there and they have become an arena of fierce conflict. As we saw in the previous chapter, even in Hapao there is a large economic and social distance between the class of people who complete university or equivalent tertiary education, speak English and travel overseas as migrant laborers, and the class who finish their education at the elementary school level and remain at home. Furthermore, as I discuss in Chapter 3 with regard to Hungduan municipality as a whole, the average annual income of villagers in Hapao, the wealthiest *barangay*, is five times that of those in Bangbang, the poorest *barangay*. This type of social and economic inequality is clearly visible between villages located on the national highway (where road access is good) and those that are remote from it. Banaue, in particular, is connected by a surfaced road to the North Luzon Expressway and has direct bus services to Metro Manila and Baguio. It has become the wealthiest city in the mountains of Ifugao.

Research on the 'real world of NGOs'

Hilhorst's research is based on her participant observation during three years as a contracted staff member with an NGO supporting indigenous women's empowerment and development in northern Luzon, both at the head office and in the indigenous villages where the NGO was working. Her main argument is that the field of 'indigenous women and development' is constructed through the interventions, responses and negotiations of a multitude of actors from indigenous communities, NGO communities, domestic and foreign intermediaries, and regional and national governments, each of whom has a different understanding of what is going on and different expectations. Furthermore, these communities are certainly not internally homogeneous, but are stratified based on differences in wealth. The 'real world' is constituted by the concurrent intermixture of this multiple, multi-tiered plurality of different constituents. By focusing on quotidian political processes, Hilhorst presents a detailed portrait of the way the 'real world of NGOS' is mutually constructed through negotiations between these constituent groups and organizations or, rather, of the agents and individuals affiliated with them. However, some of the NGO staff who she covered in her research have criticized her severely for the perspective and the political stance she adopted while discussing and analyzing the reality of everyday life at an NGO from the inside. They have also attacked her research ethics and the politics of her ethnography. These criticisms include allegations that her perspective and stance are deeply tied up with neocolonialism, that she did not seek permission or advice or consult anyone before she published the results of her research as an ethnography, and that she showed little consideration for the adverse political effect that her ethnography might have on her research subjects.[8]

Hilhorst responded in an epilogue that appears after the final concluding chapter of her ethnography. She summarizes the main criticisms levelled against her in a long letter she received from this NGO and defends herself

---

8 When Hilhorst signed the contract to become a member of the NGO's staff, she explained that she would be conducting research for her doctoral dissertation at the same time. When her dissertation, 'Records and Reputations: Everyday Politics of a Philippine Development NGO' (Hilhorst 2000), was complete, she provided a copy to the NGO's headquarters. The NGO responded with a long letter of protest, alleging that she had skillfully manipulated her research subjects and taken advantage of their goodwill for her own purposes. They criticized her for ignoring the broader context and selectively highlighting fragments of trivial conversations to suit her story while failing to understand the situation. They alleged that her activities dealt a major blow to the movement for democratization. The NGO criticized her basic stance and framework for understanding, noting that 'the historic gains of Cordillera peoples in assertion of their rights...were gains as part of the National Democratic movement. If Ms. Hilhorst does not accept Cordillera realities, she should at least respect it. She may not impose her misplaced theorizing on us'; they further urged that she should have 'let the Cordillera situation speak for itself' (quoted in Hilhorst 2003: 228).

on each point. First, she claims to have only settled on the real example of the NGO world as a doctoral dissertation, let alone as a book, after she had finished her research and after much reading and writing. Second, she says that when she first started working and researching during her contract period as a staff member, it would have been impossible to predict the results of her research and therefore to obtain permission beforehand. Finally, she states that the book is simply one perspective on some of the things that occurred as part of the management and activities of the NGO and that while she takes a different view of the history of the development of the popular democratic movement from that of people in the movement, no single representation has a monopoly on the truth (Hilhorst 2003: 3–1, 227–9).[9]

Research on utilizing traditional knowledge with GIS technology

Like the three abovementioned ethnographies, Rhodora Gonzalez considers the way Ifugao society interfaces with external political and economic systems (specifically, external actors like the prefectural and national governments and NGOs). Her doctoral dissertation, 'Platforms and Terraces: Bridging Participation and GIS in Joint-Learning for Watershed Management with the Ifugao of the Philippines' (Gonzalez 2000), incorporates her own experiences with policies to conserve the rice terraces, irrigation canals and watersheds and the effective implementation of a reforestation project as a component of these policies. As a member of staff at the Ifugao branch office of the Philippine Rural Reconstruction

---

9 Hilhorst also claims that within the context of the Philippines as a whole, the popular democracy movement is like a David facing a very powerful Goliath. Nevertheless, when you focus on the everyday activities of NGOs, deep power imbalances clearly also exist within them. She claims that her ethnography enables a critical reading of this culture. After the September 11, 2001, terrorist attacks, people in the Philippines who were involved in political activities were also labeled as terrorists or supporters of terrorism and it became easier to suppress speech and political activity. Hilhorst credits her own approach as contributing to Western understandings of the real world of NGO activities in this oppressive atmosphere, thereby facilitating further support for them from the West.

The NGO where Hilhorst worked was the Cordillera Women's Non-governmental Organization, a pioneering organization supporting indigenous women. Since the end of the Marcos administration, it has remained loosely under the umbrella of the CPP-NPA-aligned National Democratic Front.

Movement, the Philippines largest development NGO, Gonzalez spent thirteen months from 1997 promoting the maintenance and use of a Geographical Information System (GIS) with the residents of four villages centered on Bangaan, 130 kilometers east of Banaue on the Mayoyao road. During the project, the villagers displayed considerable interest in using GIS. The technology led them to deepen their appreciation and collective understanding of the current environmental conditions in their villages and of the rice terraces, canals and forests. Gonzales introduces a successful example of using GIS in Maryland in the United States, where the technology has facilitated collective understandings and the harmonization of the multiple realities experienced by multiple users in the context of environmental protection. She concludes that a similar approach is possible in Ifugao. Based on her practical experience in two villages, Gonzales found that GIS facilitated 'bridging', 'harmonization' and 'commonality' between the pictures of the world held by several users of the environment. Based on the results of her research, Gonzales (2000: 162–8) proposed a plan for environmental protection based on coordinating and utilizing both traditional knowledge and GIS.

Whereas Conklin (1980: 27) found that the soils and water supply to the rice terraces were in very good condition in the 1960s and 1970s, Gonzalez points out that by 2000 Ifugao Province had the worst landslides and related problems in all of the Cordillera Administrative Region (the six mountainous prefectures of northern Luzon plus the city of Baguio). She explains that the seeds of this environmental degradation were already sown when the American colonial administration first began in Ifugao in the early twentieth century, but the situation deteriorated rapidly over the last twenty years of the century. For example, declining forest cover led to landslides, which in turn clogged irrigation canals, leaving them unable to function. During the El Niño drought from 1997 until 1998, many of the watersheds that feed the rice terraces dried up, leading to water shortages. In 1998, when there were heavy rains associated with La Niña, many of the rice terrace walls collapsed (Gonzales 2000: 82–3).[10]

---

10 Ifugao has an average annual rainfall of 3,700 milliliters. It is the watershed for the Magat Dam, Luzon's largest dam (1.25 billion cubic meters) and its largest source of hydroelectric power (3.6 million megawatts). However, the huge quantities of earth and sand that have flowed into the dam due to deforestation and frequent landslides in the catchment have shortened the dam's expected life, from initial estimates of

Gonzales suggests a number of reasons for the serious crisis facing rice terrace cultivation. First, the penetration of Christianity and the modern political systems means that the *monbaki* and traditional leaders have lost influence and cannot exercise leadership over communal labor practices such as maintaining irrigation canals and repairing terrace walls. Second, as young people have become better educated, they show little interest in agriculture. Third, the ability to earn an income through non-agricultural means or through labor migration means that people are losing their motivation to practice agriculture. Fourth, the forests are not managed adequately. In summary, the root of the problem is a decline in the social system that has supported terrace agriculture. Even if the central and prefectural governments provide infrastructural fixes by restoring canals and repairing terraces, it will not constitute an effective policy (Gonzales 2000: 11–15, 78–87). Gonzales advocates for the use of GIS for integrated environmental protection instead of this kind of top-down infrastructure investment. Of course, sharing and transmitting spatial information and understandings is nothing new for the Ifugaos. In the past when their communities were more cohesive, it was done as a matter of course. However, the creation of a shared space where villagers can exchange opinions about conservation with one another through the computer screen and make the issues visible using various maps and charts is revolutionary. Gonzales suggests that it might be a starting point for a solution to the problems and might open up the possibility of a new cooperative game.[11]

---

100 years at the construction stage to a mere forty years. The loss of watersheds will have a serious impact on Philippine society as a whole (Gonzales 2000: 7–8, 13).

11 The specific projects Gonzales worked on were the development and implementation of monitoring systems for the Bangaan rice terraces and the development of GIS for a reforestation project in Ducligan, which was led by the natural resources management committee. She summarizes the progress of these projects and their results as follows. (There are still no detailed maps of Bangaan like the ones complied by Conklin (1980) (15,000:1) and Ducligan lacks both detailed maps and soil distribution maps. This means that the problem of constructing an accurate GIS remains to be dealt with, something Gonzales recognizes.)

In 1995 Bangaan was identified by the government's Ifugao Terraces Commission as one of eight high-priority rice terrace regions in the municipality of Banaue that were in need of repair. In anticipation of future repair projects to be carried out by the government and NGOs, the local Philippine Rural Reconstruction Movement office selected the target rice terraces with the agreement of local people. In order to prepare appropriately for the efficient

The 1991 eruption of Mount Pinatubo and rural revitalization

As I discuss throughout this chapter, I have been deeply involved in the 'Global' reforestation and social development work in Hapao and with IKGS, a Japanese NGO that supported the work. As a result, my participant observation has gone beyond the usual anthropological methodology of conducting research on the culture and way of life in a village while spending an extended period living among its people. Instead I have been a participant and an observer in a literal sense. I have been drawn into their problems and movements and become an active participant, conducting my research from the inside. My role might best be described not as that of a neutral and objective researcher, keeping my distance from the object of the research, but as a concoction of participant observer, movement collaborator, supporter and embedded reporter.

As I mention earlier, my active participation in the field began with the eruption of Mount Pinatubo on June 15, 1991. Ten days earlier there was also an explosion at Fugendake on Mount Unzen in Japan. The pyroclastic flows that followed cost the lives of forty-two people, including volcanologists, reporters and local firefighters. The eruption of Mount Pinatubo had 600 times the power of Fugendake and was the worst eruption in the twentieth

---

implementation of the repairs, maps were prepared using GIS of the integrated terrace system as a whole (*payah-cha*, the rice terraces taken as a whole from the highest levels, where water enters from the irrigation canals, to the bottom of the terraces) and relevant data was also included (owners and cultivators of each terrace, existence of irrigation or erosion). After the work was completed, Gonzales (2000: 128–40) used a global positioning system to supervise and carry out the actual repair works with the cooperation of the villagers.

In Ducligan, the *barangay* implemented a reforestation project in 1996, but it ended in failure with a sapling survival rate of less than 10 percent. The reasons for failure, according to the villagers, were water shortages, lack of follow-up maintenance after planting, outbreaks of pests, fires spreading from slash and burn agriculture, and poor soils. Based on this input, Gonzalez and the deputy governor proposed at a planning meeting that bamboo be used in a future planned reforestation project, but the villagers indicated a strong preference for native mahogany and *Alnus* species because these species are suitable for woodcarving. However, even if these native species were originally suited to the region, environmental change means that they may no longer be the most well adapted. However, Gonzalez respected the villagers' wishes and used the GIS to find potential reforestation sites best suited to these species. The reforestation was then carried out in consultation with local villagers (Gonzales 2000: 142–55).

century. The ash that rose high into the air smothered the whole globe, interfering with the sun's rays and reducing global temperatures for that year by an average of nearly one degree. More than ten years earlier, for twenty months between 1977 and 1979, I lived in the indigenous Aeta village of Kakilingan in the southwestern foothills of Mount Pinatubo, where I conducted fieldwork that looked at society, culture and religion. The Aetas are a Negrito people who closely resemble the African San people (Bushmen) in appearance. They are short of stature with an average height of 150 centimeters for Aeta men and 140 centimeters for Aeta women. They have dark brown skin and frizzy, curly hair. Other than steel cooking pots, kettles and hatchets, salt and cloth, which they obtained by trading the products of the forest, they lived an almost totally self-sufficient life in the mountains. Their staple foods were tubers, beans and corn grown in swiddens. They supplemented their diet with wild vegetables, hunted for birds and bats with bow and arrow, sometimes also taking small animals, and ate fish from the rivers. During the last glacial period (approximately 20,000–30,000 years ago) the seas retreated and the archipelago that is now known as the Philippines was mostly accessible by land from the continent. The Aetas are the descendants of a group that migrated at that time. They are truly indigenous in the sense of the Japanese word *senjū* (in residence before) as I discuss in Chapter 7.

 The Aeta people who lived around Mount Pinatubo in the 1970s did their best to avoid contact and interaction with the outside world of the lowland Christians. Within their own lifeworld in the mountains, they lived a simple and frugal existence. However, the 1991 eruption brought cataclysmic change to the natural environment of the mountain foothills. The village of Kakilingan, where I lived, is about ten kilometers from the summit of Mount Pinatubo and the ash and debris from the eruption covered the village in a layer of ash fifty to sixty centimeters deep. Moreover, when the torrential rains of the wet season came in each of the following years, the ash and debris that had accumulated on the sides of the mountain created lahars (volcanic ash and mud flows) that swept down the mountain along the course of rivers. Within a few years, the village, which was located on the bank of a river, was buried in a layer of ash and debris tens of meters thick. There was nothing left to remind them of their life before.

 At that time, about 20,000 Aetas were living in the foothills of Mount Pinatubo scattered across a number of small hamlets. Almost all these hamlets were buried in volcanic ash. The closer to the summit of Mount

Top: The lowland Christian village of Aglao downstream from Kakilingan is largely underwater of the newly emerged dammed lake formed by a lahar (volcanic ash landslide) from Mount Pinatubo slopes.

Bottom: A lahar from Mount Pinatubo buries rice paddies, farms and houses of lowland Christians on both banks of the Santo Tomas River. Kakilingan is located at the foot of the mountain in the far center of the photograph. (March 18, 1993)

Pinatubo they were located and the higher the elevation, the more the people who lived there had tended to maintain their traditional way of life. They were the ones who suffered the worst damage from the eruption. The closer they were to the summit, the source of the eruption, the greater the amount of volcanic ash that rained down upon them. In the higher and lower parts of the foothills, almost all the villages sustained catastrophic damage. This brought the Aeta people down from the mountain to take refuge in tents that had been set up for disaster victims. About six months to a year later, they moved to the new settlements established by the government, where they relied on food aid to survive. In principle, a small plot of land was attached to each house given to each family in the new settlements. However, the plots were rocky and the soils were parched and deficient in nutrients. The people were unable to live by growing food alone. Some Aetas went to work on construction sites in nearby towns or in Olongapo, the capital of Zambales Province. Others worked as cheap day-laborers for the lowlanders, doing various odd jobs and agricultural work.

The Aetas of Kakilingan lived in the tent village for about six months, after which they found their own permanent homes on public land about twenty kilometers from Mount Pinatubo (in the district of Kanaynayan, Municipality of Castelijos), where they built a new village for themselves. Although I say they built it, the village of Kakilingan was itself a new village built in the mid-1970s by the Ecumenical Foundation for Minority Development (EFMD), a small Christian NGO. This NGO encouraged the Aetas who were still practicing swidden agriculture in the mountains to come down from the mountains and practice settled agriculture. To support them in this, they used bulldozers to prepare the ground for a new village, reclaimed some agricultural land, and distributed individual plots and caribou (water buffalo) to the settled Aetas. They also carried out various development projects.

For the first few years of the project, the main drivers were the director, agricultural specialists and NGO staff who also lived in the village. However, at the beginning of the 1980s the Aetas who had settled in the village established their own association, the Aeta Development Association (ADA). EFMD and ADA worked together to conceptualize, plan and implement various projects. The aid organization Hilfswerk der Evangelischen Kirchen Schweiz (HEKS, Swiss Church Aid) consistently provided the main source of funding. Some years before the eruption, volunteers from Japan Overseas Cooperation Volunteers (JOCV) were dispatched to work with EFMD in fields such as agriculture and animal husbandry, community development, and hygiene and health. They spent a two-year period in the field, which could be extended up to three years. At the time of the eruption, two volunteer specialists in animal husbandry and health and hygiene were assigned to the village. Fresh volunteers were dispatched after the eruption. The Aetas, NGO staff and JOCV volunteers brought their own skills and resources to bear during the emergency evacuation that followed the eruption, during the disaster relief effort, and throughout the reconstruction and building of the new Kanaynayan village (Nishimura 2001).

Flowing directly from these efforts, with Japanese aid a reforestation project using *kudzu*-vine was implemented after the eruption. This project involved planting *kudzu*-vine from Japan on the foothills that had been wasted by ash and debris from the eruption. Once the *kudzu*-vine had grown and covered the ground with its leaves, the slopes were then reforested with fruit trees, building timber species and other species in order to restore the forest cover. The aim was to enable the Aetas who were settled in Kanaynayan or other settlements to return to their home on Mount Pinatubo. The driver

Student volunteers from the Sasayama Homei Senior High School and Aeta workers fill used paper cups with soil in order to germinate *kudzu* seeds. (March 26, 1999)

was a small NGO called IKGS that was established in Hyōgo Prefecture for this purpose. The project was the result of an idea to invert local thinking about *kudzu*-vine, a parasite hated in the agricultural mountain ecosystem of Sannan, and use it to revive the town.

With its long history of forestry and the cultivation of traditional medicine, the municipality of Sannan had made 'renewal through traditional medicine' a pillar of its rural revitalization strategy. As a part of this, the local civic center began organizing a series of regular talks under the title 'Scientific Lectures on Local Conditions'. In June 1992, exactly one year after the eruption of Mount Pinatubo, Professor Tsugawa Hyōe of the agriculture department at Kobe University was invited to give a talk on 'Putting Our Town's *Kudzu* to Good Use'. In the lecture, Tsugawa considered how best to utilize the *kudzu*-vine that had, despite its medicinal uses, became the 'hated parasite' of the municipality's main industry of forestry due to its tremendous rate of growth. The lecture provided the stimulus for the formation of a *kudzu*-vine Vine Craft Group, whose members were mostly members of the lifelong learning promotion committee at the civic center, to start making baskets for flower arranging and other handicrafts using the *kudzu*-vine. Tsugawa's suggestion that *kudzu*-vine's vigor and rapid reproduction would make it perfect for greening the volcanic ash wastes on the foothills of Mount Pinatubo led to the creation of a movement to collect *kudzu*-vine seeds from Sannan and send them to Pinatubo.

They decided to first plant the tenacious *kudzu*-vine on the wastes to stabilize and rehabilitate the soils, as well as to cover the surface of the ground to prevent dust clouds and protect it from the sun's rays. Once the *kudzu*-vine was well established, they would then commence reforestation.[12]

---

12 During the planning stage, there was some strong opposition to planting *kudzu*-vine due to the risk that its extremely rapid growth might lead it to spread beyond the disaster area and destroy local native plants, leading to a complete change in the composition of the local flora. At the end of this argument, the president of IKGS argued passionately for the use of *kudzu*-vine, stating that 'if it does happen then we will remove all of the *kudzu*-vine. If additional funding is required in order to do so, then I am ready to contribute my own money.' In the end it was decided to go ahead with the use of *kudzu*-vine.

In reality, the *kudzu*-vine seedlings that were planted on Pinatubo did not produce seed due to a difference in daylight hours and so it only spread via rhizome. This limited the spread of the *kudzu*-vine and led to the failure to realize the full scope of the project's objectives.

Committee members from a local civic center started with a campaign to harvest *kudzu*-vine seeds under the slogan 'international cooperation from the countryside, open to all'. With the full support of the town's elementary, middle and high school students and the seniors' association, they were able to harvest a large quantity of seed. In December 1993 IKGS was launched (the original name, International *Kudzu* Green Sannan, was changed to International Keeping Good Sannan in February 2001) and the revegetation and reforestation of Mount Pinatubo got underway. In 1992 JOCV volunteers Hasebe Yasuhiro (specializing in animal husbandry and breeding), who had been dispatched to work with EFMD before the eruption, and Tomita Kazuya (specializing in agriculture and rural development), who was dispatched after the eruption, began laying the groundwork for the project in the Philippines.[13]

IKGS volunteers harvesting *kudzu*-vine seeds from the snow-covered commons of Sannan. (January 1997, photo Segawa Chiyoko)

---

13 After the eruption, Hasebe spent about two months sleeping out with fifty head of cattle belonging to the ADA in Nueva Vizcaya, moving about looking for grass for them to eat. Due to his unimaginable toil and superhuman effort, the cows managed to survive the shortage of feed after the eruption.

The *kudzu*-vine seed was harvested on frosty highland plateaus and from the snow-covered mountains of Sannan, so it was not an easy job. However, the volunteers believed that their work would be of direct assistance in the reforestation of lands laid waste by the eruption of Mount Pinatubo and had a strong volunteer spirit. Members of the seniors' association took a particularly active part in the harvest and taught the children how to get the *kudzu*-vine seeds out of the seedpods and how to dry and preserve them, passing on their knowledge and techniques. Each spring and summer holiday between 1999 and 2003, ten to twenty members of the Interact Club at Sasayama Homei High School visited the Mount Pinatubo area for several days, where they took part in a work camp to help plant trees. One Aeta child was assigned to each student. They learned to communicate using gestures, hand signals and rudimentary English while eating and sleeping together, fostering an intimate exchange between them. Both the elderly and the children of Sannan took an active part in reforesting the disaster area.

The *kudzu*-vine seeds gathered in Sannan were sent to the team in the Philippines. Young Aetas were employed to construct seedling nurseries, germinate the seeds, transplant them into plastic planting pots and grow them on before finally planting them out on the wastes. Tomita undertook all the planning for the work on the Philippine side and looked after the students' work camp. Tomita went to help the Aetas rebuild their lives after the eruption as a JOCV volunteer agricultural specialist. He was dispatched to work with ADA in 1992 and extended his two-year term by a year. At that time, he also cooperated with IKGS on the *kudzu*-vine revegetation project. After returning to Japan at the end of his three-year stint with JOCV, he was dispatched once again in 1995 as the field officer for IKGS and devoted himself to the revegetation project. When he was redeployed to Mount Pinatubo, Tomita was accompanied by his new wife, Eriko, who had been dispatched to the Maldives in the same JOCV volunteer cohort as him. Since then the two have been based in the new settlement established for the Aetas on the outskirts of Subic, Zambales, with their two daughters and a son, who were born in the Philippines.

They remained living there until the time of re-writing this monograph (August 2018). It is worth mentioning that Eriko used her qualifications and experience as a midwife to establish the Barnabas Clinic in 2002, near the couple's home in the new settlement. She conducts pre- and postnatal examinations for the local people (most of whom are very poor), attends births and does general healthcare at little charge and with donations from Japan. She usually attends births in the clinic or sometimes at the mother's home, but in cases where complications are expected, the women are sent to a hospital in the town. As of August 2018, 4,960 children had been born under her care at the clinic.[14] She also conducts medical care with herbal medicines, which she purchases at Chinatown in Manila, and also applies indirect moxibustion.

My participation: from Pinatubo to Ifugao

I now relate how I became involved in disaster recovery in Pinatubo and how this led me to Ifugao, although I have to disrupt the chronology of the story to do so. When Mount Pinatubo erupted in June 1991, I had been in the Philippines since March conducting research while on a one-year sabbatical. My objective was to study the relationship between mass culture, political consciousness and social movements in Metro Manila. What was the political consciousness of people in the film, music, theatre and visual art scenes and what kind of messages were they producing? What were the common sensibilities and understandings among the people who were consuming this mass culture regarding the current state of Philippine politics and society and the relationship with the United States? These sorts of questions were of great interest to me. The people of Manila, who wore jeans, T-shirts and sneakers, drank cola, listened to American pop and watched Hollywood films had the same kinds of tastes and sensibilities as me. But there were subtle differences. I wanted to carefully observe these similarities and differences and give

---

14 The operating costs, necessary equipment and pharmaceutical supplies for the clinic are sourced through donations of money and supplies from Japan. In the beginning, the local medical association saw the clinic as a threat and tried to sabotage it. With the support of the local mayor and residents (large numbers of whom signed a petition and organized other support for the clinic), it received special permission to operate as a public clinic in 2003. Since then, the clinic has accepted volunteers and trainees from Japan and it continues to operate satisfactorily to this day. On January 18, 2007, the clinic was featured in the popular television documentary series *Jonetsu Tairiku* (Passionate Continent, Mainichi Broadcasting System). In August 2009, the clinic became independent of IKGS and under the name Clinic for Poverty it continues to provide medical services to local people.
 For more on Tomita Eriko's work, see her book (2013).

serious thought to the overlap between culture and politics, particularly the context of the movement for social reform that was then taking place.

Once I had settled in Manila and was beginning to make some progress with my research, Mount Pinatubo erupted. When I visited the evacuation centers, I found that the friends and acquaintances who helped me so much during my fieldwork in the late 1970s all talking about the difficulties of life in the temporary accommodation and of their unease about the future. Specialists in volcanology were warning that the huge quantities of ash and debris lodged on the side of Mount Pinatubo would be forced down by torrential rains during the wet season and create lahars that would cover the villages and agricultural lands downstream. They warned that the damage from the lahars would be much worse than that caused by the ash that had fallen after the explosion, and that it would happen every year for at least several years.

My Aeta friends had lost the foundation of their way of life. With no hope for the future, they were facing a dire situation. I felt that I had to repay them for the assistance they had given me during my fieldwork. This led me to start working with a number of NGOs that were carrying out emergency disaster relief, particularly the Asia Volunteer Network established by a Japanese NGO, Foundation for Human Rights in Asia. However, unlike the many volunteers who came from Japan (doctors, nurses, consultants, technical specialists, architects etc.) I had no special technical knowledge that could help the Aeta disaster victims directly. What I could do was to work with Asia Volunteer Network to compile information booklets in English and Japanese containing details about Aeta society, culture and history and the situation after the disaster, and to distribute this information to the organizations involved in the relief effort. I was also able to act as a guide and interpreter for journalists who had come to report on the situation, as well as NGO representatives, and to explain how the Aeta were living before the disaster and what had happened since. After returning to Japan in March the following year, I continued to visit Pinatubo every holiday, spring, summer, autumn and winter, for a couple of years, and then almost every year until 2017.

After two or three years, when the emergency had abated somewhat, I mainly assisted IKGS in Sannan and Tomita as they worked with the ADA on reconstruction activities, such as their reforestation project in the southwestern foothills of Pinatubo. I kept up my visits to the tent villages and new settlements of the Aeta and listened to my Aeta friends as they talked about their suffering during and after the disaster and their complaints and worries. I listened while they told me about their hopes for the future and asked for aid and I continued to communicate this information to Japan, appealing for more assistance for them. Three or four years after the eruption, the Aetas had begun to find a groove in their new lives and were able to support themselves, even if it was only at a basic level. I began to relax and decided to put together a book of the stories they had shared with me about their experiences during the disaster. I returned to the Aetas and listened once more to their various stories. I recorded them and had an assistant transcribe the recordings.

Nauyac explaining the plan for reforestation in Hapao. Kidlat is on the left and Nauyac's second daughter, Vivian, is on the right. Vivian later married a young Israeli man whom she got to know while working in Hong Kong and moved with him to Israel. (May 2, 1997)

I interviewed nearly a hundred of my Aeta friends and acquaintances and about thirty of their stories were published in a compilation by a Philippine publishing company under the title *The Orphans of Pinatubo: Ayta Struggle for Existence* (Shimizu 2001). I felt that I had done the job I was meant to do, fulfilled my responsibilities and gone some way towards repaying the debt I owed the Aetas.

Just before finishing the manuscript for the book in 1997, I happened to become a member of the selection committee for the Toyota Foundation's International Grant Program in 1996. Among the applications received that year was one from Sun Flower Co., a group of Baguio artists and cultural practitioners chaired by Kidlat, seeking a grant for a project in Hapao. This is how I once more became associated with Kidlat. I was very interested in the plan, which incorporated a reforestation movement to protect the basis of the Ifugao traditional lifestyle in the *pinugo* forests and rice terraces, promoting the transmission of cultural knowledge and video workshops to increase interest and awareness about culture. As I explain in Chapter 7, the idea for the video workshop reminded me of a similar project carried out with the Kayapó Indians in the remote reaches of the Amazon River region in Brazil. I decided on the spot to make use of the May public holiday period in Japan to visit Kidlat at his home in Baguio and ask him to talk about his ideas for the video project in more detail. I also asked him to introduce me to Nauyac. I visited Nauyac at his home in Asin Road Barangay for three consecutive days and interviewed him about his movement for reforestation, environmental protection and social development. I gave Kidlat copies of the three main essays by Terence Turner on the Kayapó and explained how they had started a movement to oppose the construction of a dam and had effectively used the videos they made and edited themselves in various ways. However, when I asked him later for his thoughts on these essays, he said that he had not really read them. Perhaps he did not want to be influenced by the example of an American anthropologist, given his desire to dissolve and reconstruct himself after being over-assimilated through the American educational system.

As I listened to Kidlat and Nauyac, my interest in their work grew. I visited Baguio once again in March 1998. On March 18, I accompanied Nauyac on his return journey to his hometown of Hapao in a jeepney loaded with his personal effects and more than ten sacks of seed from native tree species (see Chapter 5). On arriving in Hapao, I stayed with Nauyac at his home-cum-'Global' office and conducted preliminary research for about ten days.

While I call it a home and office, it is simply a one-room traditional Ifugao home less than ten square meters in size that he had moved from the *sitio* of Patpat, where he was born and raised.[15] When I first met Nauyac in Baguio, I was very eager to talk and asked him a lot of questions. After I accompanied him on his homeward journey to Hapao and stayed on at his home to start my research, he must have sensed my genuine enthusiasm. One day, while we were drinking some gin after dinner purchased from the general store next door and chatting about all sorts of things, Nauyac said to me:

Nauyac meeting with 'Global' members in front of the office-cum-home. (March 5, 2001)

15 Nauyac slept on his bed while I slept beside him on the floor on a straw mat. His loud snoring and his habit of putting the light on and reading the Bible for about ten minutes whenever he got up to go to the toilet during the night meant that I did not sleep well. There were also ticks and fleas so that during the first week of each research trip I always got horribly bitten. In terms of the experience of living in the field, it was much more difficult than being in Pinatubo in the 1970s.

It's good to see you devoting yourself to your research but you're doing that for yourself. We would also like you to lend us a hand to further our 'Global' movement. I would like you to find an NGO in Japan that can help us. That's why I would like you to formally become a member of 'Global' and take responsibility for recording and disseminating our work. I would also like to appoint you as our representative in Japan. Please take up your responsibility and do what you can for us.

A little tipsy and feeling happy and generous, I responded, 'alright, I understand. I'll handle the Japanese side.'

In March 1999 while visiting my Aeta friends living in the new settlements established for the victims of the Pinatubo disaster, I visited Tomita's field office-cum-home in Subic, Zambales. I explained the basic outline of Nauyac's reforestation movement and asked for his cooperation.[16] In March 2000 I returned to Subic and sounded him out about the Ifugao project once again. Tomita was worried because small troupes of NPA guerillas were appearing frequently in the IKGS reforestation area on Pinatubo and helping themselves to the hut established for the project. In some areas there had been bushfires, probably started by the guerillas, and he was unsure whether they would be able to continue with the Pinatubo project. Furthermore, it was now more than ten years since the eruption and he was well aware that securing further grant funding to continue the reforestation project on Pinatubo would be difficult. He was already thinking about his next project. He showed a strong interest in 'Global' and Nauyac's plans and immediately got in touch with Nauyac's wife in Baguio. The following month, when Nauyac was visiting from Hapao,

---

16 IKGS's reforestation work in Pinatubo received 19.7 million yen (about US$182,000) in funding from three funding bodies in the four years between 1998 and 2001 (16.5 million yen [about US$150,000] over three years from Japan Environment Corporation – Japan Fund for Global Environment; 2.4 million yen [about US$22,000] over three years from AEON Environmental Foundation; and 800,000 yen [about US$7,300] in one year from the Green Fund – National Land Afforestation Promotion Organization). By the conclusion of the project at Pinatubo in 2002, IKGS had collected four million *kudzu*-vine seeds. After they were sent to Pinatubo, germinated and planted out, approximately 400,000 trees were planted over 220 hectares. Every year in the spring vacation, about twenty students from the high school in Sannan went to volunteer, staying in Pinatubo for several days. There they did reforestation work, planted commemorative trees and enjoyed getting to know the Aeta young people.

Tomita went to Baguio and met with him. They reached a basic agreement about the project. Tomita went to Hapao as soon as he could. Then three IKGS directors from Japan came to inspect the site and were persuaded that the project was possible. They promised to give it their full support.

As the NGO in Sannan shifted the focus of its activities from Pinatubo to Ifugao in February 2001, it again changed the name of the organization – to IKGS Reforestation Campaign, the term '*kudzu*-vine' disappearing from the Japanese and English names. Unlike the wasted slopes of Mount Pinatubo, there was no need to use *kudzu*-vine as a groundcover and soil improver in Ifugao. It also avoided using *kudzu*-vine because it was apprehensive that in the climate of the Cordillera Mountains, which is very similar to that of Japan, the *kudzu*-vine might be too well suited to the environment and grow out of control, destroying the local ecosystem.

Nauyac's early work: laying the foundations

Before grant funding from Japan enabled him to expand the reforestation movement in 2001, Nauyac was steadily making preparations for the movement. In the early 1990s, Nauyac started to bring seeds and seedlings from Baguio and to distribute them to his friends and relatives for replanting during his several trips back to Hapao each year for matters related to his woodcarving business. He also gave them to friends to take back with them when they came down from Hapao to Baguio to deliver completed woodcarvings or run errands. From November 2–11, 1995, he organized a mass planting in his birthplace of Patpat, located midway up the mountain on the other side of the valley from Hapao. According to his own memo on this project, about 112 volunteers from the village participated. Under Nauyac's leadership, woodcarvers living around Asin Road in Baguio collected the seeds of native trees from the outskirts of the city, germinated them and then carried them up to Hapao by jeepney. Some of them only helped Nauyac to gather the seeds, while others joined him in planting out the saplings when they returned to Hapao and the neighboring village of Nungulunan.[17]

---

17 On October 24–29, 1995, he also attended an ecotourism workshop and seminar at Mount Data Lodge, a highland resort hotel in Bauko, Mountain Province. The event was attended by several dozen representatives from overseas, including the United States, Canada, Australia, Sweden, Germany, the Netherlands, Hungary, Argentina and Venezuela.

In 1996 Nauyac purchased 1,500 square meters of land on the main road in the Boyyod *sitio* of Hapao for 35,000 pesos. In May 1997 he bought a traditional Ifugao house (for 5,000 pesos) and had it transferred to this land to serve as his home and as an office for 'Global.' At about the same time, he purchased a jeepney from Kidlat's sister for 100,000 pesos for the use of 'Global' activities. He paid 40,000 pesos from his own bank savings for this jeepney but failed to pay the remaining balance. The jeepney was written off when he lent it to an acquaintance in Hapao, who drove it off the edge of a ravine. Kidlat's sister did not demand the balance after that. In 1997 he applied to formally register the Ifugao Global Forest City Movement ('Global') as a Peoples Organization with the Philippine Securities and Exchange Commission. On February 2, 1998, the commission issued the official certificate of registration (SEC Reg. No. B199800098). The goals of the organization as stated on the certificate included: (1) mass planting of trees to enable a lasting supply of raw materials for woodcarving and construction; (2) appropriate management of the watershed environment for the community and rice terraces, as well as for irrigation and hydroelectricity in the lowlands; (3) increasing the production of foodstuffs for household consumption and sale on the open market through the cultivation of rice, corn, coffee and mushrooms, as well as freshwater aquaculture; and (4) construction of an international peace park in Hungduan to commemorate the surrender of General Yamashita and the end of the war and to promote ecological and cultural tourism. Nauyac was the president of the organization and four villagers from influential families served as executive officers. Together with another three members, these eight founders contributed 500 pesos each to launch the organization with an initial endowment of 4,000 pesos. In the beginning, they had almost no money for their activities, so the villagers built seedling nurseries and held reforestation seminars as unpaid volunteers.

The funds Kidlat obtained from the Toyota Foundation paid not only for environmental surveys and documentation but were also used to support Nauyac's movement by holding seminars and workshops on reforestation and for maintaining seedling nurseries. Nauyac used his personal contacts, cultivated during his time as Barangay Captain in Asin Road, to try to obtain government funding. As a result of his lobbying, the movement received a grant of 650,000 pesos in 1998 from the government's Ifugao Terraces Commission via the Philippine Department of Trade and

International Cooperation

Top, middle: Nauyac speaking with 'Global' members at the woodworking center. (March 3, 1999; March 12, 2000)

Bottom: Nauyac consulting about the reforestation project. Third from the left in the middle row is the *monbaki* Teofilo Gano. (March 20, 2002)

Industry's field office in Lagawe. The money was used to build a center for carpentry and woodworking in Hungduan and to purchase a number of different machines to manufacture furniture (400,000 pesos). A small gallery was also built by the side of the national highway in Lamut to display and sell woodcraft items (250,000 pesos).[18] A separate grant from the Department of Environment and Natural Resources provided 100,000 pesos to build four seedling raising nurseries for reforestation in different parts of the village. In total, the movement received the huge sum of 750,000 pesos (US$16,500) in grant funds, the equivalent at the time of about 5,000 times the daily wages (150 pesos) for a worker in the village. The villagers were impressed at Nauyac's ability to attract outside funding and this generated high hopes and support for 'Global'. By April 1999, one year after it was established, the organization had 135 members.

Nauyac was also very proactive in attending regional, national and international seminars and workshops related to environmental protection and the preservation and promotion of traditional culture. For example, he attended a three-day seminar from September 15–17, 1998, convened by Foundations for People Development, with support from Japan Environmental Corporation, in Metro Manila. The seminar examined environmental design and the development of agriculture-related industries. It was Kidlat who told the organizers about Nauyac and encouraged them to invite him. On October 2–3, 1998, he participated in a workshop, 'Cultural Revival, Planning and Development for Cultural Practitioners from the Cultural Communities of Kiangan, Ifugao', at a youth hostel in Kiangan. This workshop was organized by NCCA and the National Committee on Northern Cultural Communities. Nauyac treasures a copy of a poem that was distributed at the conference and read together by all the participants. The poem reads as follows.

---

18 The woodworking center was a large building constructed by local carpenters on roadside land donated by 'Global' member and influential local Victor Melon. It was fitted out with various machines but they were inadequately maintained. Some users failed to pay to use the machines and some broke down and had to be abandoned. In less than two years, the center was no longer functioning. Furthermore, while a physical exhibition space in Lamut was established, it was not actually operated.

> Dear Apu Dios
> As the world becomes more and more a global village,
> As western culture and Manila culture penetrate our mountains,
> We fear for our cherished traditions –
> that our collective memories might be forgotten
> our chants no longer sung
> our dances and rituals despised
> our storied no longer told
> Until we ourselves forget who we are
> Until we ourselves become ashamed of who we once were.
> Apu Dios, thanks for the NCAA
> For helping preserve our culture and identity
> For helping us remember who we are
> And be proud to pass our identity to our children.
> Apu Dios, we thank you for our own people gather[ed] here
> For those among us who courageously stem the tide
> of an [incipient] western culture deluge
> It is not that we have blocked our mountains from outside influence
> But that as we allow other cultures to enrich our own
> We bond ourselves so that our own culture may not be vanquished
> But be preserved to enrich the culture of others, [too].
> And so Apu Dios, bless all that we will do during this workshop
> Help us to help one another preserve the memory of who we are
> May this memory of who we are be a living story
> that unfolds and enchants
> that binds us with our past and guides us into our future
> that instills pride in us and makes us one people
> We pray this through Jesus Christ our Lord, Amen.
>
> (Invocation given by Reverend Father Manuel Francisco during the opening ceremony)

Nauyac has thought carefully about how best to protect and revegetate the *pinugo* forests and common lands and how to further develop the Ifugao way of life based on woodcarving and rice terrace agriculture. While searching for answers, he tried out some of his ideas in practice. He also tried to obtain new ideas by actively participating in seminars organized by government agencies and NGOs. He spent time reading and absorbing newspapers, magazines, governmental and independent reports, and newsletters put out by NGOs and other groups. He digested the ideas, vocabularies and modes of expression he picked up from seminars and written materials and combined them with his own ideas. He set himself the task of communicating what is unique about the Ifugaos and their values in a way that would be more easily understood. He consciously studied the premises underlying the speech and thought patterns of people who support social development, environmental protection and local empowerment, assimilated them and incorporated them into his own use of language. Through utilizing these carefully framed utterances he was able to speak directly to those who were in a position to support him, securing a basis of legitimacy for his movement and its activities.

Support from Japan: pluses and minuses

Nauyac's success in implementing projects and obtaining project funds from Philippine government agencies, combined with the attraction of trying to protecting the World Heritage-listed rice terraces, led to the acceptance of the IKGS project applications by three different organizations commencing in 2001. The main implementation phase of the reforestation project began shortly afterwards. The first project, 'Technical Assistance and Implementation of Reforestation in Hapao', received a grant of 2.26 million yen (about US$20,000) from Postal Savings for International Voluntary Aid to plant 25,000 saplings over fifteen hectares of land. Another project, 'Support for Sustainable Social Development and Reforestation by Filipino Indigenous Tribes: Planting Trees to Protect World Heritage', received 600,000 yen (about US$5,500) from the AEON Environmental Foundation to plant 15,000 saplings over twenty hectares. IKGS also received a grant from Japan International Forestry Promotion and Cooperation Center (a body subsidized by the Forestry Agency of the Ministry of Agriculture, Forestry and Fisheries) for 'Expert Training in Forest Management and Nursery Techniques to Protect World Heritage in the Philippine Cordillera'. This grant enabled 'Global' leader Nauyac, his lieutenant Orlando Mahiwo and one of the younger executive members, Ramon Yogyog, to travel to Sannan in Japan from October 12–23, where they received intensive onsite training from experts such as Professor Tsugawa of Kobe University at the prefectural forestry technology center and the Museum of Nature and

Human Activities in Hyōgo Prefecture. It goes without saying that the training itself was very valuable, but for Orlando and Ramon, who were both in their thirties, it was also their first visit to Japan. In addition to training in forest management and nursery techniques, they also had an enjoyable and stimulating time and gained valuable insights and ideas. They received a particularly warm welcome at a reception held by the people of Sannan and during visits to local schools. The trip provided moral support and encouragement and heightened their motivation to continue the reforestation movement in Hapao.

Left top: Villagers at the nursery in Patpat transferring seedlings from styrofoam seed trays into plastic pots. (March 9, 2000)

Right, left bottom: Returning home with seedlings at the end of the working bee. Each person will plant the seedlings in their own *pinugo* forest. (March 9, 2000)

In 2002 'Global' received a total of 9.25 million yen (about US$85,000) in grant funding from four organizations including JICA, Japan Environment Corporation's Japan Fund for Global Environment (which changed its name in 2004 to the Environmental Restoration and Conservation Agency), the Green Fund's National Land Afforestation Promotion Organization and AEON Environmental Foundation. Each grant provided funds for reforestation work over a three-year period. The organization went on to obtain a further 39.3 million yen (about US$360,000) in funding from four foundations between 2002 and 2004. It reforested 341 hectares with 295,000 saplings. However, the follow-up maintenance after planting was inadequate and, in some areas, one-third or even up to half of the saplings died. After planting, weeds need to be managed or the fast-growing weed species will overtake the saplings, choking them to death. It was the failure to carry out appropriate weed management that reduced the survival rate.

There was a division of labor between the two groups. Acting on behalf of IKGS, Tomita provided the funding, saplings, techniques and skills (by means of specialized seminars) for reforestation. The actual replanting work was carried out by 'Global'. Participants in the replanting were paid an allowance of 150 pesos (about US$3.30) per day, whether or not they were members of 'Global'. Replanting is heavy work and the payment was commensurable with it. When viewed from afar, the mountainsides seem to be covered in beautiful soft green meadows. However, when you get up close, they are actually thick with the tenacious *noro* grass (a species resembling Chinese silver grass) that grows to more than two meters high. This grass has to be cleared, the ground terraced and holes dug one by one before the saplings can be carried into the site by hand and planted.

Thanks to the support of the IKGS Reforestation Campaign and funding from Japanese private and public funding bodies, 'Global' was able to carry out organized reforestation on a far greater scale than it had attempted before. However, as a result, it came face to face with two serious problems. First, to obtain the necessary labor power to plant the large number of trees promised in funding applications, it had to employ the villagers as day-laborers. This meant 'Global' lost its fundamental character as a movement based on local self-initiative and self-help. The second and related problem was that the funding caused some negative influences on the core purpose of the 'Global' movement to shore up the foundation of the Ifugao way of life through reforestation to strengthen Ifugao ethnic identity.

International Cooperation

Top: Nauyac and Ramon undergo training at the Forest Industry Technology Center in Hyōgo Prefecture, Japan. (October 15, 2001, photo Tomita Kazuya)

Bottom: On the wall of Nauyac's home-cum-office, slogans such as 'Plant a Tree For Life' are displayed alongside messages from Japan written on decorated cardboard. (March 9, 2003)

With regard to the first problem, wage labor was used at every stage of the implementation of these grant-funded projects, from building seedling nurseries to raising saplings, clearing weeds from areas targeted for reforestation, preparing the ground, planting trees and follow-up maintenance. Anybody who wanted to work was employed at day-rates, regardless of whether or not they were 'Global' members. When Nauyac first started the movement, almost all the work was carried out by him with small groups of ten or twenty people, mostly his kindred and old friends, at their own expense. They had high ideals but little money and had no choice but to rely on volunteer labor. Indeed, not only was the work unpaid but the seedlings raised in the nurseries were also distributed at no cost to the volunteers, who planted them in their own *pinugo* forests in order to revegetate and renew them. Most of them understood that the work of 'Global' was intended to benefit them and their children and grandchildren. They worked together to build nurseries and raise seedlings based on their existing ties with Nauyac. This acted as a major restriction on growing the movement but it also meant that the participants understood Nauyac's gospel, his ideals and his ultimate purpose and they participated out of sympathy for those ideals.

However, the receipt of funding from Japan necessitated large-scale reforestation work. The sites chosen for reforestation were not privately owned *pinugo* forests but the common forests known as *bilid* and other common lands. The participants were not restricted to 'Global' members and their motivation was less sympathy and more from the expectation of earning cash through wage labor. Apart from the 'Global' executive, the majority of the membership comes from poor households who are busy working in their daily lives. They volunteered with 'Global' on the weekends once or twice a month. From the beginning 'Global' has struggled to reconcile Nauyac's high ideals with the inherent weakness of the economic base from which to realize those ideals.

Conversely, for IKGS and Tomita, in order to carry out a concentrated large-scale reforestation in the limited two- to four-year timeframe available for this kind of project, they had no choice but to pay a daily allowance to secure the necessary volume of wage labor. The villagers had to take days off from other essential work in the fields to work on the 'Global' project. Furthermore, with the money from Japan, it seemed obvious that the workers should be compensated adequately. The young people who took part also expected to receive help with their tuition for school and university or to make some pocket money. Apart from those who work for the municipal government or the school or who operate one of the general stores, the villagers rely primarily on rice terrace agriculture and woodcarving for their livelihood and have few opportunities to earn cash incomes. The payments they received from IKGS were therefore gratefully received by most villagers. Nauyac, too, was relying on the income from his business manufacturing and woodcarvings (which his wife was barely keeping afloat in Baguio) to provide for his humble daily needs, so he had no spare money. Therefore, while ideally Nauyac would have liked volunteers to drive 'Global', he accepted that many hands were needed and saw that enabling the villagers to obtain precious cash income was unavoidable. Nevertheless, his kindred and others who agreed with his ideals continued intermittently with their own small-scale reforestation to maintain the *pinugo* forests on a voluntary basis.

Core members of IKGS visiting Hapao to observe the rice terraces and reforestation in Hapao and meet with local villagers. Fujimoto Masami is in the center of the front row. Behind him is Segawa Chiyoko and the third person to the right of her is Segawa Susumu. (September 12, 2001)

Nauyac's second objective of strengthening the villagers' self-awareness as Ifugaos was deeply related to his sense of time, his historical consciousness and his way of thinking about what efficacy means. The original intention of Nauyac's reforestation movement was for the villagers to locate themselves within a continuing history that is connected with the ancestors and stretches back for generation after generation. He hoped to do so by reviving and strengthening the 'traditional' Ifugao way of life and culture, with the rice terraces, *pinugo* and *bilid* at their core. Simultaneously, he had an eye to the future in the sense that strengthening the foundations of their way of life will ultimately benefit their children and grandchildren. To plant trees and enjoy watching them grow is inseparably connected with valuing the connection between the generations and with experiencing that connection in one's mind and body.

However, the sense of time that Tomita and IKGS brought to the implementation of the project focused on the repetition of short two- to three-year funding cycles. It was essential to demonstrate a clear objective and a specific method to achieve that objective when applying for funding. Having received the funding, they needed to achieve the stated objective within the prescribed timeframe. Only by completing each individual project successfully and producing clear results could they gain recognition for their work and earn the trust of donors. This would lead to a successful application for the next grant and therefore to the continuation of the project. Tomita's dream was to be able to expand the reforestation and environmental protection project from Hapao to the entire municipality of Hungduan and finally to all of Ifugao Province. This meant he had to carry out each project strictly as it was written in the application and be able to show results. By doing so he could prove that while IKGS might be a small rural organization, it was a responsible entity that had the ability to get things done.

However, the negative effect of carrying out reforestation using wage labor was that, apart from a few examples of people reforesting their own *pinugo*, they did not take the initiative to voluntarily carry out weeding and other essential maintenance in the *bilid* after planting. The villagers did carry out some weeding in revegetation areas located near the road as they went past, but they lacked the time to carry out major weeding. This meant that weeding after planting was inadequate, and in many cases the vigorous weeds outgrew the saplings and choked them to death. Accurate survival rates for the projects as a whole are not available, but according

Top: Slashing weeds on a slope covered with *noro* grass (a tenacious weed similar to Chinese silver grass). (August 2003)

Middle: Carrying the saplings in a basket on head. (August 2003)

Bottom: Planting in Hapao. The tall man in the white shirt is Kawayan. (June 15, 2002) (all photographs Segawa Chiyoko)

to one agricultural official from Hungduan Municipality, it was probably around 50–60 percent.[19]

In addition to these two problems, a further impediment arose when Nauyac purchased a parcel of land alongside the national highway in Danghai, in the hill country between Lagawe and Lamut, and relocated there in 2000. His purpose in buying the land was to build a rudimentary house for himself where he could stay while he was on the road on 'Global' business and to build a nursery there to help spread the reforestation movement beyond Hungduan to other parts of Ifugao. At that time, not only had he developed close relations with Japan through IKGS, he was also becoming more involved in discussions with the provincial government and regional branches of national government agencies to submit applications for further projects and obtain additional funds. It takes two to three hours one-way by jeepney from Hapao, including a number of transfers, to reach these branch offices (both provincial agencies and the field offices of the national Department of Agriculture, Department of Environment and Natural Resources, and the Department of Trade and Industry). These efforts also won Nauyac backing from the former head of the Ifugao Terraces Commission and then vice-president of the Tribal Filipino Association, Mr Juan D. Dait, Jr. from the Municipality of Kiangan, who helped 'Global' to obtain 250,000 pesos (about US$5,500) from the Department of Agriculture for a fruit tree planting project. With this money, he purchased fruit tree saplings such as mango, citrus and coconut, as well as indigenous trees for woodcarvings, that were distributed among 'Global' members. Furthermore, IKGS chose the Save the Ifugao Terraces Movement (SITMo) to be its partner for the second application under the Partnership Program. SITMo's office was in Kiangan and, to reach it, it was more convenient for Nauyac to live in Danghai.

Although there had always been a plan to build a base in Danghai in order to expand 'Global', suspicions were raised over the source of the funds Nauyac used to buy the 1.3 hectares of land (120,000 pesos, about

---

19 Governmental and international aid agency reforestation projects are deemed to have been successful if the sapling survival rate exceeds 80 percent. Contract fees are paid in three stages. The first payment is made following the successful completion of clearing and preparation works in the reforestation area and the second at the time of planting. The final payment is made one year after planting, when adequate follow-up maintenance has been confirmed. If the survival rate falls below 80 percent, the amount of the final payment is reduced.

Nauyac's house beside the national highway in Danghai (top) and the decorated rock that stands in place of a gatepost. (March 11, 2003)

US$2,600), which incorporated both the land for the house and the slopes along the river behind. 'Global' treasurer Angelina Gano, in particular, made her criticisms of Nauyac public. She had long raised concerns over his failure to produce receipts for 100 percent of the money used in implementing the reforestation project and she was suspicious that he had embezzled the unaccounted-for money in order to buy the land. When I asked Nauyac about it, he said:

> I certainly didn't embezzle the money. I borrowed all of the money to buy the land from a bank in Baguio thanks to Kidlat's introduction. I put up my home uphill from the church in the Asin Road Barangay as security. However, because of the land's location with fantastic views from up high, Kidlat wants to exchange it for some other land he owns or buy it from me. Once he does so, I will be able to return all of the money to the bank straight away.

Once Nauyac got going with this new phase of the project, he was successful in obtaining external funding. However, his success had quite the opposite effect. He grew tired of the suspicion of the 'Global' members and other villagers who had lost their faith in him. When he first left for Danghai he went back regularly to Hapao but after one or two years, he started visiting less and less.[20] His nephew Orlando built his own house next to Nauyac's and he acts in Nauyac's place as the local coordinator and manages 'Global' activities in Hapao.

The JICA Partnership Program

Partnership Program (Support Type)

Of the five organizations from which the IKGS Reforestation Campaign successfully obtained funding for revegetation activities in Ifugao, the JICA funding is of particular interest. As the project developed, the organization

---

20 When he was suspected of embezzlement and misappropriation, Nauyac talked of how Jesus Christ was misunderstood by the people of his homeland and crucified on the cross. He speculated that if one takes on a big project, it is probably impossible to avoid being subject to misunderstanding and animosity. He told me a number of times that after he died the villagers would recognize his innocence and appreciate his passion for reforestation.

provided 55 million yen (about US$500,000) in two separate grants over a period of nearly five years. The grants were made under the Partnership Program, an initiative launched in 2002. Previously, JICA's international aid work centered on public works such as roads, bridges and dams and the construction of public buildings. At about the time Ogata Sadako became the president of JICA in 2003, the organization introduced a system to provide well-integrated support to Japanese NGOs working overseas.

According to a JICA pamphlet:

> the JICA Partnership Program…aims to implement development projects in developing countries planned by Japanese development partners, mainly NGOs, local governments and universities, based on their accumulated experiences and technologies in development at grassroots level…Expense for the JICA Partnership Program is a part of ODA [Official Development Aid of the government], and JICA entrusts the project to the proposing organization as a part of ODA.

Two types of funding are available under the program, Partnership Program (Support Type) and Partnership Program (Partner Type). The condition to receive funding under the former is that the applicant has a record of achievement over two or more years either domestically or overseas. For the latter, the applicant must have had expenditure of at least 15 million yen (about US$140,000) per annum over the past two years. IKGS applied first in 2002 under the Support Type for a project titled 'Constructing a Sustainable Ecosystem Through Large-Scale Reforestation in the World Heritage Rice Terraces of Hungduan, Ifugao, Philippines: Afforestation and Agro-forestry'. This was the first proposal to be funded under the Support Type program and the only one to be funded in that year. Support and advice to assist IKGS in putting together the application came from JICA Hyōgo. However, the project itself began at the very end of fiscal year 2002 (March 2003), so only 50,000 yen (about US$460) in actual funding was received in that year. This negligible amount was accessed in the very last days of the year due to JICA Hyōgo's strong preference that the first project under the scheme show some results during 2002. In reality, the 10 million yen (about US$90,000) budget over three years was spent in the second and third years of the project.

The activities and expected outcomes detailed in the application were (1) construction of seedling nurseries, carrying out training in nursery skills, revegetating degraded forests by reforesting mountainsides; (2) establishment of an association for reforestation in the target community, training of local leaders to enable them to manage the association independently; and (3) cultivating local leaders, holding seminars, creating a manual and establishing a model farm to carry out agroforestry. In practice, sixteen hectares of mountainside near the Hungduan municipal government building were reforested with 49,000 trees. A demonstration farm was also constructed in Uhaj, about halfway between Banaue and Hapao, and planted with fruit trees. Most of the grant money was spent on purchasing the saplings and labor costs. It is difficult to accurately assess just how successful the project was in implementing the initial project goals. Based on my own evaluation of the project, my impression was that with limited funds of 10 million yen, IKGS tried to satisfy the villagers' hopes for the project and did its best by trying a number of different approaches.

It is worth mentioning the three female Japanese students who each took a year's leave of absence during their third or fourth year of university to participate in the project. They rented a house in Hapao for approximately ten months and lived there with a young female 'Global' volunteer. They worked very hard and received the same 150 pesos per day (300 yen) as did the villagers. Each had participated in a one-week work camp at Pinatubo when they were high school students and had been deeply affected by the feelings of satisfaction and fulfilment derived from volunteer work and by their interaction with the Aeta children. As university students, they made further visits to Pinatubo and later came to Ifugao to volunteer. As I discuss in detail in Chapter 4, the Hapao area was occupied by the main force of the retreating Japanese troops at the end of the war. The villagers fled into the mountains but many lost their lives. On the Ifugao side, the memory of war is still fresh and it is spoken about regularly. By contrast, practically the only Japanese to have visited Hapao since the end of the war were groups looking for the bones of the Japanese war dead or searching for the fabled Yamashita gold and a few tourists who came to see the rice terraces. The villagers' image of Japan and the Japanese is therefore tied up with their image of the Japanese soldiers and was not particularly favorable. Unlike many lowland Filipinos, not one migrant worker from Hapao has been to Japan and little information about contemporary Japan reaches the village.

The three Japanese university students were from Niigata, Hitotsubashi and Ritsumeikan Universities (Ōtake Asuka, Nagasawa Maiko and Hasegawa Midori). They came to live in the village and helped devise

Top: Agroforestry project in Uhaj, Banaue. The slopes are planted with fruit trees while the flat land at the bottom left of the photograph is used for vegetables. (March 12, 2005)

Middle: Project sign erected at the project site with Santos Bayucca, who produced it, in front (beside the Hungduan–Banaue road). The children do not throw stones or aim their slingshots at it so it is in excellent condition. This shows that the project is welcome in the area. (March 9, 2004)

Bottom: Replanting on common lands on the hillside near the Hungduan municipal offices. The site is visible from the road so people see it as they go about their day. This photo was taken at the roadside. (March 6, 2004)

various schemes for reforestation, environmental protection and raising the standard of living. Regardless of how useful they really were with the reforestation and social development work, the general impression the villagers had of them was expressed in words such as 'when I see them working I can really feel their altruism expressed in volunteering, their friendly feelings for us and their complete devotion to their work. It made us come to love the Japanese and significantly improved my image of them.' The chance to get up close with and interact with these kind and decent young women in real life was greatly welcomed by the villagers and was a big factor in the image and feeling of goodwill they developed for Japan and the Japanese.

Unfortunately, on October 16, 2004, while they were staying in Hapao, the motorized tricycle (a motorbike with sidecar used to carry passengers and luggage) in which they were traveling from Hapao to Abatan came off the road. Irene, an Ifugao volunteer from Abatan village who was living with them in the volunteer dormitory in Hapao, was driving when they left but one of the Japanese took over halfway. She lost control of the handlebars and the vehicle slipped from the side of the road down into the ravine. The bottom of the ravine was some fifty to sixty meters down. If they had fallen all the way to the bottom, the villagers said, there probably would have been nothing they could have done to save them. Fortunately, at several meters down, the tricycle became caught on a tree, which brought it to a stop, preventing major injuries. Nevertheless, Ōtake received severe bruising to her entire body. After receiving first aid at a clinic in Hapao, she was taken to a hospital in the Ifugao capital of Lagawe. Tomita received an emergency call at his home in Subic, Zambales, where he has been based since the work in Pinatubo. He leapt into his car and drove to Lagawe, transporting her straight to the Makati Medical Center, a general hospital in Manila. When she was discharged a couple of days later, Ōtake stayed at Tomita's house, where she was confined to bed for about a week. For nearly two years after the accident, she had difficulty taking a deep breath due to the pain.

The villagers ascribed the cause of the accident to the fact that numerous Japanese soldiers had died looking for water at the place where the women had stopped. They had no doubt that the spirits of the Japanese soldiers had called the young women down into the ravine. At a healing ritual conducted for Ōtake on her return to Hapao, the *monbaki* explained that she was possessed by the spirit of a young Japanese soldier who wanted to

Top: JICA evaluation team inspecting an outdoor rabbit run in Uhaj. (March 9, 2004)

Bottom: Japanese volunteer Nagasawa Maiko checking on the rabbits with local staff at the rabbit enclosure near the municipal offices. (July 21, 2004)

marry her. This confirmed the villagers' own interpretation and became the accepted account of what happened. Ōtake herself accepted the story at face value, but strangely felt no fear or ill-will towards the spirits of the Japanese soldiers. Before she came to Hapao she knew nothing about the war or about the retreat of so many Japanese soldiers to Hapao. However, while living in the village she heard lots of stories about the war from the older women. The war and the Japanese soldiers had become quite a familiar presence and so she was not afraid of them.[21]

After Ōtake finished her volunteer work and returned to Japan in 2004, she graduated from university and changed her initial plan to continue on to graduate school. Instead, she formed an NGO called Aozora (blue sky) Peace Force. In July she returned to Hapao and for two years she worked in

---

21 While she was in hospital and during her convalescence, Ōtake read a number of memoirs and records about Ifugao. She came to think of her own involvement in reforestation in Hapao as an inevitability to which she had been summoned by history and that the pain in her back was, like the band the Buddha placed around the Monkey King's head in *Journey to the West* (a magical golden headband that enables the Monkey King to be controlled by a special chant), a warning to her to do the right thing.

She understood that the dull pain in her upper and lower back might never go away. However, she later consulted a Buddhist priest who came to Hungduan to look for the remains of the war dead. He gave her a mandala and a paper talisman to comfort the spirits of the dead and recommended that she offer incense to them every morning. She followed this advice and also took up yoga. Gradually the pain lessened and she made a complete recovery. She tells the story as follows.

I had the accident after we decided to hold a workshop on Nauyac for a Japanese audience in Manila on November 24. I thought that, in addition to telling them about Ifugao, we should discuss the similarities between Japanese and Ifugao culture. We went to Abatan to take a photograph of everybody doing Ifugao wrestling. We were heading for Abatan from Hapao with Irene, who is from Abatan, when it happened. Along the way we fell into the ravine. I was never much of a reader, but after injuring myself I was lying in bed day after day. I first started to read books like *Luson senki* (Record of the War in Luzon) and *Luzon no tanima* (The Valleys of Luzon). Previously many of the Ifugao, mostly the young people I became friends with, told me how this had happened and that had happened, although they didn't experience the war themselves. I had only ever thought about the war from the Ifugao and Philippine perspectives. While I was lying there I had the opportunity to read the letters and writings of people who were soldiers at that time. For the first time I saw things from a different perspective and started to think about the war from the Japanese side. (Conversation with Ōtake Asuka, June 29, 2008)

collaboration with IKGS. There were a number of other visitors from Japan in addition to Ōtake and the young female university students, including directors of the NGO and other related individuals who made a number of goodwill visits to the village. Nauyac and some young Ifugaos, as well as SITMo president and former provincial governor Teddy Baguilat, also

Top left: Opening of an educational seminar on reforestation at the Hapao elementary school. In the center of the front row is former Ifugao governor and then SITMo director Teddy Baguilat. He is holding a color picture book, *Guardians of the Enchanted Forest*, that explains Nauyac's reforestation movement. (August 25, 2004)

Top right: Ōtake Asuka giving an educational seminar on reforestation at the Subic elementary school in Zambales Province. (September 24, 2004, photo Ōtake Asuka)

Bottom: Children and Japanese volunteers planting commemorative trees following a seminar on reforestation at Hapao elementary school. (August 25, 2004, photo Ōtake Asuka)

made the journey in the opposite direction to visit Sannan, where they spent time with local residents and school students. A connection was established between Hapao and Sannan as people traveled between the two, without stopping for long in Manila or Osaka. These visits contributed to rural renewal in both towns.

One of the three Japanese university student volunteers took responsibility for a project based on raising rabbits for meat and fur as an income source. She put forward the proposal herself and saw the project through. During the first six months, a model rabbitry was built near the volunteer hut. Baby rabbits were bred and distributed to interested people in the village to be raised in their homes.[22] Another one of the students supervised the environmental education component of the partnership project. She accompanied Nauyac on visits to elementary and middle schools, where he gave guest lectures stressing the importance of the forests and the need for reforestation. After the lecture, the students were each given a local native sapling raised by Nauyac and they planted them together to commemorate the day. Saplings were also given to anyone who wanted to plant them at home. When Nauyac gave these talks, the three Japanese students would accompany him wearing traditional Ifugao skirts. Together with Nauyac, they encouraged the children to plant trees. Sometimes they even performed Ifugao dances with him. Teddy Baguilat showed great interest in this environmental education project and also attended the seminars and lent his full support.

Partnership Program (Partner Type)

To expand the project in Ifugao, IKGS chose SITMo, an organization presided over by Baguilat, as its counterpart in a new application under JICA's Partnership Program (Partner Type) scheme. The project, 'Environmental Protection by Improving Livelihood through Grassroots Empowerment in Ifugao Province', was fortunately adopted on its first submission surely

---

22 When the young women left, she gave the remaining rabbits to anyone in the village who was interested in taking them. However, they were mostly kept in very small rabbit hutches. During the long rainy season, when it is cold and humid, most of them got sick and died. Unfortunately, keeping rabbits as a means of making an income was not widely adopted.

International Cooperation

A reforestation education seminar at Nungulunan elementary school (top). The children carrying saplings (middle) and a commemorative photograph with Japanese volunteers before planting (bottom). (March 15, 2006)

because of successful achievement of the previous one, with a budget of 45 million yen (about $410,000) over three years from 2005.[23]

In addition to continuing the existing reforestation project, the grant added a new project to build four traditional-style Ifugao lodges in Uhaj, Banaue, for ecotourism promotion and to train a group of young people to manage them. Additionally, with the full support of Hungduan's mayor, the project implemented aquaculture to raise *dojo* loach. The municipality built an aquaculture facility near the municipal offices and dedicated a number of staff members to work on the project. During his first term as governor (2001–04), Baguilat strongly promoted the aquaculture project as a local industry that could provide cash incomes and he also built an aquaculture facility near Kiangan. However, he was not re-elected at the end of his first term and the new governor, who had no interest in aquaculture, suspended the project and the facility was abandoned. Baguilat's later return to the governor's office (2007–10) coincidently overlapped with the second term of the Partnership Program. He insisted that a new aquaculture facility be built in Kiangan. A research institute was also established on the grounds of the SITMo offices with a dedicated officer allocated to it. The *dojo* loach is said to have been brought by the Japanese during the war, after which they grew in number. When the terraces are flooded, farming household conduct small-scale aquaculture with the *dojo* loach by releasing them into the flooded terraces. The mayor and the governor had high hopes that *dojo* loach aquaculture could become a reliable secondary industry for the rice farmers, located right in the middle of their existing agricultural ecosystems. They devoted the full power of their administrations to support it.

The Partner Program's original objective was to create a foundation for improving the villagers' livelihoods that would in turn enable them to carry out reforestation and environmental protection on an ongoing basis. More than half of the project funds were allocated to creating opportunities to earn cash incomes. Even though the villagers have a high degree of interest and awareness of the importance of reforestation and environmental

---

23 This was the first time Tomita was able to receive a wage as project coordinator. Until then, he made a living by renting out and driving the second-hand four-wheel drive that was donated to Eriko's clinic from Japan for various other projects. Also, Eriko's mother died in a car accident on the day Eriko graduated from nursing school. The couple has drawn on the insurance money from the accident and from her estate when emergency expenses arose.

Top: Meeting on *dojo* loach aquaculture in Lagawe convened by the Ifugao provincial government. Participants receive information on the aquaculture initiatives taking place in each municipality and training in aquaculture techniques. (June 5, 2008)

Middle: SITMo office in Kiangan. The building was originally built as an educational and cultural center for Ifugao women with money donated by an association for retired female teachers in Japan. (February 27, 2007)

Bottom: Hatching fry at the aquaculture center and next to the SITMo offices. (February 27, 2007)

protection, they lack both the spare time and the additional labor power to do much about it. The real problem the project was trying to address was how to address these fundamental weaknesses in the socioeconomic base for environmental protection.

The project was spread across five municipalities centered on Hungduan and Banaue. There were also a number of counterparts including the five municipal governments, SITMo, 'Global' and a youth group from Uhaj.[24] In terms of the aspect of the project that was intended to raise household incomes, both Kiangan and Hungduan municipalities built aquaculture ponds and hatcheries for *dojo* loach aquaculture, trained staff for loach production and installed photographic explanatory panels about production techniques in both locations. However, while they were able to establish the production system, they never secured markets for the product or established a reliable system to transport it from the point of production to the point of sale. The Philippine partner agencies (the provincial and municipal governments and SITMo) actively pursued the establishment of the production system but were unable to find a reliable mechanism for turning the product into cash. The Japanese representative, Tomita, tried to sell the fish, first in the Subic Bay Freeport Zone in Zambales, where he lives in the IKGS field office, and then to Japanese restaurants in Manila. A number of retailers expressed interest in the product. One Japanese restaurant in Subic was particularly keen. Not only did it feature the *dojo* loach on its menu, but also prepared a water tank and pump to keep the fish alive. The owner of the restaurant also began studying breeding methods. However, Tomita was unable to find a reliable way of carting the live fish the 300 kilometers from Ifugao to the restaurant at a reasonable cost. By the time the project ended, no consistent mechanism had been established to sell the fish.

In terms of the ecotourism component, a group of Japanese volunteers, separate from the university students discussed so far, spent more than six months living in Uhaj, teaching a group of interested young people how to prepare food to suit the tastes of foreign tourists and how to decorate the rooms. They also instructed them in hygiene, aromatherapy massage and other services. When the construction of the lodges began, a number of

---

24 For a detailed examination of the project and its implementation and results, see the Post Implementation Stage Evaluation that was compiled by the evaluation team I headed (JICA Hyōgo International Center 2008).

Top: Aquaculture ponds in Kiangan. (February 26, 2007)

Bottom: An aquaculture center was also established with funding from the municipality near the Hungduan municipal offices to promote *dojo* loach aquaculture. (June 6, 2008)

young people became involved in anticipation of the chance to earn cash income. They were attracted both by the daily wages and by the feeling of working together to create a space that could serve as a substitute for their traditional Ifugao youth lodges. When the lodges were complete, SITMo arranged for groups from Manila NGOs and university teachers to stay in them and sample the ecological and cultural tourism opportunities available. However, immediately after the lodges were complete, there was a lack of promotion. In 2007 just over 200 people came to stay. Like the aquaculture project, the marketing was inadequate and there was no system to attract an ongoing stream of guests.

At the conclusion of the Partnership Program project, Tomita's final report as IKGS's field representative summarized the outcomes as follows:

> The characteristic feature of this project was that while it is part of JICA, which always works in accordance with a detailed plan, it was implemented by IKGS, an NGO with a total commitment to grassroots work in the Philippines, making full use of its know-how and networks. In short, rather than sticking to the letter of the initial plan, we responded rapidly and flexibly as the project unfolded to changes in the local context, conditions on the ground and the desires of people in the field. Therefore, although the fundamental objectives and principles of the project remained the same, the counterparts and components did change a number of times. As a result, we can be proud of our success in forging appropriate links in the midst of changing circumstances and politics and the enthusiasm on the ground. The project began working at the grassroots level and over time drew in the local government, thereby increasing its potential. Furthermore, it was able to realize an ideal level of cooperation between our NGO, governments and JICA.
>
> Now that our contract with JICA has come to an end, the time has come to conclude the project. To jump straight to the conclusion, the fact is that this project did not reach IKGS's ideals. If we are to evaluate the project from the perspective of 'Who is the project for?' the local villagers experienced a temporary improvement in their standard of living, but we were unable to construct a system or mechanism to sustain this improvement and so, regrettably, the project as a whole cannot be described as a success. At the present time the project is finally starting to gather some momentum on its own. To use an analogy, it is as if the baby has stood up and taken its first tottering steps. The ecotourism initiative…appears to be relatively vibrant. So far its revenue has grown and the foundations for the enterprise have been

International Cooperation 399

The guest lodges in Uhaj built in traditional style, and children demonstrating Ifugao dances for the guests after dinner. (June 6, 2008)

established. We have also successfully demonstrated the basics of *dojo* loach aquaculture. However, in the short two-and-a-half year period of this project, aquaculture did not reach the point of becoming a stable and self-sustaining enterprise. Aquaculture was a feature of the municipal and prefectural governments' policies for livelihood improvement and enjoyed their full support. However, a reliable system for producing sufficient quantities of the *dojo* loach and transporting the live fish to market at a reasonable cost has not yet been found.

Frankly, the time and money allocated for this project was insufficient. In order to reach the objective we set at the beginning…'community-driven reforestation based on improving livelihoods' needs more time and ongoing support. It is frustrating and highly disappointing to have to withdraw at the present stage. I hope that the prefectural government and related bodies will do what they can to secure further external support and it is my fervent hope that this project will continue. (Tomita 2008)

As I stated in my executive summary in the Post Implementation Stage Evaluation report, this assessment of the implementation of IKGS's own project demonstrates considerable self-awareness and forthrightness. In a field site that was constantly changing during the implementation stage, IKGS's basic approach was to respond to the situation on the ground and to local people's needs as flexibly as possible. Personally, I fully endorse this basic approach. However, I also agree with Tomita's conclusion, that 'regrettably the project as a whole cannot be described as a success'. The reason for this, as Tomita points out, is that no system was completed that could have enabled the project to continue on its own steam and lack of time meant it had to be abandoned halfway. Of course, the project's original objectives were to complete the project within the stated three-year period (really two-and-a-half years) and to ensure that it would be sustainable. As the project commenced with this understanding, the claim that there was not enough time probably appears on the surface to be little more than an excuse. However, if one considers the very real challenges that Tomita and IKGS faced, the only possible conclusion is that the project remained incomplete due to insufficient time. First, the project's initial goals were not implemented in a top-down, highly planned way. Faithful to the idea of JICA's Partnership Program (Partner Type) scheme, the wishes of partner NGOs on the ground and of local people were taken into account. Usually, IKGS acceded to their demands and tried to find a compromise. This led to a number of changes in different components of the project. As a result, the choices made about where to focus meant that the limited time and resources available could not be utilized effectively and that the way the project was carried out was not tailored to the effective realization of the initial objectives.

Additionally, in May 2007 in the middle of the implementation period, Teddy Baguilat, the president of the partner NGO, ran for election following the sudden death of the governor of Ifugao. This meant that his NGO staff and other project workers on the ground threw much of their time into campaigning. As a result, the implementation of the joint project with IKGS was delayed by several months. Furthermore, contrary to Tomita's expectations, Baguilat's election did not necessarily have a favorable impact on the implementation of the IKGS project. Before he was elected, Baguilat had worked hard to ensure the successful implementation of the project in the expectation that he could use his achievements in his campaign at the next election. Having a pipeline to JICA in Japan and other foreign aid organizations and NGOs and being able to obtain aid money to carry out social development projects not only reflected well on him as the president of an NGO, but served as proof of the abilities that voters expected of him as a politician. Unsurprisingly, however, after he was elected governor the IKGS project became much less of a priority for him. Losing Baguilat's zeal at the top also had an influence on the enthusiasm of SITMo staff. Furthermore, in the beginning the project was only supposed to be implemented in the two municipalities of Hungduan and Banaue but it was extended to Kiangan, Asipulo and Mayoyao when Baguilat boasted in the lead-up to the election about his pipeline to JICA funding from Japan and promised to spread the benefits of the project and the funds that came with it more widely. The projects that were implemented in the three additional municipalities were small in scale (for example, building nurseries to raise seedlings for reforestation) and little actual money or effort was expended in them. As governor, the important thing for Baguilat was to show his concern for the three municipalities and to demonstrate unequivocally that the money from Japan would find its way there.

These difficulties and the lack of time meant that the project to improve livelihoods did not produce visible results. The environmental protection work that was expected to result from the additional breathing room provided by improved livelihoods was also not fully realized. Tomita acknowledges that the project concluded halfway, without realizing its objectives. However, at least in Hungduan and Hapao, almost all the villagers were familiar with the work JICA and IKGS were doing. They took an interest in the project and were relatively impressed by what it managed to achieve. It is worth noting that a change in their impression of Japan and the Japanese was a ripple effect from the project. In particular, the villagers were touched by the fact that more than ten young Japanese volunteers spent three months living and working alongside them. The villagers looked favorably on the way the volunteers integrated and their diligence.[25]

The contribution of the Japanese volunteers as a part of the project contributed to a transformation in the way local people feel about Japan and this is something we should celebrate. Therefore, in terms of my own expectations of the Partnership Program, the project was a modest yet successful example of a type of aid that seeks to enable the partners to recognize one another and achieve their goals by working together. The young people from Japan who spent between six months and a year volunteering in Hapao or Uhaj were all in their early twenties. They, and perhaps their parents too, were unaware that more than sixty-five years ago, a ferocious war took place in the Philippines or that the bulk of the Japanese military force had made its last retreat to Hapao and the Hungduan region. While they were living in Hapao, Nauyac and the other old people told them stories about the war and took them to places where tragic events took place. They came to feel that the war was not such a long-ago and far off thing. This enabled them to realize for the first time that their own volunteer work, which began with feelings of curiosity, good intentions and goodwill, was not simply a one-sided display of beneficence. They never looked down on the villagers and felt modest, humble and grateful

---

25 They were Ōtake Asuka, who arrived in March 2006 to volunteer for one year; Hasebe Hiroshi (known as *Burol*), who volunteered from June to December that year; Endō Nae (known as *Bangos*), who volunteered from September for two months; and Okamoto Kiyoko (known as *Kyaba*) and Kamijō Kozue (*Guinay*), who volunteered for one year from July 2007 until June 2008. There were several other Japanese volunteers who came for up to one month. The building of the learning center in Uhaj (later renovated to become the ecotourism facility) began with preparing the ground for construction on the cliffs above the road. The building materials had to be carried from the road to the center up a steep hill for about 200 meters. Hasebe worked on this and every other stage in the construction, including the building of the facility and contributed a lot of his own money to purchase building materials.

International Cooperation

Top: A containment wall was built around the river that runs through Hapao with funding from the Japanese embassy's Grant Assistance for Grassroots Human Security Project in 2005. (March 2, 2007)

Bottom: A billboard for the partnership project erected downhill from the municipal government building with smiling 'Global' members. (November 26, 2011, photo Segawa Chiyoko)

for the help and support they received from the villagers. Nevertheless, by learning about the history of war, they came to realize that their volunteer work today is directly connected to the historical relationship between Japan and the Philippines. A heart-to-heart connection and true dialogue developed between Nauyac and the villagers of Hapao and Uhaj and the young Japanese volunteers. It was a modest attempt to forge a future that does not neglect the past. The international collaboration by a small NGO from Sannan (IKGS) over more than ten years was the result of the efforts of very ordinary grassroots people. They bypassed Tokyo, Osaka and Manila to connect directly with another mountain people. This is a concrete example of how the spread of globalization has pulled two regions that are separated by national borders into a deep relationship with one another and how this relationship has helped to revitalize their rural towns and villages.

Conclusion: towards local leadership in social development

As I have explained in some detail in this chapter, a gulf separates the bottom-up approach to reforestation, rice terrace and forest conservation, and social development carried out by Nauyac's 'Global' reforestation movement from the government's top-down approach to rice terrace conservation and economic policy. When the rice terraces achieved World Heritage listing, the Philippine government established its own Ifugao Terraces Commission in the president's office. Beginning in 1995, the commission launched a six-year plan to restore and protect the rice terraces of Ifugao. In 1998 'Global' also received 65,000 pesos (about US$1,450) in grant funding from the commission to build four seedling nurseries and concentrate the production and distribution of saplings. The grant provided a boost to the self-directed work of the reforestation movement and led directly to further aid from Japan.

The master plan for the government's conservation project emphasized rice terrace cultivation as part of an integrated agricultural system involving terraces, swiddens and *pinugo* forests and recognized the organic connection between these elements (Orient Integrated Development Consultants, Inc. 1994, Office of the Provincial Planning and Development Coordination, and Ifugao Rice Terraces and Cultural Heritage Office 2004). Protecting watersheds for irrigation and maintaining irrigation canals, so as to support and stimulate rice terrace conservation, was part of the basic approach to development in this plan. However, it placed a far greater emphasis on creating access roads and transport infrastructure to open up the terraces and attract more tourists. Promoting the tourism industry was given center stage in development planning to protect the rice terrace environment. The splendor of the rice terrace landscapes dotted with villages with an 'exotic' culture is undoubtedly a big drawcard. But the government-initiated development projects were completely lacking in concrete ideas to provide incentives for the people who are indispensable to the conservation of the rice terraces, the cultivators themselves. From a purely economic perspective, the productivity of the rice terraces is quite poor. In proportion to the amount of hard labor needed to maintain and work them, the harvest is relatively small. The villagers can make far more money by working in hotels, restaurants and other tourism-related industries. However, the people who own and run these industries make far more money than the people who work in them. So long as rice terrace conservation and tourism are pursued through a government-sponsored regional development from above, the gap between rich and poor will only grow. Paradoxically, this places the future of rice terrace cultivation, the main drawcard for tourism, in jeopardy.

In order to combine tourism promotion and terrace landscape conservation, some kind of system needs to be developed to allow the farmers who cultivate the terraces to be included in the distribution of wealth from the tourism industry. It is equally important to approach the problem, as Nauyac has, by connecting the preservation of an integrated ecosystem of terraces, *pinugo* and *bilid* with the historical, ethnic and cultural self-awareness and pride of the Ifugaos. Attempts such as these to endow the terraced landscape with meaning and to increase public awareness need to be actively encouraged both materially and morally. The collaboration between 'Global', IKGS, JICA and other Japanese public and private entities that funded and supported this work has taken a step in the right direction.

The reasons so much support flowed from Japan to Hapao included the historical connection with General Yamashita's last stand and the glamor of World Heritage listing, but the most important factor was that Nauyac's 'Global' organization was already taking the lead to carry out reforestation on a voluntary basis. When 'Global' joined up with IKGS and obtained funding from Japan to continue and expand its work, it refused to be just a subcontractor for reforestation works or a passive beneficiary. Significantly, as equal partners in the project, it placed great importance on participation by locals and at times spoke up to ensure that the villager-led character of the movement was maintained.

As I point out a number of times, Nauyac's concept of reforestation and social development and his attempts to put it into practice were also an experiment in trying to maintain the basis for a traditional Ifugao way of life that depends upon the forest and rice terrace ecosystem and to strengthen cultural identity. Fully integrated development covering every aspect of the environmental, economic, cultural and social domains was at the core of this approach, which anticipates the social development approach explored at the beginning of this chapter. Furthermore, through a resident-led, bottom-up approach, 'Global' overcame some of the limitations of the existing participatory development approach, showing the way for the development strategies of the future. 'Global' and Nauyac retained the right to have their say and continued to play a role in the implementation of the project. This differentiates this project from the top-down approach directed from outside that has been seen in previous development projects. While they were not completely successful in their attempt, they have certainly shown us a new possibility for regional cooperation between local residents and Japanese NGOs.

10 Grassroots

Regional Networks and the Anthropology of Response-ability

I chose to examine the 'Global' reforestation movement in a small mountain village in northern Luzon because it has the potential to help us rethink our contemporary world and the kind of society we want for the future. In Chapters 1 and 9, I discuss Appadurai's (2001) emphasis of 'globalization from below' and 'grassroots globalization'. He makes a strong case for seeing NGOs as important actors in this type of globalization and as key drivers. He further maintains that NGOs, with their clear understanding of the adverse effects of globalization and their transnational advocacy and movement networks, have the potential to act as an effective brake on the inequality that is increasing both between and within societies, the deepening environmental crisis, and the economic problems attendant on the growing separation of finance from manufacturing capital (Appadurai 2001).[1] According to Appadurai, the adverse consequences of globalization are ultimately the result of the liquid and reckless nature of capital. The transnational networks through which NGOs work enables them to help counter the negative influences of globalization. In their role as a hub, they also facilitate the expansion of a radical and independent micro-level globalization at the grassroots. If we apply this perspective to the 'Global' reforestation movement in Hapao that I describe in this book, we can see it as another source of potential and hope for the future.

---

1 My understanding of globalization from below draws on the notion of 'history from below' proposed by Reynaldo Ileto in the title of the first chapter of *Pasyon and Revolution* (1979), 'Toward a history from below', and on EP Thompson's (1963) *The Making of the English Working Class*. The perspective of globalization from the periphery is touched on in Tessa Morris-Suzuki's (2000) *Henkyō kara nagameru* (The view from the periphery) and Nakamura Tetsurō's (2003) *Henkyō de miru henkyō kara miru* (Diagnosis from the periphery, looking from the periphery).

In this chapter, I summarize the main points of the grassroots transformation of peripheral ethnic groups in the era of globalization as revealed through the example of Hapao. While Hapao remains a very small community, I want to reflect on its significance for our understanding of the contemporary world. To facilitate this, I trace a history of the images and metaphors for thinking about the earth, the foundation of human existence and subsistence, since the end of the Second World War and the beginning of the Cold War. I then examine the ways in which the declarations of the end of the Cold War made by presidents Bush and Gorbachev, the fall of the Berlin Wall in 1989 and the subsequent dissolution of the Soviet Union in 1991 increased the speed of globalization, transformed the sphere of daily life, and initiated the recomposition of local community networks.[2] The village of Hapao is located high up in the mountains of northern Luzon, a distant corner of the world that is continuing to undergo rapid change and where international and local society are closely intertwined. I consider my own entry into the field, my entanglement in its fate, my active participation in the reforestation movement and the new potential such an approach has for anthropology, as well as the responsibility that it implies.

As I explain a number of times, even in remote mountain villages such as Hapao, located far from the capital in a developing country, globalization has accelerated over the past twenty years. Of course, it is true that well before the phenomenon we might call post-Cold War globalization attracted the attention of the political, economic, academic and media worlds, the people of Ifugao were already in conflict with global political and military superpowers who made contact with them. It began when Spain colonized the Philippines and sent expeditionary forces to extend its dominion over the mountainous regions. Sometimes these powers sought to placate the people and win them over, while at other times they intervened more aggressively. The Ifugao resistance to these outside interventions resulted at times in localized armed conflict.

---

2 According to Steger, since the collapse of the Soviet Union in 1991, the term 'globalization' has come to be used to mean both the unified free market that now covers the entire globe and the appearance of mass consumerism (market globalism). At the same time, there has also been the development on a global scale of a lively critique of and protest against this new reality in the form of movements for justice on the left and a jihad (holy war) by Islamic extremists (justice globalism and jihadist globalism) (Steger 2008: 10–15).

Of course, even before the coming of the Spanish (see Chapter 1), the people of Ifugao engaged directly and indirectly in trade with lowland merchants to obtain large earthenware pots, ceramic beads and agate from China, mother of pearl from the South Seas and Venetian glass beads. Hapao has always been subject to invasion and military intervention from the outside world, whether under the pacification campaign during the American colonial period, General Yamashita's retreat to the region, and the building of bases by the NPA as part of their resistance to the Marcos dictatorship (see Chapter 4). Even in their inaccessible mountain world, the people of Hapao have not lived an entirely peaceful and untroubled life.

Nevertheless, in the history of Hapao's confrontation with the great global powers, the wave of globalization that has taken place over the past twenty years is characterized by the self-initiated mass movement by the people of Hapao out of their village and even out of the country. While the villagers leave for work in order to obtain better incomes, reforestation and social development projects have been gathering pace thanks to the inflow of assistance from both governmental and private agencies, domestic or foreign, as the villagers seek to join with these projects. We can see this in the example of Nauyac's movement. Some movement leaders have been invited to travel overseas to interact with supporting organizations and report on their work on the ground. In the past, globalization was a wave that advanced on Hapao from the outside and the villagers were forced to respond with a defensive strategy to protect the basis of their way of life. By contrast, the globalization that has taken place in recent years has led them to develop offensive strategies whereby the villagers choose to launch themselves out into the world in order to obtain a better quality of life. To continue with the military metaphor, in the battlefields, where they fight both their defensive and offensive battles, they are fully engaged in a kind of hand-to-hand combat through which flesh-and-blood human beings develop deep relationships with one another and at times butt up against one another. Of course, I use the term 'hand-to-hand combat' simply as a metaphor for the sincere aspirations and bitter struggles in which individuals engage in the search for a better quality of life.

In this chapter, I understand the people of Hapao as contemporaries who, like us, live in an era of globalization. I consider their way of life as an attempt to deal with globalization and to think about the possibilities suggested by that attempt. Furthermore, because we as anthropologists are also living in such a period, we have a responsibility to renew anthropology's purpose and responsibility (in the ordinary sense) for this new era. We are all children of our times and of the land on which we were born and raised. For that reason, we must practice anthropology in the full consciousness of our contemporary context.

Spaceship Earth

The ancient Greeks knew from experience that our earth, which supports human and all other forms of biological life, has a spherical shape. When a ship approaches from the distant horizon, the first thing that an observer on the shore will see is its mast. Conversely, for an observer on a ship approaching land, the tops of the mountains will be seen first and as the ship gets closer to the land the observer begins to see the mountain slopes and foothills and finally the whole. The philosopher Aristotle (384–322 BCE) was also convinced that the earth was a sphere because when the moon enters into the earth's shadow it causes a lunar eclipse and, when it does, the shadow's edge has a round appearance.

It was Apollo 8, the first manned spacecraft to orbit the moon in 1968, that demonstrated in vivid images that anybody could understand that the earth is indeed round. In 1969 Apollo 11 landed on the surface of the moon and sent back real-time video images of astronauts stepping onto the surface of the moon. The vivid color photographs of the earth floating lightly against the jet black of space left a strong impression on the earth's people. Many instantly recognized the beauty of the mottled blue and white earth rising not above an earthly horizon but a lunar horizon against the blackness of the night and had a profound realization that the earth is a delicate vessel that can easily be scarred or destroyed.[3]

Originally, the Apollo program was a national undertaking pursued aggressively by the American military-industrial complex in the context of the fierce arms race that developed during the Cold War. After the first successful manned space flight by the Soviet Vostok 1 in April

---

3 In the film *In the Shadow of the Moon* (2008), based on edited footage from the time, Michael Collins, who was a member of the crew for the Apollo landing, talks about the warm welcome he received during his visits to different parts of the world after his return from the moon. He testifies that 'Wherever we went, people, instead of saying, "Well, you Americans did it!" – everywhere, they said, "We did it! We, humankind, we, the human race, we, people, did it!"'

1961, the United States felt the need to reaffirm its military and political supremacy. President Kennedy declared one month later that the United States would send a manned spacecraft to the moon within ten years and that its astronauts would walk upon its surface, saying that no single space project would be more impressive to mankind, or more important. Apollo 11's mission to the moon was broadcast live via satellite to living rooms in Japan, where I, too, watched the images with great excitement. Neil Armstrong's words as he stepped onto the surface of the moon, 'that's one small step for [a] man, one giant leap for mankind', spoke to me of the possibility of a bright future.

The earlier spaceflight by Yuri Gagarin also left a strong impression on my own personal history. His 1962 book *Road to the Stars* was published in Japanese translation in 1963 as *Chikyū wa aokatta* (The earth was blue) when I was an elementary student in the sixth grade. I read the book over the summer holidays and wrote a reflective essay on it for a competition. I was fortunate enough to win a merit award for the essay from Yokohama City and I attended the prize-giving ceremony at the Yokohama Port Opening Memorial Hall together with my homeroom teacher, who was a little frightening and aloof. I have completely forgotten what I wrote in that essay but I can still remember vividly the photograph on the book's cover that showed the arc of the blue earth rising over the horizon.

My own personal experience of these events provided me with a way of seeing the earth from the outside, but this experience was also a decisive one for humanity and it put me in touch with the spirit of the age. Soon after Gagarin's spaceflight, systems theorist Buckminster Fuller (1969) published a book called *Operating Manual for Spaceship Earth*. In the book he sounded a warning about the wasteful use of fossil fuels and argued for the creation of a society that would recycle and regenerate its resources and energy (Fuller 1969: 127–9). American ambassador Adlai Stevenson II also used the metaphor of a spaceship when he put forward his influential argument that life on earth was not guaranteed and was dependent upon a delicate balance. He pointed out that the earth's resources were limited and that humanity shared a common destiny. In July 1965, at the United Nations Economic and Social Council in Geneva, he used the 'Spaceship Earth' metaphor in a speech in which he said, 'We travel together, passengers on a little space ship, dependent on its vulnerable reserve of air and soil; all committed for our safety to its security and peace.' The speech, which was followed by Ambassador

Stevenson's sudden death five days later, provoked a great reaction (Ishi 2002: 9).

In 1966 the economist Kenneth E Boulding published an essay titled 'The Economics of the Coming Spaceship Earth'. In it he argued that the 'open economy' of the past had been characterized by irrationality and recklessness on the understanding that the earth's resources were unlimited. He therefore called it the 'cowboy' economy, given its similarity to the way ranchers drove the bison to extinction. Boulding (1966) argued, by contrast, that a 'closed economy' could not be premised on unlimited accumulation. Because there was a limit to the number of places where resources could be extracted or pollutants disposed of, it ought to be called the 'spaceman economy'. In 1968, one year before the voyage to the moon, director Stanly Kubrik released the science fiction masterpiece *2001: A Space Odyssey*.

The image of Spaceship Earth, which was frequently used by thinking people from the late 1960s and entered general circulation, was novel in that it expressed in a single phrase a number of arguments about the earth as a closed and cyclical apparatus for sustaining life, much like a spaceship. This apt metaphor was taken up widely in economics, sociology and political science and from the mid-1980s it developed into an ethics of coexistence with the natural environment. Ishi Hiroyuki (2002), who has studied the historical transformation in Japanese consciousness about environmental problems, has identified four stages in the development of this consciousness. The first stage, up until the 1950s, he calls the 'nature' era, when environmental problems were limited to the local area and 'common ownership' was a major concept. The second stage from the early 1960s to the mid-1980s was the era of 'the environment', when there was a groundswell of popular movements concerned about serious environmental pollution, and environmental problems began to be talked about as important political problems on a national scale. The notion of 'publicness' appeared during this period. The third stage from the mid-1980s was the era of 'ecology', when people began to feel concerned about the environment of the earth as a whole. Since the 1990s, a major value-shift has been taking place from that of the 'national public' to the 'coexistence of humanity' (Ishi 2002: 1–2, 13).

The TV Asahi documentary series '*Suteki na uchūsen chikyūgō*' (Wonderful Spaceship Earth), which was first broadcast in 1997, when production and marketing of the eco-friendly hybrid car Prius started, probably best represents the value-shift that took place in Japan during the 1990s. The series, sponsored by the Toyota Group, was distributed nationally through TV Asahi's syndicated broadcasters for thirty minutes every Sunday evening, showing (according to advertising for the program) 'examples from around the world of the measures that need to be taken to protect the global environment in these times of dramatic environmental deterioration due to global warming, atmospheric pollution and other global problems'. No doubt Toyota Group's sponsorship of the series was part of its image marketing campaign to portray itself as a company that is conscious of environmental problems. Nevertheless, via the term 'Wonderful Spaceship Earth', the series broadcast a clear message into Japanese living rooms about the two values of coexistence with the earth (reducing the burden we place on our natural environment) and coexistence on earth (living in harmony with other peoples and cultures). The clever title astutely matched the sensibility of the times (although in September 2009, after 591 episodes and twelve years, the series was finally cancelled).

Globalization and local communities

The use of the Spaceship Earth metaphor to refer to recognition of the earth as a single organic system, based on an understanding of the crisis facing the natural environment and biological systems, resembles the attempt to describe the intimate connectivity of the contemporary world in the fields of politics, economics and culture with the term 'globalization'. Globalization first came to be used as an important analytical concept at the end of the 1980s. As Robertson (1997) points out, in 1991 the *Oxford Dictionary of New Words* incorrectly classified the new usage of the adjective 'global' as 'environmental jargon'. This is a perfect example of the way understandings of globalization at the time differed from today's understanding of the economic face of rapid global flows of people, things, money and information on a mass scale. Even in the 1980s, when the world was still divided into east and west along Cold War lines, the term 'globalization' indicated an understanding, tied to an awareness of the growing environmental crisis, that crossed national borders and even penetrated the iron curtain (Robertson 1997: 20). In this sense, the term 'global' contains nuances of world consciousness and was connected with the understanding of the earth as an irreplaceable self-contained system or Spaceship Earth.

The anthropologists Conklin and Graham's (1995) detailed exploration of the Kayapó indigenous people of the southeastern forests of the Amazon River delta (population approximately 4,000) can help us to understand how this shared understanding developed. Kayapó leaders in the late 1980s opposed the Brazilian government's plan, supported by the World Bank, to build a large-scale hydroelectric dam in their home in the Amazon rainforest. They used new tactics such as videography and received support from Western NGOs that helped them carry out their spirited resistance to the plan. The peak of this opposition movement occurred at a public hearing in the town of Altamira in February 1989. Six hundred Kayapó gathered there, with the men dressed in warrior garb and bearing spears and the women with machetes. Four hundred media representatives, domestic and foreign, attended the public hearing and the Altamira Gathering that preceded it, where the Kayapó proclaimed themselves to be a proud indigenous (original) people who were willing to fight to protect the natural environment that provides the basis for their subsistence. They made the public hearing into a place to display their firm opposition to the dam for all of the world to see, rather than engaging in dialogue and negotiation with the Brazilian government. These scenes were reported in newspapers and on television throughout the world, leading the World Bank eventually to withdraw funding and the Brazilian government to postpone the construction of the dam (Turner 1991, 1993; Beckham 1989).

According to Conklin and Graham (1995), the example of the Kayapó clearly shows the potential for a new solidarity that transcends linguistic, cultural and spatial distances to emerge between people in the First World who have an interest in development and environmental issues and indigenous (original) people in the Third World. These connections are not based on the old shared identities or on calculations of economic interest but on the consciousness of a global ecological community – or what might be called a global eco-imaginary. In this imaginary, indigenous (original) peoples are no longer positioned as second-class citizens living on the periphery but as people who practice and embody the core values of environmental conservation. This led British cosmetics brand The Body Shop, whose environmentally friendly image helped it achieve spectacular growth and spread throughout the world, to use the image of the Kayapó as a symbol of nature and purity in its marketing campaigns (Conklin and Graham 1995: 696–7; for further details, see Shimizu 2003: 161–70).

The post-Second World War world, in which the world's people were divided into two opposing politico-economic systems that were somehow in a state of equilibrium, came to an end with the dissolution of the Soviet Union in 1991. As a result, the United States became the sole superpower. Its military, political, economic and cultural hegemony and influence grew by means of a multilayered network driven primarily by neoliberal economics. However, although the United States once appeared to be an 'empire' reigning over the entire world, it was rattled by the terrorist attacks of September 11, 2001, and overreacted by invading Iraq and Afghanistan, where it has remained stuck in a quagmire ever since.[4] The Global Financial Crisis that was sparked by the collapse of Lehman Brothers in 2008 showed how deeply connected and mutually interdependent the global economy has become, leading to skepticism about and opposition to the American-led economic system. American hegemony is now in decline, both on a practical level and on the level of ideology. As a result, as the world becomes ever more intimately connected through globalization, it is also simultaneously tending to become more pluralistic and multi-polar (Todd 2003).

The 'glocal' lifeworld

Despite its location deep in the mountains, since the Spanish colonial period the region that encompasses Hapao and Hungduan has been by no means a self-sufficient world, isolated from the outside. Moreover, in recent years it has become even more connected, leading to a qualitative and quantitative increase in the number of its interactions with the world outside. One important change that contributed to this was the expansion and surfacing of the road from Banaue to Hapao that began in the mid-1960s and made it possible to transit by motor vehicle. The jeepney connection with Banaue enabled the movement of people and bulk goods further and further away. When I started my research at the end of the 1990s, only a small percentage of the road was surfaced but work has continued apace and more than 50 percent of the road is now surfaced. The rapid increase

---

4 Just like in Ifugao, the mountains and the periphery still remain as hot spots where global superpowers confront one another. For a discussion of the ideal of resistance to this conflict and of the location of power, see my account of Dr. Nakamura Tetsu's work with the Peshawar society in Afghanistan (Shimizu 2007c).

in overseas migrant labor over the past twenty or so years has also created a consciousness within daily life of the villagers' connection to a network that expands beyond the seas.

Mobile telephones first appeared in the village in 2000, but at that time they could only obtain reception on the top of the hill near the municipal government building and the hospital. However, in 2006 cell phone carrier Globe Inc. built an antenna near the municipal building and mobile phone reception has since become available almost anywhere in the village. It has become fashionable for young people, albeit those from wealthier households, to wear jeans and sneakers and carry cellular phones. Those who come from poorer families aspire to such a lifestyle. Messages sent via mobile connect those who remain in Hapao with their brothers and sisters and aunts and uncles in Baguio or Metro Manila and those further afield in Hong Kong, Singapore and Taiwan. Overseas telephone calls are expensive, but it is possible to send text messages instead, which cost just 15 pesos (approximately US$0.30). Because of the high cost of making calls, people only speak over the phone in emergencies. For everyday communication they use text messages.

As their families, relatives and friends depart to work in North America, Europe, the Middle East and Asia, some even remaining there permanently (but nevertheless returning home regularly to visit bearing masses of gifts), the people of Hapao see the names of the foreign countries and cities where they work as familiar and commonplace. This leads to the development of a spatial awareness that, while ill defined, nevertheless extends across the sea (excluding South America and Africa). However, unlike the image of the world that is evoked by photographs of the earth taken from the moon or from space, the cognitive mapping of the world that exists within the villagers' consciousness is constructed from points and lines that begin in Hapao and extend to local (Banaue, Lagawe, Baguio), national (Metro Manila), regional (Hong Kong, Singapore, Taipei) and global (the Middle East, the United States, Europe, Australia) scales as they connect the village with particular cities around the world. They picture the world as a collection of enclaves on the surface of a blank map of the globe upon which their relatives and friends have left a mark, resulting in a loose network that radiates out from Hapao.

This does not simply mean that the peripheral ethnic groups who were once located outside the modern world system (Wallerstein 1974) have been subsumed within it due to globalization. The enormous numbers of migrants and refugees from the periphery of the non-Western world who enter the West and, once there, move towards the major metropolises to live and work, show that we are currently experiencing what might be called the 'peripheralization of the core' (Inda and Rosaldo 2002: 18). Even the Ifugaos, who live in the remote mountains of northern Luzon and are generally considered to engage in the most traditional of lifestyles, are actually deeply connected with the loose network of mutual interdependence created by globalization. This process, driven by neoliberalism, has organically linked the world into a whole. Life in the village is by no means separate and isolated from the outside. Most of the funds needed to pay for traditional bone-washing and funerary rites, ancestral worship and the purchase of rice terraces as prestige assets are provided by remittances from migrant workers overseas. Migrant workers tend to cover the cost of four main categories of expenditure: renovating or building new homes, educating children, supplementing the cost of living and starting a small business. The continuation of the way of life rooted in ritual practices and the rice terraces that strengthen, objectify and make visible their self-identification as Ifugaos is made possible and supported by a network that extends across the seas and includes remittances from migrant workers, aid from international NGOs and development assistance from the European Union and Japan.

In the contemporary world, there is no longer any such thing as a self-contained, autonomous microcosm on the outside of the system, which now subsumes the earth as a whole, whether in Ifugao or anywhere else. The same is true for the Pinatubo Aetas of western Luzon, whom I introduce in the previous chapter, who were once considered to be the most 'backward' ethnic group in the Philippines. The peripheral peoples who live in mountainous and remote areas far from the capital in non-Western countries, who were previously the chief object of research in cultural anthropology (the people who were known up until the 1960s as primitive or backwards peoples, then as ethnic minorities and more recently as indigenous peoples), are today also our contemporaries. They, too, in their different places and within the limits and possibilities originating from their own unique historical development paths and cultures, are facing the wave of globalization and alternately resisting it or going along for the ride. In earlier chapters I discuss the native intellectual Lopez Nauyac, whose work is based on a deep understanding of the globalizing age in which we live and of the world it has made. I explain his historical consciousness, in which globalization means the re-convergence today of unique cultural traditions that once shared the same root but have traversed different historical passages.

As we see in Chapter 8, globalization in Hapao has seen large numbers of villagers go abroad to obtain the means of subsistence and the mass influx of souvenirs such as televisions, DVD players and Hollywood films (mostly pirate copies) that they bring with them on their return to the village. Globalization develops through its inter-penetration of the local. The term 'glocalization' describes the way globalization is accompanied in each locality by an increased interest in the uniqueness and individuality of people and place and by active attempts to reevaluate and recover this uniqueness, often through performative acts of representation. Like two sides of the same coin, as networks expand across borders and the globe, they incite a return to and rediscovery of the local. In this sense, globalization and localization need to be understood as sympathetic and simultaneous movements.

According to Yamawaki Naoshi (2008), whose work involves the development of a 'global public philosophy', the neologism 'glocal' first appeared in Japan at the beginning of the 1990s. Today the term is used by a range of theorists with different ideologies. Yamawaki defines global public philosophy as 'a branch of learning that seeks to understand global and local public problems while remaining rooted in locality in the sense of the "sitedness" and "regionality" in which individuals live' (Yamawaki 2008: ii). He also differentiates a glocal environmental ethics from the way the Club of Rome looks down over the world from its comfortable seat in the developed countries. His approach is premised on an understanding that people face different environmental problems in different places and makes full use of the 'local knowledge' possessed by the poor and the people on the ground in order to address environmental problems through dialogue and deliberation (Yamawaki 2008: 47–8).

Applying Yamawaki's ideas to the cooperation between IKGS in Japan and 'Global' in the Philippines enables us to think about the connection between globalization-localization and environmental conservation from a quotidian perspective. Inevitably, in neither Sannan nor Hapao are people always fully consciousness of global environmental problems when they are busy with the minutia of their daily lives. For the people of Sannan in the remote mountains of Sasayama in Hyōgo Prefecture, the fact that some local residents took an interest in the Mount Pinatubo area in western

Top, middle: Cultural exchange and gift-giving at Sasayama Homei Senior High School l. (October 18, 2001)

Bottom: (from right) Nauyac, Randy and Orlando dancing at a social event in Sannan. At the far left is Daniel Gonzalez, an Aeta man from Pinatubo. (October 20, 2001, photos by Segawa Chiyoko)

Luzon, began to provide assistance with revegetation there and formed an NGO to carry out this work was due to their sensitivity to environmental problems as they relate to forestry, their traditional local industry. Even if the relationship between forestry and international development in their activities was somewhat haphazard, their existing concerns gave the project its initial stimulus. Without it, they would not have developed the face-to-face relationships with the particular individuals in specific places in the Philippines that in turn strengthened their interest in the work there and led them to take further action. As I explain earlier in this book, when Tsugawa Hyōe, a professor in the Department of Agriculture at Kobe University, gave a lecture in the Sannan community center, calling for revegetation of the volcanic wastes of Mount Pinatubo using *kudzu*-vine, some attendees responded by undertaking an inspection tour to the Philippines. They were deeply affected by the desolation they witnessed there, of a world covered in volcanic ash and debris. In this sense, the directness and specificity of the relationship that connected the two municipalities over national borders and oceans served as a lever to get things moving.

The consciousness of the people of Sannan regarding environmental issues centered on the town in which they live their daily lives. It did not simply expand outwards in concentric circles from the local to the national and on to the regional and the global like the ripples created by throwing a stone into a pond. Rather, the bond between these small local municipalities crosses national borders and connects them directly with one another. As they transcend the diffuse distances that define nations and regions, these municipalities resemble two enclaves that interact with one another and feel close to one another. Leaders and members of 'Global', the mayor of Hungduan and the governor of Ifugao have been invited a number of times to make friendship visits to Sannan, where they interacted with local people, and members of IKGS have been welcomed in Hapao on several visits.

While the reforestation movement on the wasted slopes of Mount Pinatubo was underway, before I became involved with Ifugao, many high school students from Japan who participated in the work camps there skipped right over Manila, even if this was their first trip overseas, to spend several days in a village where there was no electricity or running water. There they communicated with the Aeta youths using gestures, vocabulary cards and broken English and returned home having been moved by the experience. These experiences left deep impressions on them and were hard to forget. A number of former work camp participants later spent

Top: Ifugao Governor Teddy Baguilat (second from the left) dancing in Sannan, Hyogo Prefecture, Japan at the '*Mabuhay* Exchange' event. (September 14, 2003)

Middle: Governor Baguilat (left) and Mayor Pablo M Cuyahon Sr. (right), wearing Barong Tagalog, pay a courtesy visit to Sannan Mayor Adachi Umeji. (September 14, 2003)

Bottom: A group pays a courtesy visit to the head of the Tamba branch office of the Hyōgo prefectural government. (September 16, 2003, photos Segawa Chiyoko)

long periods volunteering in Ifugao as university students. One woman (Ōtake Asuka), who decided the most useful form of volunteering would be to provide healthcare, went back to university after having graduated to study medicine and became a doctor. Globalization at the grassroots has created close connections that transcend borders between people who live in two distinct points on the globe, connections that also incorporate many other points, and led to changes in the social networks and spatial consciousness that influences the lifeworlds of both.

Re-forging long-distance environmentalism

It follows that the IKGS supporters and Sannan residents involved in reforestation projects in Pinatubo and Ifugao were motivated not so much by the consciousness of a 'global ecological community' as described by Conklin and Graham but by what might better be described as a 'long-distance eco-imaginary' or 'long-distance environmentalism', terms derived from Benedict Anderson's (1993) concept of 'long-distance nationalism'. Anderson focuses on the way globalization leads masses of migrant laborers to spend long periods working overseas or to make their homes there as permanent migrants. He points out that even if they obtain citizenship in the countries to which they migrate and are able to make a comfortable life there, they have little attachment to their new country and tend to have more interest in the struggles that emerge in the homeland 'of their memory and their imagination', the place where they were born. They are liable to be tempted to participate in struggles there as propagandists, by supplying weapons or through other kinds of extra-electoral means. Anderson (1993: 189–90) worries about this long-distance nationalism and shows that the participation of these former citizens in politics inevitably leads to recklessness and irresponsibility and places them at serious risk of falling prey to shrewd political opportunists in the home country.

The way people in developed countries express concerns about environmental problems in developing countries seems similar to the way these long-distance nationalists express their affective commitment to their home countries and it provokes similar anxieties. In the case of long-distance environmentalism, too, people in the developed world who are concerned about environmental problems enjoy the comforts of the developed countries and of their support and make well-intentioned interventions intended to mitigate environmental problems in the developing countries. For example, for the Westerners who supported the Kayapó in the Brazilian Amazon or the people of Sannan who supported the Aeta and Ifugao peoples in the mountainous regions of Luzon, the frontline of the battle to protect the environment is located far away across the sea. However, the people who are actually fighting on those frontlines day and night are not the former compatriots living overseas whom Anderson evokes in his critique of long-distance nationalism, who, despite their geographical distance, are still mentally close to their homeland. For long-distance environmentalists, the people on the frontlines are poor people who live in a foreign country and culture. To put it bluntly, they are an exotic other different from themselves. If their dress or some other symbol makes their exoticism, poverty, powerlessness and need for support from benevolent outsiders clear, then it is all the more likely that they will inspire feelings of sympathy and a desire in others to help.[5]

People in the developed countries are driven to engage in support activities for people at the grassroots by a vague sense of crisis about the deterioration of our common home and a feeling of sympathy with people who are trying to conserve the environment in the field, where the crisis is more obvious. It is a feeling of solidarity and a bond that exists within the realm of the imagination, between two groups of people who are separated by vast oceans. At its core is a shared feeling, whether conscious or unconscious, that all of us, as members of the human race who happen to have been born at the same time and are living on this earth, are fated to share our journey as passengers on Spaceship Earth and therefore share the same lot. Despite the various limitations and problems inherent in this relationship, it might nevertheless be a first step to the creation of what we might call a global civil society, because it is a concern that is open to an outsider to one's own culture and society.

Appadurai (2006) points out that NGOs and other transnational networks have the potential to check the kinds of long-distance hatred

---

5 Michael Ignatieff (1998) gives a lucid account of the ways in which we become concerned about the circumstances of people who live in far-off places, which he calls 'empathy at a distance'. According to Ignatieff, even in the overwhelmingly Christian West, it was by no means self-evident that we ought to be concerned about people who live far away. As the liberal humanist imagination began to conceive of a humanity in general, developed a keen sense of reality about this concept and began to raise its voice against all kinds of sufferings in the name of humanity, it gave birth to empathy at a distance.

exemplified by the hatred and fear of Islam that developed in America after the September 11 terrorist attacks and the hatred of America in the Islamic world that emerged in response to it, and to open up a new field of what he calls international civil society. According to Appadurai, a new world is appearing as we transition from the twentieth to the twenty-first century. This is a cellular world that proliferates by creating connections and making changes, as opposed to the vertebrate world with its central nervous system made up of the balance of power between nations, military treaties, economic leagues and international bodies. This new world is a byproduct of globalization (Appadurai 2006: 127–9) and has two faces, one of which is the dark political face known as terrorism. However, Appadurai finds hope in the way long-distance politics is organized in cellular forms because it 'is not only the monopoly of rogue capitalists or political terrorists' but is in the process of creating an alternative third space of circulation that resists these powers. This second more utopian face is that of international civil society. It is made up of a network of activists who hold to fundamentally humanist aims such as human rights, poverty reduction, rights for indigenous people, disaster relief, environmental justice and gender equality. Appadurai (2006: 129–37) calls this emerging potential for a new social formation 'grassroots globalization' and it is in this process that he finds hope to build humanity's future.

The grassroots globalization that has been developing in Hapao is generating a glocal reorganization of its people's lives, as individual experiences of migrant work and cooperation with NGOs connect them to a transnational network that incorporates Japan, Asia, the Middle East and the West. This has led to a keen awareness among the people of Hapao of connections that go beyond the region to the global scale. This awareness has opened up avenues to address the deepening environmental crisis and has led them to engage in small grassroots practices that contribute to the creation of an international civil society. The development of such an awareness is a source for hope.[6]

---

6 I finished writing the manuscript for the Japanese version of this book just as the Great East Japan earthquake occurred on March 11, 2011. After the disaster, we could no longer say that Japan was safe. Across the globe, the risk of disaster is increasing. We urgently need to create transnational systems to cooperate on disaster prevention and recovery. We cannot escape the fact that we need to reform our way of life, our society and the structure of our industries, even if it means we have to compromise on our personal comforts or on our convenience as a society.

Deepening commitment and the round trip between field and home

As I explain in Chapters 7 and 9, the journey that led me to conduct fieldwork in Ifugao began when the Baguio art group Sun Flower Co., which Kidlat Tahimik chairs, submitted a funding application to the Toyota Foundation's international aid program. When Nauyac called the villagers together to take part in a program that would use indigenous knowledge to conserve the *pinugo* forests and rice terraces and kickstart the reforestation movement, Kidlat applied on his behalf for funding to hold seminars on reforestation methods. Nauyac began the reforestation movement with his relatives and old friends, using his own small funds, but in order to spread the movement to the whole village, he needed more funds in order to invite experts to give talks and to provide refreshments for the workshop participants. As part of the application, Kidlat also included his plan for a video workshop project to teach the villagers camera and editing skills so that they could document their culture and encourage the villagers to take a greater interest in their traditional culture.

I was a member of the selection committee for the foundation's international aid program at that time. I was drawn to the application when I read it and so, in May 1997, I went to Baguio to meet with Kidlat and Nauyac and talk with them about it first-hand. When I visited them at Nauyac's home, they showed me maps of the areas in Hapao where they were planning to carry out reforestation and photographs of the work they had completed so far at their own expense. I felt strongly that I wanted to go to Hapao to see their work and do some research. When I commenced my fieldwork the following year, Nauyac said that if I was really interested in their work and wanted to conduct research on it, I was more than welcome, and he invited me to collaborate with them. But he insisted that I not only do research to build my own resume but conduct it in such a way that it would also have some benefit for the people of Hapao. Specifically, he wanted me to help find a Japanese NGO that would be interested in the reforestation project and provide some assistance. He asked me to help him forge a relationship with such a group.

I was very sympathetic to what Nauyac was saying and felt that his request was a reasonable one. I therefore decided to commit myself fully to the project. As I explain in the previous chapter, what led me to make that decision was my volunteer experience working in the disaster-affected communities of Mount Pinatubo in western Luzon after the volcanic eruption, when I volunteered for eight months in a project that aimed to provide aid to the victims and help them with reconstruction. This experience changed the way I practice anthropology and as a result I decided to pursue what I call the anthropology of response-ability. This is why I did not hesitate to commit to the project in Ifugao.

The anthropology of response-ability is a style of anthropology that involves active participation in addressing the problems and challenges faced both by communities in the field and back home in the anthropologist's home country (in my case, Japan). In other words, it means working with both the people who are on the receiving end of international development assistance and those who provide it. In this approach, addressing problems, improving conditions on the ground and solving their problems are all carried out together with the research and are regarded as inseparable from it. Quite by accident and to my great good fortune, I had an experience whereby my volunteer work in the disaster-affected Pinatubo region simultaneously became a kind of fieldwork.[7] I worked with the NGOs as a volunteer but I was also a longstanding friend of the Aeta disaster victims who were the recipients of the project. This meant that I could also see things from their point of view, enabling a multifaceted approach and a deeper understanding. At that time, I did my utmost to notice and to remain mindful of the differences and similarities between the Japanese and the Philippine sides – between the two societies of the field and home. In other words, while the two sides constitute the other to their opposite, with their own paths of historical development and cultural constraints, I tried at the same time to see them as comrades living in the same era of globalization. I thought of this as an attempt to pursue the potential for a new international public that spans the sea between the two countries.

---

7 I call this fortunate because while I had grave fears that the eruption would destroy their ethnic heritage, the reverse happened and it actually brought about a rejuvenation of their people. What happened was quite unlike the process of de-culturation following the loss of the basis of their livelihoods that James Eder (1987) described in *On the Road to Tribal Extinction*. Their new way of life in the housing to which they were relocated, school education, and contact and interaction with the outside world enabled the Aetas to gain an understanding of themselves and become consciousness of themselves as an indigenous people who, as well as sharing certain physical characteristics, shared the experience of suffering and renewal after the disaster.

Over more than forty years in the Philippines, I have published four ethnographies in Japanese and two in English (one of which is an abridged translation of the Japanese version) since 1976, when I first went there to conduct fieldwork for my doctoral dissertation. I will not go into detail about them here. However, I can say that the consistent theme of my research has been the 'event' and all of my books share a number of characteristics. First, they are based on participant observation carried out over an extended period of time, usually almost ten years or more. Second, I have paid particular attention to the dynamism and processes of social change that are brought about by events. Third, my analysis places the micro-level research conducted in the field (in a village or town) in the context of macro-level phenomena and systems (the nation as a whole, major global trends) and attempts to see what light each can shed on the other. Fourth, I respond critically, both directly and indirectly, to current debates in cultural anthropology.

In all my ethnographies I try to rely upon the thoughts and perspectives of people in the field, capture their lived reality and make an accurate sketch of it, as well as a convincing analysis. I probably arrived at my focus on events more by accident than design. I also feel that my delicate work of portraying in miniature the minor events that take place in small communities has something of the artisan character of Japan's traditional crafts. The joy I experience in writing an ethnography is something like the pleasure that children experience from building models out of clay with their hands. I enjoy the feeling of working with one's fingers to give shape to a formless lump of clay and of producing something from it. This handmade quality and the pleasure I derive from it is probably why I have been able to keep writing ethnographies. Even if the reality of the field appears at first glance to be chaotic and difficult to comprehend, I always have a clear sense of its texture. To borrow Sugawara Kazutaka's (2015: 455) words, the misty landscape that one begins to perceive (of the social structure or worldview as a whole) begins to develop a clear outline and features while spending time 'entangled in a space of direct coexistence'.

My basic approach to research was always to wait for something to happen and then, when it did, to stand around rubbernecking and getting agitated together with the villagers. I also tried to look carefully at the reality of the situation and to listen to local people as I become personally entangled in the maelstrom of the event or incident. I was passive rather than active, giving myself over to the unfolding events and being swept along by them. I once regarded this approach to research, as explained in a notable episode in the beginning of Clifford Geertz's 'Deep Play' (Geertz 1973), as the ideal approach to fieldwork. It is an approach that involves shrinking oneself down so as to be almost unnoticed – ideally becoming invisible – and quietly observing without arousing any caution in the target society.

This approach can be compared with a kind of push sonar, one of the two types of sonar that aircraft carriers use to detect submarines. Push sonar senses the shockwave created by the enemy submarine's engine noise and its movement through the water. It is a passive instrument for sensing sound wave in order to determine the location of the vessel. By contrast, active sonar is an offensive method used by fishing vessels. The fish finder emits its own sound waves and locates the object by capturing the waves that bounce back when they hit their target. Metaphorically speaking, active sonar can be compared with the way police and prosecutors carry out interrogations to obtain a confession or statement from a suspect or to the questionnaires formerly used in anthropology and still used in sociology and other disciplines. This approach is suited to efficient data collection where the researcher has something he or she wants to ask or clarify in order to develop a consistent account of an incident as a whole. When the police collect evidence, they are guided by conjecture or a predetermined scenario. In research, this approach enables the researcher to quickly gather resources to prove or revise a hypothesis.

Growing up during the 1960s and '70s, the time of the student movement and the counterculture, anthropology for me was a kind of trial-and-error method for 'unlearning' as I tried to rid my old self and reconstruct myself anew. Anthropology for me was just the same as Nauyac and Ifugao culture was for Kidlat. However, during the course of my development as a researcher, my approach of focusing on a particular incident and allowing myself to get caught up in it as it developed, opening my eyes and ears and transforming myself into a kind of passive push sonar machine (hopefully a sensitive one), underwent a major change. The way I position myself within the field and the way I create and maintain relationships with people has changed significantly since the eruption of Mount Pinatubo. It is not so much that I subjectively changed my approach but that new things kept coming up one after the other. While I was being dragged along, entangled in and swept up in the situation as it unfolded, I found that I had changed my own stance as an anthropologist, in terms of both my consciousness and my behavior without even noticing it.

During that period, from the end of the 1980s through to the 1990s, the *Writing Culture* (Clifford and Marcus 1986) shock had a big influence on anthropology in Japan, as it did elsewhere. While I was still reeling from that shock, Mount Pinatubo erupted. Because some of my personal friends and acquaintances were victims, that disaster had an even greater impact on me than *Writing Culture*. Furthermore, because I was in the Philippines on sabbatical at the time, the stories I was hearing on television and in newspapers and magazines, as well as in my visits to the evacuation centers where I met with my friends, the disaster felt very close to home. I began to think that it was not the time to remain peacefully at home in the academic world, amusing myself with texts and indulging in the world of the signifier. I felt that it was time to face up to the real world that lies outside of texts.[8] I felt strongly that it was the context, the real world in which people live, that was of the greatest importance, not the world of texts, with their problems of representation and technique of writing. The real problem was not in the superstructure of consciousness and hegemony but the substructure at the base, where survival, avoiding starvation and disease, and securing the means of subsistence that enable a healthy and dignified life were more pressing problems.

That is when I became a volunteer worker with a Japanese NGO that was carrying out life-and-death healthcare projects, rebuilding livelihoods and reconstructing communities in order to help the Aeta people in their dire predicament. Looking back, I was forced by events to take a radical

---

8 Inaga Shigemi (2001), a comparative literature and culture scholar who has a profound interest in anthropology, concludes that the self-criticism and experimental ethnographic writing based on textual strategies that was brought about by the postcolonial turn in anthropology was a charade of self-justification that was confined within academia. He insists on the need to shift the questions raised at that time from an epistemic to an ethical basis (Inaga 2001: 77–8). He observes:

> their indictment of themselves for the deceptive nature of speaking for the voiceless voices, their unproductive confessions of powerlessness while remaining present in the field of 'usurping voices,' their attempts to atone for the irreproducible gifts they have received from culturally distinct others by devoting themselves to continuous self-flagellation for the injuries they have caused by representing the other, is simply a perversion that quickly transforms into a kind of self-justification that is performed exclusively within the academic community. (Inaga 2001: 96)

This condemnation strikes a little too close to home.

(even extreme) approach to the 'participation' component of participant observation, the foundational methodology of fieldwork. I still think that the basic stance that ran through my fieldwork and my writing was passivity, a lightness of being that enabled me to be caught up in situations and the ability to negate my own identity. It was that lightness that made me sensitive to outside influences and enabled me to change rather than having to remain faithful to my original approach. My approach resembles the old saying, 'he who touches pitch shall be defiled therewith'. To put it more negatively, I can be rather frivolous and thoughtless. It is quite embarrassing to have to admit to having this kind of a character. Nevertheless, it is probably this tendency that made it possible for me to adapt readily to the requirements of the moment and become a spectator to events, respond to them, get caught up in them and, through this, to come close enough to the event to perceive the shape of the reality that they produce.

In the field I listen excitedly to the small talk of daily life and the idle chatter at village assemblies. I observe and am genuinely amazed when I take part in rituals or get caught up in events. Then I ask questions and when I receive unexpected answers and explanations, the blinkers come off and my sleepy and slow-witted brain finally wakes up and gets to work. As I discuss elsewhere (Shimizu 2014: 22), when I read Ishimure Michiko's *Paradise in the Sea of Sorrow: Our Minamata Disease* (2003 [1970]) as a university student, it had a major impact on me. I had a keen sense that I lacked both the sensitivity of a poet and the imagination and creativity of a novelist. Realizing that I could become neither a poet nor a novelist, I was eager to find inspiration in my interactions in the field, to find some illumination and gain enlightenment there so that I could remake myself anew. My fascination with other cultures and with anthropology as a means of unlearning myself, which had become full of theories thanks to my exam-focused studies, closely resembles Kidlat's attempt to change himself by learning about Ifugao culture from Nauyac, entering into it and trying to change himself.

I did not take up anthropology because I felt aloof from the world. Knowing with every fiber of my being that I could never become a brilliant theorist, I have not tried to classify and comprehend reality from the perspective of theory but, rather, the reverse. I did my utmost to begin my thinking based on the lived reality of people in grassroots microcosms. I happily concede that this was due to my own lack of independence and my own frivolousness and thoughtlessness. However, today I have become quite stubborn about this and I sincerely hope that we can reconsider the direction and the potential of anthropology from such a position.⁹ I feel that one possible answer is a kind of anthropology of response-ability – that is, an anthropology that continually deepens its commitment while making the round trip between field and home.

An attempt at 'extreme' participant observation

The anthropology of response-ability is not meant to constitute a separate field within anthropology. The term is intended, rather, to emphasize the verb 'to respond' and the noun 'responsibility' in the context of an enduring relationship. It is important for the anthropologist to maintain an ongoing relationship with the people in the field and the problems they face and to thereby continue to practice anthropology flexibly while responding to changes in the field, as well as back home. Today, public anthropology is becoming popular in the United States, but it seems to be primarily a response to its domestic problems of the public good and welfare policy. Its fundamental problematics address pressing issues facing American society, such as migrants and refugees, ethnicity, race, gender, gay/lesbian/transgender/bisexual issues, education and so on (Borofsky 2007).¹⁰ By

---

9 Looking back on my own past, I went to protestant Christian private schools for elementary, middle and high school. Every morning we went to prayer, read the Bible and sang hymns. At university I also learned some of the history and philosophy of the West but it never sat comfortably with me and I never really understood it deeply. Perhaps it was because of my own discomfort about a subjectivity and self that were based in Western culture. Nevertheless, the individual, the subject and the ego that are called 'good' in the West are called 'egotism' in the Japanese Buddhist worldview. The Buddhists teach that the obsession with the ego is the origin of all suffering and pain. I have a lot of sympathy with the idea that to live is to suffer and that in order to escape from suffering you have to throw out the self and aspire to nirvana.

10 Yamashita Shinji (2014) gives a lucid explanation of the background to the appearance of public anthropology in the United States in the late 1990s. He traces its genealogy back to applied anthropology and explores its recent development in Chapter One of his edited collection. The essays in this collection also discuss various aspects of public anthropology in greater detail. Yamashita (2014: 10–11) proposes that we should avoid the term 'respond' and suggests 'engagement', along with 'collaboration', as his preferred keywords because of their implicit continuity with the methodology of participant observation and because they are also widely used in the Anglophone world. Whether we call it response or engagement, the kinds of practices that we are both trying to describe using those words are similar. It matters little what word we use to describe them. Nevertheless, where the term 'engagement' contains a strong nuance of the effort and subjectivity of the researcher,

contrast, the anthropology of response-ability that I advocate here implies both a deep commitment to the public sphere in one's home country and to the people in the field who help anthropologists with their work. It means getting actively involved in addressing important issues faced by communities and contributing to finding solutions or ways to deal with issues by acting and speaking out for change and reform with an emphasis on face-to-face relationships in the field and at home.

Anthropology is by definition a long-term enterprise that encompasses everything from the fieldwork stage to the writing of an ethnography. Indeed, it is a kind of slow work.[11] In the anthropology of response-ability that I advocate for, there is no need to treat that long journey of anthropology as a race and run towards some predefined goal at breakneck speed. Rather, the emphasis is on nurturing the relationships that develop with people in the field and responding sincerely, even while sometimes taking detours, getting lost or having a break. This responsive relationship does not come to an end with the publication of an ethnography but continues far beyond it. I am not saying that the various relationships and contributions that exist outside a narrowly defined approach to anthropological research are essential ingredients for the practice of anthropology as a scholarly discipline. Contributing to local development or solving problems will not give anthropology meaning and justification. They are not essential to anthropology as a field within the academy. You might even call this the unavoidable side-effect or residue of living in the field. Nevertheless, if you spend time in the field, it actually becomes impossible to simply dismiss or ignore the relationships that develop in your daily interactions

---

'response' implies a passive relationship (or perhaps even a sense of obligation) in which the researcher is called on by the other. Specifically, in the chronological sequence from the initial entanglement to the response to the interlocutor's call – the undertaking to change one's own positionality and the change in the relationship with people in the field that leads to serious and active engagement – I am thinking about both an anthropology that responds and an anthropologist who changes.

11 The term 'slow work' is derived from the popular terms 'slow food' and 'slow life'. It struck me as a particularly appropriate term to capture the long journey from fieldwork to the publication of an ethnography and beyond. A similar term is Numazaki Ichirō's (2012: 34) 'slow science' but anthropology is closer to the humanities than it is to the sciences. In addition, fieldwork is carried out face to face and has the character of time-consuming handicraft or artisanal work, so the term 'work' is more appropriate than 'science'. I have to thank Kimura Shūhei for giving me the reference to Numazaki's work.

with other people there. I am suggesting that we ought to acknowledge this fact. Anthropological fieldwork is carried out by means of face-to-face interactions with flesh-and-blood human beings. We inevitably become involved in relationships that fall outside the narrowly defined research. I want to say that while valuing these relationships as they develop in real time, we ought to consciously maintain and respond to these relationships in the long journey that continues even after the completion of the research and the publication of an ethnography.

When I first began my fieldwork in the Pinatubo area, I studied the local language while sitting in the corner of a classroom in a recently completed daycare center attached to an elementary school that was built by an aid organization. There were no textbooks, grammars or dictionaries for the local Zambal language. Right from the start my research was warmly received by the local people and they helped me to live in their village and taught me all sorts of things. It took me nearly ten years to complete my doctoral dissertation, including twenty months of fieldwork (1977–79). It took another four years to revise and publish the ethnography in English in Manila and in Japanese in Fukuoka, so in total the process took fourteen years from the commencement of my fieldwork. After the eruption it took another ten years to publish my second ethnography in English, Filipino and Japanese. During that time, I got a job in a university and traveled many times between my office in Japan and the villages on Mount Pinatubo and, after the eruption, to the emergency accommodation. In the case of my research in Ifugao, it took fifteen years before I was able to publish an ethnography in Japanese. The English version has taken twenty years. I can now see that it takes about ten years to complete a single piece of work. I have since returned to Pinatubo and Ifugao many times during the winter or spring vacation every year since 2012 to 2018, except 2013.

A great physical, spatial and temporal distance exists between the fieldwork stage and the publication of an ethnography, and the anthropologist travels back and forth across this distance. This endless journey is what gives anthropology both its joy and its difficulties and is connected with its strength and potential as a discipline. If the anthropologist only values the research itself, then the journey becomes a single return trip there and back. There may be a few further visits for supplementary surveys but once the ethnography is written up as a dissertation or a book, that is the end of it. Of course, it takes a number of years and quite a bit of money to keep going back again and again. It would be wrong of me to suggest that young researchers, particularly those who have completed their fieldwork and are writing their dissertations or working as casual lecturers while looking for permanent posts, work like this with its cost in terms of both time and money. However, I want to remind the reader that to practice anthropology is to walk a very long course. Many potential collaborators can be found along the way, including the villagers who help with fieldwork and make up the communities under study, the NGO staff and government officials conducting projects in the region, university lecturers and others. The relationships formed with them in the field really are once-in-a-lifetime opportunities. They might be over very quickly, but they might also continue for ten, twenty or thirty years and hence they should be cherished. Each anthropologist takes a different approach to creating, maintaining and ending these relationships.

However, in fieldwork, which is the foundation and the strength of anthropology, if we retain a humble awareness of the specificity and individuality of our individual interlocutors and communities, and of participant observation as the methodology of anthropological research, then we must be conscious of the fact that as anthropologists we are always already in the position of having to participate deeply, engage and commit to the local society. Most of the problems faced by the people who live there, including in my own field sites, relate to disasters, environmental destruction, globalization, democracy and distributive justice. These are the same problems that we face in Japan and that is why a small NGO in a mountain village in Hyōgo Prefecture made a commitment to projects in Pinatubo and Ifugao and has been providing assistance there for twenty-five years. Because I can depend upon the support of face-to-face relationships with people in both Japan and the Philippines, I have been able to continue to work in cooperation with local people and other interested groups to address these problems and respond to local needs.

Each individual anthropologist has to respond to many different interlocutors, including local people in the field, the NGO staff, and central and local government officials who work there, journalists, social movement activists and others. When they return to Japan it becomes important not to close oneself off inside academia but to create cooperative relationships with society at large. In the practice of anthropology, we have the option of making the work that begins with fieldwork and leads to the writing of an ethnography serve as a reflexive record of the relationship between three groups of actors: the anthropologist and the community in the field site, the broader society that surrounds them, and the anthropologist's own communities in his or her home society.

Towards an anthropology of difference and similarity

I use the term 'anthropology of response-ability' to refer to a whole host of meanings. Sekine Hisao (2007), in an article in the *Japanese Journal of Cultural Anthropology* titled, 'What is anthropological fieldwork?', pursues a similar approach in the field of development assistance when he advocates for a practical anthropology that emphasizes continuity between the dialogue that takes place between 'local people' and people who work in development and the work of mediators and agents that depends upon it ('connecting' work). Kimura Hideo (2007), following on from Sekine's paper, tries to address the decline in the volume of ethnographic work that is being conducted within anthropology. He insists on the potential for a new contribution based on fieldwork, anthropology's foundational methodology, that leads to the production of what he calls 'naive' ethnography. 'Naive ethnography', he explains:

> places greater importance on the ethnography's utility as a transcription of what local people said and did in the field rather than on its appeal to other academics. It stresses the concrete results of observation over theoretical consistency. It is packed with observations from the field and the accumulated results of the research presented in a format that is easily comprehensible by local people in the field. (Kimura 2007: 397)

What Kimura is really suggesting is that it is possible for the anthropologist to become 'a volunteer ethnographer'.

Both Sekine and Kimura suggest an approach to anthropology that, to use my own preferred term, responds to the various people who are in the field site. Malinowski (1984[1922]) positions anthropology as the attempt 'to grasp the native's point of view'. Similar metaphors describe the discipline as trying to read over the shoulders of local people. In these metaphors, to apply yet another metaphor, the anthropologist conceals him or herself behind the backs of the local people and tries to act as one of them, on behalf of them, to explain their experience of the world. My approach is not to hide behind the backs of the native (although, of course, there are times when one does have to do so, to avoid standing out and to listen in or catch a glimpse of what is going on) but to stand in front of or side by side with them, to sit and have a conversation face to face, to talk, ask questions and to answer their questions when asked. The anthropology of response-ability involves more than just this kind of linguistic communication. It also means doing one's best to respond when one is asked a favor or called upon to do something and to lend a hand. (Of course, a degree of caution is required. If you try to respond earnestly to too many expectations and demands, it can lead to a situation where you start getting pestered to pay hospital and pharmaceutical bills or pay school fees etc., costing both time and money.)

In the introduction to his paper, Kimura (2007: 384) makes it clear that 'the context in which we practice cultural anthropology is getting tougher and its position within the academic world is fragile. Its meaning as a branch of knowledge is in question.' I completely agree. Matsuda Motoji (2009) describes three periods of crisis for cultural anthropology in Japan under direct and indirect influences from the United States. The first wave of crisis was the overwhelming condemnation of 'anthropology's complicity with (neo)colonialism' from the end of the 1960s through the early 1970s; the second crisis from the mid-1980s was the shock that followed *Writing Culture*; the third is anthropology's failure to respond appropriately to the rapid changes in the broader context that surrounds the contemporary world and contemporary anthropology (Matsuda 2009: 12–13).

There have already been more than twenty attempts to found new branches of anthropology, sometimes in response to the abovementioned crises and sometimes independent of them. These include cultural anthropology, social anthropology, political, legal, economic, management, development, historical, psychological, religious, phenomenological, linguistic, cognitive, education, medical, ecological, environmental, practical, urban, tourism, film, public and space anthropology among others. Excluding cultural anthropology, most of these anthropologies are related to an autonomous discipline that is separate from anthropology. Their common feature is that the field in which they work overlaps with that of the underlying discipline, but they take as the object of their research a microscopic field site that they study through fieldwork. In some cases, they may also treat the research field itself as the basis for a new problematic and use anthropological methods to pursue the questions that arise from this. They closely resemble one another in that they use new perspectives from anthropology to add to fields that were already occupied by another discipline or open up a new field for research. In doing so they respond sensitively to the changing times and hunt for new objects to study.

An accurate and perhaps even slightly masochistic interpretation of these two tendencies in the new branches of anthropology is that not only are they similar but that they are both manifestations of the spirit of capitalism. In order to sell their work as a commodity, they simply improve the old model or add some functionality, sometimes even developing new products. Of course, I too live within the capitalist market system and when I look back, without even knowing it, I have internalized this way of thinking. However, I feel that, just as Confucius says in the Analects, 'one should be able to derive new understanding while revising what one has learned'. I want to reawaken once more the original spirit of anthropology and make a new beginning from there. In the United Kingdom that might mean looking at Malinowski, in the United States Franz Boas, Margaret Mead and Ruth Benedict, and in Japan Umesao Tadao and Nakane Chie. The work of these anthropologists directly addressed the urgent problems their societies faced during their time, as well as the problems that they themselves faced as anthropologists, and they spoke about these problems based on their experience in the field.

If I think about my own anthropology and attempt to legitimize it with the benefit of hindsight, I try to see the problems and issues that confront people in the field and their hopes and potential as a specific manifestation of problems faced by human societies everywhere and therefore as a source of hope. Then, while staying close to my case study, I simultaneously try to find an opening towards a resolution to these problems or at least a way of dealing with them that potentially has broader utility (even if not universal). In doing so I am less concerned about maintaining my distance from the object (the native people) and being objective and scientific. I am willing to take a risk if it means I can be of some help in finding a solution to the problems they face. I get directly involved with local people and other concerned parties and carry out practical research that overlaps somewhat with volunteer work. The key concepts in my fieldwork are to engage with urgent problems, to do research that aims to find a solution or at least a way of ameliorating these problems, the return trip between the field and home, and the micro and the macro.

Finally, making use of these key concepts, I conclude by putting forward a plan for an anthropology that I feel is already on the verge of renewal. I speak about my imaginations and dreams. Returning to the original spirit of anthropology means hoping for a better future through understanding human culture and society as a whole while taking into account both our common humanity and the uniqueness of separate cultures. Looking back over my own research, up until the eruption of Mount Pinatubo, I made a clear distinction between my own culture and other cultures and between myself and the other. I focused on the differences between the two, trying to understand the other from the inside as a people who live within a fundamentally different world of meaning. Nevertheless, while I looked at their societies from the inside and lived in their villages, the reality was that Japanese society served as the subconscious premise from which I thought about the other. The modernized, Western world served as the ideal to which I compared what I was seeing. With the modernized Japanese and Western societies foremost in my mind, I problematized the differences between myself and the other in terms of a disparity.

However, after the eruption I had a strong sense that in addition to the differences between them and us, we also had much in common. What I realized in Pinatubo and later in Ifugao was that the global system, in which Japan and the Philippines, and the different societies of Pinatubo and Ifugao, are geographically and socially positioned on the periphery, has an enormous influence on all of us and sets the limits within which we live out our lives. Just like us, they think about strategies for improving their own quality of life as individuals with agency within this broader context and, like us, they calculate the risks and the advantages and disadvantages of taking a particular course of action. Today many people decide to go out into the world in search of a better income. When they do so they live amid a different culture and change the way they think about themselves. After the damage caused by the 1991 eruption of Mount Pinatubo, the Pinatubo Aetas began to live in new, permanent housing that was built for them in the region where the majority lowland Christians live. Their way of life changed from that of nomadic swidden cultivators who supplemented their diet by hunting and gathering to workers in factories, construction sites and the informal sector. They experienced the changes that other human societies have undergone during one or two hundred years of industrialization in a period of just ten years and skillfully and flexibly adapted and responded to these changes. From my field site of Kakilingan, two young people have even gone to work in the Middle East as welders. After finishing a one-year TESDA (Technical Education and Skills Development Authority) training course, they worked at a shipyard for the Korean company Hanjin in Subic

Bay for several years and learned the skill of welding. Hanjin came to Subic after the United States naval base withdrew in 1992. This drastic transformation of once shifting-cultivators to factory workers resembles that of the Ifugao village of Hapao in the mountains of northern Luzon that I discuss in detail in this book.

From the perspective of the anthropology of response-ability and from my continuous close contact with the transformations taking place in the field, I can say that in today's world there is no longer such a thing as a self-contained microcosm on the outside of the system that now subsumes the entire globe. This is as true for the Ifugaos or the Aetas as it is for anyone. Like us, they live in the contemporary world and, while they reside in different places that rest upon different histories and cultures, they too are confronting the issues and difficulties, as well as the possibilities, that have been brought about by globalization. They choose not to refuse these changes but to make use of the new opportunities that have become available, riding the wave of globalization and taking a risk by going out into the world to improve their standard of living. As a result, they may sometimes even become our neighbors. Certainly, we are already connected via a network that is made up of any number of different passageways. Our material life is similar and we share a great many common interests and sensibilities. My dream for the young anthropologists of the next generation is for them to be fully conscious of these commonalities, aware of the deep connections that fieldwork creates between anthropologists and the people who live in the field, and to themselves become one of the passageways that connect people while actively responding to their interlocutors in the field. Through this responsive relationship, I hope that they contribute to the construction of an international public sphere (see Shimizu 2015). Of course, it goes without saying that, in doing so, they should maintain a deep understanding and respect for the other and for cultural difference.

Bibliography

References originally in Japanese

Appadurai, Arjun, 1996[2004], *Modernity at Large: Cultural Aspects of Globalization*, Minneapolis, MN: University of Minnesota Press.
Appadurai, Arjun, 2006[2010], *Fear of Small Numbers: An Essay on the Geography of Anger*, Durham, NC: Duke University Press.
Anderson, Benedict, 1983[1997], *Imagined Communities: Reflections on the Origin and Spread of Nationalism*, London: Verso.
Anderson, Benedict, 1992[1993], '"Enkakuji nashonarizumu" no shutsugen' (Long-distance nationalism: world capitalism and the rise of identity politics"), *Sekai*, September.
Anderson, Benedict, 2009, *Yashigara wan no soto e* (Beyond the coconut bowl), translated by Katō Tsuyoshi, NTT Shuppan.
Arendt, Hannah, 1958[1994], *The Human Condition*, Chicago, IL: University of Chicago Press.
Audrerie, Dominique, Raphaël Souchier and Luc Vilar, 2005, *Sekai isan* (World Heritage [orig. Le patrimoine mondial]), translated by Mizushima Eiji, Hakusuisha.
Beck, Ulrich, 2000[2005], *What is Globalization?*, translated by Patrick Camiller, Malden: Polity Press.
Beck, Ulrich, 2002, 'The cosmopolitan society and its enemies', *Theory, Culture and Society*, vol. 19, nos. 1–2.
Chanda, Nayan, 2007[2009], *Bound Together: How Traders, Preachers, Adventurers, and Warriors Shaped Globalization*, New Haven, CT: Yale University Press.
Cinematrix (ed.), 1994, *Niji no arubamu: boku wa ikoreru ki'iro 94* (Why is Yellow at the Middle of the Rainbow?), Cinematrix.
Clifford, James and George E. Marcus, 1986[1996], *Writing Culture: The Poetics and Politics of Ethnography*, Berkeley, CA: University of California Press.
Constantino, Renato, 1975[1978], *The Philippines: A Past Revisited*, Quezon City: Tala Publishing Services.
Coppola, Eleanor, 1979[2002], *Notes: On the Making of Apocalypse Now*, New York, NY: Simon & Schuster.
De Guia, Katrin, 1994, 'Remuria: sore wa kinō no koto?' (Lemuria: yesterday's story?), Cinematrix (ed.), *Nishi no arubamu: boku wa ikoreru kiiro 94* (Why is Yellow at the Middle of the Rainbow?), Cinematrix.
Endō Mizuki, 2002, 'Eizō ni yoru bunka senryaku: Firipin, Hapao mura ni okeru Kidlat Tahimik to Ifugao no jissen ni tsuite' (Cultural strategy through

film: on the praxis of Kidlat Tahimik and the Ifugaos in Hapao, Philippines), *Fukuoka Ajia Taiheiyō Kenkyū Hōkoku* (From Fukuoka: Asia-Pacific Study Reports), vol. 11.

Esteva, Gustavo, 1992[1996], 'Development' in Wolfgang Sachs, *The Development Dictionary: A Guide to Knowledge as Power*, London: Zed.

Friedman, Thomas L., 2006, *The World is Flat: A Brief History of the Twenty-first Century*, New York, NY: Farrar, Strauss and Giroux.

Fuller, R. Buckminster, 1969[2000], *Operating Manual for Spaceship Earth*, New York, NY: Simon and Schuster.

Furuya Yoshiaki, 2001, *Ishu konkō no kindai to jinruigaku: Raten Amerika no kontakuto zōn kara* (Hybrid modernities and anthropology: from the contact zones of Latin America), Jinbun shoin.

Gagarin, Yuri Alekseyevich, 1962[1963], *Road to the Stars*, Moscow: Foreign Languages Publishing House.

Geertz, Clifford, 1973[1987], *The Interpretation of Culture: Selected Essays by Clifford Geertz*, New York, NY: Basic Books.

Geertz, Clifford, 1983[1991], *Local Knowledge: Further Essays in Interpretive Anthropology*, New York, NY: Basic Books.

Giddens, Anthony, 1990[1993], *The Consequences of Modernity*, Stanford, CA: Stanford University Press.

Giddens, Anthony, 1999[2001], *Runaway World: How Globalization is Reshaping Our Lives*, London: Profile Books.

Go, Liza and Jung Yeonghae, 1999, *Watashi to iu tabi: jendā to reishizumu wo koete* (The self as journey: beyond gender and racism), Seidosha.

Gōda Tō, 1998, *Ifugao: Luzon sanchimin no juso to henyō* (Ifugao: sorcery and transformation among the highlanders of Luzon), Kōbundō.

Hamamoto Mitsuru, 2001, *Chitsujo no hōhō: Kenia kaigan chiiki no nichijō seikatsu ni okeru gireiteki jissen to katari* (Methods of constructing discipline: ritual practice and storytelling in everyday life on the Kenyan coast), Kōbundō.

Hamamoto Mitsuru, 2014, *Shinen no jubaku: Keniya kaigan chihō Duruma shakai ni okeru yōjutsu no minzokushi* (Spell of belief: an ethnography of witchcraft in the Duruma society of the Kenyan coast), Kyushu University Press.

Hara Masato, 1994, 'Eiga no jiko zōshoku, sore wa uchū o utsusu yuitsu no kagami' (Self-replicating film: the only mirror that reflects the universe) in Cinematrix (ed.), *Boku wa ikoreru ki'iro 94: niji no arubamu* (Why is Yellow at the Middle of the Rainbow?), Cinematrix.

Hardin, Garrett, 1968, 'The tragedy of the commons,' *Science*, vol. 162, no. 3859.

Harvey, David, 1989[1999], *The Condition of Postmodernity: An Enquiry into the Origins of Cultural Change*, Cambridge: Blackwell.

Hayami Yūjirō, 1995, *Kaihatsu keizai gaku: sho kokumin no hinkon to tomi* (Development economics: the poverty and wealth of nations), Sōbunsha.

Himaru Yoshihiko, 2018, 'Luson-tou hokubu sangakuchitiki Hapao-mura no shuukaku girei: tunahiki *punnok* no fukkastsu' (Harvest rite in Hapao village, northern Luzon: Regeneration of *punnok* tug-of-war), *Himaraya-gaku shi* (Journal of Himalayan Studies), no.20.

Hobsbawm, E. J. and Terence Ranger, 1983[1992], *The Invention of Tradition*, Cambridge: Cambridge University Press.

Ichiki Chiaki, 1999, *Ashin: Kaisō no hitō sen* (Asin: reflections on the war in the Philippines), Waseda sōki.
Ignatieff, Michael, 1998[1997], *The Warrior's Honor: Ethnic War and the Modern Conscience*, New York, NY: Metropolitan Books.
Iida Momo, 1980, 'Gendai teki kyogi ishiki to shite no "Uchūsen chikyū gō"' ('Spaceship Earth' as contemporary false consciousness), *Gijutsu to ningen*, vol. 9, no. 3.
Ikehata Setsuho, 1977, 'Firipin' in Ikehata Setsuho and Ikuta Shigeru, *Tōnan Ajia gendaishi II* (A contemporary history of Southeast Asia), Yamakawa shuppan.
IKGS Reforestation Campaign, 2005, *Ifugao ni mori o* (Planting forests in Ifugao), IKGS Reforestation Campaign.
Ileto, Reynaldo, 1979[2005], *Pasyon and Revolution: Popular Movements in the Philippines, 1840–1910*, Atheno de Manila University Press.
Imaizumi Kōji, 1994, *Firipin, Baguio, Kidlat Tahimik* (The Philippines, Baguio and Kidlat Tahimik), in Cinematrix (ed.), *Niji no arubamu*, Cinematrix.
Imamura Hitoshi, 2004, 'Shigen no gainen' (The concept of a resource) in Uchibori Motomitsu (ed.), *Shigen no bunpai to kyōyū ni kansuru jinruigakuteki tōgō ryōiki no kōchiku* (Distribution and sharing of resources in symbolic and ecological systems: integrative model-building in anthropology), MEXT Grant-in-Aid for Scientific Research on Innovative Areas Interim Report.
Imamura Hitoshi, 'Shigen no gainen' (Resource as a concept), Uchibori Motomitsu (ed.), *Shigen to ningen: shigen jinruigaku* (Resource and man: anthropology of resources), vol. 1, Kōbundō.
Inaga Shigemi, 2001, 'Ibunka rikai no rinri ni mukete' (Towards an ethics of understanding other cultures), Sugishima Takashi (ed.), *Jinruigakuteki jissen no saikōchiku* (Reconstructing anthropological practice), pp. 76–101, Sekai Shisōsha.
Inoue Makoto,1997, 'Komonzu toshiteno nettai-urin' (Tropical forest as commons), *Kankyou Shakaigaku Kenkyuu* (Research on Environmental Sociology), vol. 3.
Inoue Makoto (ed.), 2003, *Ajia ni okeru shinrin no shousitu to hozen* (Extinction and preservation of forests in Asia), Chuuou Houki Shuppan.
Ishi Hiroyuki, 2002, 'Comonzu to chikyū kankyō' (The commons and the global environment) in Sasaki Takeshi and Kim Tea-chang (eds), *Chikyū kankyō to kōkyōsei* (The global environment and the publicness), University of Tokyo Press.
Ishimure Michiko, 2003, *Paradise in the Sea of Sorrow: Our Minamata Disease*, revised edn, translated by Livia Monnet, Ann Arbor, MI: Center for Japanese Studies, University of Michigan.
JICA Hyōgo International Center, 2008, *Firipin kusa no ne gijutsu kyōryoku jigyō (kusa no ne shien gata) 'Aguroforesutorii ni yoru jizoku kanō na ekoshisutemu no kōchiku, sekai isan no Firipin, Ifugao tanada no hozen' monitaringu, hyōka chōsa hōkokusho kusa no ne gijutsu kyōryoku shūryōji hyōka chōsa* (Post implementation evaluation report of a Partnership Program (Support Type) project in the Philippines: constructing a sustainable ecosystem through large-scale reforestation in the World Heritage rice terraces of Hungduan, Ifugao, Philippines (afforestation and agro-forestry)).

JICA Research Insitute (ed.), 2003, *Enjo no chōryū ga wakaru hon* (Understanding trends in aid), Kokusai kyōryoku shuppankai.
Kajiwara Kageaki, 1994, 'Jōzetsu naru jiko tankyū' in Cinematrix (ed.), *Boku wa ikoreru ki'iro 94: niji no arubamu*, Cinematrix.
Kanamaru Toshitaka, 1992, *Sanretsu no hitōsen: jūgunsha no senjō taiken to kokoro no kiroku* (The cruel Battle of the Philippines: a record of the battlefield experiences and reflections of those who served), Kaichōsha.
Kataoka Sachihiko (ed.), 2006, *Shita kara no gurōbarizēshon: 'mō hitotsu no chikyū mura' wa kanō da* (Globalization from below: 'another global village' is possible), Shinhyōron.
Katō Hisatake, 2005a, *Shin-kankyō rinrigaku no susume* (For a new environmental ethics), Maruzen raiburarii.
Katō Hisatake (ed.), 2005b, *Shinban-kankyō to rinri: shizen to ningen no kyōsei o motomete* (New edition, Ethics and the environment: for a symbiotic relationship between the human and the environment), Yūhikaku aruma.
Kikuchi Kyōko, 1974, 'Cognatic shakai ni okeru zokusei to shakai seikatsu: Firipin, Kiangan, Ifugao zoku no chōsa kenkyū o tōshite' (A note on the kinship studies of cognatic society: through the case of the Kiangan Ifugao, Philippines), *Minzokugaku kenkyū*, vol. 38, nos. 3–4.
Kimura Aya, 2006, '"Tengoku e no tanada" nokoseru ka' (Can the 'terraces to heaven' be saved?), *Mainichi Shimbun*, June 13, morning edn, p. 6.
Kimura Hideo, 2007, 'Guchoku na esunogurafii: chosakuken, mukei bunka isan, borantia' (Ingenuous ethnography: patents, the intangible heritage of humanity, and volunteers), *Bunka jinruigaku* (Japanese Journal of Cultural Anthropology), vol. 72, no 3, pp. 383–401.
Koshida Kiyokazu, 1993, 'Jiritsu e no mosaku: jiriki de ikiyō to suru Firipin senjūmin Aeta' (A long way towards self-reliant community – survival power of the indigenous Ayta people of the Philippines), *Hokkaidō Daigaku Kyōikugaku Kiyō* (Bulletin of the Faculty of Education, Hokkaido University), no. 60.
Kubota Sachiko, 2009, 'Joron: fuhensei to sai o meguru poritikkusu: senjūmin no jinruigakuteki kenkyū' (Introduction: the politics of universality and difference: anthropological research on indigenous peoples) in Kubota Sachiko and Nobayashi Atsushi (eds), *'Senjūmin' to wa dare ka* (Who are 'indigenous peoples'?), Sekai shisōsha.
Kudō Ritsuko, 2004, '"Ki o ueru otoko" wa heiwa no dendōshi: Firipin Ifugao-zoku no surō & ecoraifu' ('The man who plants trees' is an evangelist for peace: slow and ecological life among Philippine Ifugao), *Shūkan kinyōbi*, no. 511, June 11.
Kumano Takeshi, 1999a, 'Ifugao zoku no dopappu sumō: Ruzon-tō hokubu ni okeru gireiteki asobi to kyōsō' (Ifugao dopap-wrestling: ritual games and rivalry in northern Luzon mountains), *Supōtsu jinruigaku kenkyū*, vol. 1.
Kumano Takeshi, 1999b, 'Firipin, Ifugao zoku to ishō no bunka' (Clothing and culture among the Ifugao of the Philippines) in Suzuki Seiji and Yamamoto Makoto (eds), *Yosōi no jinruigaku* (The anthropology of dress), Jinbun shoin.
Kumano Takeshi, 2006a, 'Firipin kaigai ijū rōdō no esunogurafii: Ifugao josei to Firipin hanayome no jitsurei o chūshin ni' (An ethnography of Filipino migrant laborers: Ifugao women and Filipino brides), *Kansai daigaku shakaigakubu kiyō* (Bulletin of the Faculty of Sociology of Kansai University), vol. 37, no. 3.

Kumano Takeshi, 2006b, 'Hokubu Luson tō Ifugao zoku no dentōteki shāmanizumu saikō' (A reconsideration of the traditional Ifugao shamanism of northern Luzon), *Kansai daigaku shakaigakubu kiyō* (Bulletin of the Faculty of Sociology of Kansai University), vol. 38, no. 1.

Kumano Takeshi, 2007, 'Ifugao zoku ni okeru nōkō girei to dochakuka shita fiesuta: gireiteki asobi no bunka fukkō wo chūshin ni' (Acculturation on agricultural rites and indigenization of fiesta among the Ifugao people: focused on revitalized ritual plays and sports), *Kansai daigaku shakaigakubu kiyō* (Bulletin of the Faculty of Sociology of Kansai University), vol. 40.

Kurihara Yoshihisa, 1950, *Unmei no Yamashita heidan: Firipin sakusen no jissō* (The fate of the Yamashita corps: the truth about the operation in the Philippines), Rokumeisha.

Majima Ichirō, 2000, 'Rekishi shutai no kōchiku gijutsu to jinruigaku' (Anthropology and the technical construction of historical subjects), *Minzokugaku kenkyū*, vol. 64, no 4.

Masamura Toshiyuki, 2009, *Gurōbarizēshon: gendai wa ikanaru jidai na no ka* (Globalization: what kind of era are we living in?), Yūhikaku.

Masuda Yoshio, 1993, *Mazeran: chikyū o hitotsu ni shita okoto* (Magellan: the man who unified the globe), Hara shobō.

Matsuda Motoji, 2009, *Nichijō jinruigaku sengen: seikatsu sekai no shinsō e/kara* (Manifesto for an anthropology of the everyday: towards/from the depths of the everyday lifeworld), Sekai shisōsha.

Matsushita Kazuo, 1992, '*Uchūsen chikyūgō* kara 20 nen, nani ga kawatta ka' (Twenty years since *Spaceship Earth*, what has changed?', *Chūō kōron*, February.

Matsuura Kōichirō, 2008, *Sekai isan: Yūnesuko jimukyokuchō wa utaeru* (World Heritage: an appeal from the Director-General of UNESCO), Kōdansha.

Meadows, Donella H., 1972, *The Limits to Growth: A Report for the Club of Rome's Project on the Predicament of Mankind*, London: Earth Island Ltd.

Meadows, Donella H., Dennis L. Meadows and Jørgen Randers, 1992, *Beyond the Limits: A Global Collapse or a Sustainable Future*, London: Earthscan Publications.

Meadows, Donella H., Jørgen Randers and Dennis L. Meadows, 2004[2005], *The Limits to Growth: The 30-Year Update*, White River Junction, VT: Chelsea Green Publishing.

Miyazawa Masashi, 2000, 'Uchūsen, chikyūgō no haibunteki seigi: yūgen na chikyū no kankyō rinri o kangaeru' (The distributive legitimacy of Spaceship Earth: thinking about environmental ethics in a finite world), *Risen*, no. 63.

Moriyama Takumi, 2007, 'Bunka shigen shiyō hō' (The utilization of cultural resources) in Yamashita Shinji (ed.), *Shigenka suru bunka* (Mobilizing culture), Kōbundō.

Morris-Suzuki, Tessa, 2000, *Henkyō kara nagameru: Ainu ga keiken suru kindai* (The view from the periphery: the Ainu experience of modernity), Misuzu shobō.

Murao Kunio, 1992, *Hitō kessen: Makkāsā jōriku to hiun no shōgun Yamashita Tomoyuki* (The decisive battle in the Philippines: Macarthur's landing and General Yamashita Tomoyuki's doom), Futtowāku shuppansha.

Muratake Sei'ichi, 1967, 'Cognatic shakai ni okeru "ie" no seisei: Firipin shoshuzoku o chūshin ni' (The formation of 'the family' in cognatic societies: the case of the ethnic tribes of the Philippines), *Sha*, vol. 1, no. 1.

Mutō Akira, 1952, *Hitō kara Sugamo e* (From the Philippines to Sugamo prison), Jitsugyō no Nihonsha.
Mutō Akira, 1981, *Gunmukyokuchō Mutō Akira kaisōroku* (Memoirs of Mutō Akira, director of the Military Affairs Bureau), edited by Jōhō Yoshio, Fuyō shobō.
Nagafuchi Yasuyuki, 1998, *Bari tō* (Bali), Kōdansha gendai shinsho.
Nagasaka Itaru, 2009, *Kokkyō o koeru Firipin murabito no minzokushi: toransunashonarizumu no jinruigaku* (An ethnography of Filipino villagers who cross borders: the anthropology of transnationalism), Akashi Shoten.
Nagata Shin, Inoue Makoto and Oka Hiroyasu, 1994, *Shinrin shigen no riyō to saisei* (The utilization and regeneration of forest resources), Rural Culture Association of Japan.
Nakagawa Gō, 1986, *Fushigi no Firipin: hikindai shakai no shinri to kōdō* (The mysterious Philippines: the psychology of a non-modern society), Nippon Hōsō shuppankyōkai.
Nakamura Tetsu, 2003, *Henkyō de miru henkyō kara miru* (Medical caring at the periphery, looking from the periphery), Seifūsha.
Nakano Satoshi, 2005, 'Firipin ga mita sengo Nihon: wakai to bōkyaku' (Postwar Japan as seen from the Philippines: reconciliation and forgetting), *Shisō*, no. 980, December.
Nishimura Mari, 2001, 'ODA to NGO no setten: seinen kaigai kyōryoku tai (JOCV) tai'in no katsudō ni taisuru Pinatubo kyūen no kai kara no enjo o megutte' (Where ODA and NGOs meet: on the support provided to JOCV volunteers by the Pinatubo support group) in Tsuda Mamoru and Tamaki Matsuo (eds), *Shizen saigai to kokusai kyōryoku: Firipin Pinatubo dai funka to Nihon* (Natural disasters and international collaboration: Japan the great eruption of Mount Pinatubo), Shinhyōron.
Noma Haruo, 2008, 'Firipin, Coruderēra sanmyaku no tanada to isan tsūrizumu no kadai: sekai bunka isan to shite no bunka keikan to chiiki shakai' (Rice terraces of the Philippine Cordilleras and some issues of heritage tourism: cultural landscape as World Cultural Heritage and the local community), *Tōzai gakujutsu kenkyūjo kiyō* (Kansai University), vol. 41.
Nomura Susumu, 1981, *Firipin shinjinmin jūgun ki* (With the Philippine New People's Army), Banseisha.
Noro Kuninobu, 2002, *Sensō bungaku shiron* (An essay on war literature), Fuyō shobō shuppan.
Nozawa Katsumi, 2004, 'Firipin no tabako sangyō' (The Philippine tobacco industry), *Kokusai kankei kiyō*, vol. 14, no. 1.
Ōe Kenzaburō, 2001, *An Echo of Heaven*, translated by Margaret Mitsutani, Tokyo: Kodansha International.
Ogawa Tetsurō, 1978, *Terraced Hell: A Japanese Memoir of Defeat and Death in Northern Luzon, Philippines*, Rutland, VT: C.E. Tuttle.
Okada Umeko, 1980, 'Ashin no midori yo, arigatō' (Forests of Asin, thank you), in Okada Umeko and Niimi Aya, *Luzon ni kieta hoshi: shūmatsu wo mita onna futari no kaisōki* (The stars that went out in Luzon: the memoirs of two women who saw the terminus), Mainichi shimbunsha.
Ōkouchi Fukyū, 1991, *'Oniheidan' Luson ni chiru* (The fall of the 'Devil Corps' in Luzon), Kōjinsha.

Ōoka Shōhei, 1971, *Reite senki* (An account of the Battle of Leyte), 3 vols, Chūōbunko.
Osawa Bungo, 2006, 'Raifusutairu shōmetsu no kiki' (The danger of lifestyles disappearing), *Mainichi Shimbun*, January 9, morning edn, p. 9.
Ōta Yoshinobu, 1998, *Toransu-pojishon no shisō: bunka jinruigaku no sai sōzō* (On trans-position: recreating cultural anthropology), Sekai shisōsha.
Peacock, James L., 2004, *The Anthropological Lens: Harsh Light, Soft Focus*, second edn, Cambridge: Cambridge University Press.
Reid, Anthony, 1988[2002], *Southeast Asia in the Age of Commerce, 1450–1680*, vol. 1, New Haven, CT: Yale University Press.
Ritzer, George, 1996[1999], *The Mcdonaldization of society*, New Century edn, Thousand Oaks, CA: Pine Forge Press.
Robertson, Roland, 1992[1997], *Globalization: Social Theory and Global Culture*, London: Sage Publications.
Sachs, Wolfgang, 1999[2003], *Planet Dialectics: Explorations in Environment and Development*, London: Zed Books.
Said, Edward, 1978[1986], *Orientalism*, London: Routledge & Kegan Paul.
Sano Shin'ichi, 1998, *Karisuma: Nakauchi Isao to Daiē no 'sengo'* (Charisma: Nakauchi Isao and Daiei in the postwar), Nikkei BP sha.
Sano Shin'ichi, 2005, 'Kakumeiji Nakanishi Tsutomu no saigo no hibi' (The last days of the revolutionary Nakanishi Tsutomu), *Bungei shunjū*, November.
Sekimoto Teruo, 1994, 'Joron' (Introduction) in Sekimoto Teruo and Funabiki Takeo (eds), *Kokumin bunka ga umareru toki: Ajia-taiheiyō no gendai to sono dentō* (The birth of national culture: contemporaneity and tradition in the Asia-Pacific), Riburopāto.
Sekimoto Teruo, 1998a, 'Fiirudowāku no ninshiki ron' (The epistemology of fieldwork) in Itō Mikiharu and Yoneyama Toshinao (eds), *Bunka jinruigaku e no apurōchi* (The cultural anthropology approach), Mineruva Shobō.
Sekimoto Teruo, 1998b, 'Bunka gainen no yōhō to kōka' (The usage and effectiveness of the concept of culture) in Aoki Tamotsu et al. (eds), *Iwanami kōza bunka jinruigaku vol. 13: bunka to iu kadai* (Iwanami lectures on cultural anthropology, vol. 13, the issue of culture), Iwanami shoten.
Sekine Hisao, 'Jinruigakuteki fiirudo wāku to wa nani ka' (What is anthropological fieldwork?'), *Bunka jinruigaku* (Japanese Journal of Cultural Anthropology), vol. 72, no. 3.
Shimizu Akitoshi, 1998, 'Hajime ni' (Preface) in Shimizu Akitoshi (ed.), *Shūhen minzoku no genzai* (Peripheral ethnicities today), Sekai shisōsha.
Shimizu Akitoshi, 2008a, 'Senjūmin to "kokumin no rekishi" no tame no joron' (Introduction to indigenous peoples and the 'history of nation'), *Bunka jinruigaku* (Japanese Journal of Cultural Anthropology), vol. 73, no. 3.
Shimizu Akitoshi, 2008b, 'Senjūmin, shokuminchi shihai, datsu shokuminchika: kokusai rengō senjūmin kenri sengen to kokusai hō' (Indigenous peoples, colonialism and 'decolonization': The United Nations Declaration on the Rights of Indigenous Peoples in International Law), *Kokuritsu minzokugaku hakubutsukan kenkyū hōkoku* (Bulletin of the National Museum of Ethnology), vol. 32, no. 3.
Shimizu Hiromu, 1991, *Bunka no naka no seiji: Firipin 'nigatsu kakumei' no*

monogatari (Politics in culture: the story of the 'February Revolution' in the Philippines), Kōbundō.

Shimizu, Hiromu, 1997, 'Kaihatsu no Juyō to bunka no henka: gendai o ikiru senjūmin no ibasho' (The reception of development and the transformation of culture: the place of indigenous peoples in the modern world) in Kawada Junzō et al. (eds), *Kōza: kaihatsu to bunka* (Lectures on development and culture), vol. 1, Iwanami Shoten.

Shimizu Hiromu, 1998a, 'Rōkaru de gurōbaru ni ikiru koto: Ifugao no mura no shokurin, kankyō hozen undō' (Living globally in the local: the reforestation and environmental protection movement in Ifugao), *Crossover* (Kyushu University), no. 8.

Shimizu Hiromu, 1998b, 'Mirai e kaiki suru kokka: Firipin bunka no katarikata, egakikata o megutte' (Back to the future way of nation building: the narration and portrayal of Philippine culture), *Ritsumeikan gengo bunka kenkyū*, vol. 9, no. 3.

Shimizu, Hiromu, 1999, 'Bunka no jikaku to imi fuyo no jissen' (Cultural awareness and the praxis of meaning making), *Museum Kyushu*, No. 65.

Shimizu Hiromu, 2002, 'Ifugao, Hapao mura ni okeru shokurin, kankyō hozen, bunka fukkō no undō' (The reforestation, environmental protection and cultural revival movement in Hapao, Ifugao) in Shimizu Hiromu (ed.), *Kankyō hozen no hōto: Firipin ni okeru NGO to komyuniti no yakuwari, kanōsei*, Final Report of Research Group 9, JSPS Research for the Future Program Integrated Research Project: Ajia no kankyō hozen (Environmental protection in Asia), 'Firipin ni okeru daitoshi chi'iki oyobi chihōbu no seibi, kaihatsu, hozen ni kansuru kenkyū' (Impact analysis of metropolitan policies for development environmental conservation in the Philippines).

Shimizu Hiromu, 2003, *Funka no kodama: Pinatubo, Aeta no hisai to shinsei o meguru bunka, kaihatsu, NGO* (Echoes of the eruption: culture, development and NGOs in the Aeta experience of the disaster and recovery after the eruption of Mount Pinatubo), Kyushu University Press.

Shimizu Hiromu, 2006, 'Rekishi wo fumaete mirai wo hiraku kokusai kyōryoku: hokubu Ruson senjūmin Ifugao no mura to Tamba no chiisana NGO wo tsunagu kusa no ne no kōryū' (International cooperation that opens the future with a foundation in the past: grassroots exchange between an Ifugao village in northern Luzon and a small NGO in Tamba), *Ryūkoku Daigaku kokusai shakai bunka kenkyūjo kiyō*, no. 8.

Shimizu Hiromu, 2007a, 'Gurōbaru ka jidai ni inaka ga susumeru chiiki okoshi: hokubu Ruson sanson to Tamba Sannan chō wo tsunagu kusa no ne kōryū, shokurin, kaihatsu no torikumi' (Regional revitalization from the countryside in the era of globalization: a grassroots reforestation and development initiative connecting a mountain village in northern Luzon with Sannan, Tamba) in Katō Tsuyoshi (ed.), *Kokkyō wo koeta mura okoshi: Nihon to tōnan Ajia wo tsunagu* (Village revitalization that crosses borders: connecting Japan with Southeast Asia), NTT shuppan.

Shimizu Hiromu, 2007b, 'Bunka wo shigenka suru imi fuyo no jissen: Firipin senjūmin Ifugao no mura ni okeru shokurin undō to jiko hyōshō' (Meaning-making practices that mobilize culture: self-representation and reforestation

in an indigenous Ifugao village in the Philippines) in Yamashita Shinji (ed.), *Shigenka suru bunka* (Mobilizing culture), Kōbundō.
Shimizu Hiromu, 2007c, 'Henkyō kara chūshin wo utsu tsubute: Afuganisutan nanmin no seizon o shien suru Nakamura ishi to Peshwāru kai no jissen' (Throwing stones at the center from the periphery: Dr Nakamura and the Peshawar Society's work to save the Afghan refugees) in Matsumoto Tsunehiko and Ōshima Akihide (eds), *'Kyūshū' to iu shisō: Kyūshū sutadiizu no kokoromi* (Kyushu as a place for alternative thought: towards Kyushu studies), Hana shoin.
Shimizu Hiromu, 2010a, 'Gurōbaruka jidai no chiiki nettowāku no saihen: enkakuchi kankyō shugi no kanōsei' (Regional networks in the era of globalization: the potential of a remote environmentalism) in Sugihara Kaoru, Kawai Shūichi and Kōno Yasuyuki (eds), *Chikyū ken, seimei ken, ningen ken: jizokuteki na seizon kiban o motomete* (Earth-sphere, life-sphere, human-sphere: for a sustainable basis for survival), Kyoto University Press.
Shimizu Hiromu, 2010b, 'Sekai isan no tanada mura ni okeru gurōbaru jidai no kaihatsu: Firipin, Ifugao senjūmin no shokurin undō to kokusai kyōryoku' (Development in the era of globalization in a village in the World Heritage rice terraces: the reforestation movement and international cooperation amongst the indigenous Ifugaos) in Nagatsu Kazufumi and Katō Tsuyoshi (eds), *Kaihatsu no shakaishi* (A social history of development), Fūkyōsha.
Shimizu Hiromu, 2011, 'Amerika no jiba no naka no jikokeisei: Yamaguchi Momoe to Koizumi Jun'ichirō wo tōshite miru Yokosuka to sengo Nihon no nejire' (Self-formation in America's magnetic field: Yokosuka and Japan's distorted postwar through the lives of Yamaguchi Momoe and Koizumi Jun'ichirō) in Fujiwara Kiichi and Nagano Yoshiko, *Amerika no kage no motode: Nihon to Firipin* (The Philippines and Japan in America's shadow), Hosei University Press.
Shimizu Hiromu and Kimura Shūhei (eds), 2015, *Atarashii ningen, atarashii shakai: Fukkō no monogatari o saisōzō suru* (A new human, a new society: recreating the narrative of reconstruction), Kyoto University Press.
Shishikura Kimirō, 1980, *Zoku Ifugao no bohyō* (The graves of Ifugao, part 2), Ikuei insatsu kōgyō.
Shrader-Frechette, K.S., 1981[1993], *Environmental Ethics*, Pacific Grove, CA: Boxwood Press.
Steger, Manfred, 2003[2005], *Globalization: A Very Short Introduction*, Oxford: Oxford University Press.
Stewart, Henry, 2009, 'Senjūmin no rekishi to genjō' (Indigenous peoples past and present) in Kubota Sachiko and Nobayashi Atsushi (eds), *'Senjūmin' to wa dare ka* (Who are 'indigenous peoples'?), Sekai shisōsha.
Sugawara Kazuyoshi, 2015, *Kari karareru keiken no genshōgaku: Busshman no kannō to henshin* (A phenomenology of the experience of hunting and being hunted: inspiration and transformation among the Bushmen), Kyoto University Press.
Sugishima Takashi, 1995, 'Jinruigaku ni okeru riarizumu no shūen' (The end of realism in anthropology) in Goda Tō and Ōtsuka Kazuo (eds), *Minzokushi no genzai* (Ethnography today), pp. 195–212, Kōbundō.
Sugishima Takashi, 2001, *Jinruigakuteki jissen no saikōchiku: posutokoroniaru*

tenkai ikō (Reconstructing anthropological practice: after the postcolonial turn), Sekai shisōsha.
Sugishima Takashi (ed.), 2014, *Fuku gēmu jōkyō no jinruigaku: tōnan ajia ni okeru kōsō to jissen* (Anthropology in plural-games situation: ideas and practices in Southeast Asia), Fūkyōsha.
Suzuki Shizuo, 1997, *Monogatari Firipin no rekishi* (Philippine history as a narrative), Chūkō shinsho.
Takagi Toshirō, 1985, *Luson senki: Bangetto michi* (Record of the war in Luzon: Benguet Road), Bungeishunjū.
Takaki Keiko, 1998, 'Review of Gōda Tō, *Ifugao: Luzon sanchimin no juso to henyō* (Ifugao: sorcery and transformation among the highlanders of Luzon)', *Minzokugaku kenkyū*, vol. 63, no. 1.
Tanaka Masakazu, 2007, 'Kontakuto zōn no bunka jinruigaku e: Teikoku no manazashi wo yomu' (Towards a cultural anthropology of the contact zone: reading 'the imperial gaze'), *Contact Zone*, no. 1.
Thompson, E.P., 1963[2003], *The Making of the English Working Class*, London: Gollancz.
Todd, Emmanuel, 2003, *After the Empire: The Breakdown of the American Order*, translated by C. Jon Delogu, New York, NY: Columbia University Press.
Tokoro Ikuya, 1999, *Ekkyō: Sūrū kai'iki sekai kara* (Crossing borders: from the Sulu Sea), Iwanami shoten.
Tomita Kazuya, 2008, *Kusa no ne gijutsu kyōryoku pātonā gata: Ifugao shū no kusa no ne empawāmento o tōshita seikei kōjō ni yoru kankyō hozen* (Final project report for Partnership Program (Partner Type) 'Environmental protection by improving livelihood through grassroots empowerment in Ifugao Province'), IKGS (mimeo).
Tomlinson, John, 1999[2000], *Globalization and Culture*, Oxford: Polity.
Tomita, Eriko, 2013, *Filipin no chiisana san-in kara* (From a little maternity clinic in the Philippines), Sekifu-sha.
Tsuchiya Naotoshi (ed.), 1965, *Yama yukaba kusa musu kabane: hitō ni sangeshita dōhō 476,000 no izoku ni sasagu* (In the mountains, the corpses are covered in grass: an offering to the families of our 476,000 fallen countrymen in the Philippines), self-published.
Tsugawa Hyōe, 2001, 'Yomigaere, midori no Pintubo' (Revegetate Pinatubo) in Tsuda Mamoru and Tamaki Matsuo (eds), *Shizen saigai to kokusai kyōryoku: Firipin Pinatubo dai funka to Nihon* (Natural disasters and international collaboration: Japan and the great eruption of Mount Pinatubo), Shinhyōron.
Tylor, Edward B., 1871[1962], *Primitive Culture: Researches into the Development of Mythology, Philosophy, Religion, Art, and Custom*, vol. 1, London: John Murray.
Uchibori Motomitsu, 2004, 'Shigen to iu genshō e mukete: jinruigaku kara no sekkin' (On the phenomena known as a resource: approaches from anthropology) in *Shigen no bunpai to kyōyū ni kansuru jinruigakuteki tōgō ryōiki no kōchiku* (Distribution and sharing of resources in symbolic and ecological systems: integrative model-building in anthropology), MEXT Grant-in-Aid for Scientific Research on Innovative Areas Interim Report.
Uchibori Motomitsu, 2007, 'Jo: shigen o meguru mondai gun no kōsei' (Foreword: the structure of the problems pertaining to resources) in Uchibori Motomitsu

(ed.), *Shigen to ningen: shigen jinruigaku* (Anthropology of resources), vol. 1, Kōbundō.
Uchibori Motomitsu, 2009, "Senjūmin' no tanjō: Indigenous People(s) no yakugo o meguru parodikaru shiron' (On the birth of 'senjūmin': a parodical essay on the translation word for indigenous people(s)) in Kubota Sachiko and Nobayashi Atsushi (eds), *'Senjūmin' to wa dare ka* (Who are 'indigenous peoples'?), Sekai shisōsha.
Uzawa Hirofumi, 2002, 'Chikyū ondanka to rinri' (Ethics and global warming) in Sasaki Takeshi and Kim Tea-chang (eds.), *Chikyū kankyō to kōkyōsei* (The global environment and the commons), Tokyo University Press.
Wallerstein, Immanuel, 1974[1981], *The Modern World System: Capitalist Agriculture and the Origins of the European World-Economy in the Sixteenth Century*, New York, NY: Academic Press.
War History Office, 1970, *Shōgō rikugun sakusen vol. 1, Reite kessen* (The Army's Operation Shōgō vol. 1 The Battle of Leyte), Asagumo Shimbunsha.
War History Office, 1972, *Shōgō rikugun sakusen vol. 2, hokubu Ruson sen* (The Army's Operation Shōgō vol. 2 The war in northern Luzon), Asagumo Shimbunsha.
Watson, James L. (ed.), 1997[2003], *Golden Arches East: McDonald's in East Asia*, Stanford, CA: Stanford University Press.
World Commission on Environment and Development (ed.), 1987, *Our Common Future*, Oxford: Oxford University Press.
Yamaguchi Masayuki, 1979, 'Rōma Kurabu e no hōkoku: Uchūsen chikyūgō no mirai no tame no senryaku' (Report to the Club of Rome: a strategy for the future of Spaceship Earth), *Kikan kagaku to shisō*, no. 31.
Yamashita Michiko, 2001, 2002, 'Firipin jin aidentitii no mosaku to kōchiku: eiga kantoku Kidoratto Tahimikku no bunka senryaku, parts 1 & 2' (The search for and construction of Filipino identity: director Kidlat Tahimik's culture strategy', *Tōkyō gaikokugo daigaku ronshū*, vols. 62 & 63.
Yamashita Shinji, 2007, 'Jo: shigenka suru bunka' (Foreword: mobilizing culture) in Yamashita Shinji (ed.), *Shigenka suru bunka* (Mobilizing culture), Kōbundō.
Yamashita Shinji, 2014, *Kōkyō jinruigaku* (Anthropology of the commons), Tokyo University Press.
Yamawaki Naoshi, 2008, *Gurōkaru kōkyō tetsugaku: 'kasshikaikō' no vishon no tame ni* (Global public philosophy), Tokyo University Press.
Yomota Inuhiko, 1993, *Denei fūun* (The state of film), Hakusuisha.
Yomota Inuhiko and Ōmori Yasuhiro, 2000, 'Tokubetsu taidan: toru koto to, miru koto no eizō taiken' (Special dialogue: filming and watching as cinematic experience', *Gekkan minpaku*, vol. 24, no. 10.

References originally in English and Filipino

Aginaya and Kidlat Tahimik, 2004, *Guardians of the Enchanted Forest*, Snannancho, Hyogo: IKGS Reforestation Campaign.
Aginaya and Kidlat Tahimik, 2004, *Ang Bantay ng Mahiwagang Gubat*, Baguio: Bale Taku Publishers.
Aguilar, Filomeno V. Jr. (ed.), 2002, *Filipinos in Global Migrations: At Home in the World?*, Quezon City: Philippine Migration Research Network and Philippine Social Science Council.
Ananayo, Jovel Francis, 1999, Insurgency and Counter Insurgency Movements: The Changes it Brought in the Socio-economic and Political Conditions in Hungduan (1960s to 1990s), a thesis presented to the Division of Social Sciences, University of the Philippines College of Baguio.
Appadurai, Arjun, 2001, 'Grassroots globalization and the research imagination,' Arjun Appadurai (ed.), *Globalization*, Durham, NC: Duke University Press.
Barton, R.F., 1962[1946], *The Religion of the Ifugaos*, New York, NY: Kraus Reprint.
Barton, R.F., 1969[1919], *Ifugao Law*, Berkeley: University of California Press.
Barton, R.F., 1979[1938], *Philippine Pagans: The Autobiographies of Three Ifugaos*, New York, NY: AMS Press.
Bonner, Raymond, 1987, *Waltzing with a Dictator: The Marcoses and the Making of American Policy*, New York: Times Books.
Bonus, Rick, 2000, *Locating Filipino Americans: Ethnicity & Cultural Politics of Space*, Philadelphia, PA: Temple University Press.
Borofsky, Robert, 2007, 'Defining public anthropology' in *Blog*, posted by Dr. Robert Borofsky, May 11, 2011, <http://www.publicanthropology.org/public-anthropology/>.
Boulding, Kenneth E., 1966, 'The economics of the Coming Spaceship Earth' in H. Jarrett (ed.), *Environmental Quality in a Growing Economy*, Baltimore, MD: Resources for the Future/Johns Hopkins University Press.
Brosius, Peter, 1999, 'Analyses and interventions: anthropological engagements with environmentalism,' *Current Anthropology*, vol. 40, no. 3.
Brosius, Peter, A. Tsing and C. Zerner, 1998, 'Representing communities: histories and politics of community-based natural resource management,' *Society and Natural Resources*, vol. 11.
Campos, Patrick, 2009, 'A portrait of Kidlat Tahimik, father of Filipino Indie Cinema', College of Mass Communication, U.P. Gawad Plaridel.
Castells, Manuel, 2001, *The Internet Galaxy: Reflections on the Internet, Business, and Society*, Oxford University Press.
Chapman, William, 1987, *Inside the Philippine Revolution: The New People's Army and its Struggle for Power*, New York, NY: W.W. Norton & Company.
Choy, Catherine Ceniza, 2003, *Empire of Care: Nursing and Migration in Filipino American History*, Durham, NC, and London: Duke University Press.
Clifford, James, 1988, *The Predicament of Culture: Twentieth-century Ethnography, Literature, and Art*, Cambridge, MA: Harvard University Press.
Conklin, Beth and Laura Graham, 1995, 'The shifting middle ground: Amazonian Indians and eco-politics,' *American Anthropologist*, vol. 97, no. 4.

Conklin, Harold, 1968, *Ifugao Bibliography*, Department of Anthropology and the Council on Southeast Asia Studies, Yale University

Conklin, Harold, 1980, *Ethnographic Atlas of Ifugao: A Study of Environment, Culture, and Society in Northern Luzon*, New Haven, CT: Yale University Press.

Constable, Nicole, 1997, *Maid to Order in Hong Kong: Stories of Filipina Workers*, Ithaca, NY: Cornell University Press.

De Guia, Katrin, 1997, Filipino Artists as Culture Bearers: Lifestyle and Worldviews of Some Contemporary Filipino Artists, Ph.D., University of the Philippines.

De Guia, Katrin, 2005, *Kapwa, the Self in the Other: Worldviews and Lifestyles of Filipino Culture-Bearers*, Pasig City: Anvil Publication.

De Jesus, Ed C., 1980, *The Tobacco Monopoly in the Philippines: Bureaucratic Enterprise and Social Change, 1766–1880*, Quezon City: Ateneo de Manila University Press.

Delgado-Yulo, Karla, 1998, 'The city of her dreams: Virginia Ortega de Guia', *Sunday Inquirer Magazine*, August 30.

Demetillo, Marilou, 1997, 'Smile, you're on "bamboo" camera,' *Manila Chronicle*, October 5 (*The Sunday Chronicle*), p. 23.

Dulawan, Lourdes, 2001, *Ifugao: Culture and History*, Manila: National Commission for Culture and Arts.

Dulawan, Manuel B., 2005, *Oral Literature of the Ifugao*, Manila: National Commission for Culture and Arts.

Dumia, Mariano, 1979, *The Ifugao World*, Quezon City: New Day Publishers.

Edelman, Marc and Angelique Haugerud (eds), 2005, *The Anthropology of Development and Globalization: From Classical Political Economy to Contemporary Neoliberalism*, Oxford: Blackwell Publishers.

Eder, James 1982, 'No water in the terraces: agricultural stagnation and social change at Banaue, Ifugao', *Philippine Quarterly of Culture & Society*, no. 10.

Enriquez, Virgilio G., 1989, *Indigenous Psychology and National Consciousness*, Tokyo: Institute for the Study of Languages and Cultures of Asia and Africa.

Enriquez, Virgilio G. (ed.), 1990, *Indigenous Psychology: A Book of Readings*, Quezon City: Philippine Psychology Research and Training House.

Enriquez, Virgilio G., 1992, *From Colonial to Liberation Psychology: The Philippine Experience*, Quezon City: University of the Philippines Press.

Enslin, Elizabeth, 1994, 'Beyond writing: feminist practice and the limitations of ethnography', *Cultural Anthropology*, vol. 9, no. 4.

Espiritu, Yen Le, 2003, *Home Bound: Filipino American Lives Across Culture, Communities, and Countries*, Berkeley, CA: University of California Press.

Fernandez, Doreen, 1996, *Palabas: Essays on Philippine Theater History*, Quezon City: Ateneo de Manila University Press.

Ganguli, Barin, 1995, *Breakthroughs in Forestry Development: Experience of the Asian Development Bank*, Manila: Asian Development Bank.

Gatmaytan, Gus, 1992, 'Land rights and land tenure situation of indigenous peoples in the Philippines', *Philippine Natural Resources Law Journal*, vol. 5, no. 1, pp. 5–41.

Geertz, Clifford, 1973, 'Deep play' in *The Interpretation of Cultures: Selected Essays*, New York, NY: Basic Books.

Giddens, Anthony, 1990, *The Consequences of Modernity*, Stanford, CA: Stanford University Press.
Gonzalez, Rhodora, 2000, Platforms and Terraces: Bridging Participation and GIS in Joint-learning for Watershed Management with the Ifugao of the Philippines, Ph.D., Wageningen University.
Hardin, Garrett 1974, 'Lifeboat ethics: the case against helping the poor', *Psychology Today*, September.
Harper, Bambi, 2003, 'Who was Enrique de Malacca? I II', *Philippine Daily Inquirer*, March 15 and 18.
Hale, Charles, 1997, 'Cultural politics of identity in Latin America', *Annual Review of Anthropology*, vol. 26.
Hall, Ronald E., 2001, *Filipina Eurogamy: Skin Color as Vehicle of Psychological Colonization*, Quezon City: Giraffe Book.
Hall Thomas D. and James Fenelon, 2009, *Indigenous Peoples and Globalization: Resistance and Revitalization*, Boulder, CO: Paradigm Publishers.
Hayama, Atsuko, 2002, *Forest Management by Local People under Changing Circumstances in Northern Philippines* (research paper submitted to JSPS Manila Project Group9).
Hilhorst, Dorothea, 2000, Records and Reputations: Everyday Politics of a Philippine Development NGO, Ph.D. thesis, Wageningen University.
Hilhorst, Dorothea, 2003, The Real World of NGOs: Discourses, Diversity, and Development, Quezon City: Ateneo de Manila University.
Hobsbawm, Eric and Terence Ranger (eds), 1983, *The Invention of Tradition*, Cambridge: Cambridge University Press.
Ileto, Reynaldo, 1993, 'The "unfinished revolution" in Philippine political discourse', *Southeast Asian Studies*, vol. 31, no.1.
Inda, Jonathan Xavier and Renato Rosaldo, 2008, 'Introduction: a world in motion', Inda, J.X. and R. Rosaldo (eds), *The Anthropology of Globalization: A Reader*, Oxford: Blackwell Publishers.
Jameson, Fredric, 1992, *The Geopolitical Aesthetic: Cinema and Space in the World System*, Bloomington, IN: Indiana University Press.
Jenista, Frank, 1987, *The White Apos: American Governors of the Cordillera Central*, Quezon City: New Day Publishers.
Keesing, Felix M. 1962, *The Ethnohistory of Northern Luzon*, Stanford, CA: Stanford University Press.
Keesing, Roger, 1989, 'Creating the past: custom and identity in the contemporary Pacific,' *The Contemporary Pacific*, vol. 1, no. 1–2.
Kerkvliet, Benedict J., 1977, *The Huk Rebellion: A Study of Peasant Revolt in the Philippines*, Berkeley, CA: University of California Press.
Kidlat Tahimik, 1986, 'Cups-of gas filmmaking vs. full tank-cum-credit card fillmaking: the challenge of Third World culture,' paper read at Duke University, North Carolina, September 29.
Kidlat Tahimik, 1997, 'Midlife choices: filmmaking vs. fillmaking' in Lorna Kalaw-Tirol (ed.), *Primed for Life: Writings on Midlife by 18 Men*, Anvil Publishing.
Kidlat Tahimik, 1999, 'The View from the San Juan Bridge: Notes ni Direk galing

sa frontlines ng Filipino-American War', *Philippine Daily Inquirer*, February 16, p.16 & February 23.
Kwiatkowski, Lynn, 1998, *Struggling with Development: The Politics of Hunger and Gender in the Philippines*, Boulder, CO: Westview Press.
Lacbawan, Isabel, 1999, *The 1999 Tungoh ad Hungduan: Terminal Report*, submitted to the National Commission for Culture and the Arts.
Lambrecht, Francis, 1932–1957, 'The Mayawyaw Ritual, 1-7', *Publications of the Catholic Anthropological Conference*, Part 1–5, Vol. IV, No.1–5, 1932–1941, *University of Manila Journal of East Asiatic Studies*, Par 6 & 7, Vol. IV & V, 1955–1957.
Leprozo, Dave Jr., 2003, 'Ifugao's *Imbayah* festival', *Sun Star*, Baguio, May 11.
Malinowski, Bronislaw, 1984[1922], *Argonauts of the Western Pacific*, Prospect Heights, IL: Waveland Press Inc.
Milgram, B. Lynne, 1997, Crossover, Continuity and Change: Women's Production and Marketing of Crafts in the Upland Philippines, Ph.D. dissertation, York University.
Medin, Douglas, N. Ross and D. Cox, 2006, *Culture and Resource Conflict: Why Meanings Matter*, New York, NY: Russell Sage Foundation.
Medina, Carlos, 2001, *106 Ifugao Abu'wab Tales Documented by Frans Lambrecht, C.I.C.M. from 1932 to 1957*, Baguio City: Saint Louis University Cordillera Research and Development Foundation.
Medina, Carlos, 2002a, *Toward Understanding Bu'gan ya Wi'gan ad Chu-li'gan*, Baguio City: Saint Louis University Cordillera Research and Development Foundation.
Medina, Carlos, 2002b, *Six Ifugao Abuwab Tales*, Baguio City: Saint Louis University Cordillera Research and Development Foundation.
Medina, Carlos, 2003, *Understanding the Ifugao Rice Terraces*, Baguio City: Saint Louis University Cordillera Research and Development Foundation.
Mojares, Resil, 1985, *Theater in Society, Society in Theater*, Quezon City: Ateneo de Manila University Press.
Nakake, Rowena, 1997, Change in Traditional Farming Practices and its Effects on Socio-Economic Conditions in Hapao, Hungduan, Ifugao, Bachelor's thesis submitted to the University of the Philippines College, Baguio.
Newell, Len, 2007, *Headhunters' Encounter with God: An Ifugao Adventure*, Lincoln: iUniverse.
Numazaki Ichiro, 2012, 'Too wide, too big, too complicated to comprehend: a personal reflection on the disaster that started on March 11', *Asian Anthropology*, vol. 11.
Orient Integrated Development Consultants Inc., 1994, *The Six-year Master Plan (1995 to 2001) for the Restoration and Preservation of the Ifugao Rice Terraces*, Manila: Ifugao Terraces Commission, Office of the President of the Philippines.
Ostrom, Elinor, 1990, *Governing the Commons: The Evolution of Institutions for Collective Action*, Cambridge University Press.
Parrenas, Rhacel Slazar, 2001, *Servants of Globalization: Women, Migration and Domestic Work*, Stanford, CA: Stanford University Press.
Parrenas, Rhacel Slazar, 2005, *Children of Global Migration: Transnational Families and Gendered Woes*, Palo Alto, CA: Stanford University Press.

Poffenberger, Mark, 1990, 'Introduction: the forest management crisis' in M. Poffenberger (ed.), *Keepers of the Forest: Land Management Alternatives in Southeast Asia*, Quezon City: Ateneo de Manila University.

Pogeyed, Manuel, 1999, 'Indigenous forest management systems in the Cordellera Administrative Region, Philippines', a paper presented during the Regional Watershed Management Course organized jointly by the DENR-CAR and SSC NATURA held at the Baguio Country Club, January 11–22.

Pratt, Mary Louise, 1992, *Imperial Eyes: Travel Writing and Transculturation*, London, New York: Routledge.

Reed, Robert R., 1976, *City of Pines: The Origins of Baguio as a Colonial Hill Station and Regional Capital*, Berkeley, CA: Center for South and Southeast Asia Studies, University of California.

Respicio, Norma, 2015a, '*Punnuk*: closing the harvest season with the tug-of-war along the River Hapao', *Summary Inventory Form No254*, National Commission for Culture and the Arts.

Respicio, Norma, 2015b, 'Tugging rituals and games in the Philippines' in Seo Do-sik (ed.), *JULDARIGI: Tugging Rituals and Games in Korea Three Other Southeast Asian Countries*, Seoul: Korea Cultural Heritage Foundation.

Respicio, Norma and Cecilia Picache, 2013, 'Harvest rituals in Hapao' in Jesus Peralta (ed.), *Pinagmulan: Enumerations from the Philippine Inventory of Intangible Cultural Heritage*, Manila: National Comm.

Rosaldo, Renato, 1980, *Ilongot Headhunting, 1883–1974: A Study in Society and History*, Palo Alto, CA: Stanford University Press.

Said, Edward, 1978, *Orientalism*, New York, NY: Vintage Books.

San Juan, E. Jr., 2000, 'Cinema of the "naïve" subaltern in search of an audience' in Rolando Tolentino (ed.), *Geopolitics of the Visible: Essays on Philippine Film Cultures*, Quezon City, Ateneo de Manila University Press.

Scott, James C., 1985, *Weapons of the Weak: Everyday Forms of Peasant Resistance*, Yale University Press.

Scott, James C., 1999, *The Art of not Being Governed: An Anarchist History of Upland Southeast Asia*, New Heaven, CT: Yale University Press.

Scott, W. Henry, 1974, *The Discovery of the Igorots: Spanish Contacts with the Pagans of Northern Luzon*, Quezon City: New Day Publishers.

Shimizu Hiromu, 1989, *Pinatubo Aytas: Continuity and Change*, Quezon City: Ateneo de Manila University Press.

Shimizu Hiromu, 2001, *The Orphans of Pinatubo: Ayta Struggle for Existence*, Manila: Solidaridad Publishing House.

Shimizu Hiromu, 'Refiguring identities in an Ifugao village: sketches of joint projects from a Filipino filmmaker, a native intellectual, and a Japanese anthropologist under American shadow' in Fujiwara Kiichi and Yoshiko Nagano (eds), *The Philippines and Japan in America's Shadow*, Singapore; Singapore National University Press.

Sollors, Werner (ed.), 1989 *The Invention of Ethnicity*, New York, NY: Oxford University Press.

Steger, Manfred, 2008, *The Rise of the Global Imaginary: Political Ideologies from the French Revolution to the Global War on Terror*, Oxford: Oxford University Press.

Strange, Susan, 1996, *The Retreat of the State: The Diffusion of Power in the World Economy*, Cambridge: Cambridge University Press.
Tahimik, Kidlat, 1987, 'Cups-of-gas filmmaking vs. full tank-cum-credit-card fillmaking', Mimeo.
Tahimik, Kidlat, 1997, 'Midlife choices: filmmaking vs. fillmaking' in Lorna Kalaw-Tirol (ed.), *Primed for Life: Writings on Midlife by 18 Men*, Anvil Publishing.
Tahimik, Kidlat, 1999, 'A view from the San Juan Bridge (Notes ni Direk galling sa frontlines ng Filipino-American War)' in *PDI*, February 16.
Tobin, Jeffrey, 'Cultural construction and native nationalism: report from the Hawaiian front,' Rob Wilson and Arif Dirlik (eds), *Asia/Pacific as Space of Cultural Production*, Duke University Press.
Tolentino, Rolando, 1996, 'Jameson and Kidlat Tahimik,' *Philippine Studies*, vol. 44, no. 1.
Tolentino, Rolando, 2001, *National/Transnational: Subject Formation and Media in and on the Philippines*, Quezon City: Ateneo de Manila University Press.
Tolentino, Rolando, 2009, 'Office of the Dean, Message' in *U.P. Gawad Plaridel 2009*, College of Mass Communication.
Trask, Haunani-Kay, 1991, 'Native and anthropologists: the colonial struggle,' *The Contemporary Pacific*, vol. 3, no. 1.
Turner, Terence, 1991, 'Representing, resisting, rethinking: historical transformations of Kayapo culture, and anthropological consciousness' in George Stocking (ed.), *Colonial Situation*, Madison, University of Wisconsin Press.
Turner, Terence, 1993, 'The role of indigenous peoples in the environmental crisis: the example of the Kayapo of the Brazilian Amazon', *Perspectives in Biology and Medicine*, vol. 36, no. 3.
Tyner, James, A. 2009, *The Philippines: Mobilities, Identities, Globalization*, New York & London: Routledge.
Vergara, Napoleon and Rodolfo Fernandez, 1989, *Social Forestry in Asia, Factors that Influence Program Implementation*, Los Baños: Southeast Asian Regional Center for Graduate Study in Agriculture
Warren, Key, 1998, *Indigenous Movements and Their Critics: Pan-Maya Activism in Guatemala*, Princeton, NJ: Princeton University Press.
Yang, Shu-Yuan, 2011, 'Headhunting, Christianity, and history among the Bugkalot (Ilongot) of northern Luzon, Philippines', *Philippine Studies*, vol. 59, no. 2.

Index

Ethnic (tribe) and religious groups

Abra 158
Aeta 356, 358–359, 362
Anglican 136
Apayao 93, 158

Baptist 136
Benguet 158
Bontoc 158

Catholic 136, 187

Ibaloi 94, 135–136
Ifugao 4, 20, 22, 24, 31–32, 34, 36, 42, 46, 93–94, 135–136, 168, 172–173, 187, 270, 274, 278, 334, 346, 348–350, 353, 417

Ilocano 53, 136, 314
Ilongot 23, 107

Kalinga 93, 158
Kankanay 94, 136

lowland Christian 4, 96, 214, 216–217, 256, 294, 296, 356

Pangasinan 136
Pentecostal 136

Tagalog 136, 216, 322

Visaya 101, 193, 262

Geographical name

Amok mountain 240
Asin Road Barangay 20, 135, 137, 139, 165–166, 171

Ba-ang 323
Baguio 20, 121, 135, 199, 306
Balete Pass 113, 115, 143
Balian 222, 242
Bontoc 94, 100, 102, 114, 120, 122, 144–145, 158, 265
Boyyod 149, 296, 307, 310, 320, 370

Cordillera Mountains 32, 94, 99–100, 102–103, 144, 158, 369, 374

Dalton Pass *see* 'Balete Pass'
Danghai 177

Gamagori-shi 149–150

Hapao 1, 4, 8, 20, 31, 45, 47, 52, 99–100, 134, 295–298, 300, 306, 322, 342–343, 407, 409
Hiroshima 154, 165
Hungduan 1, 34, 39, 45, 47, 50–52, 54, 61

Kalinga 93
Kiangan 91, 96–99, 100, 119, 124, 126

Lagawe 54, 57, 59, 84, 119, 133, 177, 298, 312, 332, 372, 382, 388, 395, 416

Mactan Island 192, 194–195
Malacca 194
Manila/Metro Manila 4, 54, 79, 216, 247, 267, 302, 306, 316, 363, 372, 416
Monument Valley 250
Mount Napulawan 118–120, 123, 154, 156–157, 164, 324, 326
Mount Pinatubo 248, 360, 418

Nabigihan 115, 120
Nagasaki 154, 165

Pangasinan 93
Patpat 149
Poitan 76

Salacsac pass 113
San Juan River 101, 235, 238
Sannan-cho 20, 202, 341, 360–361, 364, 368, 374, 392, 404, 418–419

Visaya 136

Personal name

Aguinaldo, Emilio 92, 101–102
Anderson, Benedict 132, 422–423
Appadurai, Arjun 17–18, 22, 255, 342, 407
Aquino, Benigno, Jr. (Ninoy) 212, 246–247
Aquino, Corazon 93, 189, 212, 247
Arendt, Hannah 15
Armstrong, Neil 411

Boas, Franz 283

Chungalao, Solomon 157
Conklin, Harold 34, 36, 50, 68, 70, 353, 414, 422
Constantino, Renato 190–191
Coppola, Francis Ford 179, 222

Eggan, Fred 34
Enrique de Malacca 193–194, 197, 230, 250
Enriquez, Virgilio 208, 214

Fenelon, James 21, 220
Ford, John 250

Geertz, Clifford 283

Goda Toh 43
Godard, Jean-Luc 179

Hall, Thomas 21, 220
Harvey, David 15
Herzog, Werner 222, 236, 242
Hilhorst, Dorothea 347, 350–352
Hobsbawm, Eric 132

Iglesia Ni Christo 136

Jameson, Frederic 179, 235

Kabunian 40, 160, 209, 251, 287–286
Kawayan 175, 209, 251, 271
Kidlat Tahimik 4–8, 181, 183, 187–189, 192–197, 201–204, 215, 221–224, 227–230, 237–241, 250, 252–255, 257, 259, 262, 264, 267–271, 286–289, 331
Kipling, Rudyard 106
Kluge, Alexander 179
Kumano Takeshi 43
Kwiatkowski, Lynn 347–348, 350

Lapu-Lapu 192–194, 195

MacArthur, Jr., Arthur 238
Magellan, Ferdinand 192–195
Mahiwo, Sylvano 37–39, 268, 297, 309
Marcos, Ferdinand 21, 23, 61, 74, 189, 200, 235, 249, 335, 409
McKinley, William 91, 101, 189
Milgram, B. Lynne 66, 346, 348, 350
Moriyama Takumi 280

Nakake, Rowena 38, 298, 323
Nauyac, Lopez 4, 125, 131, 253, 285–288, 339, 365–366, 368–369, 371–372, 377, 417, 419

Ōe Kenzaburō 242

Peacock, James 284
Pratt, Mary 10
Prince Akihito and Princess Michiko of Japan 202

Ranger, Terence 132
Rizal, José 213, 224
Robertson, Roland 15, 334

Rosaldo, Renato 23

Said, Edward 132
Sekimoto Teruo 284
Sollors, Werner 132
Sontag, Susan 242
Sukarno 202

Tiongson, Nicanor G 262
Tolentino, Rolando B 264
Turner, Terence 274, 366
Tylor, Edward B 283, 285

Uchibori Motomitsu 280

von Braun, Wernher 226

Wenders, Wim 242

Yamashita Shinji 280
Yamashita Tomoyuki 5, 92, 110, 118, 150, 154, 164
Yomota Inuhiko 250

Subject

365 Days with Lord 167

absorption into the local 17
abu'wab 37
accommodative values 215
Aeta Development Association (ADA) 358, 364
Age of Discovery 15
agents 351
agricultural irrigation *see* 'irrigation'
agricultural rituals *see* 'rituals'
Aichi Arts Center 260
allegorical critique of modernity 179, *see also* 'modernity'
all-out war 170
alternative cinema *see* 'cinema'
American colonial rule 106
American cultural/political hegemony 189, 205, 235, 256, 260, 415
 cultural genocide 254–255
 cultural imperialism 17
 cultural lahar (American culture descends like a lahar) 252, 254
amoebic dysentery 116
ancestors 68
 ancestor worship 52
 ancestral domains 75
anthropology/anthropologist 34, 42, 280, 284–285, 355

anthropology of commitment/
    anthropology of response-ability/
    anthropology of engagement/
    anthropology of collaboration 11,
    12, 22, 337
  cultural anthropology 131, 280
  'entangled anthropology' 12
  participatory anthropology 337
anti-Japanese guerilla *see* 'guerillas'
Aozora (blue sky) Peace Force 390
Apo 103, 108
Apollo program 410
Apu Dios/*Apo Dios* (Christian
    God) 103, 160, 373
aquaculture ponds 397
artists commune 206
Asia Volunteer Network 364
Asia-Pacific War 4, 24, 26, 52, 92,
    109–110, 127
  Battle of Leyte Gulf 92, 110, 111
  Formosa Air Battle 111–112
  General Yamashita's retreat 409
Asiatic Squadron of United States 101
Asin Woodcarving Village 88
'assimilation' and 'assassination' 187,
    189
atomic bomb 154, 165
authenticity 335
Ave Maria Church 138, 166, 171, 174

'backward' ethnic group 417, *see also*
    'second-class citizen'
Baguio artists' collective, Sun Flower
    Co. 272
Bahala na Dwende 244
baki 40, 151, *see also* 'rituals'
Balikbayan (Memories of
    Overdevelopment) 195–197, 199
bamboo model camera 258
Banal Kahoy (Holy Wood) 231, 260
barangay (the smallest administrative
    division in the Philippines) 32, 45,
    135, 325, 328, 332, 366
'*barrio* revolutionary committees' 53
base of operations for a protracted
    resistance 114

basic human needs 342
Bathala na Duwende 206–208, 221
Battle of Leyte Gulf 92, 110, 111, *see
    also* 'Asia-Pacific War', 'General
    Yamashita's retreat', 'Japanese
    armed forces'
Beatles, The 236
Benevolent Assimilation 91, 106, 189,
    205, 256
Berlin International Film Festival 179,
    261
bile 160
bilid (common forests) 76, 380, 405, *see
    also* '*pinugo*'
bird's-eye view 18, *see also* 'bug's-eye
    view'
Bolex camera 210, 238
Bolog Camp 86
bone cleaning/bone washing ritual *see*
    'rituals'
Born Again Christian *see* 'Christian'
'break mechanism' 273
bricolage 182, 224, 229, 244, 250, 265,
    332, *see also* 'hybridity'
*BUBONG! Roofs of the World,
    UNITE!* 231, 262
bug's-eye view 19–20, *see also* 'bird's-
    eye view', 'macroscopic viewpoint'
bunot (traditional haircut for Ifugao
    men) 236

Caligari Film Prize 179
canals *see* 'irrigation'
Cannyao ritual festival 138, 158
'cap and gown' 258, 260
  'cap and gown and loincloth' 260
capitalism 181, 232
Catholic Church 54
Catholicism 169
Central Cordillera Agricultural
    Programme (CECAP) 24, 58, 297
Certificate of Ancestral Domain
    Claim 345
chainsaw 76, 82
Christian 41, 138, 167, 168, 172, 217,
    265

Born Again Christian 136
Ifugao as Christian 158
lowland Christian 4, 41, 63, 96–97, 106, 214, 216–217, 256, 294, 296, 356
cinema/films
 independent and alternative cinema 252, 262
 independent and alternative cinema in the Philippines 262
 Hollywood films/movies 254–255, 363, 418
 home movie 227
Cinemalaya Philippine Independent Film Festival 261
civil defense units 349
 Civil Home Defense Force (CHDF) 54
 Civilian Armed Forces Geographical Unit (CAFGU) 60
Club of Rome 418
Cold War 14, 61, 260, 410
 end of the Cold War 408
 post-Cold War globalization 408
collaboration 6
colonialism/colonization 9, 15, 184, 208
 colonial domination 187
 colonial government of the Philippines 95
 colonial rule 94
 resistance to colonization 256
colonized sensibility 235
commercialism/commercialization 138, 213, 255
 crass commercialism 178
commitment 14, see also 'anthropology of commitment'
committee on the Ifugao rice terraces 31
Communist Party of the Philippines-New People's Army (CPP-NPA) 45, 52, 54–60, 62–63, 59–70
 Communist guerilla 174, see also 'guerillas'
 R&R area 58
 'strategic offensive' 57
 'strategic stalemate' 57
community 343, 345
 community development approach 342
 community-based forest management 345
Comprehensive Agrarian Reform Law 247–248
'compression of space and time' 293
confrontative values 215
constructionism 132, 289
contact zone 10, 127
contemporaries 8, 22, 42, 44, 409, 417
contemporary humanity 15
Contract Reforestation Program 344
cooperative associations 348
corvée labor see 'forced labor'
'cosmic vibrations' 7, 196, 213, 232
cosmos 242
 power of the cosmos 221
crass commercialism 178, see also 'commercialism/commercialization'
create a new modernity see 'modernity'
cultivating rice in the terraces see 'rice terraces'
culture
 cultural anthropology see 'anthropology'
 cultural capital 280, see also 'cultural resources'
 cultural essentialism see 'essentialism'
 cultural identity see 'identity'
 cultural imperialism 17, see also 'American cultural/political hegemony'
 cultural genocide 254–255
 cultural lahar 252, 254
 cultural practitioner 183
 cultural resources 279–282, 284–285, 293, see also 'cultural capital', 'mobilization of culture'
 cultural revival/cultural revitalization movement 1, 6, 11, 21, 27, 134, 176, 178, 279
 culture as lived experience 284
 culture as narrative 284

mass culture 178, 363
objectifing culture 172
penetration into local cultures 17
'customary practices of judging truth or falsehood by holding the hand in hot water' 105

declaration of independence 101
decolonization 6, 132, 184, 187, 206, 214
  decolonization of Americanized soul 6
  movement towards decolonization 192
defamiliarization 27, 265–267, 290
defensive posture 198
defensive strategies in the midst of globalization 9, 173–174, 293, *see also* 'strategy'
democratic space 247
development
  development assistance 24, 176, 348, 417
  development at grassroots level 385
  development projects 4, 24, 406
  development strategies 342, *see also* 'strategy'
  development theory 342
  historical processes of development 19
  women-in-development 343, 350
developmentalist dictatorship 63, 191, 212, 249, 335
dialogue 14, 59, 346, 414, 418
divination 160, 276
division of the globe 15
dojo loach aquaculture 394, 396, 400
dopap (wrestling) 43

Echigo-Tsumaari Art Field Triennale 286–287
ecosystem 25, 68, 385, 405–406
  forests and rice terraces as an ecosystem 65, *see also* 'rice terraces'
  Ifugao agro-ecosystem 49
Ecumenical Foundation for Minority Development (EFMD) 358
El Niño 353

Empire 14
empowerment 11, 350, 374
  grassroots empowerment 392
  self-empowerment 274
'entangled anthropology' *see* 'anthropology'
eruption of Mount Pinatubo 355, *see also* Geographical name index
essentialism/essentialist 132, 265, 269, 289, 346
  cultural essentialism 265
  essentialist purity 268
ethnocentrism 244
ethnography 10

fieldwork 20, 323, 337–338, 348, 356, 364
fierce feuds 161
fight against the tide of globalization *see* 'globalization'
Filipino identity 190–191, *see also* 'identity'
fillmaking 224–225
First Nations 220, *see also* 'native nations'
flexible accumulation 15
forced labor 23, 46
Fordist 224
Forest 218
  forest reservation 152
  forests and rice terraces as an ecosystem 65, *see also* 'ecosystem', 'rice terraces'
Formosa Air Battle 111–112, *see also* 'Asia-Pacific War'
Foundation for Human Rights in Asia 364
funi (sorcery) 44
Funka no kodama (Echoes of the Eruption) 338

galleon trade 95, 96
General Yamashita's retreat 409, *see also* 'Asia-Pacific War', 'Japanese armed forces', Personal name index
Geographical Information System (GIS) 353

glass beads 23
global eco-imaginary 414, *see also* 'Apollo program'
  'global ecological community' 414, 422
  'Only One Earth' 48
  'Spaceship Earth' 48, 410–413, 423
Global Forest City Movement *see* 'Ifugao Global Forest City Movement'
Global Peace Park 154, 157
global powers 127
global public philosophy 418
globalization 4, 14, 18–19, 63, 173, 197, 293–294, 334–335, 341–342, 407–409, 413, 415
  fight against the tide of globalization 178
  grassroots globalization/globalization from below 22, 28, 342, 407, 424
'glocalization' 18, 418
gold mines 93, 95
Gotad festival 330, 332
grassroots 1, 403, 407, 422
  grassroots empowerment 392, *see also* 'empowerment'
  grassroots globalization/globalization from below 22, 28, 342, 407, 424
  grassroots international collaboration 12
  grassroots people 404
Great Depression 23
guerillas/guerilla warfare 23, 26, 57, 91, 102, 124, 178
  anti-Japanese guerilla 317
  Communist guerillas 174
  guerilla war in the cultural sphere 178
'guru' 182

haciendas 162
handmade bamboo video camera 257
headhunting feuds 23, 91, 94, 100, 106
headwater forests 80
heathen 168
heathen custom 41
hegemony 17, 254, 256, 266, 429, *see also* 'American cultural/political hegemony'
  intellectual hegemony 235
  Western (cultural) hegemony 132, 230, 232–233
highlanders 217
'his (Kidlat's) own Filipino-ness' 209, *see also* 'identity'
historical consciousness 26, 293, 380
historical consciousness of Ifugao 52
history 10
'history from below' 407
Hokubu Luzon jikyū sen (Protracted war in northern Luzon) 116
Hollywood films/movies 254–255, 363, 418, *see also* 'cinema'
home movie 227, 324
hudhud chanting 332
Hungduan municipal government 67
hybridity 8, *see also* 'bricolage'

identity 25, 158, 172–173, 214, 323, 334, 414
  cultural identity 406
  Filipino identity 190–191
  'his (Kidlat's) own Filipino-ness' 209
  identity as Ifugaos 25, 28
  'my (author's) own identity' 186
Ifugao *see* Ethnic (tribe) and religious group index
Ifugao agro-ecosystem 49
Ifugao as Christian 158, *see also* 'Christian'
Ifugao ethnic dress 33, 155
Ifugao history and contemporary society 36
Ifugao leaders and intellectuals 36, 49
Ifugao lifeworld 31
Ifugao rice terraces 49, *see also* 'rice terraces'
  kindred of Ifugaos 45
  'real Ifugao' 269
Ifugao State College of Agriculture and Forestry 81
Ifugao Terraces Commission 354, 370, 382, 404
Ifugao Global Forest City Movement ('Global') 5, 26, 83–84, 155, 157, 163, 169–170, 174, 176, 330, 345, 368, 370–374, 376, 378,

382, 404–406, *see also* 'reforestation'
name 'Global' 287
Imbayah festival 332
indigenous people 4, 21, 75, 216–218, 220–221, 256, 258–260, 270, 274
 indigenous Filipino 198
 indigenous Ifugao 172
 indigenous orientation 214
 indigenousness 216–218, 268, 335
 senjūmin movements 218
Indigenous Arts and Culture Festival 172, 175
Indigenous Cultural Communities 75
Indigenous Peoples' Rights Act (IPRA) 75, 217
Indigenous Psychology and National Consciousness 216
Indigenous Psychology 216
indio-genius *dwende* 207
installation works 173, 209
Integrated Social Forestry Program 344
intellectual hegemony 235, *see also* 'hegemony'
international civil society 424
International *Kudzu*-vine Green Sannan (IKGS) 338, 361, 378–379
interpretation 131
irrigation 70, 120, 139, 152
 irrigation canals 73, 76, 80, 83, 95, 118, 161, 274, 353–354

Japan Foundation 6, 260
Japan Foundation Film Festival 6
Japan International Cooperation Agency (JICA) 5, 384, 389
 JICA's Partnership Program 12–13, 340, 385, 398, 402
Japan Overseas Cooperation Volunteers (JOCV) 358, 361–362
Japanese armed forces (Japanese Army, Japanese Navy) 23, 90, 109–110, 113–114, 116, 118, 120, 124, 126, 164, 174, 402
 Philippines Area Army (Shobu Group) 5, 92

Japanese Summers of a Filipino Fundoshi 166
jeepney 182–183, 229, 241
Jehovah's Witness 136
Jesus Christ 183, 384

Kabunian (Ifgao's God) 168
Kamikaze Special Attack Force 112
karaoke 253
Kataastaasan Kagalanggalang Katipunan ng mga Anak ng Bayan 209
Katipunan 188
kindred 45
Kulpi festival 332

La Niña 353
lahar (volcanic ash landslide) 356–357, 364
 cultural lahar (American culture descends like a lahar) 252, 254
lands of the ancestral domain 9
landscape 25
 living cultural landscapes 31
 mind's eye landscape 144
Legazpi expedition 198
Liberation Psychology 215
Limits to Growth 48
local knowledge 418
localization 18–19, 418
long-distance eco-imaginary/long-distance environmentalism 422
long-distance nationalism 422, 423
looking for the bones of the Japanese war dead 386
lowland Christian 4, 41, 63, 96–97, 106, 214, 216–217, 256, 294, 296, 356, *see also* 'Christian', Ethnic (tribe) and religious group index
lowlander elites and intellectuals 266

Mababangong Bangugot ng Aliw-Wood (Perfumed Nightmare of Holly/Pleasure wood) 205
Mababangong Bangugot ng America (Perfumed Nightmare of America) 205

macroscopic viewpoint 18, *see also* 'bug's-eye view'
malaria 116, 121
Maoist 52, *see also* 'Communist Party of the Philippines-New People's Army'
Marcos regime 246
martial law 23, 55–56, 61, 74, 191, 202, 235, 246
mass culture *see* 'culture'
mass migration of the Mongoloid peoples 15
McDonaldization 17
migrant work/migrant worker 6, 9, 21, 24, 148, 197–198, 293, 295–296, 304, 306, 310, 322
　migrant workers as national heroes 21
　working abroad 20, 67, 303, 305
military tactics associated with low-intensity conflict 349
mobilization of culture 172, 278–279, 281–283, *see also* 'cultural resources'
modern/modernity/
　allegorical critique of modernity 179
　modernization 14, 63, 132, 178, 182, 213, 229, 235, 240, 242, 282, 354
　modern Western civilization 231
　modern world 237
　modern world system *see* 'world systems theory'
　postmodernity 15
　rearrangement of the modernity 229
　Western modernity 63, 180–181, 235–236
monbaki (ritual specialist/priest) 37, 40, 81, 175, 276, 317–319, 354, 371, 388
　divination by a *monbaki* 160, 276
mother of pearl 23, 128, 409
multinational corporations 14, 16–17
muyong (privately owned forest) 73, 163, *see also* '*pinugo*'
　muyong permit 163
　muyong resource permits 304
my (author's) own identity 186, *see also* 'identity'

naivety as political strategy 230, *see also* 'strategy'
NASA 226
National Commission for Culture and the Arts (NCCA) 36, 326, 328, 330, 372
national forest reservation 151
national hero 213
National Museum of the Philippines 34, 86
Native 132
　Native Americans 192
　native intellectual 21
　native nations 220
negotiation 9–10, 22, 42, 193, 209, 248, 252, 351, 414
New People's Army (NPA) *see* 'Communist Party of the Philippines-New People's Army'
NGO 24, 352
'nostalgia for the present' 255

objectifing culture 172, *see also* 'culture'
offensive strategy 173–174, 198, *see also* 'strategy'
　offensive strategies in the midst of globalization 173
offering animals 158, 160
'One Man Band Organ' 224
'Only One Earth' 48, *see also* 'global eco-imaginary'
Operation *Shō* (Victory) One (a combined army–navy operation against the Allied forces in the Philippines) 111, *see also* 'Japanese armed forces'
'Orbit Days' 213
Organisation for Economic Co-operation and Development (OECD) 186
Orientalism/orientalist 132, 269
Our Bomb Mission to Hiroshima 166, 286
'our common home' 423
out-migration/overseas migrant workers, *see* 'migrant work/migrant worker'

pacification campaign/pacification operation 93–94, 97, 105
pagan ways 160
parabolic antenna 253, 254
participant observation 131, 337, 350, 35, *see also* 'anthropology'
participatory anthropology *see* 'anthropology'
participatory development 11, 343
peace bell 165
Peace Corps 348
peace park 154, 370
penetration into local cultures 17, *see also* 'culture'
People Power Revolution 56, 93, 189–190, 212, 246, 312
Perfumed Nightmare 6, 179, 182–183, 222, 225, 236–238, 250, 254
periphery 22, 27
 peripheral ethnicity 22, 408, 416
Philippine Constabulary 54, 60
Philippine Revolution 23, 99, 152, 162, 184, 188, 191, 238
Philippine Rural Reconstruction Movement 352–353
Philippine struggle for independence from Spain 189
Philippine-American War 99, 101, 238, 256
Philippine-Japan Friendship Highway 143
'philosopher of the forest' 218
pinugo (privately owned forests) 25, 70, 73, 131, 151, 170, 344–345, 366, 373, 375, 378–380, 404–405, *see also* '*bilid*', '*muyong*'
Plaridel prize 262
political struggle and negotiation 266, *see also* 'negotiation'
Portuguese military expedition to Malacca 193
positionality 10, 27
post-Cold War globalization *see* 'globalization'
post-Fordism 15
postmodernity 15, *see also* 'modernity'
power elites 14

power of the cosmos *see* 'cosmos'
power relations 10, 258, 267
Presidential Decree No. 705 (The Forestry Reform Code of the Philippines) 74
prestige assets 417
prestige items 322
'primitivism' 242
pusong (trickster) 290

R&R area *see* 'Communist Party of the Philippines-New People's Army'
'real Ifugao' 269, *see also* 'Ifugao'
rearrangement of the modernity *see* 'modernity'
recording of daily lifestyle 273
reforestation 1, 279, 376, 378, 404
 Ifugao Global Forest City Movement ('Global') 5, 26, 83–84, 155, 157, 163, 169–170, 174, 176, 330, 345, 368, 370–374, 376, 378, 382, 404–406
 reforestation and cultural revival movements 11, 90, 134, 139, 164, 169, 173, 178, 182, 286–287, 342–343
 reforestation project 164, 374
Regalian Doctrine 74
representation 14, 268, 283
 self-determination in matters of representation 8
resistance to colonization 256, *see also* 'colonialism/colonization'
resource 278, *see also* 'cultural resources'
response 11, 134, 269, 288
responsibility 11
returning to the people 214
revolutionary tax 55, 59
rice terraces 66, 68, 70, 78, 118, 139, 161, 170, 173, 218, 286, 293, 306, *see also* 'UNESCO World Heritage List'
 rice terrace cultivation 25, 138–139, 162, 279
rituals
 agricultural rituals 68
 baki 40, 151

bone cleaning/bone washing ritual 40, 44, 417
Cannyao ritual festival 138, 158
divination by a *monbaki* 160, 276
monbaki (ritual specialist/priest) 37, 40, 81, 175, 276, 317–319, 354, 371, 388
ritual sacrifice 168

San Juan River Bridge 101, 235, 238
sangla loan 302, 321
sariling duwende (inner playful espirit) 187
Sasayama Homei Senior High School 362, 419
satellite broadcasts 4, 253–254
Save the Ifugao Terraces Movement (SITMo) 330, 382, 391
second-class citizen 163
self-determination in matters of representation 8, *see also* 'representation'
self-empowerment 274, *see also* 'empowerment'
senjūmin movements 218, *see also* 'indigenous people'
September 11 terrorist attacks 424
settler societies 218
shaman 233
Shobu Group *see* 'Japanese armed forces'
shock therapy 266, *see also* 'strategic essentialism'
Sikolohiyang Pilipino (Filipino Psychology) 214
Sinong Lumikha ng Yo-yo? Sinong Lumikha ng Moon Buggy? 182
social development 11, 14, 279, 341, 343, 404
social development approach 342, 343
social development movement 1
social development projects 343
social position 260
social power 349

'Spaceship Earth' 48, 410–413, 423, *see also* 'global eco-imaginary'
Spanish and American colonial periods 293
Spanish colonial government 95–98
Spanish-American War 91, 99, 189
spectacle 326
spiritual guide 182
Star Wars 242
Stations of the Cross 88
strategy
defensive strategies in the midst of globalization 9, 173–174, 293
development strategies 342
offensive strategies in the midst of globalization 173–174, 198
strategic essentialism 8, 42, 176, 254, 266–267
strategies for development 342
struggle with American hegemony 256, *see also* 'American cultural/political hegemony'
swidden agriculture 23, 65, 67–68, 70, 161

terrace agriculture *see* 'rice terraces'
Third World 178, 180, 244, 260, 346, 414
TNT (*Tago Ng Tago*, meaning to stay in hiding/working illegally abroad) 300
tobacco cultivation/tobacco industry 23, 95–96, 127
tobacco tax 97
Toyota Foundation 272–274, 366
traditional culture 17, 176
traditional woodcarving *see* 'woodcarving'
traveling film 225, 228, 265
Treaty of Paris 91, 189
Tribute 23
trickster 233
true Filipino 218
Tungoh festival 177, 268, 321–324, 326, 329–330
Turumba 179, 225

Index 469

typhoon 205, 212, 240–241, 246

UNESCO 4, 31, 46, 49, 161
   World Heritage 46, 48, 127, 374, 385, 404–405
   World Heritage in Danger 73
   World Heritage List 4, 12, 31, 286, 293
   Intangible Cultural Heritage list 276–277
   World Cultural and Natural Heritage 46
'unfinished revolution' 191–192
United Nations Conference on the Human Environment 48
United States military bases 248
   Camp John Hay 200
Uniting Church 136
'unlearning' 183, 207–208, 230, 256

value under capitalism 231
video diary 232
video workshops 278, 366
Voice of America 188, 236, 254
volcanic eruption of Mount Pinatubo 248, *see also* Geographical name index

watershed 90
weapons of the weak 274

Western (cultural) hegemony 132, 230, 232–233, *see also* 'hegemony'
Western modernity 63, 180–181, 235–236, *see also* 'modernity'
Western youth popular culture 236
White Apos 107–109
'white man's burden' 106–107
Who Invented the Yo-yo? Who Invented the Moon Buggy? 198, 232
Why is Yellow at the Middle of the Rainbow? 179, 181, 184, 189, 196, 212, 244–245, 247
women-in-development 343, 350, *see also* 'development'
woodcarving/woodcarver 73, 76, 84, 135–136, 138, 161, 304, 306
   woodcarving business 66
working abroad 20, 67, 303, 305, *see also* 'migrant work/migrant worker'
world systems theory 21
   modern world system 416

Yamagata International Documentary Film Festival 4, 249
Yamashita gold/Yamashita treasure 109, 150, 386
young men's huts 105
yo-yo 196, 232

Zomia 23